John Entick

The General History of the Late War

Vol. II.: Containing It's Rise, Progress and Event, in Europe, Asia, Africa...

John Entick

The General History of the Late War
Vol. II.: Containing It's Rise, Progress and Event, in Europe, Asia, Africa...

ISBN/EAN: 9783337008932

Printed in Europe, USA, Canada, Australia, Japan

Cover: Foto ©ninafisch / pixelio.de

More available books at **www.hansebooks.com**

GEORGE II.
King of Great Britain, France &
Ireland, &c. &c.

THE GENERAL HISTORY of the Late WAR:

CONTAINING IT'S

Rife, Progrefs, *and* Event,

IN

EUROPE, ASIA, AFRICA, and AMERICA.

AND EXHIBITING

The STATE of the Belligerent Powers at the Commencement of the War; their Interefts and Objects in it's Continuation; and REMARKS on the Meafures, which led GREAT BRITAIN to Victory and Conqueft.

INTERSPERSED WITH

The CHARACTERS of the able and difinterefted STATESMEN, to whofe Wifdom and Integrity, and of the HEROES, to whofe Courage and Conduct, we are indebted for that

NAVAL and MILITARY

Succefs, which is not to be equalled in the Annals of this, or of any other Nation.

AND WITH

Accurate Defcriptions of the SEAT of WAR, the Nature and Importance of our CONQUESTS, and of the moft remarkable BATTLES by Sea and Land.

Illuftrated with

A Variety of HEADS, PLANS, MAPS, and CHARTS, Defigned and Engraved by the *beft Artifts*.

VOL. II.

Hiftorici eft: nequid falfi, audeat dicere: nequid veri, non audeat.
POLIB.

By the Rev. JOHN ENTICK, *M. A.*
And other GENTLEMEN.

LONDON:
Printed for EDWARD DILLY, in the Poultry;
And JOHN MILLAN, at Charing-Crofs.
M.DCC.LXIII.

THE GENERAL HISTORY OF THE LATE WAR.

THE campaign of the year 1756 in North America was closed with as little honour to those employed in its operations, and with less advantage to the nation, than that of the year 1755, though at a greater national expence, and with much larger supplies of men and officers from Old England. Which occasioned a serious observer of those times to remark, That the situation of affairs in North America grew more and more dangerous; and that it seemed to him, that the more the colonies were strengthened from Great Britain, the more ground they lost against the French, whose number of regular troops, this year, were much inferior to ours [a].

A. D. 1756.
The unfortunate campaign of the year 1756.

Numerous

---

[a] All the success we can pretend to boast of in the course of this war, happened in the two first years of it, when we had

A. D. 1756.

Forces how disposed.

Numerous garrisons being placed in Fort William Henry and in Fort Edward to prevent any surprize during the winter, and to defend that country within their protection from insults, the rest of the forces were quartered in barracks built for that purpose at Albany, that they might be brought

had not a fourth part of the regular troops we now have, and the French had at least an equal number in Canada, and at Louisbourg.

Our campaign in 1755 opened with an expedition against the French encroachments in Nova Scotia, with about 400 regular troops, and 2000 irregulars from Boston; which was so conducted, that the French forts upon the Isthmus soon surrendered; their garrisons were transported to Louisbourg; one of their forts upon the river St. John was abandoned, and their settlements about it broke up. The same year our own fortifications were advanced as far as Lake Sacrament, now Lake George, as in the preceding year they had likewise begun to be upon the river Kennebeck, towards the metropolis of Canada: and the French general, Dieskau, who came from France that year with about 3000 troops, and had begun his march to invest Oswego, was prevented from making an attempt upon it, and defeated in his attack upon our camp at Lake George. And in the year 1756, a large party of French regulars, Canadians and Indians, which attacked, by surprize, a party of our battoe-men upon the river Onondago, were entirely defeated by an inferior number of men.

No sooner were our forces encreased, by those which arrived here from Europe with General Abercrombie, in June 1756, but things took a very different turn. Though timely information was given, that a large French camp was formed about 30 miles off Oswego, with an intent speedily to attack it; yet that most material place was lost: General Webb not setting out till two days before it was taken.

Our next misfortune was the fate of the forts at the Great Carrying Place, just now related on page 490. Vol. I.

early

early, and with less expence and trouble than heretofore, to the seat of action. *A. D. 1756.*

Lord Loudon's conduct. As for his lordship, he applied seriously and diligently to provide for the security of the British frontiers, in the best manner his force and situation would permit, to reconcile the jarring interests of the different governments; to suppress every subject of contention, and to bring them to a temper to unite cordially, with him, in national measures, for the common interest, and to be provided for an early campaign. Yet, notwithstanding all his care, many different parts of that extensive frontier, on the back of our colonies, were exposed to the ravages of the enemy; and the defenceless settlers were frequently plundered, and most barbarously murdered, without regard to age or sex.

Its effects upon the colonies. What with the terrible forebodings of these disasters, and what with the good management of Lord Loudon, the several provinces were brought to a more settled and rational disposition. Their governors not only united with him in every proposal for establishing a harmony throughout their respective governments, and to contribute with all their ability to the support of the common cause; but they extended their endeavours to gain the Indians to the British interest: and they so far succeeded, that the Delawares, who form a line along the southern parts of Pensylvania, and had leaned very much to the French [b], were reconciled to us, and

---

[b] Their quarrel with the English was begun by the following misunderstanding:

While

A. D. 1756.

and concluded a peace with the governor of that province. The like good effect attended the treaty of

While a party of English scouters were at Shamokin, news was brought that a party of French and Indians from the borders of the Ohio were also arrived in the neighbouring parts, upon which Scaronyade, an Indian chief of the Six Nations, advised his friends the English to return back, and by all means to keep on the eastern side of the river; in consequence of this advice they did indeed return back, but instead of keeping on the east, they kept on the west side of the river, and before they had gone far they fell in with the French party, who killed four of them, and the rest escaped.

Soon after this accident, an Englishman that went to trade with the Indians at Wyoming, charged them with the murder of his countrymen, and told them, that upon them their death would be revenged; this caused a great number of Indians to assemble at Wyoming, that they might be able to make head against the English, if they should be attacked. This assembly of the Indians was again reported to the English, as the first step towards commencing hostilities against them; the English therefore, without enquiring farther into the affair, or waiting for the attack, seized as many of the Delawares, who lived among them, as they could lay hands on, to the amount of 232. One of these prisoners found means to make his escape, and gave his countrymen notice of what had happened to the Delawares.

Upon the receipt of this intelligence they were extremely alarmed, and kept scouts abroad to see if any of the English were advancing in a hostile manner.

Such was the situation of affairs, when four English arrived, who had been deputed, though somewhat too late, to examine into the misunderstanding, and to compromise it: when they had told their message, the Indians were about to enter into treaty with them, but the prisoner who had made his escape, being present, cried out, "Do not believe these men, they design only to deceive you, to make you their prisoners, or to put you to the sword." Upon this the Indians immediately seized

their

of the governor of Virginia with the Cherokees and Catawbas [c], two powerful tribes adjoining to that colony, and able to bring 3000 warriors into the field. An alliance for which we were greatly obliged to the influence of the Wolf King, who having been solicited by the partizans of France to break his faith with the English, and informed that two Shawanese and two Frenchmen, escorted by a party of Cherokees, were arrived at Halbamer fort on the 16th of November, and that the 18th was fixed upon for a meeting with the Upper Creeks, to present them with a red stick, and to engage them in the war against the English, commanded all his warriors to be ready at a call, armed with their hatchets, and painted red, fully resolved, in case he should find any of the Creek headmen disposed to listen to that proposal, to attack the Cherokees, Shawanese and Frenchmen, that came upon that errand; and there he publicly declared, "That before an Englishman should be hurt, he and every one of his warriors would sacrifice their lives to protect them." Which declaration so effectually wrought upon the Creek head-men, that they joined with the Wolf

A. D. 1756.

The Wolf King's friendship and influence.

their hatchets, and knocked them all on the head. Thus hostilities were commenced and carried on by both parties with the utmost malignity and violence.

[c] Upon which occasion the Assembly of Virginia granted 8000 l. for raising 500 men, and transporting them to New York, and to pay for servants that should inlist. And 3000 l. to cloath and maintain 350 Cherokee and Catawba Indians in our service; and 2000 l. to maintain a garrison in the Cherokee country.

King in his sentiments, and rejected and threw the red stick away; and put a stop to the intrigues of our enemies amongst the Indians on the frontiers of the most southern provinces.

A.D. 1756.

Loss of Oswego how improved in Europe by the French.

The affair at Oswego did not only disconcert our operations in America, this year, and furnish the enemy with a specious argument amongst the Indians to lessen our credit and interest; but it was magnified in every court of Europe, and published in Italian, under the direction of the French ambassador at Naples, with such circumstances, as to raise an opinion of his country's superiority in arms; to impress a favourable idea of his master's power; to sink the credit of the English courage, and to deter the Princes and States, in that part of the world, from hearkening to any proposals by a nation, unable to defend their own settlements and forts.

Nova Scotia.

On the side of Nova Scotia all things remained quiet, this whole year, since the defeat of the enemy near Chignecto. The Litchfield and Norwich, 50 gun ships, belonging to Commodore Spry's squadron off Louisbourg, took the Arc-en-Ciel, a French ship of 50 guns, and laden with 518 men, and a large quantity of provisions and stores, for the garrison of that fortress. Another French ship, the Amitie of 300 tons, with 70 soldiers on board, and 200 barrels of powder, two large brass mortars, a number of carriages for 24 and 12 pounders, and other military stores; and a large schooner with provisions for St. John's island, were taken and carried into Hallifax

The Arc-en-Ciel taken.

Hallifax harbour, by the Centurion and Succefs. Commodore Holmes cruifing with two large fhips and a couple of floops in the fame latitude, fell in with two French fhips of the line and four frigates; but could do no more than oblige them to fheer off, after an obftinate difpute; not being ftrong enough to take them; they being better failing fhips, and had a fecure port to flee unto.

A. D. 1756.

Commodore Holmes's unfuccefsful engagement.

The French account of this engagement fays, That M. Beaufier, commander of the fquadron, which failed laft April with land forces for Canada, in his return, with the Heros, the Illuftre, and the Le Corne and Syrene frigates, to Louifbourg, difcovered on the 26th of July, about three leagues S. of that port, two Englifh fhips and two frigates, who kept their wind as much as they could in order to come up with them. Beaufier taking advantage of a gale, which fprung up from the N. bore down upon the Englifh, who haftily tacked in order to ftand off. But the nature of his orders obliging him to land provifions at Louifbourg, and fearing that a purfuit would carry him to leeward of the port, he was obliged to quit the chafe and to enter the harbour. He landed the provifions and his fick men with the utmoft expedition; and next morning, by five o'clock, he got underfail in queft of the Englifh cruifers; and about noon he difcryed the two fhips, he had given chafe to the day before, which now had but one frigate in company. He crouded all the fail he could to get up with them: and they did the fame to get off. Captain Breugnon of the
Syrene

French account.

A. D. 1756.

Syrene soon came up with the English frigate, and attacked her so briskly, that she fell back under the cannon of the men of war, and was sheltered from the Syrene, which durst not follow. However this attack gave Beaufier time to come up with the two English ships, one of 74 and the other of 64 guns. He immediately engaged one of them, expecting that the Illustre, which was upon his quarter, would attack the other: but a calm coming on in that instant, hindered the latter from getting up: so that Beaufier had both the English ships upon him, and the engagement continued very warm till seven o'clock at night; when, a gale of wind springing up, and enabled the Illustre to make sail, the English took advantage of it to sheer off; leaving the Heros so disabled in her rigging and sails, and injured in her hull and masts, which had received upwards of 200 shot, besides those between wind and water, that she could not pursue them. It further says, That he spent the night in repairing his damages, in hopes of another brush with the enemy. But next morning, the 28th, he found them at such a distance, as gave him no hopes of getting up to them, and therefore returned to Louisburg with the loss of 18 men killed and 48 wounded.

English account.

Commodore Holmes on board the Grafton, off Louisburg, in a letter to the admiralty, informing their lordships of this same action, said, That having discovered the above ships from the mast-head to the N. E. directly to windward, the Grafton, the Nottingham, Hornet and Jamaica sloops gave chase

chase and made their first board to the S. they
steering directly for us till within two leagues:
that the English ships then tacked, [not to stand
off, but] in hopes to cut the French off from their
port; and that they hauled in for it. That his
ships pursued them, and brought to, about a league
from the harbour, where they were come to an
anchor, about half an hour past one at noon.
That at four o'clock he made sail to the eastward;
and at dark dispatched the Hornet to Hallifax
for some of Captain Spry's ships to come and join
him, and then stood on, as before, till three o'clock,
when he tacked and stood in for the land. That
seeing four French men of war come out of the
harbour and in chase of his ships, about eight in
the morning, he stood from them to the S. E.
about a point from the wind, [not to get off, but]
to draw them from the harbour, judging from
the expedition with which they were returned,
that they were full of men, and above his match.
That when a frigate of 36 guns fired upon the
Jamaica sloop, she returned the fire and rowed at
the same time up to the Nottingham. That on
the men of war firing at the frigate she hauled
her wind, and the Jamaica bore away to the
S. W. That about two o'clock the Nottingham
fired her stern chase at the French commandant,
which he returned with his bow, and soon after the
Grafton fired her stern chase also. That finding the shot reached each other, the Grafton
hauled up her courses, bunted her main-sail, and
bore down upon the French commodore, being
about

about a quarter of a mile from him. That it fell calm at the beginning of the engagement, he being on the Grafton's ſtar-board ſide, the other large French ſhip a-ſtern of him, and the Nottingham on the Grafton's lar-board bow, the two frigates a mile off, and the Jamaica ſloop ſomewhat more. That the French commodore, finding his error in permitting his frigates to ſheer off ſo far, made ſignals for them to rejoin him, as ſoon as the wind ſprung up, and leaſt they ſhould not come faſt enough to his aſſiſtance, he bore down to them, and was followed by his partner. That at ſeven o'clock the French ſquadron was all cloſe together: and at duſk the action ceaſed, they [not the Engliſh] ſheering off to the ſouthward, and the Engliſh ſquadron ſtanding to the S. S. E. That our men lay at their quarters all night, expecting to renew the action in the morning, but were diſappointed by the French ſhips bearing away N. W. by W. diſtance about five miles, by day light, and going away with little wind at E. S. E. right before it for the harbour of Louiſbourg. That our ſhips wore and ſtood to the W. but that theirs never offered to look at ours. That they ſailing better than our ſhips, and the wind freſhning, and the weather alſo growing hazy, were out of ſight about noon: that their chief fire was at the maſts and rigging, which they wounded and cut pretty much: and that the Grafton had ſix men killed and 21 wounded.

Hallifax fortified. At Hallifax meaſures were taken by the governor to ſecure that city and harbour from any ſurprize,

prize, by erecting three new forts with barracks; viz. one barrack on the citadel hill, 365 feet long and 35 wide, of two stories, with a wall inclosing the hill and barrack, and well mounted with cannon, to command not only the whole town, but as far as a cannon ball can penetrate into the woods. It is thought, that, when complete, 20,000 men will not be able to do it any damage, the hill being so steep, and no place for a bomb battery within reach of it.—Another barrack and fort on the Windmill hill about half a mile southward of the first, and of smaller dimensions.—And a third on the north side of the north-west arm, on the place called Pleasant Point.

<small>A. D. 1756.</small>

If we return to inquire into the state and transactions of Europe, we shall find a horrid scene of war opening in almost every nation. Even Spain, with all the professions of friendship towards Great Britain, was augmenting her navy, from the shattered state it was left in by the last war, to

<small>Affairs of Europe.</small>

46 ships of the line, carrying	3142	guns
22 frigates	568	
12 Xebecques	224	
2 Packet boats	36	
4 Bomb vessels	32	
4 Fire ships	24	
5 Galleys	25	
95 vessels	4051 guns	

<small>Spanish navy.</small>

A sea armament, that could not be prepared on any other pretence, than to be ready, when opportunity

<small>And suspicious conduct.</small>

A. D. 1756.

portunity might serve, to join with the enemies of Great Britain; and not without great suspicion[d] of some immediate attempt by the united strength of France and Spain, by sea and land, to wrest from the British crown the fortress of Gibraltar.

Depredations in the West Indies.

The Spaniards continued their depredations in the West Indies. Captain Ebbats in a sloop belonging to New York, as he turned up from the bay to go to the Musquitos, was brought to, and boarded by a Spanish guarda costa, who demanded of him an anchor and cable, &c. and upon the captain's refusal to comply with that illicit demand, seized his sloop and carried her into Port Maho. And the Crown of Spain adopted every measure to drive the English entirely out of their settlements in Campeachy and Honduras.

Spain offers to be mediator.

Yet this very nation put on the utmost appearance of candour, and went so far as to offer his most Catholic Majesty's mediation between Great Britain and France: but the terms[e] were of such a nature, that his Britannic Majesty rejected them with disdain. Which instead of immediate resentment, produced such a temper in the Spanish councils, that his Catholic Majesty ratified the

[d] Enhanced by the recent motions of the national forces in Catalonia, Valencia, &c. and the destination of the men of war, &c. from Ferrol to a port in the neighbourhood of Gibraltar.

[e] It was said, that some of the articles proposed that England should cede Gibraltar to the French and have Minorca restored: and that France should exchange Gibraltar with Spain, for that part of Hispaniola now under the Spanish crown.

convention

convention for settling the commerce and navigation of the subjects of the two crowns during the present war, which had been delayed under various frivolous pretences.

A. D. 1756. Settles the neutrality.

However, their disgust and partiality could not be smothered. They snatched at every circumstance, that fell in their way, to ground a quarel upon with the English, continuing their armaments both for sea and land with great diligence. And observing, that the court of London was scrupulously cautious not to furnish them with any pretences of complaint in Europe, they revived the dispute about the English right to cut logwood in the Bay of Honduras, not by way of remonstrance to the British court, against the practices of our traders in that wood, but by a letter dated 14th of September 1756, from the governor of Meredith to the commander or principal officer of the Bay of Honduras, setting forth, " That being informed, the English had erected fortifications, &c. on the territories of his most Catholic Majesty, contrary to treaties between the court of Spain and that of Great Britain; and further that the English were arming themselves in an hostile manner, to make the possessions, they had indulged them with, their own; he therefore ordered them to depart out of those territories, and to destroy the fortifications erected thereon, under the peril of being driven out from thence by force; unless he could shew any right or authority they had from the court of Great Britain for so doing; and that all vessels loaden with logwood

Seek a ground for a quarrel.

Resolutions to deprive us of the logwood trade

A.D. 1756.

wood, taken on that coast, should be deemed and condemned to be lawful prizes."

Neglected in England.

This menacing order was transmitted to England; but was not thought of such moment, as to engage the ministry in an open breach with Spain at this time; and the logwoodmen were left to the mercy of the Spaniards, should they not be strong enough to defend themselves in their just and lawful ancient possessions.

Not succeeding by this scheme to provoke the pacific temper of the British ministry, there fell in their way two accidents at home, which they managed with great dexterity and openness to convince us of their partiality towards the French, and to draw from us a resentment sufficient to justify a declaration of war.

Governor of Algeziers fires upon the English in the Bay of Gibraltar.

The first of these was an affair, that happened in the Bay of Gibraltar. A French privateer had carried an English vessel under the guns of Algeziers, the Spanish fort near Gibraltar, which had been taken and brought thither from the coast of France. Admiral Hawke, then riding, with his squadron, in the bay, and Lord Tyrawley, governor of Gibraltar, sent to the governor of the Spanish fortress at Algeziers, in the most polite manner and terms, to demand the restitution of the ship in question, that bay being within the commad of the English garrison. This message was accompanied with a number of armed shallops or men of wars boats, to board the said ship, and to bring her away, at all events. But the Commandant of Algeziers received this demand

mand with a haughtiness, that indicated a determined partiality to the Frenchman, and not without threats, in case our boats dared to attempt to board the prize. However, no menaces were sufficient to deter the English tars from executing their orders; and being peremptorily denied the justice demanded, they drew near the shore, and made proper dispositions for seizing the vessel. But, though they, in every other circumstance, paid all the deference requisite towards the Spanish fortress, the Commander thereof fired upon them, as if they had been enemies, coming to attack or to besiege him. By which one hundred and fifty English were killed and wounded. Nevertheless the sailors carried their point; cut the vessel out, and carried her off to Gibraltar.

<small>A. D. 1756.</small>

Such treatment extorted a severe reprimand from Lord Tyrawley and Admiral Hawke, who, by letter to the Commandant of Algeziers, said, " That his behaviour was contrary to the rules " of neutrality, decency and good neighbourhood: " That he should answer for it before his Sove- " reign: and that whatever application or ex- " tention one might pretend to give to the neutrali- " ty of a state, the protecting of pyrates against the " subjects of a nation, with whom one is linked in " friendship by treaties, was in no case allowed."

<small>Resented by Sir Edw. Hawke and Lord Tyrawley.</small>

The Commandant justified himself from precedents, which he urged, of captures made by the French on former occasions, and brought into that place under the protection of the guns of the Spanish fortress; and that he had done, in this case,

<small>Spanish commander justifies the action.</small>

A.D. 1756.

Complains to his court.

case, no more than his duty required him to do. He also dispatched a courier to the court of Madrid, with the particulars of this transaction, and with his complaint of the violation of treaties and the law of nations by the English sailors, in cutting and forcibly taking away the ship from under the guns of his fortress.

Approved of by his court.

The court of Spain took this affair up in a very high strain; they approved of their commandant's conduct; said it was inconsistent with the pacific professions of the court of London; and that they would not suffer such a violation of their rights and of the honour of their country to pass unresented.

Sir Benj. Keene's moderate reply.

To which our Ambassador, Sir Benjamin Keene, replied with such moderation, as convinced them, that any satisfaction would be granted, rather than to proceed to an open rupture. He admitted the custom of carrying English prizes, made by the French into Algeziers: but added, That the sea-officers at Gibraltar had long observed it with great vexation; that this was the case complained of: that he waited for more precise informations; though what he had already received was sufficient to prove the hostilities were commenced by the Spanish Commandant; and that, as for the rest, the uprightness, with which his Britannic Majesty was accustomed to behave, towards powers in friendship and alliance with his crown, left no room to doubt, but that he would give fresh proofs of his care and attention to preserve the good understanding between the two nations.

While the nation was alarmed at this incident; and the miniftry were perplexed, how to fteer between the imputation of weaknefs and timidity, for not refenting the indignity offered to the Britifh flag, in a proper manner; and the not afferting our right to the Bay of Gibraltar, againft its being made a receptacle and place of retreat for the French in time of war; and the danger of furnifhing the Spaniards with an opportunity to throw the blame of an open rupture between the two crowns, upon England; another accident happened, which, by its greater importance, fmothered the complaints about Algeziers, and difcovered more publickly the defires of the Spanifh councils to break with Great Britain. Which had, for a little while, been fufpended, by an alteration in the Englifh miniftry.

A. D. 1756.

The cafe of the Antigallican privateer and her prize.

This was the cafe of the Antigallican private fhip of war, and her prize, driven into the port of Cadiz by ftrefs of weather or contrary winds. The Antigallican privateer, of thirty carriage and fixteen fwivel guns, and carrying 208 men, fitted out at the expence of 10,453 l. by private adventurers, in the port of London, and commanded by Captain William Fofter, late a lieutenant in his Majefty's fervice, had the fortune to difcover [f] a French Eaft Indiaman (named the Duke of Penthievre, commanded by Captain Villaneuve, a very large and rich fhip of 1000 tons, and mounting fifty guns) about feven leagues off Ferrol, a Spa-

Her force.

Her prize where taken.

[f] On the 26th of December 1756.

A. D. 1756.

nish port in the Bay of Biscay, early in the morning. The French aboard the Penthievre trusting in their own strength, bore down, with the wind in their favour, which was then at south south-east, and blew from the land; and about twelve at noon, being about four leagues and half from the nearest shore, fired a gun to bring the Antigallican to, then sailing under Spanish colours; and upon hoisting English colours, the Penthievre fired a broad-side immediately, and half another, before the Antigallican fired a gun, or made any sign of hostility, except displaying her colours; by which several on board the Antigallican were wounded and killed. The Antigallican having returned the fire, a close engagement continued between both ships, as they went before the wind, with all the sail they could make from the land, for about three hours; when the French captain, and twelve of his men being killed; and the second captain shot thro' the shoulder, and seven-and-twenty more were wounded, the Penthievre struck, and submitted to be boarded by the Antigallicans; then distant about five leagues and a half from the light-house at Corrunna.

Why carried into Cadiz.

The captors would have carried this rich prize to Lisbon, as the best market for her cargo: but meeting with contrary winds, which kept them beating the seas, in that disagreeable situation, off the mouth of the Tagus for several days; and afterwards finding it impracticable ᵍ to bear up against

ᵍ Captain Foster, in his journal, relates, That upon the sixth of January 1757, he was got within the mouth of the harbour against the wind and the current into the Bay of Gibraltar, it was resolved, with the advice of the officers, to carry the prize with them into the port of Cadiz, not doubting of protection from a neutral nation, in alliance or friendship with Great Britain.

A. D. 1756.

When to their great surprize, after taking shel- Stopt. ter in this port, and the officers belonging to the Indiaman had been examined upon oath, in regard to the validity of the capture, by the consul, vice-consul and his clerk; in which depositions, wrote by themselves, and in the French language, they, amongst other things, voluntarily declared, " That they bore down upon the Antigallican with a resolution to take her, as they imagined she was an English ship; and made no doubt but that she would fall a very easy prize, because she was so much inferior in size and burden to the Penthievre; and that their ship was fairly taken, and they were lawful prisoners of war; nor did they imagine, that the legality of the prize would

harbour for Lisbon; when a strong gale coming on, split the prize's main-top-sail, and drove her out to sea, which made it necessary for his ship to follow her out, and to send a boat on board her with small sails. That they, from that time, beat to windward, till the 22d, endeavouring to make Lisbon, but could not: that he then resolved to bear away for Cadiz, it being the first port they could make, in their great distress, the prize not steering, her sails all in pieces, both ships so leaky, that the pumps were almost constantly going, bread almost expended, not above ten days provisions left; and he had advice from the St. Alban's man of war, that there were five sail of French men of war cruizing upon the coast.

B 3 ever

ever be opposed or contested; or that the neutrality of the Spanish crown was at all offended at this engagement;" yet orders were sent from the court of Spain to the governor of Cadiz, to detain both ships, **the privateer** and **the Duke de Penthievre, and their contents;** upon a remonstrance from the commandant-general of Galicia, and the French consul complaining, that Captain Foster had attacked and taken the said prize, contrary to the laws of nations and neutrality, within the limits of a Spanish fort; and praying that his Catholic Majesty would demand restitution thereof, and satisfaction for so gross and national insult.

Why.

While the Antigallican had been beating the seas, this application, **supported by the captain and pilot of the port of Corrunna, and such other witnesses, as the French faction could easily pick up to swear any thing against the English,** was greedily espoused by the Spanish ministry, who, without waiting for the lights, which were necessary to determine justly on this affair, proceeded directly against the capture, in a council of war, and upon the first advice of its lying at Cadiz, the Spanish ministers, with the King's knowledge, issued orders to stop both the Antigallican and her prize, **before the council had gone through the examination of the complainants, or so much as summoned the captors to make their defence.**

Protested against.

In pursuance of this order the governor of Cadiz, on the 19th of February, sent for the English consul, and told him, that he was obliged to send troops on board the prize to detain her. Mr. Golds-

Goldsworthy, the consul, who throughout this whole affair acted with wisdom and firmness, protested against it in the strongest manner, as contrary to treaties, and an open violation of the laws of nations. Nevertheless, the governor ordered all the artillery on the walls to be loaded, gunners to attend with lighted match; six companies of grenadiers to be ready, with nineteen rounds of shot; and two companies to board and take possession of the prize, who immediately seized on the arms, magazines, &c. in the ship: he ordered two companies also to the forts, and two more on board the Antigallican, which by Admiral Novarro's permission was refitting in the King's Dock, and laid like a hulk, with its masts, sails, arms, guns, &c. in the King's ware-house. But at last, conscious of the illegality of such a proceeding, which alarmed the whole city, the Governor, in the evening of the same day, withdrew the troops from the ships; who not willing to go empty-handed, broke open several chests, carried away every thing they could find belonging to the officers and crew, and the very beef, that was dressing for dinner.

A. D. 1756.

Forcibly entered.

Plundered by the soldiers.

At length the council of war, on the allegations of one party only, having come to this resolution, "That the violation of his Majesty's "territory, and the insult offered to it by the pri- "vateer being fully and clearly proved, the pri- "vateer ought to be stopt, the captain punished, "and the pretended prize restored to its lawful "owners the French;" the governor acquainted

Ordered to be delivered to the French.

our

A.D. 1756.

our consul, that he had orders to deliver the prize up to the French consul. Upon which Captain Foster offered to deposit the prize in his, the governor's, hands, till he should obtain a hearing at court in his own defence. The governor absolutely rejected this expedient, and said he would instantly deliver the prize to the French consul. And the captain as resolutely declared, that the English colours then flying on board the prize, should never be struck without force. Then the consul and Captain Foster entering their protests against all the prejudices resulting from this arbitrary way of proceeding, obtained by perjury and a denial of justice from the court of Spain, which Sir Benjamin Keene said, " was so irregular, un-
" reasonable, and unprecedented, that would
" neither bear light nor justification," the captain withdrew and went on board.

Resolutions of Captain Foster.

Governor of Cadiz useth force.

This resolution staggered the governor for a-while. But after consulting the admiral, who prudently refused to advise about the execution of orders, in which he was not concerned, he demanded in the King's name the America of 60 guns, and a frigate of 36 guns, to aid and assist him in the execution of the King's orders. With these the Governor committed the most shameful and cruel act of hostility, that has been heard of among civilized nations. He stationed them within fifty yards of the Penthievre, and though Captain Foster offered to receive thirty or forty Spanish soldiers on board, and said he would rather die under his colours, than strike them; because he could

Captain Foster's proposal to avoid damages.

could follow no orders, but what he received from his Britannic Majesty or the British high court of admiralty; they began to fire upon her, and so continued for three quarters of an hour, though they met with no manner of resistance. They soon shot away the ensign flying on board the prize, and then Captain Foster finding that it was determined to sink him, sent a man to strike the pendant, who was killed by the Spaniards in the very act. They after this kept up their fire, half an hour longer, for their own diversion, and fired in all 200 round, grape and double-headed shot, into the Penthievre, as she lay exposed to their cruelty, without firing a single gun: by which one English subject was killed and seven wounded.

A. D. 1756.
Spaniards fire upon the Antigallican prize.
One Englishman killed and seven wounded.

When they ceased firing, the commodore ordered Captain Foster on board his ship, told him he was no prisoner, and sent him ashore: and Captain Foster, with the consul, waited on the Governor, and asking whether he had any commands for him, was answered in the negative. Yet next morning, contrary to the laws of nations, which makes a consul's house a sanctuary for protection, the governor's adjutant took Captain Foster by violence out of the English consul's house, and conducted him prisoner to the castle of St. Catharine. As for his men, they were treated with the greatest injustice, some of them knocked down with the butt-end of muskets by the soldiers sent to take possession of the Penthievre, denied the liberty to carry their own necessary cloaths with them, forced out of the ship, when a boat could scarce

Captain Foster dragged out of the consul's house to prison.
The sailors stripped, beaten and sent to prison.

scarce be supposed to reach the shore, in dangerous weather; stripped of their cloaths and robbed of all their money by their very guards, as soon as they landed, and then were conducted almost naked, as prisoners to the same castle of St. Catharine; where they had nothing to lie on, but the bare stones, in a close dungeon, without air sufficient to breathe, or space to extend their bodies without lying upon one another. A prison which, though horrible in itself! was rendered more miserable to those unhappy men, as they had not room for the common offices of nature, nor an allowance of any thing to eat or drink, no, not so much as bread and water. So that they, treated worse than felons, must have inevitably perished, had not the English consul supplied them with provisions, till released on the fifth of March by an order from Madrid. Of which transaction the English consul at Cadiz informed Sir Benjamin Keene, by letter, " That he was in the greatest
" consternation imaginable; because, says the
" consul, I have seen the flag of my royal master
" insulted; our nation degraded, our treaties vio-
" lated; the lustre of our Sovereign's crown tar-
" nished and despised, and my house invaded;
" and, as there is no minister here of greater dig-
" nity than myself, I consider the affront and in-
" sult done and offered to my person, as an
" indignity on the sacred person of my royal
" master."

After this conduct of the governor, censured by the Spaniards themselves, who saw it to be unjust,

with it so much weight, at this juncture of time, that Sir Benjamin Keene thought the prize would be so easily obtained, that he sent an express to Mr. Secretary Pitt, whereby he acquainted him, "That on presenting a strong memorial to his "Catholic Majesty, he had obtained an order for "the prize to be re-delivered to his Majesty's of- "ficers; and all the hatches to be kept sealed, "under a proper guard: and that he hoped the "prize would be restored to Captain Foster in a "few days; as the depositions of the French of- "ficers were so strong, that the French could "not have any thing to say, that could prevent "her being deemed a just and lawful prize." But all this expectation vanished, upon the first intimation of that opposition in the British cabinet, which on the fifth of April [h] delivered the Spanish ministry from the terror, which Pitt's very name carried in all his dispatches, in the cause of justice, for the dignity of the crown and the interest of his country. And during the interval before that right honourable person was reinstated, the Antigallican captors were treated in the manner above-related, and totally deprived of their property.

A. D. 1756. Its effect.

How altered when Mr. Pitt was turned out.

Thus stood our situation with Spain; which, under the sacred character of a mediator, and of a strict neutrality, was publickly prostituting

Our situation with Spain.

---

[h] The day on which the Right Hon. William Pitt, Esq; by his Majesty's command, first resigned the seals of Secretary of State for the southern department.

justice

A.D. 1756.

justice and the laws of nations, in favour of our enemies, insulting the British flag, robbing British subjects of their property, and depriving them of their liberty in the most arbitrary, cruel and hostile manner, and with the utmost diligence making preparations by sea and land for an open rupture.

The measures of France.

France, on her part, flushed with the success of every scheme she had laid to deceive, and to distress, Great Britain, strikes every nail, that seemed to drive, and to extend their plan of operations. The French ministry, convinced that the completion of their advantages, and dominion in North America, depended chiefly on measures, either, to dispute the sovereignty of the seas with the mistress of the ocean; without which it would be impossible for them to supply their armies in the new world with effectual succours, to protect their own settlements, and to extend their conquests; or, to draw Great Britain into a continental war, by which the national treasure, that might be required for a naval and American war, should be dissipated and exhausted; so as to weaken the British power by sea, and to divert her attention from a vigorous pursuit of the principal object, for which this nation took up arms; or, to devise some improvement to their long-practised scheme to make us weary of the war, by engaging our ministry to maintain a prodigious navy in commission and fit for service, inactive and locked up in our harbours, and to pay large subsidies and numerous land forces in a situation, that

that could only serve to increase our load of taxes, and the already prodigious national debt; which would fill the people with discontent, and oblige them, sooner or later, to submit to an inglorious peace; their first care was to throw the weight of their strength into their naval department; and many attempts were made to keep the sea open, for the purposes of protecting their trade and islands from insult; of transporting soldiers and the necessaries of war to North America; of interrupting our navigation and commerce; of defeating our measures for the support of North America, and of threatning the British isles themselves with invasion and conquest.

<small>A. D. 1756. Attention to their marine.</small>

Their efforts by sea were made with vigour and great propriety. A navy was preparing, with the utmost diligence, to contend with ours; while the court proposed to ruin our trade, and to interrupt our navigation, by the extraordinary encouragement they gave to private ships of war.

<small>Their navy, and how employed.</small>

Within a few weeks after the declaration of war at Paris, the world was presented with the following state of the French marine, published by authority.

Mr. Perrier de Salvert's squadron.

Ships	Captains	Guns
Le Courageux	Perrier	74
Le Prothee	————	64
L'Amphion	————	50
L'Aigle	————	50
Le Fleur de Lys	————	30
L'Emeraude	————	28

At

32 THE GENERAL HISTORY OF

A.D. 1756.

At Brest.

Ships	Captains	Guns
Le Comete	——	30
L'Amethiste	——	30
La Blonde	——	30
Le Brune	——	30
Le Zephyr	——	30
L'Hermoine	——	26
La Valeu	——	26
La Fidele	——	26
La Friponne	——	26

M. De La Galissionere's fleet.

Ships	Captains	Guns
Le Foudroiant	D. L. Galissioniere	80
Le Temeraire	Glandeves, Chief d'Esc.	74
La Couronne	La Clu, Chief d'Esc.	74
Le Redoubtable	Beaumont	74
Le Guerrier	La Brosse	74
Le Content	Sabran	64
Le Triton	Mercier	64
Le Sage	Duruen	64
Le Lion	St. Agnan	64
L'Orphee	Raimondis	64
Le Fier	D'Herville	50
L'Hipopotame	Rochemaure	50
La Junon	Beaufier	46
La Rose	Costebelle	30
La Pleide	——	26
La Gracieuse	Marquizan	24
La Nimphe	Callian	24
La Topaze	Carne	24

The Marquis de Conflans's squadron.

Ships	Captains	Guns
Le Soliel	The Marquis	80
Duc de Bourgogne	——	80
Le Tonnant	——	80
Le Superbe	——	74
Le Defenseur	——	74
Le Dauphin Royal	——	70

Le

THE LATE WAR.

Ships	Captains	Guns	A.D.
Le Juste		70	1756.
Le Hardi		66	
Le Bienfaisant		64	
Le Sphinx		64	
L'Inflexible		64	
L'Eveille		64	
Le Capricieux		64	
L'Arc en Ciel		50	
La Diana		30	

For carrying soldiers to America under Mr. Beauffie.

Ships	Captains	Guns
Le Heros	Beauffier	74
L'Illustre	Montelas	64
Le Leopard		60
Le Sirene	Breugnon	30
Le Licorne	Rigaudiere	30
La Sauvage		30
La Concorde		30
L'Amarante		12

At Brest and Rochfort.

Ships	Captains	Guns
Le Formidable		80
L'Entreprenant	B. R*. Salvert, Chief d'Esc.	74

On a cruise.

Ships		Guns
La Thetis		24
La Mutine		24
La Pomone		24
Le Cumberland		24
La Galathe		24
L'Heroine		24
L'Anemone		12

Cape Breton and Martinico.
Mr. D'Aubigne.

Ships	Captains	Guns
Le Prudent	D'Aubigne	74
L'Aquilon		60

* B. R. Brest or Rochfort.

Vol. II.   C   L'Ata-

A. D. 1756.	Ships	Captains		Guns
	L'Atalante	——	——	34
	Le Palmer	B. R.	Keruforet	74
	Le Bizarre	B. R.	Urtubi	64
	L'Opiniatre	B. R.	Moelieu	64
	L'Actif	B. R.	Choiseuil	64
	Le St. Michel	B. R.	Caumont	64
	L'Alcion	B. R.	Jonquire	54
	L'Appollon	——	——	50

At Toulon.

Le Hector	——		74
Le Vaillant	——		64
L'Achille	——		64
L'Hercule	——		64
L'Oriflame	——		50

Upon the Careen.

L'Intrepide	B. R.	Rersain	74
Le Conquerant	——		74
Le Magnifique	——		74
Le Sceptre	——		74
Le Florissant	——		74
L'Algougeux	——		74
La Floride	——		74
Northumberland	——		68
Le Dragon	B. R.	Willeon	74

In different docks.

L'Ocean, finished	——		80
Le Centaure, ditto	——		70
Le Diademe	B. R.	Rasilly	74
Le Zodiaque	——		74
Le Minotaure	——		74
Le Souverain	——		74
Le Glorieux	——		74
Le —— (not yet named)	——		74
Le Belliqueux	Oroillirs B. R.		64

Le

Ships	Captains	Guns	A. D. 1756.
Le Celebre	———	64	
Le Robuste	———	64	
Le Solitaire	———	64	
Le Terrible	———	64	
Le Aigrette	———	30	
La Vestable	———	30	
La Minerva	———	24	
L'Oiseau	———	24	
Le Protecteur, building	———	74	
Le Fantasque	———	64	
Le Modeste	———	60	
La Defiance	———	30	
La Surprize	———	30	

Le Warwick, taken from the English, 1756, of 60 guns, mounting now but 50, in America, with M. D'Aubigne.

By this list it appears that the navy of France, in June 1756, consisted of one hundred and eleven ships of the line and frigates, and that they were so stationed and managed, as to find employment for the grand navy of England. A sufficient number of large ships were kept in the ports of Brest and Toulon, at an easy expence, neither manned, nor victualled, till ordered out for service; with which they put us to very great expence of large squadrons, to watch their motions in the Bay of Biscay and the Mediterranean; a service attended with so many hazards, that it was with great good luck in us, that the enemy even suffered any loss by it, or were ever so locked up, as to prevent their exports of men and ammunition for America, sailing and reaching the places

A.D. 1756.

of their destination. But it was attended with many great disadvantages on our part. For, it is a greater victory to decoy the enemy into his ruin by delay, &c. than to beat him in an open fight; because, thereby not only his strength is destroyed, but his treasure the sinews of war, is consumed.

In the West Indies.

Their next care was to threaten our sugar islands with a powerful squadron in the West Indies: which might serve to surprize and seize upon those defenceless colonies, or to weaken our naval strength by the necessity, Great Britain would be under, to keep a superior naval force in those seas, where our security must depend only upon the superiority of our navy, against an enemy, that can retreat into strong fortified harbours; when, in case of an accident, a British squadron, or ship, can find no place of shelter from a pursuing foe, in any of our islands.

Cruisers.

Their cruizers were so numerous, and properly stationed for intercepting our merchantmen homeward and outward bound; to ruin our African trade, and to favour their own convoys, to and from America; that it required more men of war to check and to defeat their proceedings, than a ministry, that was continually afraid of an invasion, dared to appoint for that purpose. And that the King's ships should perform, and confine themselves, as much as possible, to their orders to protect their own navigation, and to employ the English navy, the French King published an edict for the encouragement of privateers to distress our commerce, and to deprive us of the grand resource

Their encouragement of privateers.

of

of our riches, without which it could not be possible for us to support the war.

That edict remitted the *tenth* share of every prize, which was always before this war claimed by the French admiralty; and ordained that besides the whole produce of the prizes, the captors should enjoy a bounty [i] out of the royal treasury, for every gun and man taken from a merchantman, or man of war, or privateer. The King also promised to reward such captains or officers, that should behave well, with commissions in his marine, according to the circumstances and strength of the ships they should have engaged: and he further promised a premium to the owners of privateers,

---

[i] 100 livres per gun from four to 12 pounders, taken from merchantmen.

150 livres per gun of the same bore, taken from privateers.

200 livres per gun of the same bore, taken from men of war.

150 livres per gun 12 pounders and upwards, taken from merchantmen.

225 livres per gun of the said bore, taken from privateers.

300 livres per gun of the said bore, taken from men of war.

30 livres per head for every prisoner taken out of a merchantman.

40 livres per head for ditto out of a privateer,

50 livres per head for ditto, out of a man of war.

The same bounties to be paid for every man on board at the commencement of any engagement.

The said bounties to be augmented by *one fourth* for all such privateers or men of war, which shall be taken by boarding, and

The said bounties wholly to appertain to the captain, officers, and crew; to be divided amongst themselves according

vateers, and to take their ships, under certain circumstances, at prime cost [k]. In regard to prizes made by ships fitted out upon the King's account, the officers and crew were thereby indulged with one third part of the neat produce of all merchant ships, or more according to circumstances; besides other bounties [l]. He further promised, that privateers

to the share they are to have in the produce of the prize, and pursuant to their agreement at the time of entering on board; the money to be paid to the captain, or his representative.

[k] Ships of 24 guns or upwards, that shall have been built for privateering, shall be taken by the government at the prime cost, if they be not employed that way, or at the estimated price, if they have been so employed, when they shall be no longer authorised to cruise on the enemies. And also all ships of 24 guns or upwards, that shall be taken by privateers, and which shall be fit for service, except the captors shall chuse to make use of them themselves, or sell them along with the effects of the prizes.

In order to indemnify the owners of those ships which shall take any privateers or men of war, of the damage they shall sustain by such engagements, the following premiums are to be paid them:

100 livres per gun from 4 to 12 pounders.
200 livres per gun from 12 lb. to upwards.
20 livres per head for every effective man on board at the beginning of an engagement.

[l] They shall have besides, the same bounties as those given in the 2d article in favour of the privateers, except for men of war, for which there shall be paid 300 livres per gun, from four to 12 pounders, 450 livres per gun from 12 pounders and upwards.

The said sums to be augmented by 1-4th, when the said frigates or men of war shall have been taken by boarding.

privateers which should sail in company with men of war, or join them at sea, should have their share both in the produce of the prizes, **as well as of the bounties,** of all ships that **should be** taken in conjunction, in exact proportion to the guns they shall carry, with regard to the difference of the bore, size of the ships, or strength of the crews. That privateers should be exempt from all taxes or duties **whatsoever on provisions, artillery, ammunition,** and all **other necessaries for** their construction, victualing and armament: That the officers and volunteers on board of privateers, that have distinguished themselves, should be dispensed with from the usual time **of service on board the men of war,** in order to their being made captains. That the officers **and sailors on** board of privateers that should be **wounded and** disabled, should be intitled to the sea half-pay, and that the widows of those killed should be intitled to pensions. This edict also ordained that the wages of sailors run from a ship of 24 guns, as well as their share in prizes, should belong to the owners: and finally, That captains of privateers, should not on any account **ransom any ship,** except they should have already **sent in three** effective prizes, since their last going out.*

A. D. 1756.

* *N. B.* By these encouragements the sea presently swarmed with privateers, which did infinite damage to our trade and took great numbers of our merchantmen. They were even so audacious, that on the 4th of July, about one o'clock in the morning, a privateer from Boulogne ventured within a few yards of Dover Pier, and cut an English privateer away, most of her men being a-shore.

These

A. D. 1756.

Preparations for a land war.

How favoured in Germany.

Against Hanover, &c.

Pretences of an invasion kept

These preparations and armaments for the sea were accompanied briskly with much more extraordinary preparations for war by land. The treaty of Westphalia, which France had so often violated to pull down the House of Austria, was now made a stalking horse to carry her army without opposition into Germany: and the heiress of Austria, who is indebted to Great Britain for the existence of her family, against the natural enmity of France, adopted, and submitted to be a cover for, the French monarch's real intentions to invade the territories of our German allies, and embroil her most faithful and powerful friend in a continental war, by inviting Lewis to take part in her quarrel, or rather secret hatred of the King of Prussia. For, this was the first pretence for the motions of the French army across the Rhine; to preserve the peace of Germany and to keep all foreign forces out of the Empire: though the French ministers did not scruple to avow the resolution of their King to invade the electoral dominions of his Britannic Majesty: and the situation of his magazines, the cantonment of his troops on the frontiers of Flanders, and other dispositions on the side of Westphalia, were evident tokens, that the French King's immediate view, in joining with the Empress Queen against the King of Prussia, was to facilitate the execution of his own designs upon the allies of Great Britain.

This army also served another purpose. Having nothing to fear on the part of Spain, nor from the frontiers of Upper Germany; and possessed of

the

the secret, which had so often, on former occasions, kept the whole strength of England locked up at home; fifty or sixty thousand men or more, and artillery, were drawn down to the coast of the channel; and boats of a new construction were built, and squadrons were appointed to convoy them over to some convenient place in England. Amazing how this soporific dose of politics affected the heads of the nation! The name of a flat-bottomed boat terrified the children, the women and the beaux; and the French were well paid for their invention by the expence we were at to watch their motions, while we neglected, or omitted to employ our fleets and armies in vigorous and national measures.

A. D. 1756. up, with flat-bottomed boats.

Having thus disposed of their internal strength, the French provided, in the next place, to prevent any disagreeable and unseasonable disputes, with the maritime neutral powers, about the conditions of a free navigation; and thereby endeavoured to engage neutral ships in their service, when the circumstances of the war might make it dangerous or impracticable to carry on a communication with their colonies, and to supply their naval department with such necessaries, as could not be got in their own territories, and without which a naval war could not be supported. For, amongst other things, it will appear afterwards, that the King of France assumed a right to licence Dutch ships to trade with, or to carry the produce of, their islands, from which, in common with other nations, they had been always excluded in times

French settle the terms of navigation with neutral states.

of

of peace; and the Dutch, in return for that favour, assumed a right, which they pretended to claim upon the faith of treaty, with England, to carry the goods of our enemies: though at the same time that French ordinance [m] laid them, and all other neutral nations, under the severest prohibition not to carry British property.

British measures.

Great Britain, whose interest it was to take the most effectual measures to defeat the designs and schemes of France; and whose navy greatly exceeded the naval power of that nation in every circumstance; both as to number of ships, weight of mettal, men, and stores of all sorts; instead of seeking and annoying the enemy; covering our colonies, and protecting our navigation and trade; confined the naval strength of this island to the expensive and almost useless cruising in the Bay of Biscay and in the Mediterranean: and to squadrons at Antigua, the leeward islands, and at Jamaica, inferior to the French under d'Aubigny, near the former station, and to de Salvert hovering about the latter.

Its navy, and how employed.

East India neglected.

There was a small squadron commanded by Admiral Watson, as related before, in the East Indies; but so much neglected as if that part of the world had been excluded from the common blessings of the administration: for, war had been declared upwards of two months, before any ship was sent to give notice of it in that region.

[m] Dated 8th July 1756.

Though the very exiſtence of our ſugar planta- tions, and our Tobacco colonies in North America, depended upon the ſecurity of our ſettlements in Africa; from whence they are ſupplied with labourers or ſlaves: and though the French had begun to encroach upon our rights, on the coaſt of Guinea, and there was great reaſon to apprehend, they would at length wholly execute the ſcheme, they had long laid, of getting poſſeſſion of the whole; our ignorance of our own intereſt, or our negligence, or our injudicious parſimony had almoſt given them an opportunity to complete that work : as will appear from the ſtate of our African ſettlements from the year 1730 to the year 1756 incluſive. In 1730 the African company applied to parliament for relief, and obtained 10,000 l. per annum, till the year 1746, when it was ſuſpended on account of the ruinous condition of the company's affairs, they being 130,000 l. in debt, their forts and caſtles in ruins, and their credit and reputation loſt. In 1749, the traders to and from Africa, between Cape Blanco and the Cape of Good-Hope, were incorporated, by act of parliament, but prohibited trading in their corporate capacity, and from having any transferable ſtock, or borrowing money on their common ſeal : and a majority of a committee of nine were empowered to make orders concerning the forts and factories, and to appoint governors and officers [n].

A. D. 1756.

Africa neglected.

State of our African trade.

From

[n] Thus the old African company was aboliſhed, and received in compenſation from the houſe 112,142 l. 3 s. 3 d. for their

A.D. 1756.

From this time the parliament revived and paid the grant of 10,000 l. per ann. and increased that sum to 16,000 l. per ann. for the support and repair of the forts and settlements. Nevertheless this important coast was suffered to run to decay, as appears by a true state of the forts, at this time, in the note below*; and by the weakness of the naval power, which did now consist of no more than two men of war in those seas. So that five men of war might have driven the English quite out of Africa; to the utter ruin of our sugar colonies.

N. American coast neglected.

Our strength on the coast of North America at such a critical juncture (when the intercepting of the enemies troops and warlike stores, bound for New France, would have answered the end of a victory, and more effectually disconcerted their operations on that Continent, than the completest

---

their charters, lands, forts, castles, slaves, books, papers, and all other effects. See p. 37. Vol. I.

* 1. James Fort in the river Gambia, though mounted with 36 guns is not able to resist an European enemy.

2. Anamaboe Fort, not finished.
3. Tantumquerry, 13 guns. ⎫
4. Winnebab Fort, 16 guns. ⎬ Not defenceable against an European enemy.
5. Accra Fort, 36 guns. ⎭
6. Wydah Fort, deserted.
7. Commenda Fort, 31 guns, ⎫
8. Succondee Fort, 29 guns, ⎬ Out of repair.
9. Dix Cove Fort, 30 guns, ⎭
10. Cape Coast Castle, 40 guns, ⎫
11. Fort Royal, 12 guns, ⎪
12. Phipp's Tower, five guns, ⎬ Only in a state to keep the natives in awe.
13. Q. Ann's Point, five guns, ⎭

victory

victory in those deserts on the back of our plantations; and when Newfoundland was exposed to a surprize from Louisbourg), was so deficient for the service required in those parts, that we have seen the narrow escape of Holmes's squadron being carried into that port.

A. D. 1756.

The whole attention of the ministry continued still to turn upon domestic defence. The mouth of the Thames and Portsmouth, were the favourite stations of the capital ships, and of greatest part of our navy; while the ocean was left to the care of our privateers; under very great encouragements [p].

Fleet kept at home.

Our land forces continued upon the increase, augmented with new regiments, and with additions to the old ones. But the only use to which such numerous troops were put, was to assist in the dissipation of the national treasure, by extraordinary parades and encampments, where there was not the least appearance and expectation of meeting with an enemy. The grand trains of artillery, which marched, on those occasions, from the Tower of London, served only to confirm the people in the mean opinion, they entertained of a ministry, that could not by any provocations from the enemy, or by the remonstrances of the nation, be induced to make a better use of their strength in money and arms, than to exhibit raree-shews at an expence and with an army, that was able to attack, and should have been employed in vigorous measures against the enemy.

Land forces augmented. For what purpose.

[p] See Vol. I. page 414.

A. D. 1756.

The sense of the nation.

The sense of the nation, on this occasion, may be properly represented by the following description of the march of the train through London to Cobham, on the 19th of July, given by a political observer of that transaction [q], "I, says he, and, at least, 300,000 more idle spectators, can vouch for a good round sum of money laid out on the train, which past from the Tower of London, over the bridge to the inland village of Cobham, in Surry. An expedition, that will eat up three or four such sums, as the plate and dice acts [r] can produce; and has been longer in agitation than the succours for Mahon took up; under a ministry, which at a time they want every penny raised by parliament, and are distressed for ways and means for further supplies, to repel the common enemy, lavishly throw away their hundreds of thousands in a field where there is no enemy.—Many other disagreeable ideas crowded into my thoughts.—But there was one reflection most predominant, occasioned by the appearance of such an immense croud of spectators, that lined the streets and roads. Could London, early on a monday morning, spare, from the necessary business and callings in that metropolis, so many thousands, and Britain be destitute of strength to repel a foreign enemy? Could a raree-shew draw them from their occupations, and it be supposed they would remain passive, or flee before the invaders

---

[q] See Monitor, N°. 50.

[r] Part of the ways and means for raising the supplies in the last session of parliament.

of their liberty and property? On the contrary, it was with the utmost pleasure, that I observed all degrees, and both sexes, young and old, wishing for an opportunity to give real proofs of their loyalty and courage, and that they might live to see the money, they paid in taxes, effectually applied, not in pageantry and mock expeditions, but in defence of our colonies and settlements abroad: **in our commerce and** dominion by sea: and in a well regulated and disciplined militia."

A. D. 1756.

So that, if we sum up the whole of the service done with the vast sums granted by parliament in the last session, it amounts to no more than keeping on foot a large body of mercenaries and foreign forces within this kingdom.—An inactive campaign in North America, which deprived us of the most important forts we had to cover our plantations, and to stem the power of France, on that continent.——A squadron, on that coast, not able to prevent succours from Old France to Louisbourg and Canada.—A total neglect of Newfoundland.—Squadrons too **weak to resist** any attempt upon our sugar islands, and upon our settlements on the coast of Africa.—A supine neglect of the East Indies.——A fleet in the Mediterranean, that could undertake no affair, nor **find a more** important object for its employ, than hunting a few Tartans, loaden with provisions for Minorca.——And a still more inactive fleet beaten to pieces in the Bay of Biscay.——A few cruisers to guard the channel and to watch the French ports, without any success, except the

How the great supplies were expended.

surprize

A.D. 1756.

surprize of a small island, near Guernsey, defended by about 100 men, taken by Captain How, in the Dunkirk, and three frigates; and the capture of a great number of ships. But with such a neglect of our own trade, that, our loss in merchant ships fell very little short of the captures made from the French by both our privateers and men of war[s].—Our fleets had fled before our enemies;

---

[s] 251 ships were taken from the French, amongst which there were the following remarkable ships:

The Arc-en-ciel, a man of war of 50 guns.

A Martinico-man valued at 250,000 dollars, taken within two leagues of Cadiz, by the Experiment.

The Fortune, from Rochfort to Mississippi, 450 tons, with 140 soldiers and 30 women.

The Duke of Anjou with stores, and the Grand St. Ursin with 130 soldiers, for Louisbourg.

Two ships from the coast of Africa, with 980 slaves.

A ship with provisions for Cape Breton.

A large French Guinea-man.

One privateer of eight guns, eight swivels, and 86 men. Another of 20 guns, 200 men. Another of 10 guns and 90 men. Another of six guns, 60 men. Another of 20 guns and 195 men. Another of eight guns, 18 swivels, 100 men. Another drove a-shore on the Bahama islands. Another of eight guns, 10 swivels, 75 men. Another of four guns, six swivels, and 40 men. Another of 16 guns, 16 swivels, and 230 men. Three more privateers of 10 guns and 56 men. Another of 12 guns, 12 swivels, and 24 men.

A frigate of 36 guns with stores for Canada.

230 ships were taken within the same space of time by the French. Amongst which was the Warwick man of war of 60 guns, and four privateers. One ship with 200 soldiers for New York, and another with 88 people on board for Newfoundland. Which, allowing for the difference of value between

"perhaps it never was more neceſſary to tell it without reſerve. This is the object of the moſt humble and moſt reſpectful remonſtrance, we have the honour to bring to the foot of your throne."—"But though the meaſures of evil is nearly full, let us yet hope that the time will ſoon arrive, in which thoſe gentlemen, by whoſe erring conduct, our calamities are brought upon us, will rather than ſee the ruin complete, have pity on the public weal, and ſave the ſinking bark. Let us require this, the leaſt of reparation, and the mildeſt of requeſts, that they will now become atoning volunteers for themſelves and their country, in withdrawing from ſcenes of buſineſs, to inactive ſolitude, that by their councils and influence, they may no longer interrupt the ſucceſs of our arms, or farther diſgrace the dignified name and annals of this once victorious land.

"Let Minorca and America, oppreſſive taxes, and a complaining people, the nation's debt, and declining credit, private intereſt, and general ſafety, the approaching ſeſſions, and the expiring year, all remind and leſſon them to obey the precept. Then may we hope to ſee victory wait upon our arms, and peace, in a little time, reach out her olive-branch, plenty diſplay her horn, and glory, honour and happineſs, adorn our iſle."

In the midſt of this national diſcontent the advices from Germany increaſed our fears. The Empreſs of Ruſſia affected to be highly diſcontented with the treaty his Britannic Majeſty lately made

A. D. 1756.

The Czarina diſguſted with Great Britain.

A. D. 1756.

Renounces her treaty.

Accedes to a treaty with France.

The Empress Queen assembles her forces.

Endeavours to exculpate herself about her treaty with France.

Accuses the King of England and King of Prussia.

made with the King of Prussia, without her knowledge or her ministers. She went so far as to give it for the reason of renouncing the late treaty [u] with Great Britain. And accordingly she rejected the tender of the first payment of the stipulated subsidies. Not only so, but her Czarish Majesty acceded publickly to the treaty of Versailles; and put those very troops in motion to execute the schemes laid down by the whole confederacy against the King of Prussia, which Great Britain had agreed to take into her service [w] in order to prevent foreign, especially French, troops entering into Germany. And the motions of the King of Prussia, and his sudden and extraordinary military dispositions obliged the Empress Queen to assemble a more considerable body of troops, to be ready at all events against a surprize; who complained, by her ministers at foreign courts, That her good intentions had been misrepresented, as if the friendly alliance lately concluded between her Majesty the Empress Queen and his most Christian Majesty, contained secret articles, calculated for the total suppression of the Protestant religion, and to influence the election of a King of the Romans, and that, upon such false suggestions, there had been a proposal made for a league of the protestant courts against the house of Austria.

This declaration from the Empress Queen was answered both by the King of Great Britain, in

[u] See page 135 and 204.   [w] Ibid.

quality

quality of Elector of Hanover, and the King of Prussia: by their respective ministers at the Diet of the Empire.

A. D. 1756.

His Britannic Majesty, in quality of Elector of Hanover or Brunswick Lunenburg, answered, "That he had, with great surprize, heard that some people had affected to put a wrong construction upon the object of the treaty of friendship, which he concluded some time ago [x] with the King of Prussia, and that they have even endeavoured to represent it, as a matter wherein the state of religion was concerned; that nevertheless the whole Empire was sensible, he has always made it a rule to support the rights of each, without any distinction of persons; to maintain justice; to enforce the execution of the laws and constitutions of the Empire; to protect its liberties and the public peace; and to contribute to keep up in the Germanic body such a system, as appeared most conducive to its safety. That in consequence of these principles, he had neglected nothing, that might most effectually tend to the support of the house of Austria, even to the being ready to sacrifice all that was in his power. That the differences, which had risen between Great Britain and France, about their possessions in America, having given birth to a design in the latter power, to attack the Electoral dominions of the house of Brunswick Lunenburg; which was sufficiently known, by the little care they took to make a

King of England's answer.

---

[x] See this treaty on page 256.

D 3

mystery

A. D. 1756.

mystery of such a project, so capable of creating troubles in the Empire; his Britannic Majesty, who addressed himself to the Empress Queen, requiring the succours stipulated by treaties, was not only unable to obtain them, but at the same time found the court of Vienna as little inclined to grant another request, altogether as reasonable: which was to employ her good offices towards altering the dispositions of such of the states of the Empire, as, through indifference, seemed to favour, in some measure, that intended invasion. That his Britannic Majesty thereby found himself under a necessity of concluding an alliance with the King of Prussia, for the security of their respective dominions, as also for preserving peace and tranquility in the Empire; protecting the system established therein, and defending the rights and privileges of the members of the Germanic body; without any prejudice to either of the religions, exercised in the Empire; the contracting parties having had no views in that treaty, but such as were perfectly consistent with those salutary objects.

" That while matters stood thus, the world was surprised with the unexpected event of the treaty of alliance, which her Majesty, the Empress Queen had been pleased to conclude with a potentate, who, for above two centuries past, has dismembered the most considerable provinces of the Empire; has attacked and invaded her Archducal house; has fomented troubles and divisions in Germany; and has made such means subservient

THE LATE WAR.

vient to her own ambitious views, by usurping whatever lay convenient for her: that the inconveniencies and dangers, which this new treaty must necessarily be productive of, will, in time, be made manifest; and that as the thing is not of such a nature, as to require that one should any longer make a mystery of it, his Britannic Majesty has thought proper to explain himself clearly on this head, in order to dissipate the prejudices, which may have been created by false ideas and suggestions."

Soon after this declaration, made by his Britannic Majesty, the King of Prussia made his also, beginning with " his surprize to hear the Empress Queen endeavouring to persuade the public, that he was the aggressor, and given occasion for the great military preparations making in her dominions. To discover the falsity of which charge, said he, it will suffice to observe the points of time when the motions amongst the forces of each party began.

" It is notorious, added that Monarch, that the court of Vienna began her armaments in Bohemia and Moravia in the beginning of June, soon after signing the treaty with France, and at a time, when neither the Empress Queen, nor any of her allies, had any ground to apprehend a surprize. That his Prussian Majesty had greater reason to be attentive to these dispositions, as he received advice, at the same time, of the march of a considerable body of Russians towards Courland: and that those dispositions had determined

A. D. 1756.

King of Prussia's answer and measures to prevent a war.

him

him to detach a few regiments into Pomerania, with orders to halt, as soon as he should hear that the Russians had marched back. That the present armaments could not be ascribed, with any sort of grace, to this motion of the Prussian forces; because the march of a body of Prussians into Pomerania ought naturally to give the court of Vienna no more umbrage, than the march of some Austrian regiments towards Tuscany, could give the King of Prussia.

"That while the preparations of war were carrying on with the utmost vigour in Bohemia and Moravia, his Prussian Majesty contented himself with putting his fortresses in Silesia into a posture of defence, against a sudden attack, and marching some regiments towards his provinces in Westphalia. That to that very day he had not sent a single regiment into Silesia; that no garrison had marched out to take the field; no camp had been formed, neither had there been any motion made towards the territories of the Empress Queen. That he could appeal for the truth of these facts, to the court of Vienna itself; which in its circular letter alledged only uncertain reports, that had been confuted by the event, for no camps have been formed, nor pitched on, upon the borders of Bohemia or Moravia, as the Empress Queen pretended she was informed there would be.

"That notwithstanding the King of Prussia's pacific conduct, the Empress Queen had continued her armaments, ordered troops to march

from

from her most distant provinces, and assembled a formidable army in Bohemia and Moravia. That in such a critical juncture, when the court of Vienna was stirring up all the powers in Europe against the King, calumniating his proceedings, and giving bad interpretations to his most innocent measures; when offensive measures were taken against him; and the court of Vienna was amassing warlike stores and provisions in Moravia and Bohemia, making powerful armaments and forming camps of 80,000 men in its dominions: when lines of Hungarians and Croatians were posted on the frontiers of Silesia, and camps were marking out on the King's limits: when peace resembled war, whilst, at the same time, the Prussian troops were quiet, and not a tent pitched on their side; the King of Prussia thought it was time for him to break silence; and these military motions obliged him to demand of the court of Vienna, by his minister, M. de Klinggraffe, a friendly and sincere explanation, with regard to those military preparations: whether they were designed against the King of Prussia? or, what were the intentions of her Imperial Majesty? But the answer given to that demand being, "That in the present "juncture the Empress Queen had found it ne- "cessary to make armaments, as well for her own "defence, as for that of her allies, and which "did not tend to the prejudice of any body;" was so very ambiguous, dry and unsatisfactory, that it gave his Majesty a suspicion of a design formed against his dominions: especially as the

prepara-

A. D. 1756.

preparations in Bohemia and Moravia were continued, and doubled: That, things being thus circumstanced, it was natural for the King of Prussia to consult his own interest and safety; and that he believed, no body could justly blame him for taking measures to avoid being surprized and crushed in his own territories.

"He further challenged the court of Vienna to point out any other object of the King of Prussia's armaments, but the defence and security of his own dominions. But that it was very easy to discover some other views, than self-defence and security in the armaments of the Imperial court: and that he still left it to the choice of the Empress Queen, to have peace or war.

"The King of Prussia, he said, being dissatisfied with the Empress Queen's first answer, ordered his minister to demand a catagorical explanation from that Princess; wherein he expressed himself to this effect: That if her Imperial Majesty's pacific intentions were really as pure and sincere, as she pretended, in all places, they were, it would be easy for her to convince the King of Prussia thereof: that she need only give his minister a clear, precise declaration, free from all ambiguity and equivocation, and that would restore the public tranquility. And further, that he was willing to believe, on the assurances of her Majesty, the Empress Queen, that her late treaty with his most Christian Majesty contained no other articles, but what had been published; and that he promised himself, from the integrity of

her

her Imperial Majesty, that she would agree to no project, that might be contrary to Protestantism: But that she could not be dissatisfied to find the protestant princes upon their guard in such a critical juncture, as the present, when the validity of the act of security, given by the hereditary Prince of Hesse Cassel, for maintaining the established religion, is openly attacked, and a discovery has been made of the secret intrigues of Count Pergen, the Emperor's minister, and of Baron Kurtzrock, to carry off that Prince, and to take him from under the authority of the Landgrave of Hesse Cassel, his father, who had publickly complained thereof, but could obtain no satisfaction, &c."

His Prussian Majesty being ready to take the field at all events, ordered M. Klinggraffe to represent to the Empress Queen, "That after his master had dissembled, as long as he thought consistent with his safety and his glory, the bad designs, imputed to the Empress, he could not suffer himself longer to disguise any thing; and that he had orders to inform her, That the King was acquainted with the offensive projects formed, by the two courts, at Petersburgh: that he knew they had engaged to attack him unexpectedly with their united force; the Empress Queen supplying 80,000 men, and the Czarina 120,000: and that this design had been deferred hitherto, for no other reason, than the want of recruits for the Russian army, and mariners for their fleet, and the defect of corn in Livonia, necessary for their support;

port: that the King once more made the Empress the offer of peace or war: that if she chose peace, he expected a clear and formal declaration, consisting of a positive assurance, that she had no intention to attack the King either this year, or the next: and that he should look upon any ambiguous answer, as a declaration of war.

The Empress Queen's reply.

The Empress Queen disdaining, as she said, to be thus dictated to by a Prince of the Empire, returned a more haughty, and less satisfactory, answer to so just and equitable a demand, than the former; and in such terms, as left no doubt of the bad intentions of the court of Vienna. She retorted upon the King of Prussia the accusation of military preparations: "His Majesty the King of Prussia, said she, had been already employed, for some time, in all kinds of the most considerable preparations of war; and the most disquieting, with regard to the public tranquility; when on the twenty-sixth of last month, that Prince thought fit to order explanations to be demanded of her Majesty, the Empress Queen, upon the military dispositions, which were making in her dominions, and which had not been resolved upon, till after all the preparations, which his Prussian Majesty had already made." She appealed for the truth of these facts to all Europe: and then continued and said, "That her Majesty, the Empress Queen, might have declined giving explanations upon objects, which did not require them; that however she had been pleased to do it, and to declare with her own mouth, to M. Klinggraffe,

Klinggraffe, in the audience she had granted to him on the 26th of July," "That the critical "state of public affairs made her look upon the "measures, which she was taking, as necessary for "her own safety, and that of her allies: and "that, in other respects, they did not tend to the "prejudice of any one: that her Majesty, the "Empress Queen, had undoubtedly a right to "form what judgment she pleased on the circum- "stances of the times: and that it belonged like- "wise to none but herself, to estimate her dan- "gers: That besides, her declaration was so clear, "that she could never have it imagined, that it "could be thought otherwise: That being ac- "customed to receive, as well as to practise, the at- "tentions, which sovereigns owe to each other, "she could not hear without astonishment, and "the justest sensibility, the contents of the memo- "rial presented[y] by M. Klinggraffe: That this "memorial was such, both as to the matter, and "the expressions, that her Majesty, the Empress "Queen, would find herself under a necessity to "transgress the bounds of that moderation, which "she had prescribed herself, were she to answer "the whole of the contents. But nevertheless, "she was pleased, in answer thereunto, to declare, "That the informations, given to his Prussian "Majesty, of an offensive alliance against him, "between her Majesty, the Empress Queen, and "her Majesty, the Empress of Russia; as also,

---

[y] On the 20th of July.

"all

A. D. 1756.

"all the circumstances and pretended stipulations of the said alliance, were absolutely false and invented; and that no such treaty against his Prussian Majesty did exist, or ever had existed: and concluded with retorting the dreadful events of the war upon his Prussian Majesty,"

The moment his Prussian Majesty was advised of this conduct and resolution of the court of Vienna, he gave orders for his troops to enter Saxony; determined, if he was obliged to enter into a war, to remove the calamities thereof, as far from his own dominions, into the enemy's country, as he possibly could.

King of Prussia's troops ordered to enter Saxony.

When this vigorous step had shewn the Empress Queen that he was resolved not to be trifled with; the King of Prussia, hoping that his readiness for a war, and his immediate taking the field, might bring her to a better sense and disposition, he once more applied by his minister at Vienna, with a promise to recall his forces; provided she would solemnly declare that his dominions should not be invaded. But this was productive of no better effect, than his former demands. He accordingly proceeded with his army.

King of Prussia's ultimate attempt to prevent a war.

Let us stop a moment, and duely weigh the answer given by the Empress Queen to the demand of the King of Prussia; to which that King did ascribe the necessity of having recourse to arms; and on which was kindled the flames of a long and bloody war.

Remarks on the answer given by the Empress Queen to the King of Prussia.

The Empress Queen appeals to all Europe for the truth of certain facts, to which she affixes a

primary

primary hostile intention, disposition and preparation in the King of Prussia. These facts amount to no more than the march of four regiments of Prussians into Pomerania, on advice that the Russians were very numerous and in motion upon the frontiers of that part of his dominions, in the month of June; and his orders also to put the fortresses of that counry, into a state of defence. Which is a most weak fact or reason to be assigned for the assembling 80,000 Austrians in Bohemia and Moravia; though it is here taken up to palliate the bad intentions of the court of Vienna. The King of Prussia did also send three regiments of foot from Westphalia to Halberstadt, when he learned, that the Austrian army was assembled in Bohemia. But he did not order a single regiment into Silesia; keeping his troops quiet in their garrisons, without horses and other necessaries for an army, which is to encamp, or preparing for an invasion, that he might avoid every thing, that could give umbrage to the court of Vienna.

However the Austrians having caused another camp to be marked out near a town, named Hotzenplotz, on a spot of ground laying between the fortresses of Neisse and Cosel, and their army in Bohemia making dispositions to occupy the camp of Jaromits, within four miles of Silesia; the King of Prussia thought it time to take such steps towards providing for his own safety and supporting his dignity, as in wisdom, good policy and power he was able: whereby his Majesty was so far from deserving the imputation of any offensive intention

against

A. D.
1756.

against the House of Austria, that, it is evident, he contented himself with negociating, while the Empress Queen was diligently and vigorously arming against him; and that his military preparations were only in consequence, and far from being equal, to those of the Austrians. So that the appeal to facts, on which the court of Vienna laid so much stress, recoils with greater force against themselves, and sets their ill designs in a much fuller light.

Where her Imperial Majesty asserts that she had given the Prussian resident a *clear* declaration in answer to his memorial, it is very evident, that it was impossible from thence to understand who were meant by her allies, threatned with war? For, it could not be thought, that the King of Prussia would be so weak, as to attack either France, or Russia, with only the four regiments sent into Pomerania. Or, is it very clear, that the Empress Queen would not attack Prussia, by saying, she did not intend to prejudice any body. His Majesty only desired that he might, by name, be assured to reign unmolested by her arms: and as she refused to give him that assurance, her declaration was *not* clear, and he was justified to take such measures, as he was able, to defend himself, and to put it out of the power of his enemy to hurt him.

But the Empress Queen condescendeth to declare, That all the circumstances and stipulations of the alliance with Russia, pretended to be destructive to Prussia, were absolutely false and invented,

vented. To be sure this is a clear or direct accusing the King of Prussia of asserting a falshood, and a fiction of his own. But it is to be feared, that, notwithstanding this accusation or declaration comes from the mouth of an Empress Queen, it will be found to carry in it an equivocation or mental reservation unbecoming the meanest subject. If we examine this clause upon circumstances only, it will be found that there was certainly a concert or conspiracy between the two Empresses, against some body. In the beginning of June the Russian troops approached the frontiers of Prussia. An army of 70,000 men was formed in Livonia, at the same time the Austrians assembled in Bohemia, under the name of an army of obfervation: and when the Russian troops received orders to return into their quarters, not being able to march forward for want of corn; the Austrian camps were also put off till next year. But his Prussian Majesty had more substantial proofs of the conspiracy formed between Austria, Russia, and Saxony against his person and dominions; a conspiracy, that had been forging ever since the year 1745 [z].

His Prussian Majesty had in his own possession most authentic proofs of their treaties, at that very time, he ordered his resident at Vienna to intimate his knowledge of those dangerous practices between the two Empresses and Saxony, for his ruin; which shall appear in their proper place;

[z] See Vol. I. page 262, 263, 264.

A. D. 1756.

but he would have been contented to hear the court of Vienna reduced to the necessity of denying projects, which could do no honour to their moderation; and to stave off a bloody and expensive war, with a promise not to be attacked either in that, or in the next year.

This request, not to be molested for two years, by one, that had a right to claim the security of peace by the faith of treaty, he had not violated, and was desirous to keep, was far from being impertinent or imperious; and it was the most essential article in the memorial. It was a matter of right; and a condition, without which war must certainly commence: yet this is the precise article to which no manner of answer was given. A silence, that sufficiently discovers the real intentions of the court of Vienna.

Endeavours to make the King of Prussia the aggressor.

Thus, the court of Vienna, by haughty and disdainful answers, endeavoured to provoke the Prussian monarch to seek for safety by the way of arms; in order (as we have seen in the conduct of France towards Great Britain) to find a pretext to throw the breach of faith upon him. And he was, in the end, obliged to act in an hostile character: but neither Prussia, nor Great Britain, can be deemed aggressors, where States or Potentates are detected in hostile practices or intrigues, under the security of the sacred name of peace [a].

The

[a] By *aggression*, is understood every act, which is diametrically opposite to the sense of a treaty of peace. An offensive league;—the stirring up of enemies, and prompting them to make

The Prussian army put into motion, his Majesty's minister at Dresden demanded [b] a private audience of the King of Poland Elector of Saxony, and delivered himself to this effect, "That his royal master the King of Prussia, finding himself obliged by the Empress Queen to attack her, and to march into Bohemia through the territories of Saxony, he accordingly in the name of the King of Prussia, demanded a passage through the electoral dominions of his Polish Majesty, promising that they should observe the strictest discipline, and take all the care of the country, that the circumstances would permit; and that his Polish Majesty and his royal family, might at the same time depend upon being in perfect safety, and of having the greatest respect paid them on the part of his Prussian Majesty. He then added, that there could be no room for surprise that the King of

King of Prussia demands a passage for his army through Saxony.

make war upon another power;—designs of invading another Prince's dominions;—a sudden irruption:—All these different circumstances are so many *aggressions*; although the last, only, can be properly called an *hostility*.

Whoever prevents these aggressions, may commit *hostilities*; but is not the *aggressor*.—In the succession-war, when the troops of Savoy were in the French army in Lombardy, the Duke of Savoy made a treaty with the Emperor against France:—The French disarmed these troops, and carried the war into Piedmont:—It was therefore the Duke of Savoy, who was the *aggressor*; and the French who committed the first *hostilities*.—The league of Cambray was an *aggression*:—If the Venetians had, then, prevented their enemies, they would have committed the first *hostilities*; but they would not have been the *aggressors*.

[b] On the 29th of August.

E. 2   Prussia

A.D. 1756.

Pruffia should take such measures, at the present conjuncture, as might prevent a return of what happened in the year 1744; and that the necessity, which the King his master was under of acting in this manner, could only be imputed to the calamity of the times, and to the behaviour of the court of Vienna."

His Polish Majesty's conduct and answer.

His Polish Majesty, conscious of the private engagements, between himself and the confederate Empresses, against the King of Pruffia, and of his own inability to dispute the demand made by the Pruffian minister, answered, "That, as he was at peace with all the world, and under no engagement relative to the present object, with any of the powers actually at war, or with any of those about to enter into it, he did not expect a requisition in the form it had been made to him, neither could he conceive the end of making such a declaration; but that he should give an answer upon this subject in writing, and hoped that his Pruffian Majesty, contenting himself with a quiet passage, would neither forget the respect due to a sovereign, nor that, which all the members of the Germanic body reciprocally owe to each other."

Assembles his troops.

But, dreading the consequences of admitting the army of a doubtful friend, and of a Prince, who had thrown out sufficient hints of the discoveries he had made in the negociations of the Saxon cabinet, to his prejudice, his Polish Majesty collected his whole force, with all the diligence his circumstances would permit, in order to command some respect, and, at least, to make some

some stand against the worst attempts, till his confederates might send him such relief, as the nature of his distress and of their common cause required. These troops already raised, as the King of Prussia had intelligence, to favour the designs of the high contracting powers against his Majesty, were ordered to fortify themselves in the strong fortress of Pirna.

In the mean time his Polish Majesty ordered a written answer to be delivered to M. de Malzahn, which declared, "That his Majesty the King of Poland, desiring nothing more ardently than the peace of the Roman Empire, was extremely displeased to hear of the differences between the House of Austria and Brandenburgh, so as to occasion the march of the Prussian troops into Bohemia: but that he did not refuse the requisition of a passage for these troops through his dominions, provided they did no damage in their march; and that his Polish Majesty did rely for this, and that the Prussian troops should observe a strict discipline, upon the declaration of his Prussian Majesty." He further said, "That he expected his Prussian Majesty should previously make known at what time, through what place, and in what numbers, his troops were to pass, in order that the King of Poland might appoint commissaries, and give them instructions how to direct the troops in their march: that he hoped his Prussian Majesty, as a friend and good neighbour, would pay a regard to the bad situation of the country, and the scarcity occasioned by the indif-

Gives a written answer to the King of Prussia's demand.

ferent harvest, that year; that he would cause ready money and a market price to be paid by his troops for every thing his troops might want; and that he would let their stay be as short as possible." Then his Polish Majesty confessed his surprize at his Prussian Majesty's observing in his declaration, that the reflection of what happened in the year 1744 should occasion his taking measures against the like events; the difference of the situation of affairs, at that time and this, being very great. For the King of Poland has the strongest reasons to keep steadfastly to the treaty of Dresden; in conformity to which he had assiduously applied himself to cultivate the friendship of the neighbouring powers, and that upon this principle he flattered himself, that the King of Prussia would rest satisfied of his intention *not to take any part in the differences that have arisen between his Prussian Majesty and the Empress Queen*; which he had already several times declared to the Prussian minister, and did confirm by these presents: concluding, that such strong assurances, as these, ought to satisfy the King of Prussia, and prevent his requiring any thing of his Polish Majesty, or his subjects, contrary to the liberty of a Prince of the Empire, or that should oblige him to have recourse to the Germanic body and the guarantees of the treaties of the peace, for the due execution of those treaties [c]."

The

[c] This declaration was sent to the King of Prussia by Lord Stormont, the British minister, accompanied by the Count of Salmont, one of the Saxon ministers. His Prussian Majesty

The insincerity and fallacy of this declaration was too palpable to escape the discernment of his Prussian Majesty, already in possession of the real intentions, and inimical agreement of the court of Dresden, with the Empress Queen and the Empress of Russia: and as it was the very thing he expected in answer to his requisition, his Majesty had taken such previous measures, as to be prepared immediately to execute the first part of his plan, which was to disarm one of his most dangerous enemies: for, tho' Saxony could not be looked upon in a capacity to cope with the strength of Prussia, the contiguity of the Elector's dominions with Brandenburg, and the situation of that Electorate was such, that it would have been a continual inlet for the confederates, and a barrier against his Prussian Majesty's attempts upon Bohemia: so that by seizing upon Saxony, his Majesty got clear of an almost domestic foe; opened a ready way into Bohemia; and secured a re-

A. D. 1756
How received by the King of Prussia.

Reasons for seizing upon Saxony.

jesty received them very politely, heard their proposals, and told them, " That he heartily wished the King of Poland would confirm these sentiments by his actions: That he desired nothing more, than the neutrality proposed to his Polish Majesty; but that in order to render that neutrality more secure and less liable to variation, it would be proper for his Polish Majesty to separate his army, and to send the troops he had assembled at Pirna, back into quarters; and that, after he had given this proof of his upright intentions, he himself would take a pleasure, by an equal condescension, in shewing an equal disposition to give real marks of his friendship for his Polish Majesty, and to concert with him, what measures might be proper to be taken, according to the situation of affairs.

E 4 treat

A. D. 1756.

treat in case of a miscarriage. Be that as it will; the fate of Saxony was determined to answer the designs of Prussia.

Resolution to disarm the Saxons.

His first object, therefore, being to disarm the Saxon troops, already formed in a body, with their King at their head, he was to drive them into such a situation, as might disable them from action, or from joining either the Austrians or Russians, in case of an attempt, from either, or both of those powers, to succour and rescue the King of Poland; as he had reason to expect would be done. In this expectation the King of Poland with his two sons, Xaverius and Charles [d], retired from Dresden, as a place the least tenable, and fled before his invader to a camp between Pirna and Konigstein, entrenched and provided with a numerous train of artillery, deemed impregnable, and the only place in his electorate to make a stand against a formidable enemy, and to preserve a communication with his ally the Queen of Hungary [e]. And in this opinion the King of Prussia

[d] The Queen and the rest of the royal family remained at Dresden.

[e] The Saxon army having been raised, and this strong camp marked out and fortified, in so extraordinary a manner, when no enemy appeared, to require such an armament, gives great reason to suspect the pacific intentions of the King of Poland towards Prussia; and that finding by the demands made by the Prussian resident at Vienna, that the intrigues and agreement of Saxony to his prejudice were discovered, the King of Poland, conscious of his own guilt, had taken this measure to provide for his own safety against such a visitation.

proceeded

proceeded with his operations. He entered Saxony at the head of an army powerful enough to drive his Polish Majesty from his capital; which, at all events, he was resolved to get into his possession, it being the only place to find the originals of those copies he had obtained, of the confederacy against him; and he arranged the rest of his troops in such a manner, as to give no suspicion of their real destination to favour his designs upon the fortress of Pirna: his chief commanders themselves not being trusted with any more than temporary instructions for their motions.

Thus, while the main army was employed in the surprise of Dresden, and reducing the open country, and the untenable places, to the Prussian dominion; two considerable armies were formed in Upper and Lower Silesia, to occupy the passes communicating with the circles of Bunczlaw and Konigin-Gratz: besides another body assembled at Glatz. By which means he could cover Silesia from any attempts made by the Austrians; and he could advance into Bohemia, without interruption, in case he found it necessary to meet the enemy on their own territories; one of which seemed to be the most probable intention of his Prussian Majesty: but this disposition was no more than a piece of good generalship, to keep the enemy fixed upon a wrong and distant object, while his Majesty gained time to carry his main design into execution. So that, when Prince Ferdinand of Brunswick, entrusted with the command of the forces

Measures for securing the passes towards Bohemia, &c.

A. D. 1756.

forces upon the frontiers of Bohemia, was advanced to Gros-Kugel, and not before, he had instructions to turn off, and to take the rout of Leipsic: and, when he had got possession of this city, he received further orders, to continue his march along the Elbe, to get behind Pirna, to cut off the avenues, through which the Saxon army was supplied with provisions, and to attempt every thing to distress and shut the Saxons up, and to prevent their junction with, and their relief from the Austrians. All which that Prince performed in the most precise and effectual manner, for the service of his royal master.

To cut off all communication with the Saxon camp.

King of Prussia's manifesto.

When the King of Prussia entered the Saxon territory, he published a manifesto, "pleading the necessity, to which he was driven by the equivocal conduct and dangerous views of the court of Vienna, for taking such a disagreeable resolution to enter the hereditary dominions of his Polish Majesty, Elector of Saxony, with an armed force: and at the same time protesting, in the presence of God and man, that nothing should have induced him to take such a step against a Prince, for whom he had the greatest personal respect and friendship, had he not been forced thereunto by the laws of war, the fatality of the present combinations, and the necessity of providing for the defence of his own dominions. He then put the Saxons in mind of his tenderness towards their Sovereign, in the year 1744, and remonstrated against those councils, which engaged him to favour the enemies of Prussia: adding, that it was

from

from the apprehensions of being exposed again to their intrigues, he was compelled to pursue such measures for his own safety, as prudence had dictated: but at the same time, he affirmed, in the most solemn manner, that he entertained no hostile intention against his Polish Majesty, or any of his dominions: that his troops did not enter Saxony as enemies, being under command to observe the best order and most exact discipline: and concluded with protestations of his ardent wishes for the happy moment, in which he might restore the public tranquility, and his Polish Majesty's hereditary dominions, which he was obliged to seize by way of pledge for his own safety."

Prince Ferdinand's declaration, &c. at Leipsic.

At Leipsic Prince Ferdinand apologized for his hostile visit, by another declaration or manifesto, " which promised, in the name of his Prussian Majesty, to consider and defend the Saxons, as if they were his own subjects; and he assured them, That he had given precise orders for his troops to observe exact discipline." But the severity, with which the following resolutions of these visitors, under the name of friends, were attended, soon convinced them, that his Prussian Majesty was determined to treat that electorate in the same manner, as the dominions of an open enemy.

His first mark of friendship exhibited itself in an order for the inhabitants of Leipsic to provide his army with provisions, at a losing price, on pain of military execution. This was immediately followed, in the evening of the same day, by an order

A. D. 1756.

der for the payment of all taxes and customs to the King of Prussia; by seizing on the custom-house and excise-office; and by obliging the merchants to open the magazines of corn and meal for the use of his army.

King of Prussia's conduct at Dresden, towards the Queen.

At Dresden, which city had been deserted by the King of Poland, and his military power; and was entered without opposition by the King of Prussia; an officer was ordered by his Majesty to wait upon the Queen of Poland, with the strongest assurances of respect and security for her person and family; but soon after he returned with a peremptory demand for the keys of her husband's royal archives, cabinets and treasures: To which she was at last forced to submit, notwithstanding her utmost endeavours to divert his Prussian Majesty from such a violent and unprecedented action, under the roof of her own palace. His Majesty ordered the fortifications of Wirtemberg to be blown up; and Torgau to be fortified, at which place he established the seat of government under a Prussian ministry [f]: for the same officer, who demanded the keys of her Polish Majesty, acquainted the ministers of state and members of the council, that the King of Prussia should have no occasion for their service, but would appoint proper persons to fill, and discharge the duties of their places and offices. Baron Wyllech was ap-

Erects a new administration, &c.

[f] All offices for public business, belonging to the Prussian army, were established here. The cash and treasure of the army was kept here, and this was the place where contributions and duties of all kinds were ordered to be paid.

pointed

pointed the Pruffian governor of Drefden; he made prifoners of all the Saxon officers found in that city, and obliged them to fwear not to ferve againft the King his mafter, before they could be releafed; and he tranfported down the Elbe to Magdeburgh all the artillery, arms and other military ftores, which had been privately laid up in the arfenals and magazines of the capital.

A. D. 1756. Seizes upon all Saxon officers and military impliments.

The King of Pruffia, keeping his eye ftill principally upon the military power of Saxony, which had cooped themfelves up juft in the fituation he hoped to find them, fixed his head quarters at Seidlitz, about half a German league from the Saxon camp at Pirna; fo as to be at hand to intercept all convoys of provifions for that camp, and to favour the operations, with which he had charged Prince Ferdinand of Brunfwic, who, as obferved before, had marched along the Elbe, and formed a chain with the royal army, that extended on the right towards the frontiers of Bohemia, feifed the paffes, that lead to the circles of Satzer and Leutmeritz in that kingdom, where Prince Ferdinand took poft without refiftance.

His head quarters.

Advantageous cantonment of his troops.

Such was the diftrefs of the Saxons, when his Polifh Majefty applied, in a memorial addreffed to all the courts in amity with Saxony, for redrefs, which was couched much in the fame ftile and manner, as that addreffed to their High Mightineffes, by the Saxon minifter at the Hague.

King of Poland, Elector of Saxony's circular memorial againft thefe proceedings.

" To reprefent to you, high and mighty Lords,
" a ftate free, tranquil and neuter, invaded by
" an enemy, who covers himfelf under the name
" of

A. D. 1756.

"of friendship; who without alledging the least complaint, or any pretensions whatsoever; but governing himself solely by his *conveniency*, makes himself master, by armed force, of all the towns, and even of the capital; dismantles places, such as Wirtemburgh; fortifies others, such as Torgau: this is but a feeble sketch of the oppressions under which the faithful subjects of his Majesty groan; the burghers disarmed; the magistrates carried off to serve as hostages for the unjust and enormous contributions for provisions and forage [g]: the public coffers seised, the revenues of the Electorate confiscated; the arsenals of Dresden, of Leipsic, of Weisenfels and of Zeist broke open, the artillery and the arms plundered and transported to Magdeburg; yet all these were no more than preliminaries to the unheard of indignity offered to the Queen; whose virtues alone ought to have commanded respect from her very enemies. It was from the sacred hands of that Princess the archives of state were forced, by menaces and violence; notwithstanding the security, which her Majesty might promise to herself, under the protection of all laws human and divine; and notwithstanding the reiterated assurances given to her in the name of the King

[g] The deputies, that went from Leipsic to prince Ferdinand's head quarters, were conducted to Torgau, and there detained, as security for the obedience of the regency of Leipsic, and for the payment of the duties and contributions of that city.

"of

"of Pruffia, that not only her perfon and refi- A.D. 1756.
"dence fhould be abfolutely fafe; but that even
"the Pruffian garrifon fhould be under her or-
"ders."

"This auguft and tender mother of her faith-
"ful fubjects, who, to make a facrifice to the
"happinefs of the Saxons, had remained at Dref-
"den, expected, in the midft of tumult, to go-
"vern in fecurity the ftates of her auguft confort,
"who, prompted by cares equally important,
"had hafted away to head his army, to defend
"his injured honour, and to give to the zeal and
"love of his people, what they had ground to
"expect from the valour and firmnefs of fo mag-
"nanimous a Prince: But fhe has been deceived:
"fhe is not only deprived of the government;
"the activity of the privy-council is alfo taken
"away; and, inftead of the legitimate govern-
"ment, an arbitrary *directory* is fubftituted, which
"acknowledges no other right, but its own
"will, &c."

Whatever advantages his Pruffian Majefty gained Its effects.
over the confederates againft him, by this forcible
pufh to difarm Saxony, and by treating a country
with the rigour of martial power, which had given
him no vifible caufe of complaint; the King of
Poland, Elector of Saxony, by infifting upon his
own innocence, and the natural right he had
to the protection of the laws of nations, from an
invader of his dominions in time of profound
peace; and by expatiating upon the perfidious
and tyrannical conduct of his Pruffian Majefty

and

A.D. 1756.

and his officers, raised the attention of all Europe, and furnished those, who were most desirous to break with Prussia, with a laudable motive to arm in defence of distressed innocence and injured Majesty. Even those, who wished well to the Prussian hero could scarce reconcile his conduct, on this occasion, with justice, and some of his best friends disavowed their knowledge of this expedition, and condemned it.

In England.

None were more surprized than his Britannic Majesty, Elector of Hanover, Prussia's faithful ally. It was easy to foresee the difficulties, in which this would embroil his Prussian Majesty: none of which were so much as suspected, when the treaty between Great Britain and Prussia was signed [h]. And our King, as Elector of Hanover, was so far from being in the secret of this invasion, or of the motives which the King of Prussia had to seize upon Saxony, that he publickly disavowed, and in some sense protested against that irruption.

The reply of the King of Prussia to the Saxon memorial.

Europe, in this confusion, was immediately presented with a circular memorial, by way of reply, in the name of his Prussian Majesty; wherein it was declared, "That the imputations in the Saxon memorial were calumnies raised and aggravated without truth, and without decency; that nothing more than the usual taxes had been raised on the subjects of the Electorate, and that they had been fully paid for every thing, they had fur-

[h] On the 16th of Jan. 1756.

nished:

nifhed: that it was equally contrary to truth, where it was afferted that the refpect due to the Queen was violated, by demanding of her certain papers, the copies of which he was already poffeffed of, but which it became neceffary for him to have in the original, in order to prove unanfwerably, the plot, that was formed to ftrip him, not only of Silefia, which the Emprefs Queen referved entirely for herfelf; but likewife of the dutchies of Magdebourgh and Croffen, and the circles of Zullichau, Cotbus and Schwibus, which was the portion allotted to the King of Poland." But this was only a temporary apology, to prepare the world for thofe unanfwerable proofs, which he foon after caufed to be publifhed; and fhewed both the wifdom and juftice of a conduct, fo greatly difapproved, at firft, as to ftigmatize him with the name of a public robber.

A. D. 1756.

The Emperor was engaged by his Confort to exert the utmoft efforts of his power, to deter the Pruffian Monarch from proceeding. As head of the Empire he iffued a decree, admonifhing and commanding him to withdraw his troops from Saxony, on pain of being proceeded againft according to the laws of the Empire: He abfolved all the vaffals of the Empire found in his fervice from their oath of fidelity, and commanded them to leave the Pruffian ftandard. And by a third decree he forbade all the princes, ftates, and other members of the Empire to fuffer their fubjects to enlift themfelves in the Pruffian fervice, or otherwife to give him any kind of affiftance.

The Emperor's decree againft him.

He

A. D. 1756.

He then enumerated all the violences set forth in the Saxon memorial, with many aggravations; and concludes with this remarkable clause, "For these causes we most seriously command and enjoin your Majesty, as Elector of Brandenburgh, by virtue of our Imperial dignity, and the power of supreme judge, to desist, without delay, from all rebellion, hostile invasions, violences and breaches of the peace, in the Electorate of Saxony, and other states of the Empire; to withdraw immediately your troops, and to break up and dismiss your army, which is so dangerous to the states of the Empire, and the common tranquility; to restore every thing that has been taken; to repair, without reply or demur, all damages and costs, and to make, as soon as possible, your most humble report of the manner, in which all this has been executed. As for the rest, we shall forthwith proceed to what is enacted by the laws of the Empire, in punishment of the grievous crime committed by your Majesty, as Elector of Brandenburg, against us and the whole Empire, by a rebellious enterprize, dangerous to the community, and at the same time provide for the future security of all the Empire [1]."

In the mean time the Austrians attempted to supply the Saxon army at Pirna with provisions. But the convoy was attacked and routed by a de-

---

[1] Dated at Vienna, September 19, 1756.

tachment of Prussian hussars, who carried off a considerable number of loaded waggons. This was the first act of hostility between the troops of Austria and Prussia.

A. D. 1756.

The French court, as yet, made no movement with arms, but spit their venom in the following circular rescript to all foreign courts; in which it is said, "That his most Christian Majesty cannot but consider the requisition made by the King of Prussia to the King of Poland, Elector of Saxony, for the passage of his troops through that Electorate, as nothing less than a declaration, that he is determined to usurp that, to which he has neither absolute right, nor equitable claim.

The French declaration against the King of Prussia.

"That by this usurpation, committed in a time of profound peace, against the Elector of Saxony, at the time when that Prince relied, with unsuspecting security, upon the faith of the treaty of Dresden, and the assurances of friendship, which the King of Prussia had given him, the King of Prussia had violated the public peace, the treaty of Westphalia, all the laws and constitutions of the Empire, and every tie by which the members of the Germanic body are united.

"That the establishment of the system formed by the King of Prussia, in concert with the court of Great Britain, was the most unjust, and most injurious, that can be imagined, and such as left no room to expect, that any measures should be kept with those powers, either by land or sea, as they had violated all laws, both human and divine.

"That

A. D.
1756.

"That this conduct ought to exclude the King of Pruſſia from all benefit that he might receive from any defenſive alliance; and therefore his moſt Chriſtian Majeſty doubts not, that the ſtates which are now in alliance with him, will think themſelves abſolved from every obligation to afford him any ſuccours, and that they will aſſiſt his moſt Chriſtian Majeſty and his allies, in every meaſure that may be purſued for their mutual defence, the ſupport of the general intereſt of Europe, and the giving a proper ſanction to the mutual contract by which one nation is attached to another."

The declaration of the Empreſs of Ruſſia againſt him.

The court of Ruſſia was more explicit; whoſe declaration being dated September 4, 1756. at St. Peterſburg, a conſiderable time before they could hear of the invaſion of Saxony by the Pruſſian army, ſhews, that the diſcovery of the alliance againſt the King of Pruſſia was known at Peterſburg, and its conſequences apprehended; and that the Czarina was prepared to march her forces upon the firſt alarm of an attack made upon any part of the confederacy: for ſhe commanded the Ruſſian miniſters reſiding at foreign courts to declare, "That as the ſole intent of the preparations, which the Empreſs ordered to be made, laſt ſpring, was to enable her to fulfil her engagements with her allies, in caſe any of them ſhould be attacked, the preparations were ſuſpended, both by ſea and land, as ſoon as there was ground to hope that that caſe would not ſoon happen; in order that the whole world might be

con-

convinced that her Imperial Czarish Majesty was no less forward to defend her allies, when threatened with an attack, than backward to throw Europe into an alarm without an extreme necessity.

"That the King of Prussia, far from doing justice to the Empress's sentiments, on this head (though he remained quiet, whilst preparations were making by Russia, and even some time after they had ceased) had all of a sudden begun to make such powerful armaments, as gave room to apprehend that the flames of war would immediately burst out.

"That nevertheless Russia, to avoid the multiplying of fears, for furnishing the King of Prussia with a specious pretext for disturbing the public tranquility, had made no motions; in hopes that the King of Prussia, in imitation of this example, would not stir up such troubles: but that this Prince, having continued to arm with all his might, and without any interruption, and without alledging any other reason than the idea he had formed to himself of an apprehended attack, had thereby sufficiently intimated that he sought only a pretext to disturb the peace of Europe.

"That, in fact, it is incontestible, that when the King of Prussia was pressing his armaments with the greatest vigour, those of Russia had long ceased; *and that those of the Empress Queen did not begin, till the successive motions of the Prussians and the augmentation of their forces* [k] gave room to think Bohemia and Moravia were in danger; inasmuch as it was no secret that the King of Pruſſia was diſguſted at the treaty of Verſailles; though this Prince, when he ſigned his treaty with England, gave himſelf no concern about what the court of Vienna might think of it.

"It is, therefore, clear to her Imperial Czariſh Majeſty, that the King of Pruſſia ought to be conſidered as the firſt author of the troubles, that are going to break out, though he has affected to publiſh, that he took all theſe meaſures only to defend himſelf againſt his enemies, who had no exiſtence, but in his own ſuppoſition: that, nevertheleſs, it is from this ſuppoſition he has thought himſelf entitled to demand of the Empreſs Queen an explanation with regard to her warlike preparations, adding, in a manner not altogether decent, that if her anſwer were not to his liking, he proteſted before God, he would not be anſwerable for the conſequences.

"That in conſideration of all theſe circumſtances the Empreſs can no longer CONCEAL her *real ſentiments*, nor forbear declaring, that as ſhe cannot behold with indifferency any [l] attack made

---

[k] This is a notorious miſrepreſentation of the fact, as appears from the circumſtances related in this Hiſtory, on page 52. &c. Vol. II.

[l] This ſuſpicion could ariſe from no other circumſtance, than a conſciouſneſs of the diſcovery, made by his Pruſſian Majeſty, of the partition of his dominions in the confederate treaty; for it was not poſſible to hear of what had paſſed in Germany.

on the dominions of her allies, particularly those of the Emprefs Queen of Hungary, and the Electorate of Saxony, fhe will furnifh fpeedy and powerful fuccours to the party unjuftly attacked, and will not think herfelf in any wife refponfible for the confequences, which the prefent menacing conduct of his Pruffian Majefty may draw after it, &c."

A. D. 1756.

Whether we animadvert upon the date of this refcript, we fhall difcover the infincerity of her Czarifh Majefty; her difguft with England, for entering into an alliance with Pruffia, which fhe had previoufly been engaged to crufh, and that her real fentiments were not formed upon the prefent appearances, but upon the long prepoffeffions fhe had entertained in prejudice to the King of Pruffia, at the inftigation of the Emprefs Queen and the Saxon court, and concealed hitherto under the name of friendfhip; till neceffity obliged the confederacy to pull off the mafk in their own defence. And whoever attends to its fubftance, will find a vein of contradiction and fallacy run through the whole; advancing facts, which are not confiftent either in point of time or truth.

Remarks on this declaration.

His Pruffian Majefty, however, neither intimidated by the formidable alliances, which already appeared againft him, nor deterred from his purpofes, by the thundering decrees of the Imperial authority, which he defpifed with as much contempt, as our Henry VIII. did the thunder of the Vatican againft his proceedings in the reforma-

Refolution and conduct of his Pruffian Majefty.

F 4

A.D. 1756.

formation; attended strictly to the accomplishing his first attempt, to get full possession of Saxony. So that, the more determined his enemies appeared to oppose his arms, he exerted the power in his hands to defeat their most sanguine intentions. The Russian rescript, and the Austrian dispositions for the relief of the Saxons, served only to accelerate the total ruin of his Polish Majesty. They convinced the King of Prussia, that nothing less than a total reduction of that party of the confederacy against him could do him any service. And accordingly being master already of every other part of that electorate, he was determined to force the Saxon army at Pirna, by a strong blockade, to surrender to his arms for want of provisions, of which there was great scarcity in their camp; or to fall under his sword, if they should attempt to force their way through the lines of circumvallation.

The Empress Queen's efforts to rescue the Saxon army.

By this means the fate of the Saxon army, in which rested the last appearance of their country's independency, was daily reduced to worse and worse: and, as the Empress Queen could not but see her own danger increase through every advantage gained by the Prussian monarch over Saxony, the greatest effort was preparing, on her part, with the utmost expedition, to deliver the Saxons out of their ruinous situation, and with their force united to her army, under the command of Count Brown, whose courage, skill and conduct were in high esteem, to attack the Prussian army.

Could

THE LATE WAR.

Could this have been safely done, it, perhaps, might have had it's desired effect. But it was scarce to be thought, that a Prince, who had found out the most secret intrigues of the cabinet against him, would be regardless in the most important crisis, about what was agitating against him in the field. He was as well provided with spies and emissaries about the court and camp of his enemies, as with arms to defend himself. There was not a motion of the enemy, that could escape his Majesty's penetration. His personal knowledge of the corography, or face of the country, between him and the Austrian army, supplied him with the most minute ideas concerning every motion; of the importance of every pass; and the danger of every defile: which, assisted with early intelligence of their rout and strength, furnished him with mighty advantages, and determined him to disconcert their measures and operations, by forcing the Austrians to a battle, before they could reach the place of their destination.

A. D. 1756. Defeated by the vigilance, &c. of the King of Prussia.

With this view, the Prussian heroe had detached, from time to time, as many troops from his army in Saxony, as could be spared at the blockade, to secure the passes; and to assemble, under the command Veldt Mareschal Keith, who had orders to enter Bohemia, and to encamp near the small town of Aussig, and not far from the army commanded by Count Brown; after he had reduced the town and palace [n] of Tetchen; which was

Resolves to attack the Austrian army in Bohemia.

---

[n] Situate upon a rock, and belonging to Count Thun.

considered

A. D. 1756.

considered as a frontier fortress against Saxony; and made the garrison of one captain, one lieutenant, four subalterns, and 12 soldiers prisoners of war.

The importance of this resolution.

Here we have in sight an action, which by its consequences may be looked upon to be the most decisive of any during the whole war; because upon its success, on the part of Prussia, the fate of Saxony was determined, and a way was opened for his Prussian Majesty into Bohemia: and this battle, which was to open the first campaign of a most bloody war, was fought by two generals or commanders in chief, who were originally subjects of the British crown.

Count Brown, the Austrian General.

Count Brown, who was at the head of 60,000 Austrians, was an officer of Irish extraction, that had recommended himself to the Imperial court by his courage, vigilance and conduct, first in Italy, and especially in their last war with the King of Prussia, and was honoured with this great command for the regard paid to his merit.

Marshal Keith, the Prussian General.

Veldt marefchal, or field marshal Keith, who commanded under the King of Prussia, on this occasion, was the younger son of George Keith, Earl Marshal of Scotland, born in that kingdom in 1698, and at 17 years of age he entered with his brother Lord Marshal into the rebellion, which broke out in Scotland, in the year 1715. At the battle of Sheriffmuir he appeared in arms, in favour of the Pretender, and was wounded in the neck; but so slightly that he was not sensible of it, till he was undressed to go to bed. The defeat of his party drove this young adventurer, with many more, to

seek

seek their fortunes abroad. He followed his brother into Spain, and obtained a commission in the Irish brigade, commanded by the Duke of Ormond, lately fled to that kingdom, under apprehensions of being called to an account for his misconduct towards to the House of Hanover, at the latter end of Queen Anne's reign. In this situation the Hon. Mr. Keith continued 10 years; when tired of such an inactive state, where there was no prospect of distinguishing himself by feats of arms, he obtained recommendations to the Empress of Russia, then reigning, who received him with particular marks of distinction, and honoured him with a commission of Brigadier General: and soon after advanced him to the rank of Lieutenant General.

A.D. 1756.

The war between Russia and Turkey, which broke out in that[n] reign, afforded opportunities enough to display his courage and abilities in the military art. He was in all their battles, and was wounded so much in the heel at the taking of Ockzakow, where he was the first that mounted the breach, that they were obliged to carry him off the field of battle.

His esteem at Petersburg increased; and, upon the return of peace, the Czarina sent him to the court of London, in quality of her ambassador extraordinary. On which occasion overtures were made to Sir Robert Walpole, prime minister, to recover this veteran officer for the service of Great

[n] Of Czarina Catherine I.

Britain:

A. D. 1756.

Britain: but neither his own personal qualifications, nor the excuses, which might be alledged in his favour, from his age and the influence he was under, at the time of his taking up arms against his lawful sovereign; nor yet the applications made in his favour by several powers, that interested themselves in his proposal, could prevail. He was even obliged, when he appeared at court, to personate a Russian both in dress and language: for his Majesty would not suffer him to speak at an audience, without an interpreter.

His embassy being finished, General Keith returned to Petersburg and was caressed by the Czarina more than ever. In the war with the Swedes, he was sent into Finland; and by an act of generalship, he with a body of only 5000 men, with which he attacked the Swedes in flank, gained the victory of Wilmanstrand, when the enemy had almost made sure of the day; and dispossessed them of the isles of Aland in the Baltic.

After the peace of Abo, in 1743, he was appointed ambassador extraordinary to compliment the King of Sweden, on the election of a successor to the crown. But the splendor, in which he appeared on this occasion, at Stockholm, reduced his finances so much, that, upon his return to Russia, finding it impossible to maintain the dignity of a marshal, to which post he was now promoted in the army, with the pay of that country, by accepted of an invitation from the King of Prussia, who treated him with the honour due to his birth

and

and merit; gave him a pension over and above his pay, and admitted him his companion in a private tour through Germany, Poland and Hungary, and other places, in disguise.

King of Prussia takes the command of the army.

His Prussian Majesty, notwithstanding his good opinion of the merit, and great confidence in the fidelity of M. Keith, resolved to be present in a battle of so decisive a nature: accordingly his Majesty set out on the 28th of September from his camp at Sedlitz, and took upon himself the future conduct of the forces encamped at Aussig in Bohemia, which consisted of no more than 25,000 men.

How he disposed his troops in Bohemia.

The King without delay put the army in motion, as soon as he arrived in M. Keith's camp, and resolved to march in quest of Count Brown. He formed a vanguard of eight battalions, ten squadrons of dragoons, and eight squadrons of hussars: and putting himself at the head of this body, his Majesty proceeded to Tournitz, with orders for the remainder of the army to follow him in two columns; one by the way of Proscoboc; the other by the way the vanguard had marched. Being arrived at Tournitz, he marched with the vanguard to Welmina, where he arrived an hour before sun set, that same day: and could see the Austrian army with its right wing at Lowoschutz, and its left extended towards Egra.

Occupies the field of battle.

Having learned the true situation and disposition of the enemy, his Majesty, that very evening, and in person, occupied, with six battalions, a hollow and some rising grounds, which commanded

A.D. 1756.

ed Lowofchutz, and gained fome other advantages, which he made ufe of next day, to favour his march, and his attack againſt the Auſtrians.

The army arrived at Welmina in the night, and were ordered to form into battalions and ſquadrons behind one another, and to remain in that poſition all night. His Majeſty ſpent the reſt of the night in his cloak before a little fire at the head of his troops, and at day break (on the 1ſt of October) he took his principal general officers,

Reconnoitres the ground, and forms his lines.

and ſhewed them the ground he had propoſed to occupy with his army; viz. his infantry, which formed the firſt line, were ordered to occupy two high hills and the valley between them: the ſecond line was formed with ſome battalions: and the third line conſiſted of the whole cavalry.

Great overſight of the Auſtrian General.

The Auſtrians, whoſe ſecurity, founded upon a wrong ſuppoſition, that it would be impoſſible for the Pruſſians to form ſuch a deſign upon their camp, had occaſioned their neglect of thoſe heights, now prepared to diſpute thoſe poſts with their Pruſſian viſitors: ſo that notwithſtanding the King loſt no time in ſtrengthening the wings of his army upon thoſe hills; and the ſame diligence and precaution was uſed by the infantry in eſtabliſhing

Attack the Pruſſians, as they formed.

their poſt, at the right; yet the enemy's Pandours, Croatians, and grenadiers, gave the left ſo much trouble from the vineyards, incloſed with ſtone walls, that it was obliged to fall immediately into an engagement,

The Pruſſians advance.

However the Pruſſians advanced with great reſolution and as great order, as poſſible, till they

came

came to the declivity of the hills towards the enemy. From which station they could see the town of Lowoschutz filled with infantry; a large battery of 12 cannon in front, and their cavlry formed chequer-wise and in a line between Lowoschutz and the village of Sauschitz.

Not being able to make further discovery of the enemy's disposition and strength, on account of a thick fog, which intercepted their sight, his Majesty sent to reconnoitre, and finding that he had judged rightly of the enemy's disposition; and that his own infantry was in possession of the hollow in the manner he had ordered, he resolved to begin the attack with his cavalry to drive back the enemy's horse, which stood in their front. Accordingly he formed his cavalry before his first line of infantry, and attacked the enemy's immediately with such vigour, that they were soon broke. But as the enemy had placed a great body of infantry in hollow places and ditches, with several pieces of cannon, behind the horse, the Prussians found themselves greatly exposed to their fire, the further they pursued the advantage of their arms; and were obliged to return and form again under the protection of their infantry and cannon; the Austrian cavalry not daring to pursue them.

The Prussian horse being formed again, they returned to the charge, with such resolution and courage, that neither sixty pieces of cannon, nor a powerful body of infantry lodged in the hollows and ditches to support the cavalry, could prevent

them

them from totally defeating the whole Austrian cavalry, and forcing the infantry from their station.

When this charge was performed, the King ordered his cavalry up to the hill again, and drew them up behind the infantry: and as soon as this could be effected, the cannonading still continuing, and the enemy making all possible efforts to flank the left of the Prussian infantry, the King ordered the battalions of the first line to turn to the left: then the battalions of the second line filled up the intervals; so that the cavalry was brought to form the second line, and to support the infantry. At the same time, by a masterpiece of generalship, the whole left of the infantry, marching on gradually, wheeled about; attacked the town of Lowoschutz in flank, in spite of the cannon and the prodigious infantry of the enemy; set fire to the suburbs; carried the post, and put the whole army to flight.

Victory declares in favour of the Prussians.

Marshal Brown, finding his men were greatly dispirited by such a scene of blood, the number of killed and wounded amounting to 6000 and upwards, and deprived of several general officers, amongst whom was General Radicati killed, and Prince Lobkowitz taken prisoner, he returned with his whole force to the other side of the Egra, and took his camp at Budin.

King of Prussia maintains the field of battle.

The King of Prussia kept the field of battle, and established his head quarters at Lowoschutz; though his whole army did not exceed 25,000 men; whereas the enemy's consisted of 60,000.

The battle continued from seven in the morning till three in the afternoon. The loss of the Prussians was 2000 men killed and wounded: one general of infantry, two major generals of cavalry, and one colonel of the Gens d' Arms, killed: and according to the Austrian account some hundreds were made prisoners, amongst whom were a great many officers. The loss of the Austrians slain in battle and made prisoners, is not ascertained by their general, but the Prussian account makes it between six and 7000 killed and wounded: 500 were taken prisoners, with five pieces of cannon and three pair of colours.

A. D. 1756.
The loss of both sides.

The loss of a battle, with so great a superiority in numbers; and of such importance at the first stroke of a war, that, in all probability, was to determine the fate of the King of Prussia, or his enemies, required as good a gloss, as possibly could be invented, to palliate the miscarriage. Accordingly the court of Vienna published another account of this day's event, under the name of a relation sent to their Imperial Majesties by Marshal Brown. In which the Marshal sets out with an erroneous account of the strength of the Prussian army, which he makes to consist of 40,000 men. He then tells them, That the battle began at seven o'clock on the 1st of October, and that the Prussian canonade was such, that the like had never been heard: that the Prussians finding their efforts vain against the firmness of the imperial troops, began to throw hot balls into the village of Lowoschutz, and set fire to it: and that the Imperial

General Brown's favourable account of this battle.

A. D. 1756.

perial infantry finding themselves between the fire of the village and the enemy's attack, were obliged to quit the eminence on the right of the village to form themselves in the plain: after which the fire slackened, and ceased entirely at three o'clock in the afternoon. He further affirmed, That he remained the whole night upon the field of battle, and that his Prussian Majesty had retired behind it.

Remarks on these two accounts.

But all this art availed nothing. For, let the Austrians boast ever so much of their **advantage** in this day's action; it is certain their whole **plan was defeated**, as well as their army. What did Brown assemble that army for? Was it not **to succour** his Polish Majesty, and to relieve, and, **if** possible, to deliver the Saxons out of their confinement at Pirna? Was he in a capacity to perform that service after the action of this day? What did the King of Prussia offer him battle for in Bohemia? Was it not to disable him from marching to the relief of the Saxons under his blockade? Did this action answer that purpose? If the King of Prussia obtained his purpose; and Brown could not accomplish his errand, on which he was sent by their Imperial Majesties; and all owing to the event of this day's action, we may safely admit, That however bravely the Austrians behaved; how equal soever the forces of the belligerants were, and how considerable soever the loss of the Prussians might be; and whether they maintained the field of battle or not; victory declared in favour of the Prussian hero: and,

as

as such, his Prussian Majesty had a right to claim it: and he notified the same to all the world: of which we have the following note under his Majesty's own hand, who dispatched a messenger to the Queen mother with these few words: "October 1st, This morning I gave battle to the Austrians. Great generalship was displayed on both sides; and the fate of the day was doubtful for some hours: but at last it pleased God to give us the victory."

There being no prospect of surprizing, or of drawing the Austrian army to a second engagement, and it being of no service to leave behind him an army, without some view of immediate advantage; which chiefly depended upon the reduction of the Saxon forces at Pirna, his Prussian Majesty ordered his victorious troops to return to Saxony, and to join that body of his forces employed in the blockade of the Saxon camp: this additional strength excluded all hopes of relief, by the way of Bohemia: and, their provisions being exhausted, the extremity of want forced them, either to attempt an escape by stratagem, or to lay down their arms and surrender themselves to the King of Prussia.

An escape was most eligible, could it be contrived with any hopes of success. A plan was proposed for it, and approved of by Marshal Brown. The success depended upon secrecy and punctuality in all parties concerned. Marshal Brown promised to favour their design, and to cover their flight. He in person undertook this

King of Prussia's return with his army to Saxony.

Saxon army's distressed condition.

Plan contrived for their escape.

G 2 difficult

A. D. 1756.

Marshal Brown tries to favour their escape.

difficult and important service: and, with a considerable body of horse, he marched from the camp at Budin, to the neighbourhood of Konigstein °; where he met General Nadasti, who had arrived the day before with 6,000 irregulars; which he posted in such a manner, as to prevent eight Prussian battalions, encamped on that side the Elbe, at Lomer, from being joined by the Prussians, that were posted at Schaudau.

M. Brown, on the 11th acquainted the King of Poland with his arrival at Litchtendorf near Schaudau; and desired they would execute their part of the plan proposed for their escape, by marching out the next night. Accordingly, on the 12th at night, the Saxons secretly threw a bridge of boats over the Elbe, near Konigstein: and, under favour of a very dark night, having removed almost all their heavy artillery to Konigstein, they struck their tents, and by seven in the morning, the whole Saxon army had passed the Elbe unmolested and undiscovered: and the fog was so thick, that it was eight before their decampment and escape was known at Sedlitz. But had the Austrian General, as he ought to have done, reconnoitred the country, through which he was to escort these fugitives, he would have found, that his Prussian Majesty did not rely solely upon the strength, nor vigilance of his blockade. Veldt Marshal Keith had secured all the passes, and lined the defiles: so that, as soon as the Saxon

The Saxons attempt to escape.

° Upwards of 16 German miles.

advanced

advanced-guard had with much difficulty got about half way up a steep mountain, and the other part of them were shut up in a narrow plain, over against Konigstein, they were convinced that it was impossible for them to proceed, and to force their way through the posts occupied by the Prussians: who now surrounded them, without artillery, and without provisions, on every side: and when it was too late, they were convinced that they had been permitted to march into this toil, that they might be taken with less hazard and difficulty.

A. D. 1756. Stopt in the way.

His Polish Majesty, who remained behind in his castle of Konigstein, to wait the issue of this retreat, being informed of the deplorable situation of his troops, wrote the following letter to his general the Veldt Marechal Count Ratowski:—" It is not without extreme sorrow I under-
" stand the deplorable situation, which a chain of
" misfortunes has reserved for you, the rest of my
" generals, and my whole army: but we must
" acquiesce in the dispensations of providence,
" and console ourselves with the rectitude of our
" sentiments and intentions. They would force
" me, it seems, as you give me to understand by
" Major General the Baron de Dyherrn, to sub-
" mit to conditions the more severe, in proportion
" as the circumstances are become more necessi-
" tous. I cannot hear them mentioned. I am a
" free monarch: such I will live: such I will die:
" and I will both live and die with honour. The
" fate of my army I leave wholly to your discre-
" tion. Let your council of war determine whe-

Their King's orders for their surrender.

" ther

"ther you must surrender prisoners of war, fall by the sword, or die by famine. May your resolutions, if possible, be conducted with humanity: whatever they may be, I have no longer any share in them: and I declare you shall not be answerable for aught but one thing, namely, not to carry arms against me or my allies. I pray God may have you in his holy keeping. Given at Konigstein, the 14th of October 1756. AUGUSTUS REX."

The army resolve to capitulate.

By this letter the Saxon general had full and discretionary power to surrender, or to take such other measures, as he and his officers should judge most conducive to the preservation of the soldiers; and being informed, that Marshal Brown, despairing of success for their relief, and not in a capacity to use force, or to keep his ground, had retired towards Bohemia about noon, that same day, and that a Prussian detachment was following and harrassing him; the Saxon general and his council of war, came to an immediate resolution for a capitulation, of which the following is a copy in the terms requested by them, and settled by the King of Prussia; where we find the disagreeable article, pointed out in the King of Poland's letter to General Rutowski, obliging the Saxon soldiery to enter into the Prussian service, to serve against his Majesty's allies.

Article I.

THE army of the King of Poland, Elector of Saxony, as posted at the foot of Lilienstein, shall surrender to the King of Prussia prisoners of war.

Ans.

Anf. *If the King will give me that army, 'tis needless to make them prisoners of war.*

II. The generals, the field-officers, the persons employed as commissaries and purveyors, and all the other officers of the army, shall keep their baggage and effects, as well those they have actually with them, as what they may have left in other places; and the subaltern officers and soldiers shall be allowed to keep their cloathing, arms, and knapsacks.

Anf. *All that can be preserved or recovered of their baggage shall be faithfully restored to them.*

III. His Prussian Majesty is chiefly requested to cause the army to be furnished with the necessary provisions and forage; and that he would be pleased to give proper orders for this purpose.

Anf. *Granted, and rather to-day than to-morrow.*

IV. The generals, commandants, and all persons ranking as officers, engage themselves, in writing, not to bear arms against his Majesty the King of Prussia till peace be restored; and they shall be left at liberty to stay in Saxony, or to retire whithersoever they think proper.

Answ. *Those that intend to enter into my service must from this very moment have liberty to do so.*

V. The life-guards and the grenadier-guards shall not be included in the first article; and his Prussian Majesty will be pleased to appoint the place in the Electorate of Saxony, or in the territories depending thereon, where the said two corps shall be distributed. The field-marshal Count Rutowski, as captain of the grenadier-

A.D. 1756.

nadier-guards, the Chevalier de Saxe, in quality of commandant of the life-guards, and all the other officers of those two corps, verbally engage, and even in writing, if desired, not to make, under any pretext whatever, nor without the approbation of the King of Prussia, any change in the quarters that may be assigned them.

Answ. *There is no exception to be made; because it is known that the King of Poland did give orders for that part of his troops, which is in the said kingdom, to join the Russians, and to march for this purpose, to the frontiers of Silesia; and a man must be a fool to let troops go, which he holds fast, to see them make head against him a second time, and to be obliged to take them prisoners again.*

VI. The general and field officers, and all the officers, shall keep their swords; but the arms, belts, and cartridges, both of the subalterns and soldiers, horse and dragoons, &c. shall be carried to the castle of Konigstien, together with the colours, standards, and kettle-drums.

Ans. *Kettle-drums, standards, and colours, may be carried to Konigstein; but not the arms: no more than the cannon belonging to the regiments, the warlike stores, and the tents. The officers, no doubt, shall keep their swords; and I hope that such of them, as are of a willing mind, will make use of them in my service.*

VII. The same thing shall take place with regard to the field-artillery and the provision-waggons.

Ans. *Granted.*

VIII. His

VIII. His Prussian Majesty shall give assurances A. D. 1756. that no officer or soldier shall be obliged, against his will, to take on in his army; and that, after peace is restored, they shall all be sent back to the King of Poland; and, on the other hand, his Polish Majesty may not refuse dismission to the generals, and the other officers of his army, who may engage in any other service.

Ans. *Nobody need trouble his head about* this. *No general shall be forced to serve against his will: that's sufficient.*

IX. As to what is to be furnished to the lifeguards and grenadier-guards, if his Prussian Majesty pleases, we shall agree about the manner of proceeding therein, and settle, at the same time, with that Monarch the funds, out of which the salaries of the generals, officers, and other persons attendant on the army, are to be paid monthly, according to the estimates, that shall be drawn up by major-general Zeutsch, commissary at war.

Ans. *It is very reasonable I should pay those, who will serve;* and this payment shall be made out of *the clearest* receipts of the contributions. As to the generals, *they shall be treated like men, who have honourably served;* and it will be very easy to provide for their subsistence.

X. His said Majesty should also explain himself about the quarters and subsistence to be granted to the several regiments of cavalry and infantry, as well as to the engineers and artillery-corps.

Ans.

Anf. *I take upon me the maintenance of the army; and it shall be paid more regularly than heretofore, on the same footing as my own troops.*

XI. The King of Prussia will be so good as to order when and how the generals, and the whole army, without exception, with the baggage, shall file off from the post, in which they are at present.

Answ. This point may be settled in a quarter of an hour. One must chuse the most commodious road, and the places nearest at hand for giving them subsistence.

XII. His Prussian Majesty will be pleased to allow the necessary measures to be taken for removing and lodging the sick, that are incapable of following the army, and that they may be properly attended.

Anf. Granted.

XIII. The generals, the field and subaltern officers, as also the soldiers, who have hitherto been made prisoners, or have been left behind, shall be included in the present capitulation.

Anf. Granted.

Done at Ebenbert, *at the foot of* Lilienstein.　　*Signed,* Rutowski.

XIV. [*A separate article.*] I am authorised to oblige the army to lay down their arms; but I have no authority to free them from the oath of allegiance they have taken, nor to oblige them to take another. As for all the rest, it is left to his Prussian Majesty's disposal. Lieutenant-general

Winter-

Winterfield made me hope this Monarch would have made no difficulty to grant one squadron more of the life-guards. His Majesty will be so good as to resolve about the fortress of Konigstein, where the company of cadets and the grenadier-guards are at present with his Polish Majesty.

Done the 16*th of* Oct. 1756.

Signed, RUTOWSKI.

Ans. *Konigstein must be a neutral place during the course of the present war.*

Signed, FREDERICK.

A. D. 1756.

The Saxons, convinced of the bad policy of their court, to draw upon themselves the vengeance of so powerful a neighbour, by their hostile intrigues with Russia and Austria; the former of which was too far distant to promise them any seasonable help, and the latter had been already defeated, in their most vigorous attempt to succour them under their late blockade, submitted, with less objection than expected, to the proposal of enlisting themselves under the Prussian banner; and they were accordingly received into the pay of his Prussian Majesty; took the oath of fidelity to the conqueror, and were incorporated amongst the Prussian troops.

Saxons enlist under the King of Prussia.

With the loss of his military strength his Polish Majesty also lost that firmness and resolution, set forth in his letter, of *dying* rather than yielding to terms unbecoming a free Monarch. From this hour, it may be said, the Elector of Saxony abdicated

The King of Poland and family retire from Saxony.

abdicated his throne. He and his Queen, with the royal family, content with the appearance of royalty, which the King of Pruffia ordered they fhould have, fuffered themfelves to be difmiffed, under a proper guard, and efcorted to Warfaw in Poland: and Saxony thereby fell under the government of the King of Pruffia. An event which, as it was the moft confiderable for ftrenthening the King of Pruffia, could not have been obtained without the utmoft difficulty and danger, and obliging the Pruffian Monarch to ufe fome further means to effect it, than might have been confiftent, either with his ftrength, or found policy, had his Polifh Majefty ftood out, and put his foe upon the neceffity of driving him from his throne and out of his electorate by mere force. Had his army only laid down their arms; had they been difperfed, or difbanded by their own Sovereign's authority, it would have greatly embarraffed the King of Pruffia, how to compel them to enter into a foreign fervice, unto whom he now acquired a right by capitulation and the laws of war: and the embarraffment would have been greatly increafed by a refolute continuation of the Elector's adminiftration of his own government; which the King of Pruffia would fcarce have forced out of his hands, when the Saxon army had been difbanded. But the ruinous confequences of this capitulation and abdication are fo apparent in the progrefs of the war, that there is no need of further reflexions; and we fhall difmifs the fubject with this addition, to what has been already obferved,

Margin notes:
A. D. 1756.
Saxony falls under the government of the King of Pruffia.
By bad policy.

served, That the French ministry endeavoured to cast the whole blame of this invasion upon the alliance newly signed between Great Britain and Prussia, and spared no pains to persuade the Roman Catholic Princes, that their alliance was formed with a particular intention to destroy the Romish interest and religion in Germany. This countenanced the convention, which was now made with the Emperor, and which regulated the number and service of forces to be sent from France into Germany. The Prussian minister was ordered to quit Versailles immediately [p] : and the French King declared his resolution to maintain the public peace of Europe against all, that should attempt to break it; and especially to support the pragmatic sanction, the treaty of Westphalia, and the Romish religion.

A.D. 1756.
The use made of this by the French.
To propagate a religious war.
A convention with the Emperor.

At home, the repeated accounts of the vigorous efforts made by the French, to carry their point in America, and the notorious neglect or mismanagement of our colonies; and, at last, the account of the loss of Oswego, and of its dependences and consequences, being arrived, his most gracious Majesty, convinced by the abortive enquiries into former miscarriages and unaccountable losses, that it was in vain to endeavour any longer to mend his administration by such palliatives, as had been recommended to him, resolved upon satisfying his people by removing from his councils some, that had rendered themselves most

Domestic affairs.
State of the nation.

---

[p] And the French minister withdrew privately from Berlin.

A. D.
1756.

obnoxious to the nation, and calling up to his service and cabinet others, recommended by the unanimous voice of his subjects.

The discontent of the nation [q] cannot be better expressed than in the addresses to the King, and in the instructions to the representatives in parliament, during their recess [r]. It was vastly increased by our additional calamities: and appeared more and more in the uncommon difficulty, with which a subscription, opened at the exchequer for the sum of 500,000 l. was after many days filled; occasioned by the little prospect of having matters mended in the hands of those, who had done so little with the immense sums raised for the service of the current year; the only service done the nation having been performed by our privateers, which were fitted out with surprizing spirit, not only by merchants, but by parishes and private clubs or societies, who seemed to vie with each other in the means to distress [s] the enemy; and thus turned

---

[q] Amongst other tokens of this discontent with the ministerial measures, we may rank the refusal of quarters, in winter, to the Hessian forces, at the breaking up of their camp; there being no law then to oblige us to quarter foreign troops.

[r] See these addresses and instructions on p. 418, &c. of vol. I.

[s] One remarkable instance of the bravery of our privateers has been already given in the affair of the Antigallican; another happened, and about the same time, between the Terrible and Vengeance, of which the following is the account wrote by John Withy, third lieutenant of the Terrible.

"On Thursday, December the 23d, we saw a sail at daylight in the morning, we being then in the lat. of 47° 10′ long.

turned the war, carried on at the public expence, with so little success, to the advantage of individuals.

His

long. 11° 20'. west from the Lizard. We immediately gave chase to her, and she made all the sail she could from us; and about twelve at noon we came within gun-shot of her. We fired a gun to bring her to, which she returned with her stern-chase, and hoisted French colours. She continued firing at us, and we at her, 'till almost two o'clock, before we could get up close along side of her, when, we firing a broadside into her, she struck, and we found her to be a ship from St. Domingo bound for Nantz, laden with sugar, coffee and indigo. We lost in this engagement our fourth lieutenant and three men. We put on board her our first lieutenant and fifteen men, and were convoying her for Plymouth: but on Monday, December 27, in lat. 48° 30'. long. 6° 30'. from the Lizard, at day-light in the morning, we saw two sail bearing south by east from us, distance four leagues: we observed the largest ship to bring the small one to, and speak to her, and in about an hour after we saw the large ship bearing down for us, the wind being then at south-east. We then hawled up our main-sail, and laid our mizen-top sail aback, our prize being too far a-stern for her to come up with us. We then cleared ship, and got every thing ready for engaging; we likewise mustered all hands, and found we had no more than one hundred and sixteen, officers, men, and boys, that were able to stand to their quarters, the rest being either dead, or sick below with a distemper called the spotted fever, that raged among the ship's company. The enemy bore down upon us with English colours flying, 'till within pistol-shot of us: then she hawled up her courses, handed her top-gallant sails, and hoisted French colours. We had our people at their quarters on the starboard-side; but our prize being a heavy laden ship, she could not keep in a line with us, but fell to leeward; which the enemy observing, took the opportunity to run between her and us, and fired her larboard broad-side into our prize, which she returned.

The

The GENERAL HISTORY of

A. D. 1756.

His Majesty in the first place, to convince his British subjects, that he would rely on their courage and

The enemy then ranged on our larboard quarter, and fired her starboard broadside into us, which almost raked us fore and aft, and killed and wounded a great many of our men. With the way that she had ranged close up along side of us, our yard arms were but just clear of one another: and as soon as we got all our guns to bear upon her, we fired a whole broadside into her, our guns being all loaded with round and grape-shot, which made a very great slaughter among them. We both fell close along-side of one another, and lay so for the space of five or six minutes, her fore chains a-breast of ours; but she was afraid to board us, and we had not men enough to board her. As soon as we had sheered clear of one another, we exchanged our broadsides, which proved very fatal to us both, for there were a great many killed and wounded on both sides. But what did us most damage in killing our men, was their small arm men in their tops: they had sixteen men in the main and fore-tops, and eight in the mizen-top, who were constantly killing our men, and we had not men to send into our tops. We lost every man we had on the quarter-deck, either killed outright or else miserably wounded, except the captain and two men more; and the captain they shot through the body after he had struck. They likewise killed and wounded all that were in sight on the main-deck, but me, and eight or nine men more; and I had a very narrow escape, for a musket-ball grazed my right cheek, and gave me a slight wound; besides which, I was blown up with a powder flask. So that in this short, but bloody engagement, we had upwards of fifty men killed outright, and about forty wounded, and never an officer on board the ship, but myself, but what was killed outright, or dying of their wounds. The French used us very ill, stripping us of every thing, and some of our people they left almost naked. They turned our first lieutenant, and all our people, down in a close confined place forward, the first night that we came on board, where twenty-seven of them were stifled before

I

and zeal for the defence of his person and realm, ordered his Electoral troops to embark for Germany; and admitted the expediency of a national and well-regulated militia, in case of danger from an invasion: and then proceeded, as far, as he in prudence thought adviseable, at present, to make such alterations in his ministry, as might please his people. He began with a new commission for executing the office of treasurer of his Majesty's exchequer; by which the Duke of Newcastle, the first Lord of the treasury, was obliged to make way for his Grace William, Duke of Devonshire [t], and the Right Hon. Henry Bilson Legge was made chancellor of the exchequer, instead of Sir George Little-

A. D. 1756.
Hanoverian troops sent away.
Change in the ministry begun.

---

before morning; and several were hawled out for dead, but the air brought them to life again; and a great many of them died of their wounds on board the Terrible, for want of care being taken of them, which was out of our doctor's power to do, the enemy having taken his instruments and medicines from him. Several that were wounded they heaved overboard alive. The first and third captains of the Frenchman were killed in the engagement, with their captain of marines and sixty men outright, and seventy wounded, several of whom died of their wounds, while we were on board. The frigate is called the Vengeance, belonging to St. Malo: mounted 34 guns nine and twelve pounders, and 350 men when we engaged.

"P. S. By an account I have had from our lieutenant of marines that was in St. Malo's hospital, the French all died of their wounds before he came to Dinant."

[t] Nov. 16. The King appointed his Grace William, Duke of Devonshire, the Right Hon. Henry Bilson Legge, Robert Nugent, Esq; the Hon. William Ponsonby, commonly called Lord Duncannon, and the Hon. James Grenville, to be commis-

Littleton, Bart. By another commiffion for the marine department, the place of the Lord Anfon, firft Lord of the admiralty, was filled by the Right Hon. Richard, Earl Temple [u]: The Right Hon. George Grenville was made treafurer of the Navy.

Parliament meets.

His Majefty's fpeech.

On the fecond day of December his Majefty, thus intentioned, and, in part, difentangled from a miniftry, to whofe mifmanagement the prefent anxieties, difquietudes and misfortunes were generally afcribed, met his parliament, and, by a gracious fpeech from the throne, in a great meafure obviated all applications, which the reprefentatives of the people had been inftructed to make by their conftituents.

His Majefty told his parliament, That he had called them together in a conjuncture, which highly required their deliberation, advice and affiftance: and that he trufted, under the guidance of Divine Providence, that union and firmnefs in his affectionate people, would carry him, with honour, through all difficulties, and finally

---

commiffioners for executing the office of treafurer of his Majefty's exchequer, in the room of the Duke of Newcaftle, Sir George Littleton, Bart. Piercy Wyndham Obrien, and Henry Furnefe, Efqrs.

[u] The King appointed the Right Hon. Richard, Earl Temple, the Hon. Edward Bofcawen, Temple Weft, and John Pitt, Efqrs. George Hay, doctor of laws, Thomas Orby Hunter, and Gilbert Elliot, Efqrs. to be commiffioners for executing the office of Lord High Admiral of Great Britain and Ireland, and of the dominions thereunto belonging.

vindi-

vindicate the dignity of his crown, and its undubitable rights, againſt the antient enemy of theſe kingdoms. He aſſured them that the ſuccour and preſervation of America could not but conſtitute a main object of his attention and ſolicitude: and that the growing dangers, to which our colonies might ſtand expoſed, from our late loſſes [w] in thoſe parts, demanded reſolutions of vigour and diſpatch. He added, That an adequate and firm defence at home, had poſſeſſed the chief place in his thoughts, and that in this view he had nothing ſo much at heart, as that no ground of diſſatisfaction might remain in his people. Therefore he recommended to the care and diligence of his parliament, the framing a national militia, planned and regulated, with equal regard to the juſt rights of his crown and people, as what in time might become one good reſource to that end, in caſe of general danger. He obſerved, That the unnatural union of councils abroad [x]; and the calamities, which in conſequence of this unhappy conjunction, might, by the irruptions of foreign armies into the Empire, ſhake its conſtitution, overturn its ſyſtem and threaten oppreſſion to the proteſtant intereſt there; and that ſuch events muſt ſenſibly affect the minds of this nation, and had already fixed the eyes of Europe on this new and dangerous criſis. He then informed them, That he had ordered his

[w] Of Oſwego, ſee page 476, &c. vol. I.
[x] In the alliance between Auſtria and France.

A. D. 1756.

Electoral troops home to his German dominions; and declared, That he would with pleasure rely on the spirit and zeal of his British subjects for the defence of his person and realm. He recommended more vigorous efforts in the prosecution of the war, though attended with large expence, to a less effectual, and therefore less frugal plan of war. Thus said he, " I have placed before you the dangers and necessities of the public: it will be your care to lay the burdens you may judge unavoidable, in such a manner, as will least distress and exhaust my people." And concluded with these remarkable words, " Unprosperous " events of war in the Mediterranean, have drawn " from my subjects signal proofs [y], how dear- " ly they tender my honour and that of my " crown; and they cannot, on my part, fail to " meet with just returns of unwearied care and " unceasing endeavours, for the glory, prosperity " and happiness of my people."

Satisfactory.

This speech, (though it manifestly shewed the ascendency of some of the old leaven about the throne, by soliciting a parliamentary approbation of such measures, as his Majesty hereafter should acquaint them would be necessary, to support his electoral dominions, and our allies in Germany, against the effects of that unnatural union of councils at Vienna and Versailles, and against the irruption of French, Russian, or any other foreign armies into the Empire, to shake its constitution,

[y] In their addresses above recited. See p. 418, &c. Vol. I.

to overturn its fystem, and to opprefs the proteftant intereft) gave more public fatisfaction than
heretofore; becaufe therein were promifed feveral
great and national advantages; and his Majefty
feemed willing to throw himfelf entirely into the
arms of his Britifh fubjects.

A. D. 1756.

The Houfe of Commons addreffed his Majefty on this fpeech, with more unanimity, and, indeed with more freedom of expreffion, than had been known for fome years. After tendering their thanks for his gracious fpeech, they expreffed how far they were excited by duty, and warmed with gratitude, to acknowledge from their hearts the paternal care and royal condefcenfion of his Majefty, in pointing out from the throne, fuch a plan of force for our defence, as beft tended to the fatisfaction of the people, and in particular a well modelled national militia, as one proper fecurity for his Majefty's perfon and realm. They profeffed, that in their prefent arduous circumftances, they next after Divine Providence, re-
lied on his Majefty's wifdom and magnanimity; and put him in mind of the Britifh efforts, in times paft, under Princes, whofe firft glory was to found the ftrength of their government in the contentment and harmony of their fubjects. They promifed, that being thus united and thus animated, their Houfe would chearfully fupport his Majefty through all difficulties, and vindicate, to the utmoft, the dignity of his crown and its un-
dubitable rights, againft the ancient enemy of thefe kingdoms: and they trufted that his Ma-
jefty,

Commons addrefs.

A. D. 1756.

jefty, thus ftrengthened at home, would find himfelf rever'd abroad, and in a condition to fupport that weight and confideration in Europe, which belong to a King of Great Britain; notwithftanding the unnatural and unhappy union of councils, which had formed, on the continent, fo new and dangerous a crifis. They declared their concern at the fad events of war in the Mediterranean and in America: and affured his Majefty, that they would take thofe affecting matters into their moft ferious confideration, not imputing blame to any unheard: and that they would, with all confidence, alacrity and difpatch, fecond his Majefty's royal care for the fpeedy fuccour and prefervation of America, under the growing dangers, to which thofe invaluable poffeffions ftood expofed.

Lords addrefs.

The Houfe of Peers addreffed his Majefty in much the fame profeffions, declarations, promifes and affurances; but by the addition of thanks for his Majefty's condefcenfion to fend away his electoral troops, there arofe a warm oppofition, to that claufe only, by the Lords, who had oppofed the bringing thofe forces into England.

Mr. PITT made fecretary of ftate.

This unanimity between the King and parliament was followed by another token of his Majefty's regard for his people. On the fourth of December, the third day of the feffion of parliament, the feals were given to the Right Hon. WILLIAM PITT, Efq; who, the delight of the nation, fucceeded to the office of fecretary of ftate, in the place of Mr. Fox.

The Right Honble WILLIAM PITT, Esqr.

On this occasion every advocate for their country looked with pleasure towards the throne: every friend of liberty exulted with joy, to see the happy day, when, they thought Majesty had discovered the cloven foot; was come to a resolution to emancipate himself from those, who had brought upon him dishonour, disquietude and misfortunes; and had been graciously pleased to signify his royal intention to rely upon the deliberation, advice and assistance, not of a FACTION, but of a parliament inspired by a people, with unanimity and firmness, who had never failed to carry their Princes through all difficulties with honour, when Majesty had relied on their assistance, and not forfeited their confidence by misapplication of their money, or in pursuit of measures, which threatned their liberty, and debased their credit. A people descended from that race of men, which in all ages had distinguished themselves for their loyalty and courage: who once won the French crown in the field of battle, and brought their King to grace the triumph of our Prince: who more than once, in our own memory, reduced them to sue for peace; and who vindicated the dignity of the British crown and its indubitable rights, against the ancient and natural enemy of this realm, when France was in a much better capacity for invading and conquering our territories.

How conspicuous was the disquietude, which corroded the royal mind, at the gloomy prospect of his American colonies? when he discovered the little regard paid to their security, and the ill-concerted

concerted means of carrying thofe faint efforts into execution; which the clamours of the people, and the neceffity of keeping up appearances had obliged his late minifters to make. What could he do more than declare his own intention, and point out the danger and means of defence?

How manifeft does it appear in this fpeech, that Majefty had been laid under a reftraint; and that his wifdom, in providing an adequate and firm defence for this kingdom, had not been permitted to exert itfelf; when he takes the firft opportunity to recommend to his parliament, the forming a national militia; notwithftanding the unwearied labour, and the many bafe infinuations, with which the faction, that lately furrounded the throne, endeavoured to diffuade him from trufting his perfon and kingdom to the courage and fidelity of his Britifh fubjects.

On former occafions this militia fcheme had been treated in the great affembly of the nation, not with that regard, as its utility and importance deferved. We now fhall foon find that this countenance, given to it by his facred Majefty, difpelled that cloud of mifreprefentations, in which it had feveral times mifcarried: and brought forth that natural ftrength of our conftitution, which, by becoming one of the greateft fecurities to this kingdom, diftinguifhed the reign of George II. and this parliament for their wifdom and goodnefs.

It was never known that a Britifh monarch, who endeavoured to gain the confidence of his people, was deceived in his expectations of being revered at home, and enabled to support that weight and confideration in Europe, which belong to a King of a powerful, free and independent nation: but it is the little regard fome Princes have to their promifes, which gains themfelves fo little regard; fearch the annals of all ftates, and it will be found, That it is generally from thofe, with whom they have contemptuoufly broken their faith, that Princes have met with the greateft oppofition and mifchief. *A.D. 1756.*

How different was our fituation at this juncture? The people were difatisfied with the conduct of the miniftry: his Majefty in a great meafure removed that caufe of complaint. They implored juftice on the caufe of their misfortunes and loffes: his Majefty promifed [z], "That he would not fail to do juftice upon any perfon found wanting in their duty:" They petitioned for a national militia, and the fpeedy exportation of foreign forces out of this kingdom: his Majefty has recommended the former to his parliament; and given orders for the return of his electoral troops to his German dominions; being convinced that the ftability of his throne, and the ftrength of his fceptre, depend upon the fpirit and zeal of his Britifh fubjects. *Remarks on the King's conduct.*

The new minifter's elevation gave fo general a fatisfaction, that confiding in his abilities and integrity, the country gentlemen, in parliament, *Country gentlemen join the new minifter in parliament.*

[z] See his Majefty's anfwer to the city of London's addrefs.

who

A. D. 1756.

who had been a watch and remora to the proceedings of the court under former administrations, united heartily with the Right Hon. William Pitt, Esq; in every measure to strengthen the hands of government. By this means every motion, he made in parliament, was carried without opposition. In the mean time, the minister did every thing possible to confirm the opinion conceived of him. He applied diligently both to prevent any attempts upon this island, and to annoy the enemy, and to find them employment enough to defend their own coasts: Scotland had always been their chief expectation to create trouble within ourselves. This had been frequently done by spiriting up and assisting the clans, whose chiefs were proscribed for their connections with the exiled family of Stuart, and whose connections continued, rather through necessity, and want of the means of reconciliation with their lawful Sovereign, than any real affection for the Pretender, as had occasionally been proved by the fidelity of some of them, that served under English commissions in the last war. It was therefore proposed to his Majesty, to admit and to invite, by proper encouragements, the suspected part of the Scotch Highlanders into his pay. By this adoption his Majesty recovered a respectable body of subjects, who for many years had withdrawn themselves from his protection, and had been ready, upon all occasions, to join with, or to favour the designs of France upon England. By this expedient the seeds of rebellion were improved into the service

Conduct of the new minister.

His attention to prevent Scotch rebellions.

Advantages arising therefrom.

of our country: and those very Highlanders, that used to be a terror on former occasions, and required an army to be always kept in readiness, to prevent their rising, in favour of a foreign power, and had often defeated our best concerted measures against France, by their invasion of England; were now converted into regular and national forces, and approved themselves to be both brave and faithful, in every service of Great Britain, wherever they were commanded. Thus France had nothing to hope for in Scotland, by way of diversion to our vigorous measures. Where there could be found no men to favour a descent, it was impracticable for an enemy to invade us through the desolate [a] highlands of North Britain: and thus England was delivered from an extraordinary expence of a northern army, and enabled to employ those troops, whose service the Highlanders (that were aforetimes our terror) supplied in distant climes, in the execution of such plans, as we shall find ruined our enemies, and could not have been performed without such an additional force. As by this means a door was opened for repentance; so they who had been forced to live in exile, were now engaged, by the strongest ties of gratitude and interest, to support the present family.

Having carried this important point for preserving the peace and tranquility of the north; the minister joined heartily in the establishment of

A. D. 1756.

Destroys the French interest in Scotland.

Heartily favours the establishment of a militia.

[a] By a moderate computation there have been raised in this country 20,000 men for the land service: and by the impress bills, not less than 10,000 able bodied seamen.

A. D. 1756.

A change of measures.

a regular and well-disciplined militia, and in several other bills, which passed into laws during this session of parliament, for the internal defence of the nation, the more effectual annoyance of our enemies, and for retrieving our credit in Europe, and our misfortunes in America. Our fears of an invasion were immediately dissipated: our fleets were no longer kept to guard our ports: expeditions were preparing to insult the enemy's coasts; and, instead of consuming the vast sums of money, which had been thrown away, in mock campaigns, at Cobham, Byfleet and other parts of this island, last summer, and in the importation of foreign troops; due attention was paid to the motions of France on the Continent, and to the danger of our allies and interest in Germany; so far as might be done without prejudice to the American war, which was kept always as the chief point in view by the minister; all other measures being made subservient to that great and important object.

Message to the parliament about Admiral Byng.

His Majesty mindful of his royal word, that justice should be done upon any person found wanting in their duty, a message was sent to the Commons concerning the imprisonment of Adm. Byng, and the proceedings against him; who otherwise, perhaps, might have endeavoured to avail himself of his privilege, as a member of parliament. In consequence of which, the House being satisfied with the proceedings of the court,

the

the admiral was brought to his trial and suffered [b].

The parliament entred immediately upon measures to strengthen the hands of government. The land forces were augmented from 35,000 to 49,749 effective men, including 4008 invalids. The seamen were settled at 55,000 men, including 11,419 marines; with sufficient provision [c] for their maintenance. His Majesty was also enabled to perform his agreement with, and to provide for his Hessian and Hanoverian forces [d]. Besides which, they granted ample sums for garrisons:

A. D. 1756.

Men for the land and sea service.

[b] See p. 442 to 458, Vol. I.

[c] Viz. 2,860,000 l. for the sea service, granted on December 16: and 1,213,746 l. 3 s. 10 d. for the land service, granted 23 December 1756.

[d] For the HESSIAN Troops.

	£	s.	d.
Dec. 23. For 6544 foot with the general and staff-officers and train of artillery, from Dec. 25, 1756, to Feb. 24 both inclusive	23,335	17	11
Feb. 24. For 6544 foot, &c. from Feb. 25, to April 26	22,959	10	2
April 25. For 6544 foot, &c. from April 27, to May 27, 31 days	11,667	18	11
May 10. For the German pay for 6,600 foot, &c. from May 28 to Dec. 24	46,597	9	0
——For the German pay for 1,400 horse, &c. from April 27 to December 24	25,078	0	0
——For the German pay for 3,300 foot, &c. from April 22 to December 24	27,273	14	0
——For the German pay for 700 horse, &c. from August 23 to December 24	6,119	9	6
——For the remount and levy money for 700 horse and 3,300 foot	37,296	17	6

——For

sons: for the ordnance: for levying new regiments: for forming and maintaining an army of observation in Germany, and fulfilling his Majesty's engagements with the King of Prussia: for the support of the British forts on the coast of Africa: for the relief of South Carolina and Virginia; the support of Nova Scotia and Georgia: for enabling the East India company to keep a military force in their settlements[e]: and for several other uses and contin-

	£	s.	d.
——For making good his Majesty's engagement with the Landgrave of Hesse Castle	60,766	1	0
——For defraying the charge of an advanced subsidy to ditto	26,007	5	6
——For the remaining moiety of the remount money for 1400 horse	13,475	0	0

For HANOVERIAN Troops.

	£	s.	d.
Dec. 23. For 8,605 foot, with the general and staff-officers, and train of artillery, from Dec. 25, 1756, to Feb. 25, 1757	33,025	1	6
Feb. 24. For 5,726 foot, &c. from Feb. 25, 1757, to March 26	9,494	3	9
March 29. For defraying the expences of the march of the Hanover troops, in pay of Great Britain, both at their coming here, and their return back to Germany	31,959	13	6
[e] Jan. 17, 1757. For the ordinary of the navy, including half-pay to sea officers	223,939	7	7
March 7. Towards the buildings, re-buildings, and repairs of his Majesty's navy	200,000	0	0
March 29. Towards paying off the debt of the navy	200,000	0	0
Dec. 23, 1756. For forces and garrisons in the plantations and Gibraltar, and for provisions for the garrisons in Nova Scotia, Newfoundland, Gibraltar, and Providence	423,963	16	10

——For

contingencies: which supplies, in the whole, amounted to 8,350,325 l. 9 s. 3 d. for the payment

A. D. 1756.
Supplies granted.

	£.	s.	d.
——For the pay of the general and staff-officers, and officers of the hospital — —	47,060	15	10
Jan. 17. For the charge of the office of ordnance for land-service for 1757 ——	161,557	1	10
Jan. 20. For defraying the exceedings of ditto in 1756, not provided for — ——	228,196	4	7
Feb. 10. For defraying the charge of two Highland battalions of foot ——	46,022	5	0
March 7. For defraying the charge of four regiments of foot on the Irish establishment, serving in North America and the East Indies, and augmenting O Farrel's regiment of foot —— —— —	48,926	2	6
——For the reduced officers of the land forces and marines —— —— —	33,000	0	0
Mar. 10. For defraying the remainder of the exceedings of the office of ordnance for land service for 1756 —— ——	47,869	2	4
April 4. For defraying the extra expences of the land forces in 1756 —— ——	111,570	19	7
Feb. 10. For defraying the charges of the civil establishment of Georgia, and other incidental expences, from June 24, 1756, to June 24, 1757. — ——	3,557	10	0
Feb. 21. For assisting his Majesty in forming and maintaining an army for the defence of his Electoral dominions and those of his allies, and to enable his Majesty to fulfill his engagements with the King of Prussia	200,000	0	0
—— For supporting Nova Scotia for 1757, upon account —— ——	28,789	5	0
—— For defraying the expences incurred by supporting that settlement in 1755 ——	15,381	4	0
May 19. For defraying the extraordinary expences of the war in 1757 ——	1,000,000	0	0

——For

A.D. 1756.

of which sum there were funds established to the amount of 8,689,051 l. 19 s. 7 d. which was an overplus of 338,726 l. 10 s. 4 d. to prevent any deficiency that might happen in the guinea lottery, this year, first attempted; or in any other branch of the ways and means.

Hessians quartered by act of parliament.

All the necessary business was dispatched with equal zeal and expedition. The Hessian troops having been denied winter quarters by the publicans, who could not be compelled to receive them by law; and they having suffered extremely by the severity of the winter; one of the first cares of the parliament was to prepare a bill to make provision for quartering foreign forces, which past without opposition, and was signed by commission on the 17th of December 1756. By this act these foreign troops were, in every respect, to be treated, as the native troops of this kingdom, till their return [f].

Bills passed for the marine service.

Two bills were at the same time brought into the House of Commons: the one for regulating

	£.	s.	d.
——For the relief of his Majesty's subjects in North and South Carolina and Virginia, in recompence for services, on account ——	50,000	0	0
——To the East India company to enable them to keep a military force in their settlements in the East Indies, in lieu of a battalion of his Majesty's troops withdrawn from thence ——— —— ——	20,000	0	0
——For supporting the British forts, &c. on the coast of Africa —— ——	10,000	0	0

[f] A pardon was granted to deserters in the land service, on condition, they should return before the last day of January 1757, by proclamation, dated December 31, 1757.

the marine forces while a-shore; which differed from the mutiny act only in giving the Lords of the Admiralty power to grant commissions for holding general courts martial, and to do every thing, and in the same manner, as his Majesty is empowered to do by the usual mutiny bill. The other was for the more speedy and effectual recruiting his Majesty's land forces and marines, whereby justices of the peace, commissioners of land tax, magistrates of corporations and boroughs were invested with a power to meet, under certain directions from the war office, in their respective divisions; and at their meetings to *enlist* volunteers for the land service, on or before the 1st of May, with a bounty of three pounds to be paid by the receiver general or collector of the land tax; and on condition of being discharged at the end of three years, if the war should then be ended, otherwise at the end of the war: and to *impress* into the said service, all able bodied idle and disorderly persons, who did not exercise and industriously follow some lawful occupation, or had not subsistence sufficient to maintain themselves: for whom they were also empowered to search, &c. [g] And it ordained that all men thus apprehended, adjudged within the description of the act, and approved by the military officer in attendance, should be delivered to that officer, who should pay 20 s. for each unmarried man, and 40 s. for a man with a wife or family, to be applied to the use of the

---

[g] See the clause on p. 218. Vol. I.

parish:

A. D. 1756.

parish; provided there was no informer, who was intitled to 10s. of the money. The act further ordained, That they should not imprefs any man troubled with a rupture or any other bodily infirmity; nor a reputed papift, nor one under the fize of five feet four inches tall, nor under the age of 17, nor above the age of 45, nor any one qualified to vote for a member of parliament: and that no man thus imprefled should be intitled to his difcharge till he had ferved five years, or till the end of the war. It was further provided, That no private foldier enlifted under this act, might during the time he should remain in Great Britain, be difcharged without the confent of the colonel or field officer commanding the regiment; or, if a marine, without the confent of the admiralty; the officer difcharging him in any other manner, to be cafhiered.

Remarks on thefe acts.

These acts paft without oppofition; though at a time when there might not have been the like neceffity for a powerful augmentation of our forces, nor an equal opinion of the minifter's love

For prefling.

for his country, the power given, at large, to the feveral denominations of men, in this commiffion, without diftinction, or regard to their abilities and private characters, to imprefs their fellow fubjects, would have met with a ftrenuous and reafonable oppofition; as it put the liberty of the fubject, fome times, and in fome places, in the power of a worthlefs, over-bearing and felf-interefted magiftrate.

The

GENERAL TOWNSHEND.

The bill for regulating the militia, was mentioned so early in this session of parliament, as on the 4th day of December, by Colonel GEORGE, (now General) TOWNSEND, eldest son of the Lord Viscount Townsend, whose patriotic spirit could never shine with greater lustre than in his unwearied and disinterested endeavours to plan, and to carry this constitutional act through the House, under the auspices and aid of the King's recommendation, against that natural aversion to militia forces, which still subsisted amongst some men in power, and of great influence in both houses of parliament; and whose military abilities and conduct will give us frequent occasion to mention him with honour to his country. But the many difficulties, which the gentlemen charged with its formation had to encounter, and the competitions of interests they had to reconcile, drove its first reading off till the 26th of January: and, after mature deliberation, and several alterations to satisfy the most cinic opposition, this bill so well considered, and recommended from the throne itself, underwent diverse material amendments, before it was fit for the royal assent. The most disagreeable alteration was the reduction of the number of men to one half[h] proposed by the House of Commons. This occasioned some warm debates in the lower house: but after several conferences, the patriotic members having been deprived of the assistance of Mr. PITT, who had been

A. D. 1756.

For the militia.

[h] Viz. to 32,340 men, for England and Wales.

forced

A.D. 1756.

forced to resign the seals, gave way, rather than furnish the opposition with a plausible pretence to throw the bill out. To which restrictions and alterations we may impute those imperfections, that, in many particulars, have crampt the due execution of the militia act; which past the royal assent on the 28th of June[1].

A

---

[1] *An abridgment of the act for better ordering the militia forces in the several counties of that part of Great Britain called England, passed 28 June 1757.*

Whereas a well ordered and well-disciplined militia is essentially necessary to the safety, peace, and prosperity of this kingdom.

Be it enacted, That from the 1st of May 1757, the lieutenants of counties shall arm and array proper persons; and the lieutenants shall appoint their deputy lieutenants, and give commissions to lieutenant colonels, majors, and other officers, whose names shall within a month, be certified to the king.

The lieutenant of every county shall have the chief command of the militia of that county.

In each county shall be appointed twenty or more deputy lieutenants, if so many can be found qualified, each of whom shall possess 400 pounds a year, in freehold, copyhold, customary estate for life, or an estate for some long term of years, determinable upon lives, or shall be heir apparent of a possession of 800l. a year. A lieutenant colonel, or major, shall be possessed of 300 a year, or heir apparent to 600. A captain shall possess 200 a year, or be heir to 400, or to be the son of one who possesses, or at his death did possess 600 a year. A lieutenant shall possess 100 a year, or be the son of one who possesses or at his death did possess 200. An ensign shall possess 50 pounds, or be the son of one who possesses or at the time of his death did possess 100. One moiety of the estate in all these cases, lying within the county.

In

A bill of such consequence to the liberty of the subject against the practices of a ministerial power, and

A. D. 1756.

In counties where twenty deputy lieutenants with proper qualifications cannot be found, it shall be sufficient to appoint so many as can be found.

A right to the immediate reversion of an estate leased out for lives on a reserved rent, producing to the lessee the clear yearly rent of 300 pounds, shall be considered as equivalent to an estate of 100 pounds a year, and so in proportion.

An ensign or lieutenant may be promoted to be a captain; and a captain or major may be promoted to be a lieutenant-colonel, on extraordinary occasions, on account of merit.

The King may displace any deputy-lieutenant or officer, and the lieutenants shall appoint others in their stead.

Every deputy or officer shall give in his qualification to the clerk of the peace, and take the oaths to the government, within six months after he shall begin to act, on penalty of 200 l. on deputy lieutenants, and all above the degree of captain; and 100 l. on captains and those under.

Peers are exempted from serving by themselves or substitutes; but they and heirs apparent of peers, may be appointed deputy lieutenants, or commission officers, and their qualifications need not to be left with the clerk of the peace; but on taking the oaths, &c. they may act without being otherwise qualified.

A commission in the militia shall not vacate a seat in parliament.

At the end of every four years a number of officers shall be discharged equal to the number of those, who, duly qualified, shall sollicit for admission.

To each regiment an adjutant shall be appointed, who has served in the regular forces, in which he shall still retain his rank; and to every company of the militia, shall be appointed two or more serjeants (in the proportion of one serjeant to twenty private men) out of the regular forces, who shall be intitled to the hospital of Chelsea. And serjeants appointed from

and carried with so much resolution, may be looked upon with surprize. But when we consider the popularity

from that hospital shall be re-admitted on producing certificates of good behaviour.

No persons selling liquors by retail shall be capable of being a serjeant of the militia.

The number of private men serving in the militia shall be; for

County	Number	County	Number
Bedfordshire	400	Nottingham county and town	480
Berkshire	560	Oxfordshire	560
Bucks	560	Rutlandshire	120
Cambridgshire	480	Salop	640
Chester and Chester county	560	Somersetshire	840
Cornwall	640	Southampton county and town	960
Cumberland	320	Staffordshire and Litchfield	560
Derbyshire	560	Suffolk	960
Devonshire and Exon city	1600	Surry	800
Dorsetshire and Poole	540	Sussex	800
Durham	400	Warwick county and Coventry	640
Essex	960	Westmoreland	240
Gloucestershire, Gloucester city, and Bristol	960	Worcester county and city	560
Hereford	480	Wilts	800
Hertford	560	York city and West Riding	1240
Huntingdon	320	York North Riding	720
Kent and Canterbury city	960	—East Riding and Hull	400
Lancashire	800	Anglesea	80
Leicestershire	560	Brecknock	160
Lincoln county and city	1200	Cardigan	120
Tower Hamlets	1160	Caermarthen county and town	200
Middlesex, rest of	1600	Carnarvon	80
Monmouthshire	240		
Norfolk and Norwich	960		
Northamptonshire	640		
Northumberland, Newcastle on Tyne and Berwick	560		

Denbigh

popularity of the object, and the immediate exigencies of the state at this critical conjuncture, it appears

A. D. 1756.

Denbigh	280	Montgomery	240
Flintshire	120	Pembrokeshire and	
Glamorganshire	360	Haverford W	160
Merionethshire	80	Radnorshire	120

There shall be no more than one captain, one lieutenant, and one ensign, to 80 private men.

Where the proportion of men directed by this act to be raised in any county shall be judged by the lieutenant to be too large, the privy-council, on application, may regulate it.

The lieutenant of each county with two deputy lieutenants, or three or more deputy lieutenants in the absence of the lieutenant, shall meet on the 12th of July 1757, and on the first thursday in June, in every subsequent year, and require the head constables to deliver in a list of all the men between the age of 18 and 50, in their several districts, except peers, officers of the militia, officers of the regular forces or garrisons, members of either university, clergymen, teachers of separate meetings, peace and parish officers, articled clerks, and apprentices, and seamen, noting in the list the men labouring under any bodily infirmity.

Every deputy constable, or other petty officer, shall transmit to the head constable the list of his division, having first affixed it to the door of the church or chapel for one Sunday.

On the day appointed for receiving these lists, the lieutenants and deputy lieutenants shall settle the number to be taken from each hundred, or division of the county. They shall then subdivide themselves, and three or more deputies, or two deputies with one justice of the peace; or one deputy with two justices, shall meet within a month in every subdivision, to hear the complaint of those, that think themselves entitled to exemption; and upon any just cause shall correct the lists. They shall then settle the number to be raised in each parish, and chuse the individuals by lot; and within three weeks afterwards

A.D. 1756.

appears that fear was the prevailing motive, which deterred the greatest sticklers and the most factious opponents

wards, the person so chosen shall appear before them; each of whom shall take the oaths, and enter into the militia for three years, or bring one to serve as his substitute, or forfeit 10l. and be liable at the end of three years to serve again.

Three deputies, or two deputies and a justice, or one deputy and two justices, shall meet in their several subdivisions occasionally at other times, and annually on the Tuesday before Michaelmas; and if any person 35 years old shall shew just cause for his discharge, it shall be granted, and another chosen by lot in his room; and the vacation by death shall be filled up in the same manner.

A militia man removing to another parish, shall serve the remainder of his time in the new parish.

New lists of men qualified for service shall be made every year.

A new body shall be chosen every third year, so that all persons duly qualified may serve in their turns, each for three years.

A list of the persons serving in each parish shall be transmitted to the lieutenant.

An officer neglecting to return his list, or making a false and partial list, shall be committed for a month to the common goal, or be fined not more than five pounds, or less than 40 s.

Every private man serving for himself shall be exempted from statute work, from serving peace or parish offices, or in the regular forces.

He that has served three years shall not serve again until by rotation it comes to his turn.

Married men having personally served in the militia, if called out in case of invasion or rebellion, shall be entitled to the same privileges of setting up trades in any place of Great Britain or Ireland, as by act 22 Geo. II. is granted to mariners or soldiers.

A

opponents of the new ministers, from treating the militia bill with the same ill-usage, as on former occa-

A quaker refusing to serve shall hire another in his stead; and if he neglects, a sum shall be levied upon him by distress, sufficient to hire another man.

Within one month after the return of the lists, the lieutenant and two deputies, or without the lieutenant three deputies, shall form the militia of each county into regiments, consisting of not more than twelve, nor less than seven companies of forty men each; appointing the commissioned and non-commissioned officers to each company.

They shall be exercised thus: On the first Monday in the months of March, April, May, June, July, August, September, and October, they shall be exercised in half companies; and on the third Monday in the said month in companies.

And once every year, on the Tuesday, Wednesday, Thursday and Friday of Whitsun-week, they shall be exercised in whole regiments.

No man shall be exercised in half company or company more than six miles from his own house.

Notice of the time and place of meeting shall be sent by the lieutenant and two deputies, or, without the lieutenant, by three deputies, to the high constables, and by them to the petty constables, who shall fix them upon the door of their respective churches.

The lieutenant shall appoint at pleasure a regimental clerk, a serjeant-major out of the serjeants, and a drum-major out of the drummers.

If it should be thought inconvenient, on account of fairs or markets, to exercise the militia on the day set by this act, order may be made by three deputies, or two deputies and one justice, or one deputy and three justices, for exercising them on any other day, Sunday excepted.

In counties where the militia do not amount to seven companies, and therefore cannot make a regiment, they shall be formed into a battalion, under the lieutenant and one field-officer,

A.D. 1756.

occasions, and obliged them to permit a few patriots to carry a point, so contrary to their natural inclina-

officer, one adjutant who shall be a subaltern in the army, a serjeant-major, a drum-major, and a clerk shall be appointed them, and they shall be exercised as a complete regiment.

Where a whole company or a half company cannot be brought together, they may be exercised in smaller numbers, as the lieutenant or deputy shall direct.

One commissioned officer shall attend the exercise of the half company, and inspect their arms and accoutrements.

The arms and cloaths of the militia shall be carefully kept by the captain of each company in chests, provided by the parish where they are deposited. The muskets shall be marked with an M and the name of the county.

The King's lieutenants, or the colonels, may seize, or remove whither they shall think proper, the arms, cloaths, and accoutrements, when necessary to the public peace.

Any person intrusted with the custody of any arms or cloaths, delivering them out, unless for exercise, or by command of his superior officer, or by the order of any justice of the peace, under his hand and seal, may, by two justices, be committed to the county goal, for six months.

No pay, arms, or cloathing, shall be issued, nor any adjutant or serjeant be appointed, till four-fifths of the men shall have been chosen, and the officers have taken out their commissions.

The officer, who superintends the exercise, shall call over the list, and certify to a justice the names of those, who are absent from exercise. The justice shall examine the excuse offered, and if it be insufficient, shall punish the defaulter for the first offence by fining him 2s. or setting him in the stocks for an hour; for the second he shall fine him 4s. or send him to the house of correction for four days; for every offence afterwards he shall fine him 6s. and if it be not paid, send him to the house of correction for any time not exceeding a month.

If

inclination. Besides, they were beaten upon their own principles: they had no argument or device left,

If any man shall be convicted upon oath, before a justice, of being drunk at the time of exercise, he shall forfeit 10s. or sit an hour in the stocks.

He that shall be convicted on oath, before a justice, of insolence or disobedience to his officer, shall, for his first offence, be fined 2s. 6d. and in default of payment be sent to the house of correction for four days; for the second 5s. or committed for seven days; and for every offence afterwards be fined 40s. and committed to the house of correction for any time not more than a month, nor less than fourteen days.

If any man shall sell, pawn, or lose his arms or accoutrements, he shall be fined a sum not exceeding three pounds, or in default of payment be committed to the house of correction for one month; and if he cannot then raise the sum required, for three months.

He that shall neglect to return his arms in good order after exercise, the same or the next day, shall be fined 2s. 6d. or be sent to the house of correction for seven days: If he neglect to return them by Monday after Whitsun-week, he shall forfeit 5s. or be sent to the house of correction for fourteen days. And the person entrusted by the captain with the care of the arms and cloaths, who shall omit to complain of such neglect, shall forfeit 20s.

The soldier or non-commissioned officer, that shall be absent from his annual exercise, shall forfeit 10s. a day, or be committed to the house of correction for a month.

If any non-commissioned officer shall be convicted, upon oath, of being negligent in his duty, or disobedient or insolent to the adjutant, or other superior officer, he shall be fined by a justice a sum not exceeding 30s. or, in default of payment be committed to the house of correction for fourteen days, and may be discharged by the lieutenant.

Whoever shall unlawfully buy or receive any arms, or accoutrements belonging to the militia, shall incur the penalty

of

A. D. 1756.

left, (except they had pulled off the mask and availed themselves solely upon a suspicion or jealousy of five pounds, and in default of payment be imprisoned for three months, or publickly whipped, at the discretion of the justice

No man shall be censured for absence occasioned by attending an election.

The militia are to be subject in military affairs to their own officers, and in civil to the civil magistrate.

All parish officers are required to assist the lieutenants and justices.

In case of actual invasion, or upon imminent danger thereof, and in case of rebellion, the King first notifying the occasion to parliament, if then sitting, or in their recess to the privy-council, and to the people by proclamation, may direct the lieutenants, or any three deputy-lieutenants, to draw out their regiments, who shall march, by his Majesty's order, to any part of the kingdom, under the command of such generals, as he shall appoint, receiving, during the service, the same pay with the regular regiments of foot, and the officers holding the same rank with the regular officers of the same denomination. The militia, during the time of service shall be liable to the law martial then subsisting; and any man wounded shall be entitled to the hospital of Chelsea. A militia-man not appearing, or refusing to march on such occasion, shall forfeit 40 l. or be committed to the county-goal for twelve months.

In case of actual invasion, or upon imminent danger thereof, and in case of rebellion, if the parliament be not sitting, nor its adjournment or prorogation to expire in fourteen days, the King may summon it to meet on any day, upon giving fourteen days notice; and they shall meet accordingly for the dispatch of business.

The militia and regular troops shall be tried by courts-martial, each by their own officers.

The militia during their annual exercise shall be billeted as regular troops.

In

jealousy of the people's discontent at their misconduct,) to reason away the utility and expediency

A. D. 1756.

In case of invasion or rebellion, justices, upon order from the King, or any chief commission officer of the militia, shall issue warrants to the chief constables of hundreds to provide carriages for the arms, cloaths, accoutrements, powder, &c. which carriages shall be paid in ready money by the officer demanding them, after the following rates: A waggon with five horses, or a wain with six oxen, or with four oxen and two horses, 1 s. each mile; a cart with four horses 9 d. a mile; and so in proportion. Persons having such carriages are required to furnish them for one day's journey only. Any chief constable neglecting his duty in the premises, shall forfeit a sum not exceeding 40 s. nor less than 20 s. to be levied by distress.

The militia shall not, on any occasion, be compelled to go out of this kingdom.

In all cities, or towns, which are counties within themselves, and have been accustomed to raise their own militia, the lieutenant or chief magistrate shall appoint five deputy lieutenants, who shall exercise the same power as the other deputies. Of these smaller counties the deputies, colonels, lieutenant colonels, and majors, shall possess lands to the value of 300 l. a year, or a personal estate of 5000 l. captains 150 l. or two thousand five hundred pounds personal estate; lieutenants and ensigns, 50 l. a year, or 750 l. personal estate. One half of the real estates of the officers of county towns must be in such city or town, or within the county at large, to which such city or town is united for the purposes of this act. The penalty for acting, if not qualified, is, for a deputy-lieutenant or field officer, 100 l. for all under, 50 l.

All fines and forfeitures shall be paid to the regimental clerk, and made a common stock in each subdivision; of which an account shall be given to three deputies, or two deputies and one justice, or one deputy and two justices, who shall apply it to the erection of buts, and the provision of gunpowder, to be

A. D. 1756.

ency of this military and conſtitutional eſtabliſhment. They could not alledge, as heretofore, That there was any danger or appearance of internal commotion, and inſurrections in favour of an exiled family. So that they were conſtrained to give their aſcent to a meaſure, which they had always dreaded, as the moſt effectual bar to miniſterial tyranny. Whereas the new miniſters, by thus arming the people for the internal defence of the nation, diſcovered their intention to execute ſome diſtant ſervice with the national troops, that required a powerful military force abroad.

How the militia act was obſtructed in its execution.

The oppoſition to this conſtitutional bill was not confined to either houſe of parliament. Every art was made uſe of by thoſe, who ſet their faces

be uſed in ſhooting at marks; and the remainder ſhall be diſtributed in prizes to the beſt markſmen, or employed in any other way for the uſe of the militia.

Perſons committed to the houſe of correction upon this act ſhall be kept to hard labour.

Proof of qualification, in all ſuits, ſhall lie on the defendant.

No order made, by virtue of this act, by a lieutenant, deputy, or juſtice, ſhall be removed by *certiorari*; nor execution be ſuperſeded thereby.

Where a pariſh extends in two counties, its militia ſhall ſerve in that county where the church ſtands.

Thoſe, who are trained and muſtered in the docks, ſhall not be obliged to ſerve in the militia.

All former acts relating to the militia are repealed by this act, except in caſes, which are herein directed to be ſubject to former acts.

The other clauſes in this act (which is to remain in force five years) contain proviſions reſpecting the privileges of particular places.

againſt

THE LATE WAR. 143

against it in parliament, to prevent its being carried into execution. Many lieutenants of counties would not arm and array proper persons; and others found means to evade the law, and to excuse themselves. Men of property were deterred from accepting commissions; and such a dislike to this new service was every where propagated, amongst the lower and middling class of people, that in counties, whose lieutenants were well disposed and well officered, it was with the utmost difficulty to raise the common men by ballot; and scarce any where could it be performed, for some time, without discontent and riot; especially amongst the farmers and landholders, who, of all men, should be least suspected of joining in any opposition to a measure, so necessary for the safety of their estates, from foreign invasions and domestic insurrections. The masters were frightned with an opinion, that the militia would rob them of their servants: and the labouring men were terrified with the suggestion, that they would be misused, and sent to fight the battles of some foreign prince or state; or transported like felons to the plantations in America. Prejudices were thus formed in their minds, which could hardly be removed with the most serious and laboured representations of the expediency of the act, and of the insidious discourse of those, that set them against so salutary a law. Amongst which there appeared a letter, in the name of a deputy-lieutenant of a county, addressed to his tenants and neighbours, and recommended to the perusal of

A. D. 1756.

How removed.

all

all the people of England, in order to obviate and remove such ruinous misrepresentations, and seting forth the importance of the act, and the necessity of its being duly executed.

Importance and necessity of the militia.

"I will tell you, said he, plainly what I think "necessary to be told you at this time, when "every mistake may be of most pernicious con-
"sequence to us all. When I first heard of the
"discontents and riots of some of the poorer
"people, which are so greatly to their disgrace
"and disadvantage; I could scarce believe it was
"possible, that they could have arisen from the
"execution of the late act for a militia; a thing
"so moderate in the duty, and so desired by the
"voice of the nation.—You may expect a full
"explanation of the benefit you are likely to re-
"ceive from it: and to do you justice, neigh-
"bours, I do not know any set of men, more
"likely to yield to reason, when it is honestly
"laid before them, than the farmers of England.
"—But before I say any thing of the absolute
"necessity of some law of this kind, I must set
"you right as to some notions, that I find are
"industriously spread amongst you by the ene-
"mies of our country, as though the militia-men
"were to be carried out of the kingdom, and
"forced to serve abroad. But this is a wicked
"falshood: for you may see, by the act itself, that
"unless there be an actual invasion, you are not
"to march even out of your own counties; but
"that you are never to be sent out of the king-
"dom, upon any pretence whatsoever. Our re-
"gular

"gular armies are to fight your battles abroad:
"you are only to defend yourselves, your wives
"and children, which, no doubt, every man is
"always ready to do, at home. This is the pro-
"mise, upon the unshaken faith of parliament,
"which cannot be broken.—Besides, you are
"not subject to the command, as men that fight
"for their pay—you receive no money at en-
"gaging: you engage only by the common duty
"of all Englishmen: and you are not to be of-
"ficered as others; but to be commanded by the
"gentlemen of your own county, who, if what
"you are wickedly told were the case, would
"think it as hard to be decoyed out of the king-
"dom, or to be laid under any unreasonable dif-
"ficulties, as you possibly can."

"I shall proceed to lay before you the reason
"why you are to be armed at this time, and to
"be exercised with particular care: It is, because
"your King and country stand in need of an
"army of defence, to relieve you from the ex-
"pence and danger of maintaining a too numer-
"ous soldiery: it is to put arms into the hands
"of a free people, who have, by various
"practices of state, been deprived of the means
"to defend themselves, upon any emergency,
"ever since the restoration: it is to convince you
"of his Majesty's confidence in your fidelity,
"and in his opinion of your innate courage and
"bravery: and, in particular, it is because dan-
"ger, at this present time, hovers over your

"heads

"heads from the power and malice of your confederate enemies, much more to be dreaded than any, which have ever yet threatned us.— The French, who, for a hundred years paſt, never ceaſed a moment to contrive our ruin, are, after many defeats, coming forward again, and now aiming at us ſuch a blow, as would, if it took place, lay us at once on the ground. They are aiming to cut off our colonies at a ſtroke: Colonies peopled by our brethren, Engliſhmen, and our own fleſh and blood, and therefore infinitely dear to us: colonies, the main ſupport of our trade, by which the market for our corn, and all the produce of our lands is kept up. Of which the French King is ſo ſenſible, that he thinks, if he could deprive us of theſe valuable poſſeſſions, he might reduce us to beggary and ſlavery."

"Our Sovereign, the beſt and braveſt of Kings, has reſolved to defend theſe colonies with the utmoſt vigour, as he will every thing elſe that belongs to us: the French King, on the other hand, meeting with a vigorous reſiſtance in our colonies, does not confine his ſchemes to that part of the world, but ever ſeeks to enter into the heart of our own country; to deſtroy every thing with fire and ſword, and to bring on us every ſort of miſery, that a powerful and enraged enemy can contrive or execute. 'Tis to prevent all theſe evils, that the law in queſtion is provided: So that had it ten
"times

"times the hardships, that are complained of, whereas it contains no hardship at all in reality, it ought to be joyfully and thankfully accepted. For, shall we refuse arming ourselves, when not only our honour, our prosperity, and our safety, but our liberty and our very being depend on our exerting ourselves, our natural and constitutional strength manfully."

"This is not all: every one may not be aware of our condition, and of the power of that enemy we have to contend with. The French King's country contains many millions of people more than we have: and he is absolute master of the lives of all those people, and of every thing they have: when he pleases he drains the last penny from their purses; and takes the last man from their villages and factories. A power, that makes him dangerous enough at all times: But an affair has happened, which makes him much more dangerous than ever."

"The Queen of Hungary, whom, in the last war, we saved from being entirely destroyed by the French, equally unmindful of justice and gratitude, has now joined all her forces with those very French, for the sake of oppressing the King of Prussia, instead of joining us against the common enemy. The Queen of Hungary is mistress of Flanders, which has always been looked upon as a country of great consequence to us, because it covers the states of Holland, and lies directly opposite to our coast. Now she
"has

"has delivered this barrier into the hands of the
"French, to pay them for the affistance they
"give her in her unjuft defigns. From which,
"three mifchiefs happen to us; firft, they have
"thofe towns, that look directly into the mouth
"of the Thames, by which they may do our
"trade great prejudice. Secondly, the French
"take us in on another fide, and have fo many
"more ports from whence they can invade us:
"and thirdly, as they now lie next to the Dutch,
"by having Flanders given up to them, they
"overawe them in fuch a manner, that they dare
"not come to our affiftance. So that now our
"whole dependance muft be only upon God and
"our own courage."

"I know that great reliance is juftly had on
"the defence we may juftly expect from our
"navy, and from the regular army, we have in
"pay. But this army is only a handful in com-
"parifon to theirs: and what is our fleet or our
"army to cover a coaft of 15 or 1600 miles,
"the circumference of the ifland of Great Britain.
"If then the French could efcape our fleet, and
"enter our country in a hoftile manner, what, in
"fuch a cafe, would you do? Think, fpeak and
"act like Englifhmen! Is there a man amongft
"you, who would leave the defence of his wife,
"his children, his king, his country, and his re-
"ligion to any mercenary foldiers in the world?
"I am perfuaded, you would yourfelves go into
"the field. Had we an hundred thoufand men
"in arms, you would ftill be afraid that, in fuch

"an

" an interesting conjuncture, they were not half
" sufficient. Such is the spirit, which is, I am
" confident, still in my countrymen: and a noble
" spirit it is! But let not our spirit hurry us away
" from the consideration of those things, without
" which no spirit can be serviceable. You are
" called upon to fight, when all that can be dear
" to you as Englishmen, as men, as protestants,
" is at stake! You are going to fight for all this,
" without knowing what you are to do against
" men, whose trade it is to fight, and who have
" been perpetually exercised in the use of arms."

A. D. 1756.

" I know very well, that no men are naturally
" more brave than you are: But in man bravery
" is not enough: strength is not enough: there
" must be skill; there must be practice; or the
" greatest strength and courage signify very little.
" Suppose the stoutest, bravest man in the coun-
" ty, who in his whole life had never handled a
" cudgel: what figure, pray, could he make against
" a little slight fellow, that by long practice was a
" good cudgel-player? undoubtedly you will
" say, a very poor figure. Just so is the very
" strongest bravest man in the world to one, who
" is trained up to be a soldier. And every man
" must be, and ought to rejoice in being a sol-
" dier, when the real danger of his country calls
" upon him; and he ought to spare no pains to
" compass it."

" Therefore as your danger was well known,
" and as your desire and courage to defend your-
" selves were likewise well known, the wisdom
" of

A.D. 1756.

"of the government has thought fit to make
"you capable of protecting yourselves, by putting
"arms, in an orderly manner, into your hands,
"and by inftructing you in fuch a difcipline, that,
"when you are perfected in it, you need not,
"under the protection of heaven, fear any force,
"that the enemy can fend againft you."

"This is the defign of the militia; and it is
"nothing elfe. If you think it a reftraint on
"your liberty, to be obliged to ferve in this
"manner; I pray you to confider, that there is
"not one of you, that thinks it a hardfhip on
"his child to fpend a laborious fervile appren-
"ticefhip of feven years, to learn a trade, by
"which to gain a fmall livelihood: and will you
"then pretend to grudge a few days in a year to
"learn a profeffion, honourable to all, abfolutely
"neceffary to yourfelves, and the only thing
"that can preferve your lives, properties, reli-
"gion and liberty, without which all the reft is
"nothing. Or will a man pretend to fay, That
"he loves his country, and values his freedom,
"and refufes to take reafonable pains to learn
"to defend that, and every thing elfe, that an
"honeft man ought to value."

"But I have fomewhat particular to fay to
"thofe, who refufe, to put themfelves in a pofture
"to defend their country, through cowardice or
"lazinefs. If through their bafenefs the enemy
"fhould happen to prevail, they would, after be-
"ing ftripped of that liberty, which they pre-
"fume to abufe, and know not how to value, be
"forced

"forced to bear those arms for a tyrannical op-
"pressive master, which they now refuse to em-
"ploy in their own defence. The law is the
"only protection of liberty: and, just so much
"as every man murmurs at wholesome laws and
"regulations; so much as he evades them by ar-
"tifice; so much as he riots to destroy them by
"violence, exactly so much is he a promoter of
"arbitrary power, and so much is he a French-
"man in his heart. Could our forefathers look
"down upon these discontents and disturbances,
"and were told, That you rioted, because you
"are born under a King, who in his goodness is
"willing to put arms into your hands for self-
"defence, and whose government is taking pains
"to instruct you how to use them against your
"natural enemies the French: that they were
"giving you arms and skill to fight, lest you
"should be conquered by those, whom your fore-
"fathers had so often conquered; they would be
"confounded at your ignorance, startle at your
"folly, upbraid you for your ingratitude, cow-
"ardice and laziness, and disown you for the
"descendants of English heroes."

Such was the language, such the arguments and persuasions required in the patriots, to inform the understandings of the people, in their respective neighbourhoods, and to dissipate the fears raised in their minds by that leven of the old ministry, which now began to work powerfully again in every department; and would have deprived the nation of the advantage of that service-

able

A. D. 1756.

able militia, during the late war, had not the same spirit, which carried the bill through the legislature, exerted itself in the execution of this salutary law.

Measures taken by the new ministry.

The hopes conceived by the new ministers and the nation, from the effectual execution of the militia bill, put them upon ways and means to employ the standing forces of the kingdom in services, for the interest of their country and their own honour. Large draughts were designed for North America, and Louisbourg was the first object of their operations. For this purpose a squadron of ships of war was ordered to be equipped, at the proper season, to sail under the command of Admiral Hawke, with a powerful land force under his convoy. A squadron was also dispatched to the East Indies, under the command of Commodore Stevens, and our interest in the West Indies was consulted, by sending a squadron to Jamaica, under the command of Admiral Coates.

A. D. 1757.

About this time the public were informed, that Admiral West had wrote to the secretary of the Admiralty, desiring to resign his command and to come to town, upon Admiral Byng's condemnation: and to Lord Temple, then first Lord of the Admiralty; to whom he further explained himself on the said subject. As these letters convey the private sentiments of one, who is looked upon to be the most material evidence on Mr. Byng's trial; who was the second in command on the affair, for which Mr. Byng lost his life, and who

received

received such distinguishing marks of the royal favour after his return to England, it would be concealing, or, at least, not giving the whole truth, which is the duty of an historian, as much as of an evidence, should we suppress, or deny them a place in this history.

A. D. 1757.

While Mr. Byng was under confinement for trial, the Lords of the Admiralty manifested his Majesty's approbation of Admiral West's conduct, by appointing him to the command of a secret expedition, with orders to hold himself in readiness to sail. But on the very day sentence of death was passed upon Admiral Byng, Mr. West wrote to the secretary of the Admiralty:

Admiral West's letters relative to Mr. Byng's sentence.

SIR,   Magnanime, 27 Jan. 1757.

"WITHOUT entering upon the merit of
" Admiral Byng's behaviour, or deciding
" at all upon it, one way or other; yet the sen-
" tence passed this day upon him (the substance
" of which I have seen) makes it impossible for
" me to help declining the very honourable and
" distinguished command their lordships have been
" pleased to appoint me to: I must, therefore,
" beseech and entreat their lordships to confer it
" on some person more worthy, since I can only
" be answerable for my loyalty and fidelity to my
" king, and resolution of doing what appears to
" me for his service, which it seems *an officer may
" not want, and yet be capitally convicted for his mis-
" conduct or inability of judging right:* and I am
" not so presumptuous, as to imagine, that my
"actions

To the Lords of the Admiralty.

A.D.
1757.

"actions can always be so rightly governed; nor
"am I altogether certain that the *judgment of others*
"*is infallible*; and as in other cases the conse-
"quences may be fatal, I must therefore repeat
"again my most earnest request, that their lord-
"ships will be pleased to appoint some other per-
"son to my command, and grant me their lord-
"ships permission to come to town."

By the same conveyance, he sent as follows to Earl Temple:

To Lord Temple.

"My Lord,   Magnanime, Jan. 27, 1757.

"HOwever honourable, or however advan-
"tageous the situation I am placed in may
"be; yet I am determined and fully resolved to
"forego any thing rather than serve on terms,
"which subject an officer to the treatment shewn
"Admiral Byng, whom the court-martial have
"convicted, *not for cowardice, nor for treachery*;
"but for MISCONDUCT: an offence never, till now,
"thought capital; and now it seems only made
"so, because no alternative of punishment was
"found in that article, they bring him under.—
"Strange reasoning!—to *acquit* him of the two
"points *cowardice* and *disaffection*, to which that
"article can *only* have respect.—Since, though
"*negligence* is mentioned, yet can it be only in-
"tended to refer to one or the other of those two
"crimes, *negligence* PROCEEDING *from disaffection*
"*or cowardice*. And I well remember this was the
"opinion of the House of Commons, when the
"bill was before them; for which reason no alter-
"native

" native was left in that article, which otherwise
" there would have been.—Courts martial I have
" always underſtood to be courts of honour and
" conſcience; and therefore why gentlemen ſhould
" think themſelves tied by the letter, or to act
" againſt their opinion, I know not; but enough
" of this at preſent. I ſhall only make one ob-
" ſervation more, in regard to that part of their
" ſentence, wherein he is ſaid *not to have done his
" utmoſt to relieve St. Philip's caſtle* [b], without
" pointing

A. D.
1757.

[b] Admiral Weſt in his evidence on the trial of Mr. Byng, being aſked, concerning the poſſibility of any ſhips of the fleet, or frigates getting cloſe to the caſtle of St. Philip on the 19th in the morning, ſaid, He believed it was not poſſible: for that the ſhips, ſent for that purpoſe, ſeemed to endeavour it as much as was in their power. And being further interrogated relative to the ſame object, whether he apprehended the enemy were maſters of Mahon harbour, he replied, " I do apprehend that the enemy were ſo far maſters of Mahon harbour, as to prevent the Engliſh fleet from making uſe of it with ſecurity to themſelves." And in regard to the propriety of throwing in the land forces, He declared it his opinion that it would have been improper and highly inexcuſeable, when the enemy was in ſight, as it would have weakened the force of the Engliſh fleet, and expoſed it to that of the enemy, which was at that time ſuperior: that had thoſe land forces been thrown into St. Philip's, the ſhips would not have been fit for action and to engage the enemy's fleet, nor ſufficient to defend the caſtle againſt the enemy, in ſuch a manner, as for them not to have ſurrendered.

Captain Amherſt declared, that all the ſhips in the fleet, when the ſignal was made for battle, bore down, and thoſe ſhips, which were in action, did engage as cloſe as they could get; amongſt which he particularly mentions the Culloden and the ſhips in her van; and as the weather was very good he apprehended,

that

"pointing out, which way it could have been re-
"lieved by him, which indeed they would have
"found difficult enough to have done.

"As that the rear would have engaged as near as the van did, had the French laid to, instead of making sail on, presently after Mr. Byng began to engage.

Captain Lloyd being *asked* concerning the occasion of the Admiral's ship backing, and the delay it made, *answered*, "That he thought the Trident's being under the Admiral's lee bow, was the occasion of his backing, and, in course, so much time was lost in getting down,"

Captain Philips being asked, If each ship in the rear had crowded sail in proportion to their distance from the enemy, they could not have got as near the rear of the enemy within the time, or a little space of the time more, as the van closed the van of the enemy? answered, That he thought all the sail they could have made would not have brought them down so soon as the van. Though they might have got down in a little time more. (*But then the French, when they saw that, made sail on*, as Captain Amherst relates.)

Captain Gardiner of the Ramillies deposed, That the Trident being abaft the larboard beam of the Ramillies, did so impede the Ramillies in going down to the enemy, that the Admiral must have gone down without his force, which was not his intention: that the signal was out for the line of battle a-head at that time, and the rear division went down very regular after the Trident and Princess Louisa got into their stations. Being asked, Whether it had not been a more speedy and regular method to close the enemy, to have made the signal for the line a-breast? the Captain said no; because it would be improper for ships to go down in a line a-breast, to attack ships that are laying in a line a-head, when they can go down with their bows to them; i. e. a slanting course to them: and therefore he was of opinion, That the rear did take the proper method to come down to the enemy. And being further interrogated, Whether he meant, as to the course steered

"As I have taken my firm and final resolution to resign the command, and have wrote very strongly

A. D. 1757.

on the enemy, or the sail carried? he answered, "Both: but this, said he, is matter of opinion which I shall hereafter avoid entering into, as there are many superior judges here to me."

He was also of opinion, That the rear would have engaged as near the enemy as the van did, had the French fleet staid: "that it was Admiral Byng's intention to engage the Chief Escadre, the third ship from the enemy's rear, and not to throw away his shot, as the enemy did, till he came near the enemy: "that the Admiral stood on, till it was imagined on board the Ramillies, that every ship, if she had gone properly down with a slanting course, could have gone down to the ships, they should have engaged, of the enemy, with their broadsides to them: "that he recollected this particularly to have heard the Admiral say, when the Ramillies was a-breast of them, that that was his intention: "that the Admiral ordered the guns to be shotted with round and grape shot, two shot in the guns below, and proposed to set top gallant sails on seeing the French going away; and that he heard him express, at that time, his unhappiness at not having a sufficient force to make the general signal to chase; as he thought he could materially have distressed the enemy in the situation they then were in, if, said he, *I had two or three ships more.*"

Joseph Belwaird, master of the Ramillies, said, That he had orders to steer such a course down on the enemy, as to cut off the third ship of the enemy's rear, which ship the Admiral expressed his intention to engage, and that they should have gone near on the enemy, if that accident, of the Trident, had not happened.—Admiral Norris interrupted him by saying, That was matter of opinion.—Being asked, whether the ships could have preserved a line of battle in going down to the enemy, as well with the top gallant sails, as without them, as the weather then was? answered, That as the weather then was he could have carried them; but that he left it to the judgment of the court, whether a croud of sail is proper to preserve the order of battle,

when

A. D. 1757.

"ſtrongly, on that head, to the board, I muſt intreat your lordſhip to facilitate it; and I am, Yours, &c."

Laſt year, at this ſeaſon, the cry was about the danger of a French invaſion. This was

The French ſcheme for the year 1757.

when ſhips are in a line a-head ſo cloſely connected together, as at the diſtance of half a cable, and at the brink of coming to action, when the enemy is waiting.

Colonel Smith being examined in reference to the priſoner's courage, ſaid, That he was near the Admiral's perſon during the whole time of action; that he perceived no backwardneſs in the Admiral during the action, nor any mark of fear or confuſion, either from his countenance or behaviour, but rather the reverſe: that he gave his orders very cooly, and without the leaſt confuſion: that he did appear ſolicitous to engage the enemy: to aſſiſt his Majeſty's ſhips, that were engaged with the enemy; and both this Colonel and others teſtified, That they never, after the day of action, heard any murmuring or diſcontent among the officers or men, on any ſuppoſition that the Admiral had not done his duty; and Mr. Lloyd, ſurgeon of the Ramillies, ſaid, that the men were quite the reverſe from any diſcontent, &c.

All which compared with the reſolutions of the court martial, which *acquit* him expreſsly of *cowardice* and *diſaffection*; and with the 25th reſolution, which ſays, that " the court were (*unanimouſly*) of opinion, that while the Ramillies was firing, in going down, the Trident and ſhips, immediately a-head of the Ramillies, proved an *impediment* to the Ramillies's continuing to go down;" may properly account for thoſe paſſages in Admiral Weſt's letters, where he ſays, " I am not altogether certain that the judgment of others is infallible," and where he is determined and fully reſolved to forego any thing rather than ſerve on terms, which ſubject an officer to the treatment ſhewn Admiral Byng.

N. B. General Fowkes has been reſtored to his rank in the army, and to a command in Ireland, by his preſent Majeſty.

thought

thought a proper foporific for the men in power at that time, to keep the ftrength of the nation inactive at home. The alteration in the miniftry, and the proceedings of the parliament, this winter, made the French alter their fcheme. They were informed of the new minifter's abilities and enterprifing activity. They could not expect to frighten him into a refolution to employ all our force, as his predeceffors had done, to guard the coaft of thefe kingdoms from a defcent; and they were perfectly convinced, that the voice of the people was for an offenfive war, and that they were alfo willing to fupport the King in a vigorous profecution of it. Therefore, their plan for the year 1757, was to divert Great Britain from the main object of the war in America, by provoking us to become principals in the German war.

A. D. 1757.

With this view we find the French took all their meafures. And on the 17th of February his Majefty fent a meffage by the Right Hon. WILLIAM PITT, Efq; one of the principal Secretaries of State, fignifying, "That it was always with reluctance that his Majefty afked any extraordinary fupply of his people; but that, as the united counfels and formidable preparations of France and her allies threaten, with the moft alarming confequences, Europe in general; and that as thefe moft unjuft and vindictive defigns were particularly and immediately bent againft his Majefty's Electoral dominions, and thofe of his good ally the King of Pruffia, his Majefty did confide on the experienced zeal and affection of his

His Majefty's meffage about his Electoral dominions, &c.

A.D. 1757.

King of Prussia.

his faithful Commons, that they would chearfully assist him in forming and maintaining an army of observation, for the just and necessary defence and preservation thereof, **and to** enable his Majesty to fulfil his **engagements** with the King of Prussia, **for the security of the Empire, against the irruption of foreign armies, and for the support of the common cause."**

Disagreeable to the nation.

How the parliament received and honoured this message, by granting all his Majesty requested, has been already related [b]; but it was not **done** without a great outcry and clamour amongst the people without doors; who, on this occasion, talked very freely against the projected army of observation in Germany, which they deemed a prelude to a ruinous continental **war,** that, sooner or later, might starve our **operations** by sea, and in America, and at **the same** time distress the nation with an accumulation **of taxes, and** an additional **load** of debts. However, the popularity of the minister, who, with his adherents, omitted nothing to discourage German measures; and the compassionate arguments urged in favour of Hanover, **by the** advocates for a continental war, threatened, **by the** enemy **of** our nation, on our account only, reconciled them **to** an acquiescence; if **it could** not bring them to approve a measure, **which** leaned so apparently towards a re-adoption of those continental measures; upon **a** bare suspicion of which any other ministry would have totally forfeited the confidence of the people. In a word, the expediency of supporting Hanover and assist-

Allowed to be expedient.

[b] See the supplies on p. 125, &c. Vol. II.

ing

ing the King of Pruſſia was allowed; and meaſures were taken immediately to carry the neceſſary reſolutions into execution. Two hundred thouſand pounds was granted for the relief of his Pruſſian Majeſty ᶜ. His Royal Highneſs the Duke of Cumberland was appointed to the chief command of the army to be raiſed in Germany, to obſerve the motions of the French: and he ſet out accordingly for Hanover, on the 9th of April, from London. The French army of 80,000 men, the choiceſt troops of France, under the command of M. de Eſtrees, having already paſſed the Rhine, ſeized upon the town of Embden and whatever belonged to the King of Pruſſia in Eaſt Frieſland, and by ſlow marches made the beſt diſpoſitions to over-run his Britannic Majeſty's Electoral dominions; and fixed upon Munſter for the Marſhal's head quarters. There was another army of 25,000 men, ſent from France, under the command of the Prince of Soubiſe, which at the ſame time was employed in the reduction of Cleves, Meurs and Guelders, &c. after which ſervice, it was ordered to join the Imperial army of execution, againſt the King of Pruſſia and his allies.

But ſuch was the equity and precaution of his Britannic Majeſty to give no real cauſe, or appearance of provocation, to any power, to invade his German dominions, that in theſe circumſtances, when a formidable French army was advanced to their frontiers, his Majeſty would not ſuffer his troops to take the field, till he had publiſhed to

A. D. 1757.

The equity of his Britannic Majeſty.

ᶜ See the note on page 127. Vol. II.

A. D.
1757.

the world the juſt motives, which compelled him to repel force by force, and to defend him againſt the invaſion of his enemies by thoſe means, Providence had put in his power.

His motives, as Elector of Hanover, for appearing in arms.

"His Britannic Majeſty, Elector of Brunſwick Lunenburg, on this occaſion declared, That he had uſed his utmoſt endeavours to prevent the war, which had riſen between him as King of Great Britain and the crown of France, and to accommodate the differences, which occaſioned it, by way of negociation: That when he found theſe endeavours to be ineffectual, he ſtill laboured to keep the war, which he could not prevent, within narrow bounds, that it might not interrupt the tranquility of his dominions in Germany, much leſs the other States of Europe, who had no concern in the quarrel: That in conſequence of this pacific diſpoſition, and becauſe in autumn, 1755, it was become more probable than ever, that France, to revenge the ſuppoſed injuries, which ſhe had received from his Britannic Majeſty, would attack his dominions in Germany, his Majeſty in the beginning of the year 1756, concluded a treaty with the King of Pruſſia, by which he had great reaſon to hope his pacific deſigns would have been rendered effectual; as by this treaty, purſuant to the deſign of it, it was probable the King of France would be diſappointed in his views [d]: and

[d] This leads us to the reaſon of our ſubſidiary treaty with Ruſſia in 1755, which by this aſſertion, appears to have been made with a view to prevent any attempt upon Hanover, by the King of Pruſſia in alliance with France. See Vol. I. p. 134, 135, 202, 203, 255, 256.

though

though a new war ᵉ has broken out unexpectedly ᶠ, since that time his Majesty had carefully avoided taking any part in it. That it was impossible for the dispassionate and impartial, after considering the conduct of his Britannic Majesty on this occasion, not to see the injustice of all the motives and pretences of France for invading the electorate of Brunswick, which is under the protection of the Empire: That, if these pretences were founded upon the war, which had broke out between England and France, it would be easy to shew, that this war, both with respect to its causes, and its end, is entirely foreign to his Majesty, as Elector of Hanover, and to his Hanoverian dominions: and that as to the second war, which had been kindled in Germany, the crown of France, as guarantee of the treaty of Westphalia, had not the least pretence on one hand, to act against the States before-mentioned, so long as his Majesty cannot be charged with any breach of the said peace; and on the other, France, as an ally and auxilliary of the Empress Queen, cannot justly act against a member of the Empire, who is not at war, nor has the least difference with her Imperial Majesty. But that, as France has notwithstanding entered the Empire on the side of Westphalia, with a numerous army, which after hav-

A. D. 1757.

ᵉ Between the King of Prussia and the Empress Queen, and her allies.

ᶠ As to his part: for his Britannic Majesty declared his total ignorance of any such intention of the King of Prussia's invading Saxony and Bohemia, till it was actually done. See p. 80.

ing garrisoned the Imperial city of Cologne, is advancing farther and farther into the Electoral States of Brunswick; as it has already entered and raised contributions in the Bishoprick of Munster; and as his designs against the estates of his Britannic Majesty in Germany, are too manifest to be doubted, he was compelled by indispensible necessity, to assemble and march an army to avert, with the assistance of the Most High, all violence, injustice and usurpation, upon his own estates and those of his neighbours: That, to prevent the ill consequence of false and artful insinuations, his Majesty thought it highly requisite thus to declare to the whole world, that he was very far from having conceived any design to act offensively against any of the States of the Empire, or even against the crown of France: and that by the armament, and the march of his troops, to which he was compelled, he had no view, nor desire, but to repress by the divine assistance all invasion, violence and hostilities; and, if such should happen, to do, as an original member of the Empire, what shall be just in the sight of God and of man, and what is required of him by the states, which the Almighty has placed under his protection: That he was confident, no person could mistake or misinterpret that conduct, into which he had been forced upon the principles of self-defence: and that he particularly confided in the faith and friendship of his co-estates in the Empire, that they would not discountenance his views in their favour, of keeping the calamities of war at a di-

stance

stance from their frontiers; but that they would rather facilitate and support them: that being well assured his Majesty's troops would observe the most exact discipline, he hoped, they would in return, give them proofs of their good will, particularly by furnishing them, for ready money, with such provisions and forage, as they should want: and lastly, that they would not furnish his enemies with these or any other necessaries, or accommodations, that might be prejudicial to his Majesty's dominions or their own."

This declaration was immediately followed by assembling the army of observation, which consisted of Hanoverians, Hessians and some other less respectable States, to the amount of 40,000 men, under His Royal Highness the Duke of Cumberland, who established his head quarters at Bielfeldt, and there concerted the plan of operations with the general officers, that were to act under him. But what could be expected from so weak a force, and a measure, which by no means could be said to be agreeable to the English, at whose expence this army was to be supported; and at a juncture of time, the more unfortunate for such an undertaking, as it was to be carried into execution and supported by the old ministry restored, whose credit with the nation was so entirely sunk, and whose attachment to continental measures, at the risk of their national interest, had been so often proved, that every wheel of the state turned heavily from the day they resumed the management of public affairs.

The

A. D. 1757.

The conduct of the new ministers.

The disinterestedness of that part of the ministry, which had been called to the helm, in the late promotion, appeared on every occasion, in the senate and in the cabinet. Great counsellors of state (whose predecessors had made it a constant rule to maintain their power by consulting the inclinations and passions of their sovereign, and patronizing no measure either in parliament, or at the council board, but what tended to extend the prerogative, and to bring the people into a state of dependency upon the crown) who were determined to shew, that, as they had not bargained for their places, nor surrendered their principles by capitulation, he is the best servant of the crown, that maintains his independency and candour in office, with the strictest regard to the interest of his country. Thus the first time, for many years, the interest of the nation became the touchstone of every measure proposed by the administration. Men, that could not be tempted to depart from their integrity, that kept themselves disembarrassed, and set no further value upon their power, than it enabled them to serve their King and country, debated every measure in the presence of their sovereign, without fear of his dislike and resentment; and in parliament they remembered, that they sate in that august house, not as servants to the crown, but as representatives of the people, and guardians of their liberty and property; and that it was their duty to oppose every design, which appeared prejudicial to the subject.

However,

However, this behaviour expofed the patriot minifters to great mifreprefentations by their affociates out of the old miniftry, who ftill continued about the throne, and made their addrefs to his Majefty by exaggerating the oppofition to thofe meafures, efpoufed moft warmly by his Majefty, in behalf of his Electoral dominions, and injurioufly reprefenting the new minifters to be lukewarm in promoting other meafures, which the national fervice required. So that by opportunity and importunity, and by conveying falfe ideas, injurious to the characters of Mr. PITT and his adherents, in the late promotions to the miniftry, they obtained their peremptory difmiffion from their feveral offices; at a conjuncture of time, when wifdom, integrity and firmnefs were more neceffary than ever.

A. D. 1757. Mr. PITT refigns the feals.

A pen cannot depict the prefent deplorable ftate of the nation in this real diftrefs; without anally, but who required powerful aid from us; engaged in a war with the moft formidable enemy in Europe, and in a war hitherto unfuccefsful; without any fyftem in its councils for carrying on the war to effect, and with a miniftry in whom the nation could not confide: when the military virtue of our anceftors feemed to be degenerating for want of proper difcipline and fervice; our operations againft the enemy at a ftop, and the rage of faction was every where confuming the little remains of patriotifm.

The deplorable ftate of the nation.

At court the enemy feemed to be entirely forgot. There was no attention to any thing, but who could get, and keep the beft places. The

A. D. 1757.

Treachery suspected.

Fleet delayed.

Attack of Louisbourg resolved upon.

enemy was permitted to execute every plan, without opposition: and, if it may be equitable to judge from circumstances, that can be proved by events; there was great reason to suspect that Mr. PITT's plan against Louisbourg, was not kept with that secresy, amongst the parties entrusted with its destination, as becomes a cabinet-council: nor carried so unanimously in the cabinet, as to prevent any private intrigue to render it abortive. For, the equipment of this armament was by one means or other delayed till it was too late, either to attack Louisbourg, or to favour any plan of operations by Lord Loudon and the Provincials, on the continent of North America. This fleet did not get from Cork before the 8th of May; and then, instead of Admiral Hawke, it sailed under the command of Admiral Holbourne. Our attention to the security of our settlements in North America might be easily foreseen by the French. But the plan for taking Louisbourg, which we shall see was the principal object of the French armament at this conjuncture to prevent, could scarce have entered their thoughts, had it not been intimated to the enemy; and, perhaps, as soon as it had been resolved upon at St. James's; or it would have been impossible to have provided so expeditiously for its defence.

The resolution to attack Louisbourg, at the same time the French were to be driven from the Ohio, and their other encroachments on the continent of North America, was taken soon after his Majesty committed the direction of his national affairs

affairs to Mr. PITT: and the preparations were begun to carry it into execution soon after Christmas. The French, truly sensible of the importance of Louisbourg, immediately equipped, with the utmost expedition, three several squadrons to cover and defend Louisbourg, and to strengthen their forces on the continent. One, of nine ships, sailed from Brest on the 30th of Jan. 1757, with a body of troops on board, under the command of M. de Beaufremont; who steered for the West Indies to reinforce the French garrisons in that quarter, and to wait the first opportunity to get into Louisbourg after the breaking of the ice. This was followed by another squadron of five ships, which sailed under M. du Rivest, about the beginning of April, with a number of troops, warlike stores and provisions on board, from Toulon; escaped Admiral Saunders stationed off Gibraltar, and arrived at Louisbourg on the 4th of June. A third, consisting of 14 ships, sailed on the 3d of May, (a week before Holbourne departed from Cork) under the command of M. du Bois de la Mothe, from Brest, with a number of soldiers on board, and presents for the Indians, and arrived at Louisbourg on the 29th of June; whereas the English fleet did not arrive at Hallifax, the place of rendezvous, before the 9th of July; when both the season, and the superior strength of the enemy, made it impracticable to carry Mr. PITT's vigorous and seasonable plan into execution, with any hopes of success.

A. D. 1757.

How prevented

A. D. 1757.

Three factions in the state.

There were three factions now formed amongst the great men of the nation: Of which it will be necessary to observe, That one of them, which had the greatest parliamentary interest, and the greatest interest also with the monied people, consisted of such as had grown into place and power under the old ministry; were greatly respected by the King, for their long and adulating services and compliances; but weak in some material points; and not at all popular.—Another faction, whose parliamentary strength was much inferior to the former, had the character of better abilities, and an interest at one court able to balance that of the old ministry, by means of a then powerful connection; yet they were more unpopular; and that very powerful connection made them much less respected at another court; and still worse with the generallity of the people; whose jealousies had been industriously raised and increased by sarcastical hints and whispers. A third faction formed itself, without the aid of parliamentary, or court influence; almost entirely upon the popularity of their leader, whose abilities recommended him to their esteem, who had no other views than a redress of grievances. His eloquence and disinterestedness could not be denied by his enemies: and the nation placed their whole dependance upon his wisdom, integrity and love for his country.

These factions differed extremely in regard to power: though the two former were near agreed in the general scheme of their politics. They looked upon the increase of power in France, as

the

the greatest of all evils: and therefore thought it absolutely necessary to maintain a balance of power, or to seek the safety and liberty of Great Britain in the general safety and liberty of Europe. This system had drawn them, many years, into close connections with the powers on the continent, **by large** subsidies and inconsistent treaties, and even by fighting their battles in foreign quarrels. This furnished an argument for a standing army: and prevailed with them to employ **our** navy in subserviency to the continental **system.** They were also peculiar in their notions about our constitutional liberty. Both parties declared against arbitrary power, and admitted the usefulness of parliaments. **They** pretended **to be stanch** friends to the constitution; and strenuous assertors of the legal rights of the people: **But,** under a mistaken notion of government, they deviated into the very principles and practices, they publickly dis**avowed.** They threw the ballance of power into the crown, which our constitution requires to be equal in all its parts. They, for this purpose, extended the influence of the court by creating numerous lucrative places and employments at the disposal of the crown. By the **means of** these places, they **secured** a majority in parliament; and so long as they could preserve this majority, they gave themselves no concern about the esteem and approbation of the people. It was assembled to raise money for them, to do as they pleased with it; and that judicature, which ought to **be a** terror to bad ministers, skreened them from punishment,

nishment, if impeached by the nation for their misconduct.

The third, which, for distinction sake, let us call the popular party, did also think it necessary to set bounds to the power and influence of France, amongst the neighbouring states: But these differed much about the means; and were for making the operations, of which necessity, or sound policy, might oblige Great Britain to take a part in, upon the continent, to be entirely subservient to our naval strength, as a more natural and less expensive plan of politicks. They said, that they could depend in the most hazardous and desperate service, on the naval commanders: because their way of life, and natural ferocity of manners, secured them from that luxury and effeminacy, (which is the corruption of those, who abuse their leisure in dress, gaming and female intrigues) and instilled into them a spirit of duty and glory. So that, the fleet being the natural strength of this nation, their thirst after conquest and fame is the same as the people's at home, who act upon national principles.

It was urged in defence of this system, That our situation, as an island, prescribes to us a conduct very different from all other nations: That our strength and our support is in our navy and trade; and that, as they mutually support each other, they ought to go hand in hand. But that, if we abandon our natural element, we should then turn our back to our real interests, and enter into an inextricable labyrinth of continental

poli-

politicks: if we take a share in every controversy; if we consume our treasure in retaining the friendship of petty princes and states; if we lavish British blood in German quarrels; we are so far from attacking France, to our advantage, that we expose ourselves to ruin by our ill-judged efforts, on the strong side of the enemy.

They further argued, That while Great Britain preserves a superiority at sea, there can be no danger arise from the superiority of the French on the continent: that we can always cut the sinews of the enemy's strength, by destroying their trade and commerce; that there can be no fear of an invasion, from the country that has no marine to support it: that a standing army of mercenaries is dangerous to freedom; and might be made useless by a well-regulated militia: and that a government, like ours, connected by its very essence with the liberty of the subject, can never be in want of paliamentary influence, bribery and corruption, or any other supports of despotic power. For, where rulers govern well, the people will do their duty.

Great as the esteem had been for the right honourable gentleman, who was at the head of this party, before his late promotion to the important trust of the steerage of the state; it was most surprisingly enhanced by his conduct, and the union of parties brought about by his wisdom, during his short administration. The healing balsams, he was continually pouring out of the abundance of love for his country, had already cured her wounds,

How the public esteem increased for Mr. Pitt.

revived

A. D. 1757.

revived her spirits, and made her ready to face the enemy in the most advantageous and promising manner. The more benefit was received through his counsel and direction, the more odious his predecessors in office and trust appeared in the opinion of the public. So that at his dismission from the direction of the national affairs, it would be difficult to affirm, whether the voice of the nation echoed more in his, and in the praise of his associates in office and disgrace; or in the accumulative invectives thrown out by all degrees against them, whom they had disliked and complained of before, for their mal-administration, and to whom they now imputed all the misfortunes, which were expected to follow this change in the ministry.

Its effects on the old ministry.

It appeared now most evidently, That the faction, against whom the addresses to the throne had delivered themselves so openly, had been compelled to take Mr. Pitt and his adherents into the ministry, to prevent the consequences of those instructions, which the people had given to their representatives in parliament. For, had his Majesty been prevailed upon, by the votes or addresses of his parliament, to dismiss his timid, inactive and inglorious ministers from all places of trust, and from his councils and presence, there must have been an entire end of their power. By this means they prevailed with the people to push them no farther; and by the same means they persuaded his Majesty, That they would not oppose his inclination to satisfy his subjects. But when

Why Mr. Pitt had been taken into the ministry.

when the *old ones* had thus managed the nation, A. D. in regard to their own safety; their grand point 1757. was to make this change subservient to their principal object; which was, to ruin their new associates, in the state, in the opinion of the people, and, at all events, to keep the King in a continual dislike and jealousy of their counsels and measures. When they could be thus abased in the opinion of the public and of the King; it would then have been most easy for these to resume their power, and the administration, without any opposition from the deceived nation.

But how egregiously were these statesmen out *Disappointed.* of their politicks in this affair, as well as in regard to the nation. The patriots so conducted themselves in place, that they lost none of their popularity. Their virtues became more conspicuous, more admired, more universally known: though their steady opposition to the old system of neglecting our natural strength, and the national interest, to enter into, and espouse the quarrels of our neighbours, where we can have no interest, gave their associates in power a handle to ruin them in the King's esteem; whose regard for his native country filled him with too great a desire to support Hanover and its dependences, at all events, and at the risk of the British interest.

Thus, when his Majesty had been worked up *Honours to a pitch of dissatisfaction, and to a resolution to paid to the disgraced* dismiss Mr. PITT, Mr. Legge, Lord Temple, *ministers.* &c. from his service; the people, always grateful to their benefactors and friends, received them

2   with

A. D. 1757.

with the greatest tokens of approbation, for their disinterested conduct, their firm attachment to the true interest of their country, and their unequalled abilities. The highest mark of an Englishman's blessing, above other nations, is his liberty: and the most generous token of the people's regard and love for these patriots was immediately signified by presentations of their freedom, from the most populous, most opulent and respectable corporations; with addresses of thanks to Mr. PITT and Mr. LEGGE, for their integrity and services, inclosed in gold boxes, or some other elegant materials, enriched with emblems, conveying the sentiments of their approbation and gratitude [g].

Old ministry restored.

In the mean time some of the leaders in this removal, and in the late administration, resumed the

[g] It was moved in the common-council of the city of London, to present the freedom of that city to the Right Honourable William Pitt, late one of his Majesty's principal secretaries of state; and to the Right Honourable Henry Bilson Legge, late chancellor of his Majesty's exchequer, in testimony of the grateful sense, which the city of London entertained of their loyal and disinterested conduct, during their truly honourable, though short administration; their beginning a scheme of public œconomy, and at the same time lessening the extent of ministerial influence, by a reduction of a number of useless placemen: their noble efforts to stem the general torrent of corruption, and to revive, by their example, the almost extinguished love of virtue, and our country: their zeal to promote a full and impartial enquiry into the real causes of our late losses in America and the Mediterranean: And, lastly, their vigilant attention to support the glory and independency of Great Britain, the honour and true interest

of

The Right Honble HENRY BILSON LEGGE.

the reins of government: But there was no settled ministry. A new board of admiralty, indeed was formed, with the Earl of Winchelsea at its head. Mr. Legge was succeeded in the exchequer by Lord Mansfield: but no one was appointed in the place of Mr. PITT. And the contention now grew so strong about power, and the disposal of places belonging to the crown, that the parties, who had so carefully guarded their royal master from the approaches of their rivals in the ministry, attended so industriously to their particular interests, that they neglected the avenues to the throne, and suffered the general voice of the people to plead their own cause of complaint, and to found the praises of the disgraced servants of the crown, in the royal ear. On the contrary, the affairs of the court party became so desperate, that they openly encouraged bribery and corruption; and did not stick at speaking and writing against all principles of morality and virtue, and in favour of political vice; asserting, that the most base acts of corruption, villainy and deceit are necessary in the government of a state or commonwealth.

A. D. 1757.

Their conduct.

The Spaniards, who had begun to conduct themselves with more circumspection and respect towards the English, under Mr. PITT's administration [h], resumed their partial and unjust pro-

Behaviour of the Spaniards.

of the crown, with the just rights and liberties of the subject; thereby most effectually securing the affections of a free people to his Majesty and his illustrious family.

[h] See page 28. Vol. II.

ceed-

ceedings against the Antigallican and her prize, as soon as it was understood at Madrid, that the old ministry had driven him from the seat of government, and that there was no longer any fear of our resentment [i].

The

---

[i] See page 29. Vol. II.

The Spaniards were so far influenced by Mr. Pitt's remonstrances, in this case, that an order was given by his most Catholic Majesty, to re-deliver the prize to the English.

On the advice of this order from the Spanish court, the proprietors of the Antigallican privateer wrote the following letter to the Right Honourable Mr. Pitt, though he was, at that time, dismissed from the office of principal secretary of state.

SIR,

We the managers and owners of the private ship of war the Antigallican, together with the laudable association of Antigallicans, established at the Lebeck's-head in the Strand, must think ourselves lost to all sense of honour, of gratitude, and concern for our country, were we not to take the earliest opportunity to return you our sincerest thanks, for your seasonable and ready execution of his Majesty's orders on our behalf, in regard to our ship and prize, which have been so long **detained** in the **bay of Cadiz**, by the cruel, treacherous, and **partial behaviour of the** governor, after killing and wounding several of the men, and imprisoning our officers and the rest of our crew, in open violation of the most solemn treaties, notwithstanding she was before legally condemned to us.

The easiness of our access to you, and your generous protection in our rights, and polite treatment in your office, filled every heart with joy rather to **be conceived** than expressed, as well knowing that your undertaking **this affair was more** than an omen of its success.

Your whole behaviour in the affair has been so noble, so steady, and uniform, **that we are** at a loss where to admire you **most**, in the design, **the** prosecution, or the event.

Believe

The northern powers erected their crests, and threw out several hints, no ways agreeable to the interest and dignity of Great Britain, under the plausible colour of maintaining the peace of the north. The Russians made no scruple of their resolution to express their dislike of the British alliance with Prussia, and to join the confederacy against the King of Prussia, and had already entered and committed hostilities in that King's dominions. The Swedes were enlisted under a French subsidy, and had declared their readiness to favour the designs in Germany, by the most vigorous diversion, in their declining power, on the side of Pomerania. The King of Denmark only preserved some appearance of a pacific and neutral temper; but was far from being depended upon, should he meet with an opportunity to avail himself and his dominions, by taking part with

A. D. 1757.
State of the northern powers.

> Believe us, Sir, when we say, that after paying our most profound duty to his Majesty on this occasion, we think ourselves bound in gratitude to acknowledge you as the next immediate cause of the restitution of our ship and prize; and we do with true sincerity of heart most ardently wish and pray, that his Majesty may never want a minister like you, to hear with impartiality, to advise with candour and judgment, and with the most steady resolution to procure a proper redress for the grievances of his Majesty's subjects. We are, with the utmost deference and respect, Sir,
>
> Lebeck's-head,   Your most obliged, and
> 15 April, 1757.   Most obedient humble servants.

Compare this letter with the advice sent from the English ambassador at Madrid, page 29. Vol. II. and you will find, that the expectations of the proprietors were well founded.

A. D. 1757.

the grand confederates, who began to be equally offensive to Hesse and Hanover, as to the King of Prussia. And the Emperor was accelerating, as much as the nature of his office would permit, the assembling an army of the circles, which, under the name of an army of execution, was intended to favour and even to join the Austrians, French and Russians [k]. The French were driving the army of observation before them; their arms diffused terror wherever they marched, and there was not a court in Europe, where their interest had not superceded that protection and respect the British nation had a right to demand in neutral ports and states.

Of North America.

Our affairs in North America were still upon the declivity of destruction, and by the advices received in the spring it appeared that they ap-

[k] The colleges of the empire acknowledge the justice of the complaints addressed to them by the Emperor and the Empress-Queen, concerning the King of Prussia's invasion of Bohemia and Saxony. They approved the Emperor's conduct on this occasion, as having been entirely conformable to the laws and constitutions of the empire, to the ordinance of execution, to the peace of Westphalia, and to his Imperial Majesty's capitulation. They agreed that proper methods must be taken to re-instate the King of Poland in the possession of his hereditary countries, and procure him a full indemnification for the prejudice he has suffered, and also to procure for the Empress-Queen the support and satisfaction, which she has a right to expect. At the same time the colleges of the empire resolved, that all the circles of the empire should treble their respective contingents, in order to gain these ends. *N. B.* The troops of the circles, by trebling the contingents, would have formed an army of above 100,000 men.

proached

proached nearer to the brink of ruin. For though Lord Loudon had diftinguifhed himfelf by his diligence and wifdom in eftablifhing an harmony, to unite the provinces heartily in the common caufe againft the triumphing enemy; yet fuch was the lofs of Ofwego, that the enemy were become mafters of all the lakes; and thereby poffeffed of every means, either to perfuade, or to compel the back Indians to defert, and to fight againft the Englifh. This was followed by the lofs of the friendfhip or affiftance of the Six Nations, whofe communication was cut off by the impolitic demolition of the forts at the Great Carrying Place, and by the ftopping up of Wood's Creek: and the delightful plantations on the German Flatts, and along the Mohawk river were immediately deftroyed by fire and fword. In a word, had not Fort William Henry, in which a confiderable garrifon had been placed at the conclufion of the laft campaign [1] been ftrong enough to refift the power of the French, who marched againft it, early in the year, nothing could have prevented their over-running the whole continent of North America.

The garrifon of this fort was alarmed [m], and indeed furprized with a noife and a light, at a confiderable diftance down the lake, having kept no fcouts, to watch the motions, nor fpies to dive into the operations and intentions of the enemy:

Fort William Henry ftorm'd.

[1] See page 4. Vol. II.
[m] At about one o'clock in the morning of the 19th of March.

and

A. D. 1757.

and in about two hours after, the enemy's whole army was perceived to advance regularly upon the ice towards the fort: but they were so warmly received with a brisk fire both of the artillery and small arms of the garrison, that the main body retreated; and, after making two fruitless attempts to set fire to a sloop and the battoes belonging to the fort, they with-drew at day break, leaving behind them some scaling ladders and combustibles; though they consisted of near 2000 regulars, Canadians, and Indians, and were provided with 300 scaling ladders, and all the necessaries for a general assault.

However they soon after appeared again on the lake, and with parties on each side of it, disposed in such a manner as indicated a resolution to surround the fort; but though they advanced with great bravery, for some time, through a continual fire of artillery and small arms from the garrison, they once more retreated, for that day.

On the 20th about midnight, they resumed the attack; and it was resolved to storm the place with their whole army. But this proving also ineffectual, and being driven back, they, after setting fire to two sloops, and burning most of the battoes, retreated at day-break.

Every thing appeared favourable, and about noon the French army seemed to take the rout to Ticonderoga. But all on a sudden, two men were sent back with a red flag towards the fort; from whence an officer and four men were dispatched to meet them; and they brought in one of those

those men, who had a letter from M. de Vaudreuil, commander of the French army, directed to the commanding officer of Fort William Henry, signifying " That he had sent M. le Chevalier le Merceire, commander of the artillery, to acquaint them with his resolution; and that he might give entire credit to what he should say to him on his behalf."

A. D. 1757.

Summon'd to surrender.

M. le Mercier was the other person, and was now brought in blindfolded by another officer. His message was, in substance, " That M. de Vaudreuil was averse to the shedding of human blood, and should be glad to put an end to the war: and therefore, for this good end, That, as the English, he said, had been the aggressors, by incroaching upon his most Christian Majesty's territories, and built forts on them, he proposed that the said forts might be delivered up in a peaceable manner: that the garrison should be allowed all the honours of war, and be permitted to carry away all their most valuable effects, requiring only that something might be left to gratify the Indians, from whom they needed not be under any apprehension, as there were regulars enough to protect the garrison from any violence that might offer: and concluded, that if these terms were not accepted, they would immediately make a general assault, which, should they succeed, the garrison must take the consequence."

To which the commanding officer in the fort returned this answer to the French commander, " That his fixed resolution was to defend his Majesty's

Bravely defended.

A.D 1757.

jesty's garrison to the last extremity." M. le Mercier was then dismissed and conducted back blindfolded: and soon after his arrival at his own army, the French wheeled about; and every thing was made ready for a general assault. But neither the threats of the enemy, nor their superior numbers could intimidate the garrison, though at that time very sickly. The officers behaved with the greatest vigilance, care and resolution. The men were determined to die rather than yield. So that, upon the return of the enemy to the attack, they were very roughly handled, and driven back a second time with considerable loss. Nevertheless, as if this had been a service to be executed, at all events, the French commander once more returned to the assault; and in the night made a third general attack; but with no better success. He then set fire to several store-houses belonging to the provincial troops, and to all the huts of the rangers, which burnt with great fury, but did no further damage; and afterwards burnt a sloop on the stocks, and then totally disappeared with his army.

Dislike of the ministry continues.

Nothing, but this gallant behaviour of a petty fort in the deserts of North America, offered to asswage the ferment of the nation. Every other circumstance served only to increase their indignation against the men, who had brought them into their ruinous condition; had got possession of the immense sums granted, last parliament, on the good opinion, the people entertained of the administration under Mr. PITT, and shewed the same

same disposition to squander the public money, A. D.
as they had done in the preceeding year, without 1757.
due attention to the national strength and interest.

"It is no wonder therefore that the people
"cried aloud for redress, and vigorously sup-
"ported the minority, in whose wisdom, and in-
"tegrity they could safely confide. Here, says
"a late authorⁿ, were exhibited strong proofs of
"the natural spirit of a brave and free people,
"who had been treated like slaves, by base arts
"and the most abusive language. It is a lesson
"that ought to be precious to princes, especially
"of this island; while such men were in power,
"as the people disapproved, misfortune followed
"misfortune, and the nation was divided and
"distracted: but when such men are employed,
"as they do approve, unanimity, vigour and suc-
"cess crown their efforts. Thus a King, acting
"with his people, is all power and glory; but
"without them he is nothing."

"Such was the disconsolate face of affairs, when The na-
"the general voice of an abused people roused the tional voice
"Great into fear; even those who had treated the PITT.
"general voice of the people, with contempt,
"dreaded the rod of national vengeance; and
"therefore, when the cries of injury became
"louder and louder every day, from all parts of
"the kingdom [and the partizans of L——r H——e
made the interest of the family a common cause
with that of the nation, and joined the cry of the

ⁿ See a Review of Mr. PITT's Administration, 3d edit. p. 24, 25.

people

A.D. 1757.

people in the recommendation of Mr. PITT] "they thought it high time to quit their gaming tables, and suffer a few honest, wise and vigilant men, who had spirit enough to save this country from the destruction, into which the others were going to tumble it, to approach the throne." And it is very certain, that the restoration of Mr. PITT to the office of secretary of state might have much sooner taken place, had not that right honourable gentleman desired to be excused the service, which, experience had taught him, was not to be performed with equal satisfaction to his king and to his country. Mr. PITT's aversion to continental measures had brought him into disgrace with his royal master; whose affections were naturally warped towards his native country. These measures had always been the way for recommendation to the royal favour; and yet always the ruin of the national interest; and if, once more permitted to superceed our country's cause, might prove the destruction not only of our colonies and trade; but also of the royal family on the throne. A foresight, which was so evident to the court of the P——, that they unanimously, and with most solemn engagements to support his measures and favour with the King against the faction, that had worked him out before, conjured Mr. PITT to resume the seals; intreating him, in the most prevailing manner, to save the family, to save the nation, by preventing the excess of measures, which the failings of the —— had made unavoidable, and by turning

His aversion to continental connections.

ing, what could not be avoided in the local attachments, to some national advantage.

A. D. 1757.

Here we find a temperament to prevent the misfortunes, that might arise from the two extremes, between *all* attention to the continent, and *no* attention. It was now proposed to gratify the Prince upon the throne, not with engaging in all the business of the continent without reserve, and so to plunge ourselves into real evils out of dread of possible mischiefs; but with assisting our friends and allies, on the continent, in ways and means most agreeable to our insular situation; which is, by way of diversion with our fleets, and with such land force and money, as our strength and finances, our interest, and the importance of the quarrel, shall require.

The temperament proposed.

Thus we see when the nation was almost ruined by the conflict for power, Mr. PITT, quite retired from the noise of the world, quite disembarrassed, and content to enjoy the comforts of life without further honours, than the general approbation of his fellow-subjects, as well as the consciousness of having served his King and country with wisdom and fidelity, was ready to sacrifice his private ease to the public trouble; that he might plead the cause of his country in the cabinet, as well as in the senate, and that he might give the ——— the most convincing proof of his sincere attachment to the interest of the family in possession of the crown. And further it must be remarked, That Mr. PITT, by accepting of the seals, under these circumstances, we apprehend, could not be

charged

charged with any consequences arising from continental measures, which were not in his power to prevent, in opposition to the King and the council; but only for those measures, which he advised, or did not endeavour to make them subservient to the interest of Great Britain.

Mr. Pitt restored.
The temperament being thus settled between the friends of our country and the family, with all due submission be it said, Mr. PITT yielded to their intreaties, and a coalition was formed in the best manner the present circumstances would permit; when it would have been impossible for any particular party to carry on the public business on its own single bottom. A change in the administration was brought to pass. The seals of secretary of state were given to Mr. PITT[o]. The Duke of Newcastle was appointed first Lord of the treasury. Mr. Legge chancellor of the exchequer. Lord Anson was made first Lord of the admiralty. Lord Temple was appointed Lord privy-seal, and Mr. Fox was made paymaster of the forces.

The commencement of his administration.
Here we may date the beginning of Mr. PITT's administration: and it began with the only healing measure that could be pursued. The parties themselves were satisfied, and so were their numerous friends: part of whom were put into offices of less importance. The ministers condescended to an amicable capitulation in their several opinions, which they had violently pushed in their several extremes; and from that moment

[o] On the 29th of June 1757.

the nation began to hope, the counsel to be unanimous, and spirit to revive amongst the people; for, though they blamed the Lords at the head of the treasury and admiralty board, and the paymaster of the forces, for all their miscarriages and misfortunes, their opinion of Mr. Pitt's diligence and capacity obliterated the remembrance of past errors in his associates, who seemed heretofore inflexibly opposite to him; and they trusted solely to his wisdom, for the measures to humble France.

The ministry was not only established in outward form, by this arrangement, but even in the hearts of men, as Bolinbroke says, by Mr. Pitt being allowed to be the principal director of affairs, without his assuming to become a premier. The genius of England seemed to rise with the administration, and a new soul diffused itself throughout all ranks of people; whose hearts burnt with resentment to wipe out past disgraces; and to restore the glory, honour and true character of their country [p].

Agreeable to the people.

The difficulties Mr. Pitt had to encounter at his resuming the seals, were greatly increased since his first appointment to the direction of public affairs, in December last. As the powers on the continent perceived such distractions in our nation, such divisions amongst the Great, and so little wisdom and vigour in our councils; not only the Spaniards, but the petty state of Malta, and the

Difficulties increased in the administration.

---

[p] See review of Mr. Pitt's administration page 25, 26, 27. Third edition.

Regency

Regency of Tuscany, were spirited up by the gasconades of France, and the example of Spain, in the forcible detention of the Antigallican and her prize, and thought themselves safe from the resentment of Great Britain, in their most partial actions towards our enemies: as appears in the case of the St. George private ship of war, Captain Fortunatus Wright, who in an English privateer was become the terror of the French in the Mediterranean [q]. One of his prizes, which he carried into Malta, was detained by that government, upon a false claim made by the French. And he was threatned by the Regency of Leghorn to be arrested and his privateer to be seized, for doing no more than defending himself against two French privateers within the port of Ferraio: according to the account in the note below [r]. The delay of the American

[q] He had destroyed one privateer, disabled another, and taken ten prizes.

[r] *Extract of a letter from Leghorn, March 21.*

"We advised you in our last of the departure of the St. George, Captain Wright, with four prizes, under convoy of the Jersey man of war, for Cagliari and this place. We yesterday received an express from Porto Ferraio, acquainting us of the arrival there of a prize belonging to Captain Wilson, and one of Captain Wright's, who parted with the convoy in a hard gale of wind. The insolence of the French, tho' in neutral ports, heightens to the greatest degree; as you'll think from the conduct of the captains of two French privateers that happened to be in Porto Ferraio on the arrival of the two afore-mentioned prizes; they immediately addressed the governor, requesting him to order them for sea, as being the captures of a pyrate; the governor's reply was, that as they

American armament, which he had so seasonably advised and set a foot, had given the French an opportunity to counteract their intention: and at his re-appointment to the direction of public affairs, he found the enemy more powerful both in America, more formidable on the continent of Europe, and with a more respectable navy, than at the commencement of the war. The army

A. D.
1757.

they came in under English colours, he would protect them, and ordered them, at their peril, to commit any violence; but they made light of the governor's orders, since by a vessel arrived here to day we have advice of their attempt to cut out Captain Wright's prize: the two privateers got ready for sea, with their anchors aboard, and sent their boats to cut her cable: the captain of the prize had only time to get some muskets loaded, they fired a volly at the boats, and killed one man; this alarmed the centinels, when notice was sent to the governor, who immediately ordered the two privateers to depart, upon which they went to Porto Lungoni, in the same island: they mount 18 guns each, and there are three more privateers on the coast.—— It is not surprizing that the French should attempt to treat Captain Wright as a pyrate after the example set them by this government; and we are sorry to acquaint you, that so far from obtaining any redress for the injuries done him here, to the amount of 300 l. though we are assured the strongest representations have been made to the court of Vienna, Sir Horatio Mann has wrote our consul word, that he must not think of coming into Leghorn, if he should, they will seize the privateer and lay him under an arrest. These are the menaces from a neutral power to the British flag. The Malteze have detained one of Captain Wright's prizes on a false claim made by the French. Upon the whole, we don't know what he must undergo for having been so active against the enemies of his country, as to destroy one privateer, disable another, and take ten prizes: such is our miserable situation in the Mediterranean!"

A. D. 1757.

of observation, under His Royal Highness the Duke of Cumberland obliged to retreat before M. de Estrees. The Austrian army in Bohemia augmented to 100,000 men, under Prince Charles of Lorrain, assisted by M. Brown. The Russians under M. Apraxin, to the number of 60,000, and a strong fleet in the Baltic, to co-operate with the army, were on the back of his Prussian Majesty. Besides the Swedes joined by 6000 Mecklenbourgers brought up the rear of those great armies, which had taken the field to destroy, or reduce the heir of the Marquises of Brandenbourg, who for his great abilities had made himself hated by the House of Austria.

Advantages arising from a treaty with Prussia.

The only favourable circumstance to check the ambition and arms of France was the hopes conceived from our alliance with the King of Prussia; whose great abilities and valour filled the English with such expectations from a stricter connection with him, since their own affairs teemed with disgrace and ruin, that they naturally began to wish, and even to claim an extention of the treaty with Prussia, which hitherto was no more than a *convention of neutrality, for the defence of each others German dominions,* to a treaty of alliance with the King of Prussia, *whereby his arms, in consideration of a subsidy, might be brought against France.* For, as the French had got the start of us in North America, and seemed to be in a condition to wrest that part of the new world entirely out of our possession; they that were most sanguine in the cause of our country grew more eager for an alliance with Prussia;

Prussia; that would, in their opinion, find employment for the arms of France at home, and deprive them of those means, which were necessary to push their successes in North America.

"Thus the former administration not only laid the foundation of an alliance with Prussia; but by the ill success of our affairs under their direction, they so dispirited the people, as to make them (even them, who have since declaimed against it) call out for an alliance with that monarch, who had been hitherto attended with success. So that, if the alliance, which was afterwards made in consequence of this humour, proved prejudicial to the interests of Great Britain; that prejudice or injury ought to be charged upon those, who, by their mismanagement, provoked the people to call for such alliance, as the only hope of retrieving the ill state of their affairs; and not upon the minister, who did all in his power to turn its advantage in favour of our American war [s]."

The foundation of that treaty laid by the old ministry.

The King of Prussia in possession of Saxony, and sensible of the storm gathering against him, resolved to make Dresden his place of arms, and to bear the heat and burden of the war: for which purpose he immediately set about the improvement of its fortifications, under his own inspection, and to fill the magazines and arsenals with the necessary stores and impliments of war. As to the rest of this conquered Electorate: none were permitted to keep arms, but such as actually

King of Prussia's progress in Saxony.

---

[s] See a review of Mr. Pitt's administration, page 20, 21, third edition.

A. D. 1757.

took them up under the Prussian banner: the whole country was reduced to the greatest state of slavery: And as to the attempts of the Austrians, there were such dispositions made on the borders of Bohemia, that they covered his quarters and territories effectually from any insults or surprize.

His motives for invading Saxony.

While every martial disposition was carrying on with diligence, his Prussian Majesty did not forget to publish his motives for invading Saxony, and attacking the Empress Queen. Accordingly he published a memorial, setting forth the conduct of the courts of Vienna and Saxony, and their dangerous designs against him, with the original documents in proof of them.

In this memorial it is declared, " That, the reasons, which had laid the King of Prussia under the necessity of taking up arms against the court of Vienna, and of securing the King of Poland's hereditary dominions, during the present war, were founded upon the strictest rules of justice and equity; not upon motives of ambition, or views of aggrandizement; but upon a series of projects, conspiracies and treachery, on the part of those two courts, that had obliged his Majesty to provide for his own defence and safety. That the discoveries he had made on this important subject, set this truth in a full light, and that the proofs, in his hands, amount to a demonstration of the justice of his cause, and the wicked practices of those, who have forced him to come to such sad extremities: and that his Majesty thought it incumbent upon him to procure the originals of those

those proofs, copies of which had long since come to his knowledge; that he might put it out of the power of his enemies to deny the real existence and truth of them.

His Prussian Majesty begins his proofs with a treaty of *eventual* partition of his dominions between the courts of Vienna and Saxony, wherein the contracting powers, immediately after they had signed a treaty of peace, on 25 Dec. 1745, at Dresden, in which the King of Prussia had given shining proofs of his love of peace, disinterestedness and moderation, combined to seize an opportunity to attack the King of Prussia and to divide his dominions[1]. He then exhibits a new treaty of

---

[1] 'To prove this the treaty itself is produced, which is in substance as follows:'—" Experience having but too well shewn how far the King of Prussia carries his evil intentions, in order to disturb the repose of his neighbours; and that prince having, on the one hand, repeatedly invaded and laid waste the dominions of her Majesty the Queen of Hungary and Bohemia; and, on the other side, alarmed his Majesty the King of Poland, Elector of Saxony, by divers menaces, warlike preparations, and violently passing through his territories, for which it has not been possible to obtain due satisfaction for time past, nor sufficient security for the future; it has been considered, that this double end cannot be obtained till the said formidable neighbour is reduced within narrow bounds. For these reasons, his Majesty the King of Poland, Elector of Saxony, as an auxiliary ally, and her Majesty the Queen of Hungary and Bohemia, as a party attacked and at war, have agreed, by the present seperate and secret act, to employ their joint efforts, not only to perform fully the act passed between their Majesties the 6th [17th] of May 1744, and the measures concerted in consequence of the engagements entered

A. D. 1757.

of alliance proposed by the court of Vienna to the court of Dresden, in which was renewed the treaty into by their treaty of alliance the 8th of January 1745, with the maritime powers; but likewise, that neither the one nor the other shall lay down their arms, till, besides the conquest of all Silesia and the county of Glatz, the King of Prussia be farther reduced.

And that they may previously understand one another, with regard to the partition of the conquests to be made, seeing the 8th article of the said treaty of Warsaw only settled in general terms, that his Majesty the King of Poland, Elector of Saxony, is to partake of the advantages, by having such territories as lie convenient for him; it has appeared necessary to distinguish the cases that may hereafter happen, and come to a right understanding about each of them.

Suppose then, that besides the recovery of all Silesia and the county of Glatz, they should conquer from the said King the dutchy of Magdeburg, including therein the circle of Saal, the principality of Crossen, with the circle of Zullichau belonging thereto, and the Fiefs of Bohemia possessed by that King, and situated in Lusatia; namely, Cotbus, Peits, Storckow, Beeskau, Somerfeld, and other places and districts belonging thereto. In this case, all Silesia and the county of Glatz, excepting Swibus, must return to her Majesty the Queen of Hungary and Bohemia, who, in exchange cedes all the rest just mentioned, with the district of Swibus, belonging otherwise to Silesia, to his Majesty the King of Poland, Elector of Saxony.

Supposing on the contrary, that besides the recovering of all Silesia and county of Glatz, they could conquer upon the aggressor no more than the circle of Saal, the principality of Crossen, with the circle of Zullichau, and the above-mentioned Fiefs of Bohemia belonging to him in Lusatia; then his Polish Majesty, Elector of Saxony, shall be content with this last partition and the district of Swibus, leaving in like manner to her Majesty the Queen of Hungary and Bohemia,

all

treaty of Eventual Partition of the 18 May 1745. And the court of Saxony, as he obferves, thinking it neceffary, in the firft place, to give a greater confiftency to their plan, by grounding it upon an alliance between the courts of Ruffia and Vienna; thofe two powers did on May the 22d 1746 conclude a defenfive alliance at Peterfbourg: but that the oftenfible part of it was drawn up merely with a view to conceal the fix fecret articles thereof from the knowledge of the public, the 4th of which was levelled fingly at Pruffia. In which treaty he admits that the Emprefs Queen of Hungary and Bohemia did fet out with a pro-

A. D. 1757.

all Silefia and the county of Glatz, Swibus excepted. But fuppofe, in fine, that, contrary to all expectation, and in fpite of the joint efforts above-mentioned, they could conquer, befides the county of Glatz, and the whole of Silefia, no more than the principality of Croffen, with the circle of Zullichau, and the abovefaid fiefs of Bohemia, poffeffed by the faid King in Lufatia: In this cafe, his Polifh Majefty fhall have, befides the principality, the circle and the fiefs juft mentioned, the diftrict of Swibus, otherwife belonging to Silefia.

And her Majefty the Queen of Hungary and Bohemia, engages in the ftrongeft and moft folemn manner, that his Majefty the King of Poland, Elector of Saxony, fhall have precifely the fame fecurities for thefe new acquifitions, which fhe fhall or may have for the recovery of her antient patrimonial territories, that is to fay, Silefia and the county of Glatz.

To this end the Saxon troops of his Polifh Majefty fhall remain in re-conquered Silefia, till his ftipulated fhare be effected, at leaft according to the laft of the cafes above-mentioned. After which the high contracting parties fhall reciprocally guaranty, &c.

Done at Leipfick, the 18th of May, 1745.

(L. S.) AUGUSTUS R.

teftation

A.D. 1757.

testation religiously to observe the treaty of Dresden, but that her real way of thinking upon this point in the following words, in the same treaty: " If the King of Prussia should be the
" first to depart from this peace, by attacking
" either her Majesty the Empress Queen of Hun-
" gary and Bohemia, or her Majesty the Empress
" of Russia, or even the republic of Poland, in
" all which cases the rights of her Majesty the
" Empress Queen to Silesia and the county of
" Glatz, would again take place, and recover
" their full effect; the two contracting parties shall
" mutually assist each other with, &c. to con-
" quer Silesia, &c." extends the infraction of the treaty of Dresden to any dispute, that might arise between Prussia and Russia, or Poland, and to be a sufficient ground for a revival of the rights of the House of Austria to Silesia; though neither Russia nor the republic of Poland are at all concerned in the treaty of Dresden. But it is obvious, says he, that, by this article the court of Vienna has prepared three pretences for the recovery of Silesia; and by comparing it with her conduct from that time it did visibly appear, that she thought to attain her end, either by provoking the King to commence a war against her, or by kindling one between his Majesty and Russia, or Poland, by her secret intrigues and machinations.

His Prussian Majesty produces the instructions to the Saxon ministers at Petersbourg and Vienna, to prove the time when the Elector of Saxony was invited to acceed to this treaty, and the eager-
ness

ness with which he accepted that invitation ᵘ. And then makes this observation and inference: as

ᵘ 'In these instructions, which are recited at large, are these remarkable particulars:' " As to the principal treaty between the two Imperial courts, the King is entirely disposed to accede thereto, without any other restriction, than that of the number of troops, which they have reciprocally stipulated therein, for the ordinary cases of giving succours. But the King's accession to the six separate articles, five of which are secret, require much more restriction and adjustment, with regard to the King's conveniency.

As to the first secret articles, which concerns the guaranty of the Grand Duke of Russia's possessions, as Duke of Holstein-Sleswick, and of his ducal house, the Empress of Russia will be pleased to consider how tenderly and cautiously the King must behave towards the court of Denmark, on account of his affinity and right of eventual succession; and therefore the said sovereign, as well as the Empress Queen, and even the Emperor her consort, will not, in return, refuse the King and his posterity the guaranty of the succession to the throne of Denmark, which in time may fall to a Prince of the electoral house of Saxony.

And as to the fourth article, which regards eventual and stronger measures against a new, sudden, and unexpected attack from the King of Prussia, the King acknowledges therein the prudent forecast of the two Empresses, in thinking beforehand how to concert matters together, and powerfully assist one another, if, contrary to better expectations, and notwithstanding their scrupulous attention to observe their treaties with the said Prince, the latter should invade the dominions of either of them; and in this case the King is ready enough to concur in the same measures; but as he is the most exposed to the resentment of so formidable and restless a neighbour, witness the sad experience his Majesty has lately had of it; their Imperial Majesties cannot think it strange, that the King, before entering into such a new, eventual, and extensive engage-as the court of Saxony does thus betray their readiness to enter into all the offensive engagements ment, should take better precautions, as well for his security and mutual defence, as for his being indemnified, and recompensed in proportion to his efforts, and the progress made against such an aggressor.

To this end the Count de Vicedom, and the Sieur Pezold shall ask the Imperial ministers plenipotentiaries, 1. What number of troops, in such a case, their sovereigns desire of the King; and, in return, with how many will each of them assist him? And 2dly, That this succour desired of the King be not disproportionate to the strength of his army. 3. That the two Imperial courts must promise double the number to the King. 4. That the two Empresses must each engage to keep at least such a body of their troops, in a moveable condition, and ready to march to the assistance of his Majesty, one upon the frontiers of Prussia, and the other in Bohemia. 5. That they likewise oblige themselves to let the King come in for a share of the prisoners, spoils, and conquests they shall make jointly, or separately on the aggressor, and thereby the common enemy.

With respect to this last point, and the partition of the conquests to be made, the King's ministers plenipotentiaries are to ask the Russian minister, what his sovereign's offers are; and to declare, relative to the Empress Queen of Hungary and Bohemia, that supposing this Princess were attacked again by the King of Prussia, and should recover not only Silesia and the county of Glatz, but likewise succeed in reducing that aggressor within narrower bounds, the King of Poland, as Elector of Saxony, would abide by the partition stipulated between her and his Majesty by the convention signed at Leipsic the 18th of May 1745, a copy of which the resident Pezold received, enclosed in a letter from the ministry of the 14th of November following; excepting the third degree of partition defined therein, with which his Majesty cannot be satisfied; since in case the Empress Queen should be able to conquer, besides

ments of the treaty of Peterſbourg; and as they have been ſince the peace, the revivers of the Partition treaty, made againſt the King during the laſt war; they had juſtified his Majeſty in reſenting a treaty made againſt him, notwithſtanding the general amneſty ſettled by the treaty of Dreſden; as appears from the opinion of the Saxon privy council; who upon being conſulted about this very fourth ſecret article on the 15 Aug. 1747 and the 17 Sep. 1748, gave it, as their opinion, "That the ſaid article exceeds the uſual "rules.—and if his Poliſh Majeſty ſhould approve "by his acceſſion, a principle [w] ſo repugnant to "the ordinary rules, the King of Pruſſia, ſhould "he hear of it, might charge him with a viola-"tion of the treaty of Dreſden, and their appre-"henſions from his Pruſſian Majeſty would great-"ly increaſe."

A. D. 1757.

beſides the county of Glatz and all Sileſia, no more than the principality of Croſſen, with the circle of Zullichau, and the Fiefs of Bohemia poſſeſſed by the King of Pruſſia in Luſatia, it would be neceſſary to grant eventually to the King, Elector of Saxony, a more conſiderable ſhare in thoſe conqueſts, than the ſaid principality, the circle, and the Fiefs: His Majeſty will wait for the offers of the court of Vienna on this head, and will order the Count de Loſs to negotiate thereupon; wiſhing only that the Ruſſian court would uſe its good offices to obtain, in this caſe, a better partition for the King from the Empreſs Queen, and then ſecure and guaranty to his Majeſty the acquiſition thereof.

Written at Dreſden, the
23d of May, 1747.

(L. S.) Augustus R.
C. de Br.
de Walther.

[w] That an auxiliary potentate is to be conſidered on the ſame foot as the belligerent power, &c.

A. D.
1757.

He adds that Count Bruhl was so well apprized, and convinced of this truth, that he did all in his power, to conceal the six secret articles above-mentioned. For the proof of this he cites instructions to Count Loss, the Saxon minister at Paris [x]. And, though continues his Majesty the court of Saxony deferred their acceeding to the treaty, in form; they did not fail to assure their confederates, that they were ready to accede to it, as soon as it could be done without too evident a risk, and their share of the advantages to be gained, should be secured to them [y].

Several passages of letters were extracted in this memorial, one [z] from Count Flemming to Count Bruhl, in which it is said, " That Count Uhlefield
" had charged him to represent a-fresh to his
" court, that they could not take too secure mea-
" sures against the ambitious views of the King
" of Prussia, and that Saxony more especially, as
" being the most exposed, could not be too cau-
" tious in guarding against them; that it was of

[x] June 18, 1747.

[y] General d'Arnim, when he was going to Petersbourg, in quality of minister from Saxony, was instructed to declare, " That (before his Polish Majesty's accession) the two Imperial courts should promise him, in case of an hostile invasion of his patrimonial dominions in Germany, a speedy, sure, and sufficient assistance, by means of two armies to be always kept ready on the respective frontiers, which might be able to succour him immediately, or to make a diversion according to the exigency of the case; *and in fine, that the share he is to have in the advantages that may be gained by good success in war, be positively determined.*".

[z] Dated 28 Feb. 1753.

" the

"the higheſt importance to ſtrengthen their old
"engagements, upon the footing propoſed by the
"late Count Harrach in 1745, that this might be
"done upon occaſion of the acceſſion to the treaty
"of Peterſburg; or in any other manner, which
"ſhould ſeem fitteſt for keeping it ſecret; and
"that he thought the preſent ſituation of affairs
"abſolutely required the allied courts to unite
"cloſer than ever, ſo as, that *all ſhould anſwer for*
"*each one, and each one for all.*" To which Count
Bruhl anſwered [a], "That his Poliſh Majeſty was
"not diſinclined to treat afterwards in the utmoſt
"ſecrecy, with the court of Vienna, about ſuc-
"cours, by private and confidential declarations,
"relative to the 4th ſecret article of the treaty of
"Peterſburg, provided reaſonable conditions and
"advantages be granted him." And concludes,
"That it is his previous opinion, that what was
"promiſed by the Empreſs Queen's declaration [b]
"of the 3d of May 1745, may ſerve for a baſis."
—Another out of a diſpatch from Count Flemming
to Count Bruhl, in which the former writes:
"Your excellency knows the great objections,
"which the court of Peterſburg made to us in the
"laſt war, when we reclaimed the *caſus fœderis:*
"and your excellency will alſo remember the an-
"ſwer, which their miniſters gave us, when we
"were preſſed to accede to the treaty of Peterſ-
"burg of 1746, and we ſhewed our willingneſs

[a] Dated 8 March 1753.
[b] This is the very treaty of Partition, ſigned at Vienna on 3d May, and at Dreſden on the 18 May 1745.

"to

A. D. 1757.

" to do it, upon condition *that we should not appear upon the stage, till after the King of Prussia should be attacked, and his forces divided*; that we might not from the situation of our country hazard our falling the first sacrifice."—The following passage from the Sieur Funck's dispatch of the 7 June 1753, " That having had the question put to him at Petersburg, whether his court would not take up arms, in case of a war with Prussia; and having replied, That the situation of Saxony did not permit it to enter the lists, till its powerful neighbour should be beat out of the field;" he was answered, " That he judged rightly, For, *the Saxons ought to wait till the knight was thrown out of the saddle.*"

Hence his Prussian Majesty observed, That it is evident the court of Saxony, without having acceded to the treaty of Petersburg in form, were not the less an accomplice in the dangerous designs, which the court of Vienna has grounded upon this treaty; and that, having been dispensed with by their allies, from a formal concurrence, they had only waited for the moment, when they might, without running too great a risk, concur in effect, and share the spoils of their neighbour.

In expectation of this period, continues the memorial, the Austrian and Saxon ministers laboured in concert and privately, to prepare the means of putting their intentions into execution. And as it was laid down, as a principle in the secret treaty of Petersburg, that any war whatever between the King and Russia would authorize the Empress

Emprefs Queen to re-enter and take Silefia: there was nothing more to be done, than to fpirit up fuch a war. Therefore every art was ufed to embroil the King irreconcilably with the Emprefs of Ruffia, and to provoke that Princefs by all forts of falfe infinuations, Impoftures and atrocious calumnies; as may be collected from feveral difpatches and inftructions to the Auftrian and Saxon minifters at Peterfburg.—Mr. Vicedom, the Saxon minifter, informs, "That Baron Pretlack, mini-
"fter from Vienna rejoiced, upon his having
"found means by confidential communications
"from his court, concerning various fecret prac-
"tices of the King of Pruffia to the prejudice of
"her Imperial Majefty, to raife ideas in her,
"which had carried her enmity to the higheft
"pitch; and that the two minifters of Vienna
"and Saxony concerted together the means of
"bringing about an accommodation between the
"Emprefs Queen and France, in order that the
"former might be able to make head againft the
"King of Pruffia." Count Bernes [c] exaggerated the military arrangements of the King of Pruffia: and affirmed that the court of Pruffia was concerned in a plot hatching in Sweden againft the perfon and life of the Czarina [d].

He then produces vouchers from the Saxon miniftry, who gave it as a general inftruction [e] to keep up dextroufly the diftruft and jealoufy of

[c] In a difpatch of 6 July 1747.   [d] 12 Dec. 1749.
[e] Inftructions to General d'Arnim in 1750.

Ruffia

A. D. 1757.

Russia in regard to Prussia; and to applaud every arrangement made against the latter. So that they were constantly insinuating that the King was forming designs upon Courland, Polish Prussia and the city of Dantzick:—that the courts of France, Prussia and Sweden were hatching vast projects, in case of a vacancy of the throne of Poland; and many more falsities of the same kind; so far as to affirm that he was endeavouring to set the Turk upon the back of Russia.

He observes, That these calumnies and impostures did, at length succeed in insnaring the Empress of Russia's equity and good faith, and in prejudicing her against the King, to such a degree, that by the result [f] of the assemblies of the senate of Russia it was laid down for a fundamental maxim of the Empire, to oppose every further aggrandisement of the King of Prussia, and to crush him by a superior force, as soon as a favourable opportunity should occur, and that this resolution was renewed in a great council, in Oct. 1755, with a further resolve, "To attack the "King of Prussia without any further discussion, "whether that Prince should happen to attack one "of the allies of the court of Russia, or one of "the allies of that court should begin with him [g]." All which was received with inexpressible joy

[f] On the 14 and 15 May 1753.

[g] It was at the same time resolved to erect magazines for 100,000 men, at Riga, Mittau, Lichau, and Windau. And they established a fund of 2,500,000 rubles, and an annual fund of 1,500,000 rubles, for this service.

" by

by Count Bruhl; who, in anſwer to Sieur Funck writes [h], "That the deliberations of the grand council are ſo much the more glorious to Ruſſia, in that there can be nothing more beneficial to the common cauſe, than previouſly to settle the effectual means of deſtroying the overgrown power of Pruſſia, and the undoubted ambition of that court." And again [i] he explains himſelf as follows, "The reſult of the grand council of Ruſſia has given us great ſatisfaction: the confidential communication, which Ruſſia is pleaſed to make of it, will enable all their allies, *as well as our court*, to come to an explanation about the arrangement, and meaſures to be taken in conſequence thereof. But, it cannot be taken amiſs, if Saxony, conſidering the ſuperior power of its neighbour, proceeds with the utmoſt caution, and previouſly expects its ſecurity from its allies, and to be aſſiſted with the means of acting."

This memorial then ſets forth the panic, which ſeized this Saxon miniſter upon the convention of neutrality in Germany ſigned [k] between the courts of London and Berlin, which he was afraid would ſilence all his calumnies, and ſhake his iniquitous ſyſtem, and therefore redoubled his efforts in Ruſſia in order to prevent a good underſtanding between that court and the King of Pruſſia. "A

[h] Dated the 11th of November 1755.
[i] The 23d of November 1755.
[k] On the 16th of January 1756.

A.D. 1757.

"reconciliation, says he[1], between the courts of Berlin and Petersburg would be the most critical and the most dangerous event, that could happen. It is to be hoped, that Russia would not hearken to such odious proposals; and that the court of Vienna will be able to thwart so fatal a union." However, it appears from what follows, that there was no ground for Bruhl's fears. The court of Vienna had made sure of the Czarina, and imagining that the new connections, they had entered into, this year, would facilitate the recovery of Silesia, they took their measures accordingly. Russia, armed with great strength, both by land and sea, under pretence of a treaty with England, which required, at that time, no succours. Bohemia and Moravia were covered with troops, camps, magazines, &c. agreeable to a secret convention between the two Empresses; and discontinued till next year, for certain reasons. For, whoever attends to the correspondence of the Saxon ministers will find that Prussia was the real, whatever might be the apparent object of such armaments. A report was industriously propagated at Petersburg, from several parts, under the influence of the Austrian and Saxon ministers, "That the King of Prussia, under a pretence of trade, was sending officers and engineers, in disguise, into Ukraine, to reconnoitre the country, and stir up a rebellion." Which, if believed, was, according to the treaty

[1] In his letter of the 23d of June 1756.

of eventual partition, a sufficient ground for a rupture[m]. This had such an effect, that the Russian minister of state assured secretary Passe, "That his court would soon begin the war against the King of Prussia, in order to set bounds to so troublesome a neighbour, and that the engagements of his court with England, in regard to the neutrality of Germany, did not concern the Saxon league at least, and that they would go on their own way, in keeping to the sense of the subsidiary treaty with England[n]. That they very much approved of the court of Vienna's new connections with France; which they wished might extend so far, as to support the Empress Queen, in her attempts upon Prussia, and that the order for putting a stop to the armaments of that Empire, was occasioned by the want of officers and seamen, magazines and forage[o]." Count Flemming, the Saxon minister at Vienna, informs [p] his court of a conference he had with Count Kaunitz, concerning the armaments of Russia, and the difficulty of maintaining those great armies, and the dangers that might ensue a discovery of their real object, by that crafty and sharp-sighted Prince, the King of Prussia. In the course of which Flemming was made to understand, that those armaments, whatever might be pretended in regard to en-

---

[m] Sieur Passe's letter to Count Bruhl, 28th of April 1756.
[n] His letter of the 10th of May 1756.
[o] On the 21st of June.
[p] On the 12th of June 1756.

gagements with England, were made againſt Pruſſia: that money would not be wanting nor grudged, provided they knew how to make a proper uſe of it, and that, in caſe the King of Pruſſia ſhould fall ſuddenly upon his neighbours, he would meet with his match: "for that the Ruſſians were prepared at all events." But nothing could prove the inſincerity of the Auſtrian court more evidently than a letter from this ſame Count Flemming at Vienna, to Count Bruhl, the Saxon prime miniſter, dated June 9th 1756. in which it is ſaid with great aſſurance, that there was an eſtabliſhed concert between the two courts of Vienna and Ruſſia: that the latter, in order to diſguiſe the true reaſons of their armaments, made them under the pretence of being thereby in a condition to fulfil their engagements with England: and that when all the preparations ſhould be finiſhed, they were to fall unexpectedly upon the King of Pruſſia; and another letter, dated 28th of July, which ſets the ſyſtem of Vienna in a full light, at the bottom of the page ᶜ.

This

ᶜ *Letter from Count Flemming to Count de Bruhl.*

SIR,   Vienna, July 28, 1756.

M. Klingraffe received laſt Saturday an expreſs from his court, in conſequence of which he ſent a note the next morning to Count de Kaunitz, earneſtly entreating him to appoint an hour for a conference with him. This note was delivered to the chancellor of ſtate, juſt while he was in conference with the Marſhals Newperg and Brown, and Gen. Prince Piccolomini. And as he intended to wait upon the Empreſs Queen immediately after the conference, in order to make her a report

This letter, says the memorialist, proves, that by dictating the answer to his Sovereign; Count Kaunitz

A. D. 1757.

port thereof, he sent word to M. Klingraffe, that he was indeed obliged to go to Schœnbrunn, but nevertheless he would be obliged to him, if he would hasten to him that very instant; which the Prussian minister did not fail to do. Count de Kaunitz told me in confidence, at a conversation I had with him yesterday morning, that M. Klingraffe, on his accosting him, gave him to understand, with a certain embarrassment mixed with uneasiness, that he had just received an express from his court, who brought him some orders, the contents of which he was to lay before the Empress Queen in person, and for this purpose he was enjoined to demand a private audience of her Imperial Majesty, which, he desired, he would be pleased to procure for him. That he, Count Kaunitz, made answer, that being just ready to set out for Schœnbrunn, he willingly took upon him to demand the audience he desired; but could not avoid letting him understand, that it was proper he should be enabled, at least in general terms, to give the Empress previous notice of the nature of the insinuations he had orders to make to her Majesty. Whereupon M. de Klingraffe told him, that he was charged to demand *amicably*, and by way of eclaircissement, in the name of the King his master, what was the tendency of the armaments and military preparations making here, and whether they might not, perhaps concern him; which, however he could not imagine, as he did not know that he had given the least occasion for them. That he, Kaunitz, replied, that he could not just then make any answer to that overture; that he would not fail to make a report thereof immediately to the Empress, and procure him the audience he requested; that, nevertheless, he could not forbear telling him, that he was surprised at the explanation, which the King his master required, concerning the measures taken in this country, seeing this court had expressed no uneasiness or umbrage at the great movements and preparations, which had been previously observed in his army. This minister further

told

A. D. 1757.

Kaunitz proposed to shut the door against all means of explaining and conciliating matters; and

told me, "That having set out immediately after for Schoen-
"brunn, he had reflected by the way on the answer he should
"advise his Sovereign to give M. Klingraffe; and having
"thought he perceived that the King of Prussia had two ob-
"jects in view, which this court was desirous equally to avoid,
"viz. to come to conferences and eclaircissements, that might,
"at first, cause a suspension of the measures, which they judged
"necessary to be continued vigorously; and secondly, to lead
"matters further on, to other propositions and more essential
"engagements; he had therefore judged that the answer
"ought to be of such a nature, as might entirely elude the
"King of Prussia's question; and that, in leaving no more
"room for further explanations, it should at the same time be
"resolute and polite, without being susceptible of any inter-
"pretation either sinister or favourable. That pursuant to
"this notion, it appeared to him sufficient, that the Empress
"should content herself with simply answering, that in the
"violent general crisis Europe was now in, her duty and the
"dignity of her crown required her to take sufficient measures
"for her own security, as well as for the safety of her friends
"and allies." That the Empress Queen had approved of this answer; and to shew that the King of Prussia's step and demand did not occasion the least embarrassment here, her Majesty immediately ordered the hour of M. Klingraffe's audience to be fixed for the next day, which was the day before yesterday; and after hearing that minister's proposition, just as he had imparted it the preceding day to Count de Kaunitz, she had answered him precisely in the terms above-mentioned, and then suddenly broke off the audience with a nod, without entering into any further detail. It is certain that all Vienna, being then assembled in the Empress Queen's drawing-room, as it was a day of gala, saw M. Klingraffe enter, and depart in a very few minutes, with an embarrassed countenance. I have all these particulars from the mouth of Count de Kaunitz, who

and at the same time, to pursue the preparations for his dangerous designs, in the expectation, that the

on this occasion, has talked to me with more openness and confidence than he had hitherto done, and even charged me to make use of them in my dispatches to your Excellency, but still with the greatest secrecy.

It is so much the less doubted that this answer, equally strong and obscure, will greatly puzzle the King of Prussia; and 'tis pretended here, that that Prince must be under a great deal of uneasiness, and that he has already drawn three millions of crowns out of his treasury, for the charges of his preparations and augmentations.

It is presumed, and not without probability, that his design in the demand above-mentioned was, that if he had been answered, that he himself had been the cause of the armaments made here, he would have endeavoured to leer himself of the charge, by alledging, in proof of his innocence, that for this very reason he did not only form the camps, which he has already traced to exercise his soldiers, but had ordered the regiments to separate; perhaps imagining he should lay this court under this necessity to follow his example by discontinuing likewise his preparations. However, I think he would find it no easy matter to divert it from its design by such illusions as these.

We have learned by an express who arrived last Sunday from the Count de Puebla, that notwithstanding the feigned dispositions of the King of Prussia, his troops still continued filing off towards Silesia. Besides, it is very easily understood that that Prince, by the local position of his army, which he can assemble in as many weeks as it would require months to do the same here, on account of the distance of the places where the troops are quartered, has too visible an advantage over this court, which he can put to such great expences by long and continual marches, that they would at last become intollerable: I say, it is very readily understood, that it is necessary to pursue, without interruption, the measures already begun, the King would be so far provoked, as to take some step, which might serve to make him pass for the aggressor.

He begun, in order to put themselves in the present circumstances, upon equal terms, and in a good condition; that the King of Prussia may be thereby obliged, to keep up his armaments; and the augmentations made and to be made, will exceed his faculties, and waste him gradually; "or else, in order to "prevent this inconvenience, to take a precipitate resolution; "which, I think, is the very thing expected from him."

The return of M. Klingraffe's courier, which the said Prince, no doubt, waits for with the utmost impatience, will give us more light into his dispositions. There is reason to believe, that if he thinks himself menaced, he will no longer delay coming to action, and preventing those, whom he dreads, in order to take advantage of the situation, in which this court will be 'till the end of the month of August, which is the term when all the troops are to be assembled. But on the other hand, if he remains quiet, he may be persuaded that he will not be molested or attacked, "at least not this year." However, from all the observations I make, I cannot but imagine, that this court must be very sure of the friendship and attachment of Russia. And this seems to me to be farther confirmed by a letter of the 6 D. c. from M. Swart the Dutch minister at Petersburg, to M. de Burmannia, wherein he writes among other things, that the French emissary, the Chevalier Douglas, gained ground every day.

As this cannot fail of producing an alteration in the old system of Russia, it does not appear surprising that the high chancellor Count Bestucheff, agreeably to what your excellency did me the honour to write to me in your last dispatch, has resolved to retire into the country, under the pretext of recovering his health, and to withdraw a-while from public business; as he may be willing to wait what turn affairs may take, and perhaps foresees that the hour is at hand, since the whole seems to depend on the King of Prussia's resolution; it being

He then relates the measures, he had taken to prevent a war with the Empress Queen, as already set

being certain, that if he remains quiet, that the court of Vienna will not begin to act neither, " at least this year: but
" she will endeavour, during that interval, to finish her pre-
" parations, that she may the next year be in a situation to
" take a course suitable to the circumstances and events, which
" time may produce.

" This confirms me more in the opinion, which I ventured
" to take the liberty to communicate to your excellency in
" my former letters, that our court has no surer means to
" profit by the present conjunctures, which, perhaps, never
" were so favourable during the reign of our august master,
" than by putting itself in a good posture, to the end that its
" concurrence may be courted. A friend of mine, who pre-
" tends to have his information from one of the clerks of the
" treasury, assures me, that this court has remitted a million
" of florins to Russia."

Count de Kaunitz has told me, that the advices, which your excellency had conveyed to him, of reports spread by the King of Prussia, concerning alliances to be made between him and us, as also with Russia; and, moreover, that this court was taking upon her to mediate between France and England; has already been sent to him by other hands, and consequently deserved the more attention, as well as to be contradicted; which the Empress Queen's ministers at the courts of Europe would accordingly be ordered to do. This chancellor of state further told me, there was advice, that the King of Prussia had had an intention to surprize the city of Stralsund in Swedish Pomerania; and that if this proved true, it was likely to be in consequence of the plot lately discovered at Stockholm.

If your excellency has an opportunity to make insinuations with safety at the court of London, you might perhaps do it some service by apprizing it of the danger, into which it has been led by those, who now have the greatest influence there.

A.D. 1757.

set forth [r]; and the constant refusal of giving him a satisfactory answer, in regard to his own safety: a conduct, adds the memorialist, that gave the highest degree of evidence to the dangerous designs of the court of Vienna, and forced his Majesty, who could no longer entertain the least doubt about it, to take the only way, he had left him, to avert the dangers, he was threatened with, by preventing an irreconcileable enemy, who had sworn his ruin.

It will be a hard task for that court to get out of the distress, which she has plunged herself into, and if she does not detach herself from the King of Prussia, by making her peace with France on the best conditions that can be had, the latter will go on from success to success, and from one project to another, which, in the long run, may prove fatal to the house of Hanover.

I beg it as a favour of your excellency, that you would not descend to particulars with M. de Broglie about any thing I have the honour to write to your excellency, because that ambassador holds a correspondence with M. d'Aubeterre, who has told me with some surprize, that the Count de Broglie was fully persuaded, that mischief was intended against the King of Prussia, and even accused him of distrust and too much reserve concerning the designs of the court of Vienna.

The Marquis d'Aubeterre having long solicited permission to absent himself from his post for a few months, in order to attend his family affairs, which require his presence at Paris, has at last obtained his request.

General Karoli, and not General Nadasti, as was thought, has just been declared Bann of Croatia.

I have the honour to be, &c.

C. FLEMMING.

[r] On page 55 to 62. Vol. II.

He then appeals to the impartial world to determine, which of the two ought to be deemed the aggreſſor; he who is preparing every means to cruſh his neighbour; or, he who, ſeeing the arm raiſed over his head, aiming the moſt dangerous blows, endeavours to ward them off, by ſtriking home upon the perſon of his enemy.

Then he obſerves, That the King's conduct towards the court of Saxony is grounded upon the ſame principle of indiſpenſible neceſſity of providing for his own ſecurity againſt the moſt dangerous deſigns. For, ſays he, from the beginning of the troubles, which have juſt broke out, Count Bruhl had acted the part, he had, long ſince, agreed to with the allies of his court, by borrowing the maſk of neutrality; but, in the mean time, and till he ſhould be at liberty to pull it off, he was not the leſs forward in entering perſonally into the late concert formed againſt his Majeſty: and that no ſtronger proof of this can be given, than by repeating here, what has been related above, that his miniſters did not ſcruple to make himſelf acceſſary in propagating the calumny, that the King wanted to ſtir up a rebellion in Ukraine.

That Count Bruhl loſt no time in ſettling his ſyſtem of neutrality, agreeably to ſuch principles; appears from his letter to Count Flemming, on the 1ſt of July, and conſequently two months before the King's army began to march; " That he " ſhould propoſe to the court of Vienna, to take " meaſures againſt the paſſage of the Pruſſian " army through Saxony, by aſſembling an army
" in

"in the circles of Bohemia, which border upon
"that Electorate; *and to order Marſhal Brown to
"concert ſecretly with Marſhal Count Rutowſki:*"
and from Count Flemming's anſwer, on the 7th
of July, "That Count Kaunitz had aſſured him,
"that the generals would be forthwith named;
"and that one would likewiſe be appointed, to
"concert with Count Rutowſki: that the court
"of Saxony ſhould not ſhew any trouble or un-
"eaſineſs; but rather keep a good countenance,
"*by preparing privately againſt every event.*" Where
one may judge of this concert, by the counſel,
which Count Flemming gives Count Bruhl, in his
diſpatches of the 14th of July, "to grant the
"paſſage to the Pruſſian troops; and, afterwards,
"to take ſuch meaſures as ſhould be moſt pro-
"per."

He further ſets forth, That by a letter from
Count Flemming of the 18th of Auguſt, the
Empreſs Queen explained herſelf to that miniſter
in the following terms: "That ſhe required no-
"thing, for the preſent, from the King of Po-
"land, as ſhe was very ſenſible of his tickliſh
"ſituation;—that, however, ſhe hoped he would,
"in the mean while, put himſelf in a good
"poſture, in order to be prepared at all events;
"and that, in caſe any breach ſhould happen be-
"tween her Majeſty and the King of Pruſſia, ſhe
"would, in time, not be averſe to concur in the
"neceſſary meaſures for their mutual ſecurity."

Then ſumming up the facts, the memorialiſt
ſays, That from a curſory review of all the facts,
which

which have been alledged above, it will be easy to form a just notion of the conduct of the court of Saxony towards the King; and to judge of the justice of his Majesty's actual conduct towards that court. For it does appear, that the court of Dresden has had a share in all the dangerous designs, which have been formed against the King: —that their ministers have been the authors, and chief promoters of them:—And though they have not, formally acceded to the treaty of Petersburg, that they have, however, agreed with their allies to suspend their concurrence therein, till such time only, as the King's forces should be weakened and divided, and they might pull off the mask without danger.

That the King of Poland had adopted, as a principle, That any war between the King and one of his Polish Majesty's allies, furnished him with a title to make conquests upon his Majesty; —And that it is in consequence of this principle, that he thought he could, in time of peace, make a partition of the dominions of his neighbour.

That the Saxon ministers had founded the alarm against the King, all over Europe; and spared neither calumnies, nor falshoods, nor sinister insinuations, in order to increase the number of his enemies.

And particularly that Count Bruhl had eagerly entered into the late plot of the court of Vienna, by the injurious report he undertook to propagate; —And that it has been made appear, that there
was

A. D. 1757.

was a secret concert existing between the courts of Vienna and Saxony, in consequence of which, the latter did intend to let the King's army pass, in order to act, afterwards, according to events, either in joining his enemies, or in making a diversion in his dominions, unprovided with troops.

Then the memorial concludes with this declaration, Such is the situation, the King was in, with the court of Saxony, when he resolved to march into Bohemia, in order to avert the danger, which was prepared for him. His Majesty could not therefore abandon himself to the discretion of a court, whose ill-will he was thoroughly acquainted with;—But found himself forced to take such measures, as prudence and the security of his own dominions required; and which the conduct of the court of Saxony towards him, has authorized him to pursue."

The Empress Queen's answer to these motives.

The Empress Queen made an appearance to answer the charge brought against her and her allies, in these motives; in which he chiefly insisted upon the right of self-preservation, and the proofs of a confederacy by powers, with whom he was in a state of peace, to attack him unprovided and defenceless, in order to rob him of his dominions, to which he had a just right by inheritance and treaty, and to divide them amongst themselves. But she, in her answer, evaded those two principal points; and, in general, only denied, or endeavoured to give a favourable turn to, those documents and original papers, the King of Prussia had published, in justification of the violent measures,

he

he was obliged, through neceffity, as he faid, to purfue.

To invalidate thefe motives, It is afked in the anfwer of the court of Vienna, " Do thefe pieces of correfpondence fo taken, and then publifhed in the Pruffian memorial, actually and really exift? And if they do; are their contents truly the fame, as related? And fuppofe them to be originals, Are they not falfe and fuppofititious?" " For, fays the anfwer, **thefe pretended** originals are communicated only by way of extracts, not duly connected; fome paffages being **purpofely** left out, or at leaft difguifed."

It juftifies the treaty of the 18th of May 1745, upon a notion of right, which a potentate has to renew different former conventions, according to the difference of times; and upon a fuppofition that fuch meafures, propofed to be taken in a future time of war, are not to bind, or take effect, until, according to all laws, human and divine, the parties are no more bound to peace; and the full right of fuch treaties fhould not before be entered upon, or avail. So that here the fact is confeffed, though the intention is denied for carrying the fact into execution.

" But, fays the anfwer again, the cafe of her Majefty the **Emprefs Queen** was very different from that of the **King of Pruffia**: the continual danger of an attack, fhe was in, fince the peace of Drefden, was a real concern. The experience of repeated infractions of the peace, committed by Pruffia, and followed within a few years, one by another, left **no room to** the court of Vienna

A. D. 1757.

to expect another fate: becaufe the King of Pruffia was continually arming himfelf, and augmenting his forces; though the peace was but lately concluded, and no probability of any danger; the houfe of Auftria being engaged in another war; Ruffia at a great diftance, and Saxony too weak for any enterprize: but Pruffia was fo ferious in its preparations, as made it hard to diftinguifh a time of peace and a time of actual war from each other.

It further bids the reader add, the notorious turbulent temper of the King of Pruffia, his continual intrigues with foreign courts; his contraventions; his raifing difputes amongft his neighbours; and then infers, That nothing could be expected, but that he would play his game again, the firft opportunity, and unexpectedly interrupt the moft folemn treaties of peace; and that he had only made peace, in order to prepare for another war with renewed ftrength.

" As a further juftification, it is faid, That the imperial court of Ruffia has no lefs intereft in the fupport of the houfe of Auftria, than this houfe in the undifturbed tranquility of the Ruffian Monarchy, and both courts in the defence of the republic of Poland, againft the aggrandizing views of Pruffia, and its intermeddling with the domeftic affairs of this kingdom: and therefore, that no better method could be taken to provide for the common welfare and future fafety, than the union of the two courts, which was effected by the treaty of 1746, obliging each other to unite their ftrength

for

for setting proper bounds to the over-grown power of Prussia; if this King, not satisfied with the considerable acquisitions he had made, should again proceed to commit hostilities against either of the contracting parties or their ally, the republic of Poland. So that the Empress Queen insists, that this fourth secret article, on which the King of Prussia fixes the first cause of his violent measures, was not offensive, but merely a defensive treaty of friendship, until it should happen that the King of Prussia himself, by attacking first Austria, Russia, or the republic of Poland, should oblige them to unite against him.

As to the proceedings against Saxony in particular: it is granted, says the answer, that the court of Berlin could not possibly expect any other resolutions from that court, considering the unneighbourly manner, and oppressions, both in regard to commerce and other provincial affairs, which Saxony has suffered from Prussia since the late peace: neither could it be wondered, when such a conduct has grieved the Saxon ministers to their heart, and made them to speak more freely to others about it: but that it was, in no wise justifiable to make the court responsible for those correspondences, and to treat the country with a cruelty, that may be felt for a whole century.

It further says, in regard to the motives drawn from the sentiments of the King of Poland's privy council, that these, and the other allegations, import no more than that the Electoral court of Saxony had resolved to direct its measures according to future events, waiting firſt a Pruſſian attack, and a ſubſequent diverſion to be made by its allies.

As to the proofs drawn from the correſpondence between the miniſters; it is alledged, that they were only miniſterial ſentiments, which can determine nothing, nor be admitted by way of evidence, concerning the intentions of their principals, in oppoſition to the plaineſt declarations given by the court itſelf, where the miniſter reſides. And as to the final anſwer demanded by the King of Pruſſia from the Empreſs Queen; the court of Vienna, ſays the anſwer, did not think proper to make a new declaration, in compliance with the Pruſſian dictates, after a ſufficient anſwer was given already to the firſt demand. Becauſe, the truce, propoſed for *two years*, ſuppoſed an actual war, and real offenſive circumſtances, or offenſive meaſures, agreed upon by the two Empreſſes; which the court of Vienna could not againſt truth, and the aſſurances already given, allow to be the caſe; and becauſe the obligation, by the peace of Dreſden, would, in conſequence of ſuch a declaration, have been void.—But that this court acknowledges, that it has always entertained a diſtruſt of the King of Pruſſia, and had been ever attentive to the continual armaments and unwarrantable violences committed on all ſides: neither was it now frightened by a Pruſſian aggreſſion, or deterred from its defenſive meaſures, by any threats and artifices: but that it had taken, ſince the late breach, the moſt effectual meaſures,

in

in order to make the author of the present troubles repent of his open injustice, violence and rash perfidy."

Such were the evasions; such the invectives and threats of the court of Vienna; which were far from disproving the truth of the Prussian Monarch's suspicion; or his right to those violent steps he had taken for his own security; and served only to confirm him in his opinion of the conspiracy against him, and whetted his resolutions and activity in his future operations.

How it operated on the King of Prussia.

The King of Prussia thus circumstanced; his conduct misrepresented in every court of Europe; his Electorate put under the ban of the Empire; his subjects absolved by the Imperial decree from their allegiance; threatened with an angry declaration from Russia, and from France, who had marched formidable armies to attack him, in conjunction with Austria; besides the diversion he expected from the Swedes and the Duke of Mecklenburg; maintained his winter quarters in Saxony, for that part of the army commanded by Mareschal Keith; which lined the shore of the Elbe between Pirna and the frontier; and covered Silesia from surprize with the army under M. Schewrin, who took up his quarters in the county of Glatz, till the time came for action.

The present state of the King of Prussia.

During this recess a regiment of Saxon troops, which had entered into his service, after their surrender at Pirna, and sent by him to garrison Berlin, deserted and retired into Poland, being joined by some more in their march. However, this did

Saxon troops desert.

A.D. 1757.

did not weaken his army. For, he broke all the rest of the Saxon regiments, incorporated the men amongst his own troops, and obliged the Saxon magistrates to supply him speedily with four thousand fresh recruits.

Measures to prevent the march of the Russians.

As soon as the season would admit, his Majesty, informed of the march of 130,000 Russians, which had been advancing ever since the month of November towards Ducal Prussia, with provisions only to supply their necessities, till they could reach Lithuania, reinforced Memel with three regiments of troops and a great number of matrosses; he also ordered 30,000 men, under General Lehwald, to meet the enemy under M. Apraxin; and bought up all the corn and forage of the country where the Russians were to enter, and they depended upon a plentiful supply. Which precautions had their desired effect.

Saxony how disposed.

In Saxony one regiment only was allotted for the garrison of Dresden, but the towns-people were disarmed. A detachment was posted at Konigstein, to oblige that fortress to observe an exact neutrality. The French minister was ordered to with-draw: and several gentlemen and ladies about the court were laid under restraint [s]. And all

[s] On the 10th of April Major-general Bornstadt sent for the burgo-masters and syndic of the city of Dresden, and read to them the following order of his Prussian Majesty. " You shall give notice throughout the city, that having thought fit to cut off all communication with this court; from henceforth nobody shall be admitted to the palace, except the domestics, whose service is required there. All access thereunto is interdicted

all possible care was taken by the Prussians to secure a retreat in case of necessity. For which purpose his Majesty ordered two bridges to be thrown over the Elbe early in the year, and he obliged **the Saxons to** supply waggons with four horses for that service.

Having provided for the security of his possession of Saxony, and settled all in profound quiet, his Prussian Majesty went in person to visit all his posts in Silesia, and at Neifs he settled the operations for the ensuing campaign, with Mareschal **Schewrin;** whose army, consisting of 50,000 men in Silesia, he commanded to regulate its motions with **the royal** army, so as **to act** in concert, as circumstances might require. **He** placed armies in Lusatia and Voigtland; he ordered 20,000 men, **under Prince** Maurice of Anhalt Dessau, **to** assemble at Zwickaw, **on the** frontiers of Bohemia, towards Egra; and detached 60,000 men towards Great Zeidlitz, where **their** head quarters were settled.

<small>A. D. 1757.</small>

<small>Preparations for opening the campaign.</small>

The Austrians, convinced by **the experiment** already made in the autumn, that their army was not strong **enough** to force the Prussians, had not only demanded **the aid** of their allies, but greatly augmented **their own forces, and** employed the winter in **such preparations as the nature of** the war required: **keeping a constant** attention upon

<small>By the Austrians.</small>

dicted to others: so that whosoever shall **presume to act** contrary to this order shall be taken up, and lodged **in some fortress,** without regard to quality or condition."

A. D.
1757.

Skirmishes.

the motion and measures of the Prussians. So that while the Prussian troops were making their necessary dispositions on the frontiers of Bohemia, there happened several skirmishes between them and the Austrians; with various success. On the 20th of February about four in the morning, the Austrians, in number 6000, surrounded Hirschfield, a little town in Upper Lusatia, garrisoned only by one battalion of Prussian foot. The attack was made on two redoubts without the gates, defended by two field pieces each. The Austrians, after being several times repulsed, with considerable loss, made themselves masters of one redoubt, and carried off its two cannon. But the Prussians, sallying out and harrassing their rear, killed some, and took many prisoners.

Prince of Bevern's progress.

This was improved by the Prince of Bevern; who in the beginning of March departed from Zittau with 9000 men, to beat up and destroy the dens or forts erected by the Austrians on their frontiers. In which expedition he seized upon the Austrian magazine at Friedland in Bohemia, and carried off 9000 sacks of meal, and a great quantity of ammunition; the van of his troops, consisting only of 150 hussars of Putkammar's regiment, having attacked, sword in hand, a body of 600 croats, sustained by 300 Austrian dragoons of Bathiani, at their first entering Bohemia; killed 50, took 10 dragoons prisoners, and 30 horses, without any loss or hurt, except two men slightly wounded. From Friedland the Prince of Bevern marched against Richenberg;

which

which also surrendered to his arms. From thence he returned victorious to Zittau.

A. D. 1757.

The time of action seemed to drive on a pace, M. Brown visited the fortifications of Brian and Konigsgratz; reviewed the army under the command of General Serbelloni, which had been commanded by Prince Piccolomini; and immediately upon the hearing, that the Prussians were in motion, he marched with the grand army, with an intention to fix his head quarters at Kostlitz on the Elbe.

M. Brown takes the field.

The activity of the Prussian hero, having nothing to fear from the Russians, who could not march forward for want of provisions and forage, would not permit the Austrian General to enter Saxony. It is always the best policy to carry war into the enemy's country, and to keep it as far as possible from home. Therefore, those four armies, which he seemed to have placed upon the defensive in Silesia, Lusatia, Misnia and Saxony, had orders suddenly to penetrate by four different and opposite routs into Bohemia, at one and the same time, and as near as possible. That from Saxony his Majesty commanded in person, assisted by M. Keith: Prince Maurice of Anhalt Dessau was at the head of the army from Misnia: That from Lusatia was conducted by Prince Ferdinand of Brunswick Bevern: and M. Schwerin commanded the troops from Silesia. All which was executed with that diligence and secrecy, that those four armies entered Bohemia almost without opposition; for the Austrians never suspected the least of such

The activity of the King of Prussia.

His four armies.

A.D. 1757.

a visit till they were convinced of their arrival in Bohemia.

Enter Bohemia.

M. Schwerin entered [t] Bohemia in five columns and by five different roads: and met with no opposition till they advanced to Guelder Oelse, which defile was filled with Pandours; but they were immediately attacked by two battalions of Prussian grenadiers with bayonets fixt, who routed them. Prince Anhalt Deſſau paſſed [u] the frontiers of Bohemia without any reſiſtance. Being advanced with the corps under his command within a ſhort diſtance of Egra, he attacked a poſt guarded by 400 dragoons, ſuſtained by Croats and Pandours; which he entirely defeated with great loſs to the enemy: he then detached 4000 of his troops towards Holtenberg, in order to ſeize on the important paſs of Schirdinger. On the 20th of April the Prince of Bevern entered Bohemia alſo, and got poſſeſſion of Krottau and Graffenſtein, the firſt poſt, on that ſide of the kingdom, without the loſs of a man: hearing that the enemy had approached to Kratzen, he proceeded and drove them away from thence the ſame day, and continued his march to Machendorf near Reichenberg, and not far from a camp of 28,000 Auſtrians, under the command of Count Conigſeg. Putkammer's huſſars, who formed part of a body, commanded by a Colonel and Major, fell in with a party of ſome hundreds of cuiraſſiers, poſted before Colin, or Kohleg, under the command of

The battle of Reichenberg.

---

[t] On the 18th of April.   [u] On the 21ſt of April.

Prince

Prince Litchtenstein; took three officers and upwards of 60 horse prisoners, and dispersed the rest. Night not only prevented a pursuit; but obliged the Prussian army to remain in the field till morning. At break of day they marched in two columns, by Habendorf, to attack the enemy near Reichenberg: and as soon as they were formed in three lines of about 30 squadrons, they advanced towards the enemy's cavalry; the two wings being sustained by the infantry, posted amongst felled trees, and behind entrenchments. The cavalry having a village on their right, and a wood, where they were entrenched on the left, received the canonade with resolution. But fifteen squadrons of the dragoons of the second line being ordered by the Prince of Bevern to advance, and at the same time, the wood on the right being attacked by the battalions of grenadiers of Kahlden and of Moellendorf, by the Prince of Prussia's regiment of dragoons; who, by getting clear over all the heaps of timber, and the entrenchments, secured their flanks, and entirely routed the enemy's cavalry; and Colonel Putkammer and Major Schenfeld with their hussars, though flanked by the enemy's artillery, gave the Austrian horse a very warm reception; whilst General Lestewitz attacked the redoubts, that covered Reichenberg, with the left wing of the Prussians. An action, that redounded greatly to his honour; for, though there were many defiles in the way, and the enemy was in possession of the eminences, the regiment of Darmstandt drove all before them,

A. D.
1757.

them, and with a ferocity fcarce to be conceived, bid defiance to powder and ball, and drove the Auftrians not only from the redoubts, but purfued them with great flaughter from hill to hill [w], as far as Rochlitz and Dorffell.

Its continuance and lofs.

This action began at fix in the morning, and lafted five hours; and was fupported with great obftinacy and bravery on both fides, though with great difproportion in the lofs. For the Auftrians were obliged to leave behind them feveral pieces of cannon, and feveral ammunition waggons in their trenches, to the difcretion of the enemy: and they had upwards of a thoufand men killed and wounded; amongft whom were found General Porporati and Count Hobenfelds killed, and Prince Lichtenftein and Count Mansfeld wounded: they alfo loft three ftandards, 20 officers, and 400 private men made prifoners. Whereas the Pruffians had only feven fubaltern officers, and a 100 rank and file killed; and General Normann, one colonel, four majors, three captains, feven fubalterns, and 150 rank and file wounded.

Remarks on this event.

Such a blow at the firft of the campaign was productive of feveral advantages. It diffufed vaft ideas, in every place, of his Pruffian Majefty's abilities and valour; it animated his victorious troops to face every danger; it ftruck a panic throughout the country he had invaded; it fecured a fafe and eafy retreat in cafe of neceffity; and it facilitated the execution of the whole plan of

[w] . bove a mile.

operations, which had been so gloriously begun. The news of this eclat reached England at the time Mr. PITT was dismissed, and the English bemoaned the mismanagement and timidity of their own governors; it made them more eager and clamorous for an alliance, with a power, that was every day exhibiting proofs of foresight and bravery.

A. D. 1757. Its effects in England.

His Prussian Majesty did not omit to make the best use of this victory. He himself published the account thereof at the head of his own guards, in a stile that would have done honour to an Alexander or a Cæsar, "See, my boys, said he, "a most happy beginning. Heaven espouses our "cause. The Prince of Bevern has defeated the "Austrians at Reichenberg. This promises us, "that, with God's assistance, we shall have the "like success." Words can't express the joy that diffused itself in every countenance, and the acclamations which resounded from the whole army with huzzas, and "A long life to their incomparable sovereign."

The victory published by the King at the head of his army.

An army spirited up in this manner was eager to be led on to the most arduous enterprizes. The King seizes the opportunity, and prepares to seek the main body of the enemy, and if possible, to draw them to a general engagement; though they were far superior to him in numbers, and encamped in a situation so fortified by every advantage of nature, and contrivance of art, as to be deemed almost impregnable. With this resolution he ordered the Prince of Bevern, who was joined,

Resolution to seek and attack the main army.

soon

A. D.
1757.

soon after the battle, by the army under M. Schwerin, to march with all expedition to meet him, at a certain place: and the same orders accelerated the march of the Prince of Anhalt Dessau with his army. In their rout the Prince of Bevern made himself master of the greatest part of the circle of Buntzlau, and dislodged and took a considerable magazine from the Austrians.

A stratagem to divide the Austrian forces.

Every thing succeeded to favour the junction of the Prussian forces. There still remained something to be done in point of generalship, to weaken the enemy's strength, without leaving all to the risk of the sword. His Prussian Majesty, ever vigilant and penetrating, with a sagacity, that foresaw every thing, was readily furnished with a stratagem for this purpose. His Majesty, to the surprize of every body, after the Prince of Anhalt Dessau was arrived at the camp of his destination, near that of his sovereign's army, decamped and advanced with his own part of the army to Budin, where he drove the Austrians from their advantageous camp, to Westram, which lies half way between Budin and Prague.

Succeeds.

This movement, added to the way by which he entered Bohemia, which was at a considerable distance from any of the corps commanded by his generals, so deceived the enemy, into an imagination that his Prussian Majesty had undertaken some design distinct from the object of his other armies; that they fell into the snare, and detached 20,000 men from their main army to attend upon his particular motions.

But

But after his Majesty had paſſed the Egra, and was there joined by the army under M. Schwerin, in ſuch a ſituation that they could act jointly, he made ſo ſudden and maſterly a movement to the left, as if his intention was againſt Egra, that it completed his real deſign; which cut off all communication between that detachment and the main army of the Auſtrians, ſtrongly entrenched, as above-mentioned, on the banks of the Moldau to the north of Prague; their left wing being guarded by the mountains of Ziſcka, and the right extending as far as Herboholi, under the command of Prince Charles of Lorrain, and Marſhal Brown.

Having gained this advantage to weaken the enemy's main body; it made the Auſtrians more cautious, and though they had been reinforced by an army from Moravia; by the remains of the forces defeated by the Duke of Bevern, and by ſeveral regiments drawn from the garriſon of Prague, it was reſolved not to march in queſt of the invaders, and to prevent their uniting, as in ſound policy ought to have been done; but to wait their united force in a ſtrong camp to cover the metropolis from inſult. But this caution in the enemy only ſtimulated the vivacity of the Pruſſian hero, whoſe courage was always ſharpened by difficulties. His reſolutions were not taken upon the danger, but the expediency of the action. He could not hope for ſucceſs, in his future operations, without defeating this fortified army. Therefore deſpiſing the difficulties he had

Auſtrians wait his approach.

Reaſons for attacking the Auſtrian army.

to

A. D. 1757.

to encounter in the attack, orders were given for 30,000 men to pass the Moldau, which was done, with himself at their head, on the 6th day of May, in the morning, on bridges of boats; having left the rest of the army under the command of the Prince of Anhalt Dessau, to secure the pass of that river, in case of need. Those 30,000, on their arrival a-cross the Moldau, were immediately joined by the troops under M. Schwerin and the Prince of Bevern, according to the good disposition made by his Majesty in the general plan of this invasion: and it was resolved to attack the enemy with these united forces, on the same day.

Prussian troops joined.

Advance to the attack.

In pursuance of this resolution the King ordered his army to file off on the left by Potschernitz, as the most eligible disposition for executing this grand design, by flanking the enemy. This obliged Count Brown to wheel about to the right. The Prussians however continued their march to Bichwitz; though it was a very bad way, so full of defiles and morasses, that the infantry and cavalry were forced to separate. But all those obstacles could not check the ardour of the Prussian officers and men, who on this occasion, vied with each other in passing defiles, in crossing marshes, in seizing the rising grounds, and in clearing ditches.

The battle near Prague.

A small check at the first.

However, their ardour had in the beginning of the engagement like to have ruined their cause. Too eager for action, the infantry began the attack so precipitately as to give the Austrians some advantage; which obliged them to fall back: but this

this check served only to whet their courage. The infantry immediately rallied, and advanced with an impetuosity, that was not to be resisted, attacked and entirely broke the enemy's right. The King was employed in taking the enemy in flank. But the whole plan of operations was almost disconcerted by a marshy ground, which unexpectedly stopt the advancing of M. Schwerin's army; without whose help, it was not possible to defeat the enemy. Therefore the Marshal dismounted, and entering the morass with the standard of the regiment in his hand, so encouraged his men, with crying out, " Let all brave Prussians follow me;" that they, inspired with the bravery of their heroic commander, in the 82d year of his age, and all their officers, who followed this example, pressed forward, and never abated in their ardour, till the enemy was totally routed, though their General was unfortunately killed by the first fire. The Austrian cavalry stood no more than three charges, and then retired in great confusion; the center being at the same time totally routed. The Prussian left wing filed off towards Micheley, and being there joined by the horse, renewed their attack upon the enemy retreating hastily towards Safzawa; while the right wing of the Prussians were diverting themselves with attacking the small remains of the left wing of the Austrians, and making themselves masters of three batteries. Prince Henry of Prussia and the Prince of Bevern performed wonders, making themselves masters of two batteries: and Prince Ferdinand of Brunswick took the left

A. D. 1757.

Whetted their resolution.

wing of the Auftrians in flank, while the King fecured the paffage of the Moldau with his left and a body of cavalry. However the Auftrians at firft received the enemy with great firmnefs and bravery; and did not give way, till they, after a long and obftinate engagement, were obliged to yield to fuperior abilities, and the fate of war.

Victory declares in favour of Pruffia.

After many fignal examples of valour on both fides, the Auftrians were driven from the field of battle; who attributed the ill fuccefs of the day to the advantage, which the Pruffians had of the wind, that blew the powder into the eyes of the Auftrians. Be that as it will: the King of Pruffia obtained a complete victory; took 60 pieces of cannon [x], all the tents and baggage, the military cheft, and the whole camp; ten ftandards and upwards of 4000 prifoners [y], amongft whom were 30 officers of rank; and they killed and wounded a very extraordinary number; amongft whom was M. Brown, who died of his wounds and chagrin foon after, at Prague.

Auftrian account of the lofs.

The Auftrians gave out that the Pruffians had 30,000 men killed and wounded in this action. But the account publifhed by the King of Pruffia, admits of no more than 2500 killed, amongft whom was M. Schwerin, the Prince of Holftein Beck, General d'Amftel, two Colonels and one

---

[x] Some accounts make them 250 pieces of cannon, which feems moft probable from the ftrength and extent of the camp, and the number of field pieces required in each regiment, in the time of action.

[y] Some accounts make them 10,000.

Lieutenant

Lieutenant Colonel: and about 3000 wounded, including six Generals.

A. D. 1757.

The fugitive Austrians took several roads. About 12,000 of their horse fled towards Benschau, where they afterwards assembled under General Pretlach. About 40,000 escaped their pursuers, and escorted Prince Charles of Lorrain and M. Brown into Prague: but suffered greatly in their retreat from a detachment under M. Keith, who pursued them up to the very gates of that city.

Austrian army dispersed.

Most of them got into Prague.

Two objects now presented themselves for his Prussian Majesty's attention. To avail himself of the present consternation and confusion of his enemy's troops; and to guard against the Imperial army of execution; the only force that could be brought against him with any hopes of success; and which was preparing to march for the relief of Prague and the Austrians. So that, while he took the resolution to besiege Prague; his Majesty commanded Colonel Meyer, with a battalion of Prussian pandours and 400 hussars, to cut off all subsistence for any army, that should march to the succour of the Austrians: which service he effectually performed, by destroying all their magazines, especially that considerable and valuable one erected at Pilsen. His expedition against Prague was so rapid, that he, in four days, surrounded the walls of that city, himself on one side, and M. Keith on the other side of the river, with lines and entrenchments, in such a manner, as entirely cut off all communication with the country;

Two objects to be considered.

To prevent another enemy advancing.

To besiege Prague.

A. D. 1757.

Strength of the garrison.

country; and shut up Prince Charles of Lorrain, M. Brown, two Princes of Saxony, the Prince of Modena, the Duke d'Aremberg, Count Lacy, several other persons of great distinction, and about 40,000 of the Austrian army, that had escaped him in the field and fled here for refuge: an army, it was then thought, strong enough to dispute their sovereign's cause in the field; and by no means commendable for placing their safety, within the walls of a city, where nothing but some fortunate accident, was like to deliver them from the enemy, after they had undergone every

Blockade formed.

hardship of famine, fire, and sword. So that when they saw their communication cut off, and that the Prussians were continually employed in strengthening the works of the blockade, they had formed, and had made themselves masters of Czifcaberg, a strong redoubt, on an eminence, that commands the city, without being able to recover that post, notwithstanding they had sallied out, and taken some other steps, for that pur-

A powerful sally, to clear the city of useless mouths.

pose; a design was formed to get rid of the useless mouths, which could serve only to consume the provisions, to bring on a famine, and perhaps a plague, or oblige them to surrender. This was to be done by forcing the Prussian lines: and 12,000 men were drawn out for that service; who were, with sword in hand, to open a way through the camp of the besiegers for those that were not wanted in the city: and in case an impression could be made on the lines, they were to be sus-

tained

tained by all the grenadiers, volunteers, pandours, and Hungarian infantry.

Every thing was prepared for this fally with the greatest vigour and privacy, and promised the desired success, under the cover of a very dark night. But Providence stept in between the King and his danger. A deserter, about eleven that same night, reveals the whole design to the royal ear. Heaven gave the alarm: the King in less than a quarter of an hour had his whole army under arms, and prepared to give the assailants a warm reception [z].

The Austrians, it seems, depending more on the obscurity of the night and a profound silence in their motions, than upon the use of their arms, charged the Prussian advanced posts before they were discovered; though the Prussians were forewarned of their attempt. They first attacked the camp of M. Keith, on the side of the little town, and the left wing of the Prussian army, that stretched along the Moldau; with hopes to destroy the batteries that were raising, and to gain the bridges of communication, thrown by the Prussians over the Moldau at Branick and Podbaba, about a quarter of a German mile above and below Prague. About two o'clock the enemy expected to surprize the miners: but they came a quarter of an hour after the miners had left work. However they fired a piece, which alarmed a piquet of one hundred of the Prussian guards sent to sustain the body that covered the works: but

A. D. 1757.

Betrayed by a deserter.

Fails.

[z] On the 23d of May.

A.D. 1757.

Loss.

the night was so dark, that they could not distinguish, who were friends, or foes, and so fell into confusion. This was remedied by Lieutenant Jork, who being sent with two platoons to reconnoitre the enemy, kindled a fire, the light of which discovered their disposition to Captain Rodig, who immediately formed the design of falling upon them in flank; which they performed effectually by firing in platoons, and mutually repeating the signal given by their commander. By which means, and keeping up a continual shooting, they made the Austrians believe them to be a numerous body; so that they fled with such precipitation, that many of them were drowned in the river; several deserted, and the rest returned to Prague.

At the same time the miners were attacked, a regiment of horse grenadiers, supported by the Hungarian infantry, attacked a Prussian redoubt, guarded by Prince Ferdinand of Brunswick's battalion. The Austrians returned thrice to the assault; and their musquetry kept an incessant fire upon the whole front of the Prussians, from the convent of St. Margaret to the river: by which the battalion suffered extremely.

As soon as day began to appear, the Prussians quitted their camp, to seek and to engage the enemy. They found Pandours in possession of a building called the Redhouse, at the bottom of a declivity before Wellastowitz, well barricadoed and supplied with cannon. But the battalion of Pannewitz, after two hours severe service, in the midst of a continual fire from both cannon and musquetry

musquetry drove them out; though they were not able to maintain the post; because the artillery of the city kept a continual fire upon it, from the moment it was known to be in the power of the Prussians. So that this house fell again into the hands of the Pandours.

A. D. 1757.

Thus ended the affair of this sally, which had been so well contrived. The Austrians left many [a] dead and wounded behind them; and many deserters and prisoners. It was also attended with considerable loss to the Prussians, both in officers and private men: and Prince Ferdinand, the King's youngest brother narrowly escaped, with a slight wound in his face, and a horse killed under him.

It appeared necessary to find them employment in Prague; and for that purpose especially, to hasten the approaches and to complete the batteries. The heavy artillery being arrived, four batteries began [b] to play with great execution from the banks of the Moldau. The Prince of Bevern was appointed to cover the siege with an army of 20,000 men. After a most dreadful storm of rain and thunder, as if it were to display how much more ruinous the malice of men may be, than the greatest terrors of nature, a rocket was thrown into the air, as a signal for the batteries to begin; and they discharged at the rate of 288 bombs every 24 hours, which were accompanied by vast numbers of red hot cannon balls, and other instruments of destruction. The besieged were not in

A most terrible bombardment.

---

[a] About 1000 killed and wounded.
[b] On the 29th of May in the evening.

a condition to return the fire with equal fury. Their want of proper artillery and ammunition furnished his Prussian Majesty with an opportunity, not to be expected, to pour destruction upon this unfortunate city, whose streets and squares were crouded with [c] horses, grown almost mad for want of forage; and whose houses, at last, took fire on the side of the Moldau, which heightened the misery of the citizens, and encouraged the besiegers to divest themselves of all humanity, and to practise every stratagem, to try every barbarous invention in the military art, to force them to surrender or capitulate. The bombardment never ceased night nor day. And the flames, at last got to such a head, that the fire was no sooner quenched in one part, than it broke out in another.

Thus, men, horses and houses were wrapped in flames and reduced to ashes; and the necessaries of life also consumed in this almost general conflagration; a still more moving scene presents itself. The principal magistrates, burghers and clergy were not suffered to open their mouths to the army, in the most submissive terms, in favour of their city, on the point of being reduced to a heap of rubbish. Two senators, more importunate than the rest, were hanged by order of the military power; and when the cry of the public increased for necessary subsistence, 12,000 of the most useless mouths were driven out to ask bread, or to fall under the sword, of the enemy.

[c] 12,000 horses.

Their starving condition had no weight in the reasonings of an enemy, whose success depended upon the increase of his adversary's distress. They were driven back, which soon reduced the city to the necessity of eating horse flesh. The horses which were starved for want of forage, were cut up and distributed amongst the garrison; and the citizens were glad to buy it at four pence per pound. But so long as their corn held out, the garrison was in no hurry to capitulate: of which there was yet no scarcity. Once more it was resolved to try the issue of sallys; and though they proved of no advantage otherwise, they harrassed the enemy, and obliged the Prussians, who had not a sufficient change to watch so numerous, resolute and desperate a garrison, to be always upon their guard, and might in time oblige them to raise the siege.

A. D. 1757.

Beat back.

Eat horse flesh.

Such was the critical situation of the affairs of the Empress Queen. All the passes of her kingdom of Bohemia towards Lusatia, Voigtland, Saxony and Glatz, in the possession of the King of Prussia; the flower of her armies and the chief commanders cooped up in Prague: the rest of her troops defeated, dispirited and dispersed in small parties, and flying to seek subsistence: the capital of Bohemia reduced by fire and famine to the last extremity: the army within on the point of surrendering prisoners of war: the whole kingdom without ready to submit to the will of the conquerors: all aid from Saxony entirely cut off: the Russians obliged to retreat: all the hereditary

Remarks on the critical state.

domi-

A. D. 1757.

dominions of the house of Austria open and exposed: Vienna itself not secure from a siege; and the Prussian troops deemed invincible! when two extraordinary incidents started up to convince the world that no power upon earth is to trust too much to his own wisdom and strength; and that there are resources in the womb of Providence, which if properly attended to and improved, are able to deliver us out of the most desperate circumstances.

King of Prussia's too great courage.

The irresistible success of his arms had so far got the better of the King's reason, that he suffered the small parties of the enemy to assemble in a body, in a situation [e] not less hazardous to be attacked, than the walls of Prague. He made too sure of reducing the city: and he made too light of breaking the lines and forcing the camp at Kolin, against which his Majesty, in person, marched on the 13th day of June, with a force very inadequate to attack an army of 60,000 men, fortified and commanded by a brave and experienced general. — A resolution so fraught with difficulties, that M. Keith remonstrated earnestly against this measure. The Marshal advised either to raise the siege and to attack the camp with the united forces of Prussia, or to proceed with the siege in the present manner, till the city should be obliged to capitulate, or till the Austrians in the camp should attempt to raise the siege. Because, from either of these resolutions there were hopes of success. The Prussian united forces might more probably carry their point against the

Resolves to attack the camp at Kolin.

Against M. Keith's opinion.

[e] At Kolin.

camp, than could be expected from the moft refolute efforts of the inferior ftrength of 32,000 men, which was the whole force fet a-part by the King for that fervice. And by continuing the fiege in its prefent form, he faid, it would either oblige the Auftrians within to furrender, which would leave all his Majefty's forces at liberty to act, as circumftances might require; or the Auftrians without, to quit their ftrong camp, and to attack him to their great difadvantage: for fo long as the Pruffians fhould continue within their lines before Prague, no army could attempt to raife the fiege, without fighting them upon terms nearly equal.

Sage as this counfel might be, the King's courage got the better of his judgment: elated with victory, impetuous in his valour, and depending upon the difcipline of his foldiers, in which he expected to gain the fuperiority, (againft him greatly in numbers) he bid defiance to all oppofition, depended folely on the courage and victorious arm, which had carried him through all oppofition, and delivered him out of all difficulties, and actuated with a kind of military enthufiafm, he marched towards Kolin with affurance of fuccefs.

How the King was mifled.

To humble this fpirit of prefumption, there ftarted up a General, whom the neceffities of the times recommended to a fervice of that interefting nature, which was no lefs than to fave the Emprefs Queen's dominions from entire deftruction, and to deliver her armies from the coercive power of a moft furprizing adventurer; already in pof-

A. D. 1757.

The character and conduct of Count Daun.

session of all that fertile country between the Egra and the Moldau. This was Leopold Count Daun, who had never commanded in chief before; but had acquired great experience in the most illustrious scenes of action, and under the most distinguished Generals of this century, in various parts of Europe; and particularly the favourite of the great Kevenhuller: yet, neither his connections with those great soldiers, nor his noble extraction, from a very ancient and great family, had ever procured him any favour from court; his promotion in the army being entirely owing to his merit. His way to preferment was a kind of index to his future conduct, in possession of the highest command. It was slow and silent, resolved to gain that by mere dint of superior worth, which others sought and pushed for with much intrigue, hurry and bustle, amongst their friends at court.

This was the temper, this the character of the General, who now entered the theatre of war, to stem the torrent of disgrace, and to save his country from utter ruin. His firmness, sagacity, penetration and cautiousness recommended him, at this critical juncture, like another Fabius, to check the fire and vigour of the Prussian monarch, who like Hannibal, set no bounds to his ambition and arms; and did almost ruin himself by trusting too much to his good fortune and military skill.

This General had been sent from Vienna to the grand army; and did not arrive till after its defeat. The day after the battle he had got no farther than Boemischbrod, a few miles from Prague: where

where he met a large body of Auſtrian horſe, under General Serbeloni, which, with ſome other of the fugitive corps and broken remains of the Auſtrian army, Marſhal Daun collected with an activity, that attracted the attention of his Pruſſian Majeſty; who detached the Prince of Bevern, with 20 battalions, and 30 ſquadrons, to prevent their numbers becoming formidable. A moſt prudent ſtep: and could it **have** ſucceeded, the fate of Bohemia, and perhaps of the Houſe of **Auſtria**, would have been therewith decided. But Daun acted upon more ſure principles. He was too cautious and penetrating to ſtake the ruin of his Imperial Miſtreſs on the chance of a battle, to be fought by a few diſpirited, ſhattered troops, ſunk with diſgrace, and in great want of every thing, with an army fluſhed with victory, and well ſupplied with all the neceſſaries for a ſoldier's life and for action.

A. D. 1757. Collects the ſcattered remains of the Auſtrian army. Prince of Bevern ſent to attack him.

As ſoon as it was known that the Pruſſians were in motion, to attack him, Daun retreated to the Elbe, and entrenched himſelf ſtrongly, and with great advantage of ground at Kolin; where he could receive recruits, ſent daily to his camp from Moravia, and heavy artillery from **the fortreſs of** Olmutz; and inſpire the garriſon in Prague with hopes, that he would ſoon be in a condition to raiſe the ſiege: he was likewiſe ſo ſituated that he could harraſs the enemy by cutting off their convoys; and weaken their efforts againſt Prague, **by** obliging the King to employ near a moiety of his army in watching his motions.

Daun retires to Kolin. Its advantageous ſituation.

By

A. D.
1757.

His use of this camp.

By keeping close within this camp, he had nothing to fear from the Prince of Bevern; whom he frequently alarmed by a detachment of Hungarians and Saxons under General Nadasti, who made several motions with advantage; and by another of hussars under Colonel Putkammer, who passed the defile of Czirkwitz and spread an alarm through the whole camp of the enemy: and thus by degrees, he restored the languishing and almost desponding spirits of his own troops. Besides, he rendered his situation irksome and embarrassing to a monarch of an enterprising and impetuous disposition: and did not doubt, but he should be able, by retarding the enemy's operations, and assiduously avoiding a precipitate action, until the Prussian vigour should be exhausted, their strength impaired by desertion and losses, the fire and ardour of their genius extinguished by continual fatigue and incessant alarms, to oblige the Prussians not only to raise the siege of Prague, but to evacuate the whole kingdom of Bohemia.

King of Prussia's reasons for attacking Count Daun.

The event justified his conduct. The army at Kolin increased daily in number; and consequently became more formidable to the enemy. The King of Prussia, who had depended upon the impossibility of such a numerous army subsisting so long within the walls of a city, grew daily more and more impatient, at the length of the siege; and he began, already, to foresee the fatality of permitting Count Daun's army to grow so powerful, as in a short time, it might not only be too much for the Prince of Bevern, but strong enough

enough to force him to raise the siege. This decoyed him into the snare spread by the Austrian general; who was at the head of 60,000 men, well disciplined and deeply entrenched; defended by a prodigious train of artillery, placed on redoubts and batteries, erected on the most advantageous posts; with lines and heavy pieces of cannon at every accessible part of the camp, and rendered almost inaccessible by difficult defiles at the foot of the hills.

<small>A. D. 1757.</small>
<small>Strength of the camp at Kolin.</small>

How formidable soever this appearance of the Austrian camp may be, it rather served to sharpen, than to blunt the edge of his Prussian Majesty's martial genius. He joined the Prince of Bevern at Milkowitz, about six miles from Prague, with three battalions of infantry and one regiment of cuirassiers, brought from before Prague, and with five battalions and ten squadrons he had picked up on the road, which had been employed to guard the Safawa. He also had ordered Prince Maurice of Anhalt Dessau to follow him next day with six battalions and one regiment of cuirassiers. Which was punctually done. Thus the whole force of the Prussian army, after their junction, consisted of 32 battalions and 111 squadrons of horse, dragoons and hussars, making 32,000 men, upon the nearest computation; and without further delay they advanced to seek the enemy, whom they found most advantageously posted, and covered with a very numerous artillery, upon the high grounds between Genritz and St. John the Baptist; greatly reinforced since the King's march

<small>King of Prussia marches to attack Count Daun.</small>
<small>His force.</small>

A. D. 1757.

Came to action.

march from his camp before Prague, and drawn up in three lines. It was now about three in the afternoon, when the first onset was made. The Austrians waited the approach of the enemy, as a people secure in their situation, rather than in their numbers and courage. Their artillery were placed with the utmost advantage for defence, and charged with chain and grapeshot, which poured like hail upon the Prussians, who bid defiance to difficulties and death, and marched up the hills with a firmness and intrepidity, that must have daunted and driven back any troops, that were not determined to conquer or to die. The slaughter of the advancing army was most horrible; the Prussians were obliged not only to pass through the thickest fire, that can be imagined, but to fight their way over heaps of their brave companions, mowed down by the cannon of the enemy. Yet inured to conquer, and spurning at danger, the Prussians drove their enemies from two eminences, fortified with heavy cannon, and from two villages defended by several battalions. For a while victory seemed to incline towards the Prussians; but, as they attacked the third eminence, their prodigious loss of men, the obstinacy of the enemy, and the advantage the Austrian cavalry gained, by their numbers and situation, to flank them with grape and chain-shot, the brave few that were left in battle, to contend for victory, were put into disorder, and driven back. However, preferring a glorious death in the presence of their King, to an inglorious retreat, that should cancel the honour,

nour, and wither the laurels, they had brought into the field from Reichenberg and the neighbourhood of Prague, they rallied and refumed the charge with double ardour, not only once more, but feven times fucceffively; led on by that valiant foldier and great general Prince Ferdinand; but not being in a condition to maintain the ground, where their cavalry could not act, and againft the obftinacy and numbers of an enemy, who had the advantage of fituation, artillery and entrenchments, under the command of a general of the greateft fkill and conduct, they gave it up.

The King, like a man in defpair, more willing to meet death, than to carry the caufe of difcontent in his breaft, refolves to wipe off the difgrace, which now appeared ready to fall upon his arms, through his own rafhnefs, by a more furious effort. With this refolution he put himfelf at the head of his cavalry, and attacks the left wing of the enemy, with the greateft bravery, and expofed his perfon, to animate his foldiers, in the moft perilous fituations. Yet neither valour, conduct, nor even defperation was able to mend a loft caufe. So far his tutelar genius accompanied him in this diftrefs, as to favour the retreat of the remains of the braveft army, that ever faced an enemy. The King drew off his forces from the field of blood, for this might more properly be called a carnage, than a battle, with all his baggage and artillery, in fight of the enemy, in good order, and without one attempt to purfue him.

Defperate refolution of the King.

Retreats.

A.D. 1757.

Remarkable bravery on both sides.

Thus ended that precipitate resolution, taken by his Prussian Majesty, contrary to the good advice of his faithful Keith, whose valour was tutored by experience. However, this engagement may be accounted a trial of skill and courage between the two powers concerned therein. For, almost all the officers, on each side, distinguished themselves: The Prussians, to recommend themselves under the inspection of their Sovereign, and to support the applause already gained by their victories: the Austrians, to save their country from falling a sacrifice to the jealousy and resentment of the King of Prussia. Both the King's brothers were in the field, and they did all that could be expected from the King of Prussia's brothers. Count Daun had a horse killed under him, and received two slight wounds, as he emulated the conduct of his royal adversary in every perilous situation. The losses of both armies were extraordinary in their men.

Losses on both sides.

The Prussians had upwards of eight thousand killed and wounded: many were made prisoners [f], or deserted. The Austrians had above ten thousand killed and wounded.

King of Prussia blames himself.

The loss of this battle the King attributed wholly to himself. One false motion frequently proves decisive. He exposed the infantry naked and uncovered by the cavalry, to the chain and grape-shot of the enemy's whole artillery; which was an error, that could not be retrieved, on

---

[f] Amongst whom were the two generals Treskow and Pannewitch.

ground,

ground, where the cavalry could not be brought up to cover the infantry. The Austrians did actually fly before his Majesty's victorious troops, at the beginning of the engagement: but the Prussians having neither horse nor artillery to enable them to sustain the shock of the Austrian fire, which made terrible havock amongst their ranks, it was impossible for them to do more than they did. The ardour of the conquerors being checked they were necessitated to submit to fate, and retreat, not from the enemy, who never dared to follow them, when ever they fell back; but from those engines of destruction, whose murdering fury they had no means to resist, nor numbers to supply.

However, the Prussian hero did not sink under this reverse of fortune, he supported himself with a dignity becoming a great King, who, notwithstanding this severe trial of his fortitude, and the cloud, which appeared to overcast his glory, and to darken the way to future success, was convinced of his error, acknowledged his fault, and did every thing that one, in his situation, was able to do, to extricate himself out of the present difficulty, and to continue the war with more advantage: So that whatever small blemish his military conduct might have suffered, his reputation rose higher and higher in the opinion of all judicious men, by the candid and noble manner in which he acknowledged his mistake; by the firmness, with which he bore his misfortune, and by those

those aftonishing strokes of genius and heroifm, by which he retrieved his lofs.

His letter to Earl Marfhal.

His Majefty, in a letter to Earl Marfhal, gives the beft narrative and proof of this affair. He firft does juftice to his enemy's valour. "The imperial grenadiers, fays he, are an admirable corps: one hundred companies defended a rifing ground, which my beft infantry could not carry. Ferdinand, who commanded them, returned feven times to the charge; but to no purpofe. At firft he maftered a battery, but could not hold it. The enemy had the advantage of a numerous and well-ferved artillery. It did honour to Lichtenftein, who had the direction." He then extols the courage of his own men. "Only the Pruffian army can difpute it with him." But "my infantry were too few. All my cavalry were prefent, and idle fpectators, excepting a bold pufh by my houfhold troops and fome dragoons." He then points out the caufes of his defeat: "Ferdinand attacked without powder; the enemy, in return, were not fparing of theirs. They had the advantage of a rifing ground of intrenchments, and of a prodigious artillery. Several of my regiments were repulfed by their mufquetry." Speaking of his brothers: "Henry, fays he, performed wonders, I tremble for my worthy brothers: they are too brave." He takes the blame on himfelf. "Fortune turned her back on me this day. I ought to have expected it. She is a female, and I am no gallant. In fact

"I ought

"I ought to have had more infantry.—Success, my dear Lord, often occasions a destructive confidence. Twenty-four battalions were not sufficient to dislodge sixty thousand men from an advantageous post. Another time we hope to do better.—I have no reason to complain of the bravery of my troops, or the experience of my officers. I alone was in the fault: and I hope to repair it;" was the generous declaration of his Prussian Majesty to one of his general officers.

His shattered army having made a safe retreat from the enemy's defiles and eminences; the next and immediate care was to prevent the bad effects of this day's work, should the news thereof reach Prague before he could take proper measures to secure his men, and all the matters employed in the reduction of that city. Therefore, though he had been so greatly fatigued by the service of the day, at the head of every attack, on horseback, he left his army at Nimberg, under the command of the Prince of Bevern, and with fresh horses, and an escort of a dozen huzzars, he set out in person for his camp before Prague, and arrived there in the morning without halting. He placed double sentinels at all the avenues and advanced posts, to prevent intelligence arriving from Kolin; and his orders for sending off all his artillery, ammunition and baggage, were executed with such expedition, that the tents were struck, and the army on their march, before the garrison were informed of the mighty cause of their deliverance.

His expedition and success in raising the siege of Prague.

A.D. 1757.

A sally made by the garrison.

verance. Prince Charles of Lorrain, who held the chief command alone, after the death of M. Brown, who died in Prague of his wounds received on the 6th of May, made a sally with a large body of Austrians; but could do no further mischief, than kill about two hundred of the Prussians in the rear of M. Keith's division; the corps commanded by the Prince of Prussia, having marched all night, by another rout, to join the Prince of Bevern at Nimberg, was not so much exposed to the enemy.

Prussian army takes different routs.

M. Keith made the best of his way towards Saxony; and was left by the King at the head of 25,000 men to guard the passes. His Majesty and Prince Henry his brother, made the best of their way to Pirna, with another part of the army, and encamped in that neighbourhood. The Prince of Prussia retreated into Lusatia, with his division of the army: where he was soon after, in danger of being surrounded by the Austrians, who followed him, laid the town of Zittau in ashes by a dreadful bombardment; and obliged the garrison to surrender. This called for immediate relief. His Prussian Majesty did not hesitate a moment to march from Pirna, with part of his army, and leaving the remainder under M. Keith, to guard the passes of the mountains of Bohemia, he, by forced marches, came suddenly upon the Austrians, obliged them to retire, and delivered his brother's army.

Austrians pursue into Lusatia.

Zittau bombarded.

King of Prussia marches to the relief of his brother.

His other mortifications.

The action at Kolin was not the only mortification, which his Prussian Majesty met with this summer.

summer. His territories in Westphalia were over- A. D.
run and laid under contribution, and seized by 1757.
the French, for the use of the Empress Queen:
and the army of observation, paid by Great Britain,
and lately put in motion under his Royal Highness the Duke of Cumberland, was not in a condition to stop their progress, or to make a sufficient diversion in his favour.

His Royal Highness the Duke of Cumberland The ar-
not only wanted strength to act offensively against my of ob-
the advancing enemy; but he found himself ob- under the
liged to conform to the Hanoverian council as- Cumber-
signed him, for his conduct in the command of land.
the army of observation; whose favourite object
was to keep clear of any operations and connections, which might expose their Electorate to a
criminal process in the Imperial courts; and to act
only on the defensive, with expectation that the
French would not dare to act in the hostile manner, as they did, against a German Electorate; or
that, in case of such an atrocious infringement of
the Imperial compact, for the preservation of all
parts of the Germanic body, the Emperor would
be obliged to protect them from a foreign and un-
provoked invader.

Such was the situation of his Royal Highness French ar-
at Bielfeld [g], when the plan of operations were M. d'E-
settled trees.

[g] His army consisted of thirty-seven battalions and thirty-
four squadrons; viz. three Prussian regiments, that retired
from Wesel, six battalions and six squadrons, posted at Bielfeld,
under command of Lieutenant-General Baron de Sporcken;

R 2   six

A. D. 1757.

In great want of provisions, &c.

settled between him and the Hanoverian generals; and the French army, consisting at that time of seventy battalions [h], forty squadrons [i] and fifty-two pieces of cannon; besides a body of cavalry left at Ruremond for conveniency of forage; of which the French were greatly in want, as well as of almost every necessary of life, which want daily increased by the measures taken by the Duke to retard and to discourage their advancing to the Weser: for, the nearer they approached the seat of the army of observation, the greater they found the difficulty to get provisions. The country was not able to supply all their wants, and the little that could be found was not to be carried away without opposition, and disadvantageous skirmishes; for the Hanoverians penetrated so far as the country of Paderborn, and carried off a convoy of wheat and oats, to be laid up in the Electorate of Cologne for the use of the French army.

Several skirmishes.

Wise dispositions made by the Duke of Cumberland.

Certainly no dispositions could be made with greater propriety, to convey the most advantageous ideas of the martial and political abilities of a commander in chief, than those, which his Royal Highness the Duke of Cumberland laid

six battalions at Hervorden, under Lieutenant-General de Block: six battalions and four squadrons, between Hervorden and Minden, under Major-General Ledebour; seven battalions and ten squadrons, near Hamelen, under Lieutenant-General d'Oberg; and five battalions and four squadrons, near Niemburg, under Major-General Haufs.

[h] A French battalion is from five to six hundred men.
[i] A French squadron is from two hundred and fifty to three hundred horse.

down

down, advised, and maintained to the utmoſt of his power; ſo far, we humbly preſume to ſay, as his ſtrength in the field, and his weight in the council, under which he was obliged to act, would enable and permit him to diſplay the military knowledge of his heroic genius. But, when he perceived that the French were under the deſperate neceſſity of fighting or ſtarving; that neverthelefs he could not draw them to an engagement, with the advantage he had formed to himſelf, by placing his camp between Bielfeld and Hervorden; and that the enemy, by a vaſt ſuperiority of men, would be able to get between him and the Weſer, and that they were making diſpoſitions even to ſurround his ſmall army, on the ſide of Burghotte: his Royal Highneſs withdrew his poſts from Paderborn and Ritzberg, leaving nothing of ſervice behind them, and, at length, broke up his camp at Bielfeld, to a more advantageous and ſafe ſituation; as it was impoſſible on that ground to withſtand the force of the enemy.

His reaſon for retreating from Bielfield.

No troops could retire in better order: and the corps poſted at Bielfeld, to cover the retreat, with orders, upon the approach of the French, to obſerve their motions, and to regulate their own conduct, accordingly, behaved with ſo good a countenance, that they made their own retreat good after a feint reſiſtance [k]. This opened a way for the

Retreats in good order.

---

[k] They found nothing in this town, but the remains of a magazine in flames; to which the Germans had ſet fire. But the French account of this retreat is very different, who ſay, That

A.D. 1757.

the French army to get plentiful supplies of all neceſſaries. Which enabled them to purſue their ſucceſs.

The French advance.

The allies rendezvouzed at Cofeldt, and encamped there on the 14th and 15th. The French in the mean time ſummoned the corps at Hervorden, and made a feint, as if they would attack the town, but marched off, without making any further attempt. By this time the whole French army was collected, and obliged the allies to paſs the Weſer. Which was performed with very inconſiderable loſs, and that only in the rear of the parties, as they retreated from their ſeveral poſts.

The Duke retreats beyond the Weſer.

When the Duke foreſaw that there was no ſtanding againſt the ſuperior power of the enemy, and that his chief dependance was upon the defence of the Weſer; his Royal Highneſs made the beſt and moſt active diſpoſitions to ſecure the paſſes of that

That on the 13th in the evening, Colonel Fiſcher, with his corps and ſome grenadiers attacked Bielfeld, without much reſiſtance, at firſt; that the Pruſſians in the left wing of the Duke's army, threw in a reinforcement, which made a vigorous defence. That at break of day, this left wing, compoſed of Pruſſians, Heſſians, and Brunſwickians, was attacked, defeated, and driven from Bielfeld; on which the right wing, conſiſting of Hanoverians, took to flight. That immediately after the action, the French pitched their tents on the ſpot from whence the allies had been driven. That they took ten pieces of cannon, beſides ſeveral baggage-waggons; and loſt no officer of note. And that on the ſide of the vanquiſhed party, there were ſeveral officers of rank among the ſlain, particularly the generals Einſiedel and Junckheim.

I

river,

river, which he paſſed, unmoleſted in the rear, with all his ammunition, artillery, baggage and troops, between Minden and Oldendorp, a camp being prepared for their reception, in a moſt advantageous ſituation, having the Weſer in front, and the right and left covered with eminences and moraſſes.

A. D. 1757.

In this camp, it is very clear that the Duke was determined to diſpute the paſſage of the Weſer with the enemy. But how was the world diſappointed of their expectations, when they were informed by authority, that the beſt diſpoſition, that the beſt general in the univerſe could deviſe and make, was made to ſerve no other purpoſe than to lie upon their arms, to witneſs the uninterrupted paſſage of an enemy, who had as much power to force them to retire in the country beyond the Weſer, as on the nether ſide, when they had nothing more than an army, that could not ſtand before them in the field, to encounter. Here the weight of Hanoverian councils appeared in the ballance againſt reaſon, againſt the judgment and inclination of the commander in chief. Forbearance and non-reſiſtance were now the maxims of the Hanoverian chancery. Their own innocence, inoffenſive conduct, and the juſtice and right of protection, which an Electorate can demand under the capitulations of the Golden Bull, were inſiſted upon, as arguments for the ſecurity of Hanover and its dependences againſt France, in preference to the vigorous meaſures, provided by his Royal Highneſs for defence, by way of arms,

Remarks on this ſituation.

R 4   againſt

A. D.
1757.

against an invader, that bid defiance to all laws human and divine; and, what was more than they were willing to underſtand, acted in concert with the Lord-paramount of the Empire, to deprive the allies of Great Britain of the means to favour the deſigns of Pruſſia.

The French paſs over the Weſer.

However this might be, the French were ſo little diſmayed at the Duke's well-choſen camp, that they ſeemed to be in the ſecret of the cauſe of the Hanoverian ſecurity; for, they advanced to the Weſer without delay, and paſſed that river on the 10th and 11th of July, without fear or the the loſs of a ſingle man.

Marſhal d'Etrees being informed that his magazines of proviſions were well furniſhed, his ovens eſtabliſhed, and the artillery and pontoons arrived at the deſtined places, ordered Lieutenant-General Broglio, with ten battalions, twelve ſquadrons, and ten pieces of cannon, to march to Engheren; Lieutenat-General M. de Chevert, with ſixteen battalions, three brigades of carabineers, the royal hunters, and ſix hundred huſſars, to march to Hervorden; and Lieutenant Marquis d'Armentieres, with twelve battalions and ten ſquadrons to march to Ulrickhauſen. All theſe troops being arrived in their camp on the 4th inſtant, halted the 5th. On the 6th twenty-two battalions and thirty-two ſquadrons, under the command of the Duke of Orleans, marched to Ulrickhauſen, from whence M. d'Armentieres had ſet out early in the morning, with the corps under his command, and by briſk marches got, on the 7th by eleven

at

at night, to Blanckenhove, where he found the boats which had gone from Ahrenſberg. The bridges were built, the cannon planted, and the entrenchments at the head of the bridges compleated, in the night between the 7th and 8th. The Marſhal having ſent away part of his baggage from Bielfeld on the 6th, went in perſon, on the 7th at eleven o'clock, to Horn, and the 8th to Brakel. On advice that M. d'Armentieres had thrown his bridges acroſs, without oppoſition, and was at work on his entrenchments, he went on the 9th to Blakenhove, to ſee the bridges and intrenchments, and afterwards advanced to examine the firſt poſition he intended for this army, and came down the right ſide of the Weſer to the abby of Corvey, where he forded the Weſer, with the Princes of the blood, and their attendants. The 10th in the morning he got on horſeback by four o'clock, to ſee the Duke of Orleans's diviſion file off, which arrived at Corvey at ten o'clock; as alſo that of M. d'Armentieres, which arrived at eleven; and that of M. Souvré, which arrived at noon. The Marſhal, having examined the courſe of the Weſer, cauſed the bridges of pontoons to be laid within gunſhot of the abbey, where the Viſcount de Turenne paſſed the river in 1673, and where Broglio and Chevert's diviſions paſſed it the 12th and 13th. M. de Chevert, and the Duke of Broglio being informed of what was to be done upon the Upper Weſer, made an attack upon Minden, and carried it.

Whilſt

A.D. 1757.

Lien and Embden surprized by the French.

Whilst these operations were carried on, the French Marshal detached the Marquis d'Anvel, with a strong party, to favour the designs of the Empress Queen, in East Friesland, who made himself master of Lien, and then proceeded to surprize Embden, the only sea port under the dominion of the King of Prussia, which surrendered by capitulation, without the least opposition; the garrison, which consisted of 400 men, having mutined against their officers; because they did not think themselves a sufficient force for the defence of the town. The French published ordinances for the security of the religion and commerce of the city; and for prohibiting the exportation of corn and forage out of that principality; and obliged the inhabitants to take an oath of allegiance to the French King.

The French raise contributions in Hanover.

Whatever were the real motives of the Hanoverian backwardness to attack the invaders of their country, they certainly paid dear for their inactivity or timidity. The French proceeded immediately to raise heavy contributions in Hanover[1] This seemed to convince those passive or pusillanimous advocates for non-resistance, that it was time to embrace and follow more salutary advice, and no longer to imagine, that their Electoral dominions were so secured, as to have nothing to fear from a powerful and perfidious neighbour.

[1] The French General, from his camp at Stadt-Oldendorf, sent to the regency of Hanover a requisition, dated 21 July, demanding that deputies should be sent to his head quarters to treat about contributions.

It was resolved to make a stand at Haftenbeck, within a few miles of Hammelen, where it was judged, that the ground would deprive the enemy of that advantage, they so much depended upon, in regard to the superiority of their numbers. The Duke detached 12,000 men to seize the important pass of Stadt Oldendorf; but the French had got possession of it already, and a few days after drove the Hanoverian parties from the village of Lutford. Their camp was now transferred to the fine plain of Stadt Oldendorff.

A. D. 1757. The battle at Haftenbeck.

These were only preludes to the main design of the French; which was to force the allies to battle. Accordingly, as soon as His Royal Highness the Duke of Cumberland perceived the intention of the enemy was to attack him, he drew up his little army on the height between the Weser and the woods, with his right towards the river, his left close to the woods; on the point of which he erected a battery of 12 pounders and haubitzers, supported by the hunters and two battalions of grenadiers, posted in the corner of the wood upon the left of the battery, under the command of Major General Schulenberg, with the village of Hoftenbeck in his front. There was a hollow way from the left of the village to the battery, and a continual morass on the other side of Haftenbeck to his right. In the evening of the 24th he called in all his out posts, and kept the whole army on their arms all night; on the 25th in the morning the enemy advanced in columns, and made an appearance to attack the

right

A.D. 1757.

right, the left and center; but nothing more was done than a severe cannonade, which continued all day, from a train much superior to the Duke's artillery. The next night was also spent by the allies, upon their arms: the battery at the end of the wood was repaired, and Count Sculenberg reinforced with a battalion of grenadiers and two pieces of cannon. He also ordered four more battalions of grenadiers, under Major General Hardenberg, to support that battery; caused another battery to be erected of 12 and 6 pounders, behind the village of Haftenbeck, and provided in every respect to give the enemy a warm reception: and then, at day light, got on horse back to reconnoitre the position of the enemy. And at five next morning the French renewed the cannonade; which now was levelled particularly against an Hanoverian battery, supported by the Hessian infantry and cavalry. The artillery was served on this attack with great fury and skill, and the place was defended with extraordinary resolution and incredible bravery. Between seven and eight the musquetry began to play on the Hanoverian left; and the connonading continued without intermission for six hours; when his Royal Highness ordered Major General Behr, with three battalions of Brunswick, to sustain the grenadiers in the woods if necessary. The fire of the small arms increasing, His Royal Highness detached three Hanoverian battalions and six squadrons round the wood by Afferde, who towards the close of the day surprized several squadrons of the enemy, that

they

they had not time to charge, and drove them back to their army. Yet how neceſſary and wiſe ſoever thoſe diſpoſitions were made with the grenadiers in the wood, thoſe troops, as ſoon as they perceived the enemy's troops endeavouring to penetrate that way, quitted their poſts, and joined the left wing. By which miſconduct, the French got poſſeſſion of the Hanoverian battery on the left without oppoſition. It is true this afforded an opportunity for the hereditary Prince of Brunſwick, at the head of a battalion of Wolfenbuttle guards, and another of Hanoverians, to diſtinguiſh himſelf, by retaking the battery, with their bayonets fixed, from a much ſuperior force of the enemy. But the French having got poſſeſſion not only of the woods, but of a height, that flanked both the lines of infantry, and the battery of the allies, and were able to ſupport their attack under the cover of a hill, his Royal Highneſs conſidering the great ſuperiority of the enemy, both in numbers and artillery, and that it was impoſſible to diſlodge them from their poſt without expoſing his own troops to too great a hazard, ordered a retreat, and drew off his army to Hamelen in very good order.

A. D. 1757.

This action may be ſaid to have continued three days; and was diſputed with great vigour and ſkill on both ſides, and with ſuch doubtful ſucceſs, that it is a doubt to this day, which of the armies had a right to claim the victory. As for the loſs, it was much leſs on the ſide of the allies. The killed, wounded and miſſing, did not exceed

Remarks thereon.

1454

1454[m]. The French according to their own account loft 2000 and upwards. This is certain, the French, who marched into the woods of Lauenftein, were feized with fuch a panic, that upon the bare imagination of being attacked by the Hanoverians, they fired upon one another: fo that had the grenadiers, &c. which His Royal Highnefs had wifely difpofed and ftationed in thefe woods, kept their pofts, as they in duty ought to have done, they might have improved that confternation; and by a well regulated attack upon that party of the enemy, their defeat might have been left undifputed. But the fate of this day is but one example of many, that fhews how the Hanoverian miniftry difapproved of the meafures taken by their fovereign for their defence. It is more than conjecture, that they would have been much better fatisfied to put themfelves under the protection of France, than join the moft powerful armies to defend their territories from a French invafion.

In this temper continually, they had by retreating before the enemy, prevailed with the Duke to come to fuch an iffue, that nothing but fuperior judgment in the military art, could have delivered his army, on this occafion, from falling a prey to the enemy. This was a deliverance beyond all expectation: and could his Royal Highnefs have been at liberty to retire with his army to Magdeburg, the French would have felt their lofs in this

---

[m] 327 killed, and 1127 wounded and miffing.

action

action very severely; and soon have been obliged to quit the Electorate of Hanover, or to maintain an army, that would have exhausted their finances, to cover an acquisition, not able to pay the expence.

A. D. 1757.

But the fear they now adopted for the archives, and many valuable effects, that had been carried to, and deposited at Stade, a small town near the mouth of the Elbe, prevailed with His Royal Highness to make all his dispositions and marches after this battle, to cover Stade from a surprize by the enemy, in the manner we have seen them subdue Embden. Thus he left a garrison at Hamelen and retreated to Nienburg, and then to Hoya: in whose neighbourhood he encamped the remains of his army, after sending away all his magazines, sick and wounded, in order, as he was advised, to cover Bremen and Verden, and to preserve a communication with Stade. An excellent situation for the purpose, had they, that insisted upon the measure, provided him also with an army capable of disputing the ground with an enemy, that was expected, and upon their march, to force the way. But could not be expected, in his circumstances, to have been less ruinous, than will be seen below.

Reasons for retreating towards Stade.

Sends off all his sick, wounded, and magazines.

Upon the Duke's retreat from Hamelen, it soon submitted to the French, by a capitulation, which did no credit to the garrison: for they took no care of the sick and wounded; who thereby became prisoners of war. The French dismantled the walls, and carried off 60 brass cannon, several mortars, 40 ovens, large quantities of provisions and

Hamelen surrenders to the French.

and ammunition, and part of the equipage of the Duke's army.

M. d'Eftrees fuperceeded.

Here the French halted for some time. Advice was arrived in the French army, that the Duke de Richelieu was appointed, and on his way to fuperceed M. d'Eftrees, and to take upon him the command of the French army in Lower Saxony; to which poft he had been raifed by court intrigue, through the means of Madam Pampadour, the King of France's female favourite. M. d'Etrees had immediately after the battle of Haftenbeck, detached 4000 men to take poffeffion of the Electorate of Hanover, and to lay it under contribution. The fame was done in the territories of the Duke of Wolfenbuttle, and in many places in the dutches of Bremen and Verden. But nothing

Richelieu arrives and takes the command.

more was done till Richelieu arrived; who two days after his arrival at Hamelen, detached the Duke de Chevreufe, with 2000 men, to take

Takes poffeffion of Hanover.

poffeffion of the city of Hanover; and dubbed him governor of the firft fruits of his promotion. A circumftance appears in this expedition, which gives a fhrewed fufpicion of too good an underftanding between the regency of Hanover and their French invaders: for, there was not the leaft refiftance on the part of the city; and the garrifon were permitted, after they had laid down their

M. de Contades how received at Warburg.

arms, to retire wherever they pleafed. M. de Contades, who was fent alfo with a detachment to reduce the territories of Heffe Caftle, was met at Warburg by the Prince of Heffe's mafter of the horfe, more like a friend than an enemy, with

affurassurances that the French should be furnished with every thing the country could afford; and the magistrates of Cassel presented him with the keys of their city. {A. D. 1757.}

Having thus displayed a kind of sovereignty in Lower Saxony and made all safe in the rear, Richelieu bent his thoughts towards the allied army, encamped at Hoya. His motions were watched. So that as soon as His Royal Highness the Duke of Cumberland was informed that Richelieu had passed the Aller, with a large body of troops, in the night of the 24th of August, he decamped, and ordered his army to march and secure the important pass and post of Rothenburg; which was done the next day; and he encamped again with his whole army behind the Wummer; a very strong and advantageous situation, between Rothenburg and Otterſburg. {Richelieu pursues the allied army. Advantageous camp of the allied army.}

This motion of the allies left Bremen and Verden to the mercy of the French, who immediately entered Verden[n], and detached a sufficient force to take possession of Bremen, which opened her gates to them on the 29th. Two principalities, for whose fate the Hanoverian ministry did not seem to be under much concern, as not being an original part of their Electoral dominions; but a purchase made by King George I[o]. {Bremen and Verden seized by the French.}

The French halted again, till they had seized all the posts round the Duke's army; which

[n] On the 26th of August.
[o] For the sum of 250,000 l. sterling.

VOL. II.   S   putting

putting him upon the neceffity of making another march, to prevent his communication with Stade being cut off; which the Hanoverian miniftry infifted fhould be covered, at all events; His Royal Highnefs retreated, firft, to Selfingen, and from thence under the cannon of Stade: where His Royal Highnefs was made to believe, That he fhould be able to maintain his ground, between the Aller and the Elbe, and be effectually fupported by four Englifh men of war, &c. which at that time lay at anchor off that port, in cafe the French would venture to attack his army.

A.D. 1757.
The allied army retire to Stade.

In this expectation His Royal Highnefs made his difpofitions, and took his meafures for defence; and particularly he detached fome troops with artillery to Buck-Schantz, and with orders to defend that poft to the laft extremity. But thefe hopes foon vanifhed. The French followed him ftep by ftep, and having cooped the allies up in this corner, which left no more room for the retreat of an army, that was not in a condition to advance; (or, perhaps under fuch reftraints, that the generaliffimo had it not in his power to rifk a battle; as all the world are fatisfied the Duke would have done, both now and long before, who have the leaft conception of his Royal Highnefs's valour and impetuofity, animated by the examples of the Englifh atchievements at Creffy and Agincourt) they hemmed them in on every fide, and, notwithftanding the four men of war in the river, they got poffeffion of a fort at the mouth of the Zwinga, which cut off the Duke's communication with

Meafures taken for defence.

Purfued by the French.

Gain the advantage of their fituation.

with the Elb. Under this preffure of the moft hazardous circumftances, not in a condition to fight, not in a fituation to retreat, nor covered, as it would have been of the utmoft fervice at the laft extremity, by a refpectable fquadron of men of war; and urged by the Hanoverian miniftry to accept of fuch terms of capitulation, as would fave their men, fave their archives and valuable effects, and by a neutrality clear their country from the misfortunes, that always afflict a feat of war, which, indeed, feemed to be the whole bent of their conduct; he was forced to accept of a mediation offered by the King of Denmark, for which his minifter, the Count de Lynar, was already prepared, and to fign the following convention; which it will be proper to give entire, on account of its confequences, occafioned by what the French call an infraction of the capitulation.

Oblige them to capitulate.

"HIS Majefty the King of Denmark, touched with the diftreffes of the countries of Bremen and Verden, to which he has always granted his fpecial protection, and being defirous, by preventing thofe countries from being any longer the theatre of war, to fpare alfo the effufion of blood in the armies, which are ready to difpute the poffeffion thereof, hath employed his mediation by the miniftry of the Count de Lynar. His Royal Highnefs the Duke of Cumberland, General of the army of the allies, on the one party, and his excellency the Duke de Richelieu, General

A. D. 1757.

of the French forces in Germany, on the other; in confideration of the intervention of his Danifh Majefty, have refpectively engaged their word of honour to the Count de Lynar, to abide by the convention hereafter ftipulated; and he, the Count de Lenar, correfpondently to the King his mafter's intentions, obliges himfelf to obtain the guaranty mentioned in the prefent convention; fo that it fhall be fent to him, with his full powers, which there was no time to make out in the circumftances, which hurried his departure.

Articles of capitulation.

ART. I. Hoftilities fhall ceafe on both fides within 24 hours, or fooner if poffible. Orders for this purpofe fhall be immediately fent to the detached bodies.

II. The auxiliary troops of the army of the Duke of Cumberland, namely, thofe of Heffe, Brunfwick, Saxe-Gotha, and even thofe of the Count de la Lippe Buckebourg, fhall be fent home: and as it is neceffary to fettle particularly their march to their feveral countries, a general officer of each refpective nation fhall be fent from the army of the allies, with whom fhall be fettled the rout of thofe troops, the divifions they fhall march in, their fubfiftence on their march, and the paffports to be granted them by his excellency the Duke of Richelieu, to go home to their own countries, where they fhall be placed and diftributed as fhall be agreed upon between the court of France and their refpective fovereigns.

III. His Royal Highnefs the Duke of Cumberland obliges himfelf to pafs the Elbe with that part

part of his army, which he shall not be able to place in the city of Stade. That part of his forces, which shall enter in garrison in the said city, and which, it is supposed, may amount to between four and six thousand men, shall remain there under the guaranty of his Majesty the King of Denmark, without committing any act of hostility; and, on the other hand, they shall not be exposed to any from the French troops. In consequence thereof, commissaries named on each side shall agree upon the limits to be fixed round that place, for the conveniency of the garrison; which limits shall not extend above half a league, or a league, from the place, according to the nature of the ground or circumstances, which shall be fairly settled by the commissaries. The rest of the Hanoverian army shall go to take quarters in the country beyond the Elbe; and to facilitate the march of those troops, his excellency the Marshal Duke de Richelieu shall concert with a general officer sent from the Hanoverian army, the routs they shall take, obliging himself to give the necessary passports and security for the free passage of them and their baggage to the places of their destination; His Royal Highness the Duke of Cumberland reserving to himself the liberty of negociating between the two courts for an extension of those quarters. As to the French troops, they shall remain in the rest of the dutchies of Bremen and Verden, till the definitive treaty of the two sovereigns.

A. D.
1757.

IV. As the aforesaid articles are to be executed as soon as possible, the Hanoverian army, and the corps, which are detached from it, particularly that which is at Buck-Schantz, and the neighbourhood, shall retire under Stade in the space of 48 hours. The French army shall not pass the river Oste, in the dutchy of Bremen, till the limits be regulated. It shall, besides, keep all the posts and countries, of which it is in possession; and, not to retard the regulation of the limits to be settled between the armies, commissaries shall be nominated, and sent on the 10th instant to Bremerworden, by his Royal Highness the Duke of Cumberland, and his Excellency the Marshal Duke de Richelieu, to regulate, as well the limits to be assigned to the French army, as those that are to be observed by the garrison at Stade, according to article III.

V. All the aforesaid articles shall be faithfully executed according to their form and tenor, and under the faith of his Majesty the King of Denmark's guaranty, which the Count de Lynar, his minister, engages to procure.

Done at the camp at Closter-Seven, September 8, 1757.

Signed   WILLIAM.

SEPERATE ARTICLES.

Upon the representations made by the Count de Lynar, with a view to explain some dispositions made by the present convention, the following articles have been added:

I. It

I. It is the intention of his Excellency the Marshal Duke de Richelieu, that the allied troops of his Royal Highness the Duke of Cumberland shall be sent back to their respective countries according to the form mentioned in the second article; and that as to their separation and distribution in the country, it shall be regulated between the two courts; those troops not being considered as prisoners of war.

II. It having been represented, that the county of Lauenbourg cannot accommodate more than 15 battalions and six squadrons, and that the city of Stade cannot absolutely contain the 6000 men allotted to it, his Excellency the Marshal Duke de Richelieu, being pressed by M. de Lynar, who supported this representation by the guaranty of his Danish Majesty, gives his consent; and his Royal Highness the Duke of Cumberland engages, to cause 15 battalions and six squadrons to pass the Elbe; and the whole body of hunters, and the remaining 10 battalions and 28 squadrons shall be placed in the town of Stade, and the places nearest to it, that are within the line, which shall be marked by posts from the mouth of the Luhe, in the Elbe, to the mouth of the Elmerbeck, in the river Oste; provided always, that the said 10 battalions and 28 squadrons shall be quartered there, as they are at the time of signing this convention, and shall not be recruited under any pretext, or augmented in any case; and this clause is particularly guarantied by the Count de Lynar, in the name of his Danish Majesty.

III. Upon

A.D. 1757.

III. Upon the reprefentation of his Royal Highnefs the Duke of Cumberland, that both the army and the detached corps cannot retire under Stade in 48 hours, agreeable to the convention, his Excellency the Marfhal Duke de Richelieu hath fignified, that he will grant them proper time, provided the corps encamped at Buck-Schantz, as well as the army encamped at Bremer-worden, begin their march to retire in 24 hours after figning the convention. The time neceffary for other arrangements, and the execution of the articles concerning the refpective limits, fhall be fettled between Lieutenant General Sporcken and the Marquis de Villemur, firft Lieutenant General of the King's army.

Done, &c.

The bad effects of this capitulation.

The immediate injury brought upon the allies of Great Britain by this convention, for whofe common benefit and fervice, it had been underftood both by the parliament and people, at the time the fupplies for an army of obfervation were fo readily granted, this army was embodied and put in motion; was the deprivation of that aid, which the King of Pruffia wanted, and had a right to expect, from the diverfion, the army of obfervation might have continued to make, in the field; fo as to divide the forces of the grand alliance againft him and the proteftant intereft: and the full liberty, in which the French were thereby left, to difpofe of their army to affift the Emprefs Queen in the ruin of the King of Pruffia,

Had

THE LATE WAR. 281

Had the army of observation, if it was found inadequate to the opposition it met with in the field, retired to the Prussian garrison at Magdeburg [p], which could have been done in less time, and more security; and encamped under the guns of that fortress, the King of Prussia would have been protected by the addition of 38,000 troops; the army of observation would have grown more formidable to the enemy, on account of its situation and connections, and Hanover could have had no more to fear from the French invader, than what was the necessary and unavoidable consequence of such a retreat, which ended in the shameful surrender of their arms, and a local restraint of their soldiers.

A. D. 1757. Remarks on this event.

The French delivered by this convention from all hostilities; found themselves in a condition to keep a sufficient force in the vicinity of Magdeburg, to over-awe the garrison, with which the M. Duke de Richelieu remained, keeping his head quarters at Brunswick; and to send a large reinforcement, under the Lieutenant General Berchini. He also ordered the gens d'arms and the other troops, that were in the Landgravate of Hesse Cassel, to file off to the army under the Prince of Soubize, which united force, joined with the Imperial army of execution, was intended to drive the Prussians out of Saxony, and to carry the flames of war into Silesia and the other domi-

How advantageous to the French.

---

[p] Which was no more than a little above 100 miles from Hastenbeck; whereas it is above 150 miles to Stade.

nions

Richelieu invades the Prussian dominions.

nions of Prussia. M. Duke de Richelieu then commanded 60 battalions of foot, and the greatest part of the cavalry to attack the Prussian territories, into which he, in person, also entered soon after, with 110 battalions and 150 squadrons and 100 pieces of cannon near Wolfenbuttle, in three columns; which penetrated into Halberstadt and Brandenburg, plundering the towns, exacting contributions, and committing such excesses, that would have disgraced the military discipline of a Heathen army.

The distress of Prussia.

Here we shall leave Germany and the King of Prussia exposed, and actually invaded, and his situation grown more dangerous than ever: not only the French were let loose upon him, and were ravaging his unguarded provinces, and pouring all their force towards Saxony; but the Russians resumed their march under Marshal Apraxin and General Fermor, into Ducal Prussia: The Swedes declared against a King, who at this time seemed to be unavoidably crushed; and were ready to enter Prussian Pomerania with 22,000 men. The army of execution joined by the French under the Prince de Soubise undertook the recovery of Saxony: and the Austrians were at liberty to act with all their force in conjunction with their allies, where it should appear most to their advantage.

How to be relieved.

Nothing could be more affecting than this state of our German allies. There was no human help for them, but in Great Britain. The only question was, whether it was the duty, upon the faith of treaties; or the interest of Great Britain, either in regard to her own security, or to her commerce, to assist them in this distress; and to prevent their destruction? by a confederacy, in which our natural enemy was a principal, and the most powerful party; and how far our aid ought to have extended? We shall see how this was understood by the court and people of Great Britain, much better by their future measures, than by any reasonings or speculations. A national approbation, confirmed by the unanimous voice of the people, must carry great weight on such a subject.

A. D. 1757.

At the entrance of Mr. PITT, a second time, into the administration, the affairs in Germany bore a very different, nay a reverse aspect. The King of Prussia had beaten down all opposition, and seemed to be in a fair way to force the Empress Queen to equitable terms of peace, and to establish the tranquillity of that continent. For, by breaking the Austrian link of the confederacy, it was natural to suppose that the other powers, in that league, would withdraw their forces, and relinquish their pretensions; and that the protection of the Germanic liberties, in any branch of the Roman Empire, would have become the interest and care of the whole body. The Swedes had not begun to stir. The Russ were at a stand. The army of the Empire was assembling with much dislike, so as to render their service very doubtful: And the French, whose operations and measures more nearly attracted the attention of the British nation, did not seem to be pursuing any object adequate to their prodigious armies beyond the Rhine; and therefore to be looked upon as a feint

Why Mr. PITT did not acquiesce in a German war.

A. D. 1757.

feint to draw the British councils into measures injurious to the American war.

The British court and parliament had done all, that was thought necessary and incumbent upon them, for their allies, under these circumstances. The King of Prussia asked for relief in Money. It was granted. Hanover required actual defence. An army of 40,000 veteran troops was hired for that service, and the King of Great Britain's only surviving son was sent to command it. Which, in the condition the King of Prussia was at that juncture, and, with a conduct regulated by the common interest of the allies, was sufficient to cover Hanover, and to defeat any enterprize undertaken by the French, to the prejudice of Great Britain, or of any of her allies. Besides, there was a more natural measure to divert them from an attempt upon Hanover, by finding their troops employment at home.

Proposes an attack of the coast of France.

No wonder then, that Mr. PITT did not, at first acquiesce in the German war; when neither the faith of treaties, nor any immediate danger to the interest of our nation, required further assistance on the continent. However, he resolved upon an expedition by sea, which, by insulting, alarming and landing on the coast of France, might serve both Germany and Great Britain. This was a scheme planned with the most promising hopes of success to both Great Britain and her allies. It was the best method to annihilate the strength of France, by annoying her coasts and destroying her maritime stores, while her troops were embarked

in

in the quarrels of the Germans, and she was marching her great armies to increase those disturbances. And it was the most effectual way to save Germany from the power of French armies, by cutting them out work for the defence of their maritime places at home.

The minister carried this plan of operations; but not without some feint struggles by the advocates for more vigorous measures by land. For, though they had nothing to alledge against the utility, they pretended, that it was a kind of cowardly, weak and immethodical war, unbecoming a brave people. And some of these carried their dislike so far, without doors, as to decline the commands offered to them in those expeditions; which was thought to be the secret cause why our naval armaments against the coasts of France were not always attended with adequate success. {*How discouraged.*}

The first expedition or armament of this kind was fitted out against Rochefort; which was represented to be in a very defenceless condition; and, if taken or destroyed by our arms, would give a finishing blow to the naval power of France; and at all events, would oblige the court of France to recall a considerable part of their armies from Germany to guard their own coasts from insult and ruin. {*Expedition against Rochefort.*}

The importance of this place, which is situate near, and very little inferior to, Brest in its docks, yards, magazines of naval stores, and in the number of King's ships fitted out from thence, {*Its importance.*}

was a sufficient object of an expedition, And its defenceless state was so well attested, that, it would have been deemed an oversight in a minister to neglect or to disregard the information.

Why proposed.

The original design arose from the intelligence of one Captain Clerk, a worthy, intelligent and skilful land-officer, who, in a letter to [q] Sir John Ligonier, and by him transmitted to Mr. Secretary Pitt, which was penned by Captain Clerk, by order, and in pursuance of several previous meetings and conferences on that subject, lays down the particulars, that were supposed to favour an attack or surprize on Rochfort.

" S I R,

Captain Clerk's account of its condition.

" IN returning from Gibraltar, in 1754, I went
" along part of the western coast of France,
" to see the condition of some of their fortifica-
" tions of their places of importance, on purpose
" to judge, if an attempt could be made with a
" probability of success, in case of a rupture, and
" of the French drawing away their troops to
" Flanders, Italy and Germany, in the same man-
" ner they did in the last war.

" I had heard, that Rochefort, though a place
" of the utmost importance, had been very much
" neglected. I went there, and waited upon the
" governor in my regimentals, told him, that I
" was upon my way to England from Gibraltar;
" and, that I came on purpose to see the place,

[q] Dated the 15th of July 1757.

' the

" the dock and the men of war. He was very
" polite; I was shewed every thing; went aboard
" ten ships of the line new built: and, an en-
" gineer attended me in going round the place.

" I was surprised to find, that though there
" was a good rampart with a revetement, the
" greatest part of it was not flanked but with re-
" dans; that there was no outworks, no covert-
" way, and in many places no ditch; so that the
" bottom of the wall was seen at a distance:
" That in other places where the earth had been
" taken out to form the ramparts there was left
" about them a good height of ground, which
" was a disadvantage to the place: That for above
" the length of a front there was no rampart, or
" even intrenchment; but as the ground was low
" and marshy at that place, being next the river,
" there were some small ditches, which were dry,
" however, at low water; yet the bottom remained
" muddy and slimy.

" Towards the river there was no rampart, no
" parapet, no batteries on either side. Towards
" the land-side there was some high ground very
" nigh the place, perhaps at the distance of
" about 150 or 200 yards.

" The engineer told me, that the place had
" remained in that condition for above 70 or 80
" years.

" I got no plan of the place, and put nothing
" down in writing; for I found that the whole
" town had been talking of me, and thought it
" very

"very extraordinary that I should be allowed to go about and see every thing.

"I burnt even some sketches and remarks I had by me, upon other places, that they might have no hold of me, in case they searched my baggage, and therefore could only expose themselves, as I had done nothing, but what was open, above board, and with permission.

"However, as to utility, I was as much satisfied, as if I had got a plan: in regard of the profil indeed, I have thought since, that it would not have been amiss if I had known for certain the exact height of the rampart. I think that it could not well exceed twenty-five feet. In Martiniere's Geographical Dictionary, it is called only twenty feet high; perhaps the parapet is not included.

"I told your Excellency, that I had never seen any plan of the place: but as there had been no alteration in the works for so many years, I made no question, but that some old plan of it might be found, which would correspond exactly with what I said. In the Forces de L'Europe, which I have, there is no plan of Rochefort, but I found one in the Duke of Argyle's edition, which I borrowed, and shewed to your Excellency. It agrees exactly with what I said, and with the sketch I drew of it before you, from my memory, except that a regular ditch is represented every where, which is not the case.

"The

"The river may be about 130 yards broad. The entrance is defended by two or three small redoubts, which I did not see, nor could I venture even to go down and examine the coast.

"What I mentioned to your Excellency of the method of insulting the place, considering it upon the footing of an immediate assault, I have not put down; for, though it may be reasoned upon in a general view, *yet many things can only be fixed and determined on the spot.* I was told, that there are never any troops at Rochefort, but the marines. There might be about a thousand at that time.

"By the expedition to Port L'Orient in 1746, it appeared to me, that the country people in arms are very little better than our own; and that an officer who possesses himself, might march safely from one end of a province to another, with only five companies of grenadiers, where there are no regular troops. They imagine at first, that they can fight, and their intentions are good till it comes to the point, when every body gives way almost before the firing of a platoon.

"In writing this I have obeyed with pleasure, as I have always done, your Excellency's commands.

"I am, &c.

R. CLARKE."

A.D. 1757.

Laid before the council, &c.

The verbal account of this project being thus reduced into form, it was laid, by Mr. PITT, before the Lords of the cabinet; and the matter thereof afterwards made the subject of two nights conversation; Sir John Mordaunt and Major-General Conway examining, and almost cross-examining Mr. Clerk, concerning every matter contained therein, and a great deal more that the letter led to, particularly about laying a ship to Fort Fouras[r]; about the proper artillery that would be necessary to attack Rochefort in form; and about the future destination of the armament against Port L'Orient, Bourdeaux, &c. in case either of success at Rochefort and Aix, or of the impracticability of its first object.

The plan examined.

Pilot examined.

In these conferences or consultations they not only canvassed Mr. Clerk's intelligence, and examined him closely as an engineer, that had been upon the spot, but they examined Joseph Tierry, a French pilot, touching the practicability of an attempt upon Rochefort, Fouras, and the isle of Aix; who, in the presence of Lord Anson, Sir Edward Hawke, Lieutenant-General Sir John Mordaunt, Major-General Conway, Lord Holderness, Mr. Secretary Pitt, General Ligonier, Admiral Knowles, and Captain Clarke, declared, That he was a French protestant, and had been a pilot twenty years, and upward, on the coast of France, and had served as first pilot on

---

[r] See Major General Conway's evidence on the trial of Sir John Mordaunt.

board

board several of the French King's ships: that he had been twenty-two months on board the Magnanime, and had brought that very ship several times into the road of the Isle d'Aix: that he was well acquainted how to go in and out of the said road: that the channel between the islands of Rhée and Oleron is three leagues broad, and that he *had turned it in and out* in the Magnanime: that the shoals, which are to be avoided, are near the land; and that the breakers could be seen at a considerable distance. He further said, that the shoal, called the Boiard, is not very dangerous; because the breakers shew its situation: that the entrance into the road of Aix is not so difficult, as to require a pilot to bring in great ships; and that there is good anchorage, both within the road and out at sea, in twelve and fourteen fathom water, quite to Bayonne.

A. D. 1757.

Being interrogated particularly concerning the isle of Aix, Tierry declared, That the isle of Aix measures about six English miles in circumference; that there was a kind of village, consisting of about forty houses or huts, with a battery of twenty-four or twenty-six guns, twenty-four pounders, but no fortification on the island: That the largest ships might come very near it; and that the Magnanime alone might destroy the said battery in a very short time.

Being examined in regard to the approaches that might be made with our ships and men against Rochefort, he answered, That though the river is very narrow, the largest ships could go up as far

A. D. 1757.

as Vergerot, two English miles from the mouth of the river: that men might be landed to the north of a battery called de Fourras, out of sight of the fort, on a meadow where the ground is firm and level, and within random shot of the ship guns: that from the landing place to Rochefort, is five English miles; the road dry, and not traversed or impeded by ditches or morass: and that the city is almost surrounded with a rampart; but that on both sides, in that place, which ends at the river, there is no wall, for the length of sixty paces; the inclosure being only a bar or palisade, and the ground, to come up to the palisade, not intersected by any fosse.

This pilot added many more particulars; and underwent a long and close examination for two hours together; throughout which he established the facts with a readiness and presence of mind, that few men in higher life are equal to [b].

The actual force of France.

Their next consideration was to examine evidences, concerning the internal strength, or the land force then actually in France, and where stationed. For this purpose, there was produced a memorial of the actual force of France by land, and the services, on which it was employed, in the year 1757. Mr. PITT informed the generals appointed for this expedition to the coast of France, and met at Lord Holdernesse's house, that the memorial to be considered did come through Lord Holdernesse's department, and had been intro-

[b] See Sir John Mordaunt's trial, page 9, 29, &c.

duced

duced by his Lordship at a meeting, where Sir John Mordaunt and Major-General Conway were present: that it was a paper on which much reliance was had by the King's servants; as coming from one of their most considerable correspondence, to which they gave much credit.

The memorial sets forth, " That the French
" army, at the beginning of the present troubles,
" consisted only of 157,347 men, not including
" the militia and the invalids: and that it was
" composed in the following manner:

" French foot	98,330
" Artillery	4,100
" Foreign foot	25,589
" King's houshold horse	3,210
" French horse	14,520
" Foreign horse	960
" Dragoons	7,680
" Hussars	800
" Light troops	2,158
	157,347

" That in the month of August 1755, an aug-
" mentation was made of four companies of forty-
" five men each, in every battalion of the King's
" regiment; and of four companies of forty men
" each, in every common battalion of French
" foot, which made in all 29,620 men: and
" that about the same time there was an augmen-
" tation made in the dragoons, which made up

"every regiment four squadrons of 640 men,
"making in all 2560 men. That in the month
"of December, of the same year 1755, there
"was also an augmentation made of ten men to
"every company of horse, in all 5560 men;
"without reckoning the royal volunteers and
"Fischer's corps, which were also augmented, ac-
"cording to the best advices, with about 680
"men, or thereabout, the number not being ex-
"actly known. So that these several augmenta-
"tions amounted to 38,420 men; and conse-
"quently, that the French army did then amount
"to 196,000 men, without reckoning the militia
"and the invalids. They also had raised two new
"regiments in the county of Liege; but notwith-
"standing that, their regular troops were under
"200,000 men.

"Of which the islands of Minorca and Cor-
"sica, with the colonies in America, take up
"25,000 men, at least: Three or four thousand
"men were embarked this spring for differ-
"ent services in the two Indies. M. d'Etree's
"army, if the regiments were complete, would
"amount to 92,000 men; and M. Duke de Riche-
"lieu's to 32,665; and 6 or 7000 men must be
"allowed for garrisons at Toulon, Marseilles,
"Cotte, Antibes, &c. for the protection of that
"part of the coast.

"That according to this calculation there must
"be 160,000 regular troops employed, and no
"more than about 40,000 men remain for all
"the garrisons from Sedan to the frontiers of
"Swis-

" Swifferland; and alfo for thofe of Roufillon and
" Guiame, without fpeaking of Flanders and the
" coaft.
" Then reckon about 20,000 placed from St.
" Valery to Pergue, and there is all the reafon to
" believe that there can be no more than 10,000
" men ftationed from St. Valery to Bourdeaux."

A. D.
1757.

The object being fixt, after a due enquiry into the fituation and ftrength of the place, and of the internal weaknefs of the coaft; the next ftep was for the minifter to provide a ftrength equal to the fervice, and to expedite the execution thereof with the greateft fecrefy and difpatch.

The preparations for this expedition.

The following fhips and commanders were immediately appointed for this expedition.

In fhips.

Rates	Guns	Men	Ships	Commanders
1ft	100	870	Royal George	Matt. Buckle
2d	90	780	Ramillies	James Hobbs
		770	Neptune	James Galbraith
		750	Namur	Peter Dennis
	84	770	Royal Willm.	Witt. Taylor
	80	700	Barfleur	Samuel Graves
3d	80	666	Prfs. Amelia	Stephen Colby
	74	700	Magnanime	Hon. R. Howe
	74	700	Torbay	Hon. A. Keppel
		600	Dublin	Geo. B. Rodney
	70	520	Burford	James Young
	64	500	Alcide	James Douglas
	60	420	America	Hon. Jⁿ. Byron
		420	Achilles	H. L. Barrington
		420	Medway	Hon. Ch. Proby
		420	Dunkirk	Robert Digby

T 4

5th

Rates	Guns	Men	Ships	Commanders.
5th	32	220	Southampton¹	J. Gilchrift
6th	28	200	Coventry	Carr. Scrope
Frigate	18	120	Cormorant	Benj. Clive
		120	Poftillion	William Cooper
		120	Beaver	Edw. Gafcoigne
	16	80	Pelican	James O'Hara
	14	80	Efcort	Charles Inglifs
Bomb	8	60	Firedrake	Owen Edwards
		60	Infernal	Jas. Mᶜ Kenzie
Firefhip		45	Pluto	John Lindfey
		45	Proferpine	Francis Banks
Bufs	6	45	Canterbury	Tho. Lampriere

¹ The Southampton having taken a frigate in the way to Bafque road, was ordered to carry her prize into port, and by that means was prevented in the further executing of the orders of this expedition. The account of this engagement does honour to the Britifh naval hiftory, as here defcribed by an eye witnefs. This French frigate of 26 guns and 200 picked men, being a prime failor, was fent out to watch the motion of our fleet; but falling in the calm, and not having equal number of boats to tow her, the Southampton came up with her; who at firft made a feint of fheering off; Captain Gilchrift was at breakfaft, and cooly ordered his men to breakfaft alfo, making off, gave him time to prepare, and the Frenchman crowding all his fail, eagerly purfued; when the Southampton laying to, to receive him; never was there a more refolute engagement for twenty minutes, the officers of the French were all killed, two of them by the fame fhot of a blunderbufs, by Captain Gilchrift's own hand; the men fought each other with handfpokes; and when the French had ftruck, what remained were fo able feamen, that they derided the mean appearance of ours, though their conquerors. The Southampton received fo much damage in this action, that fhe was obliged to return to England to repair.

45 Medway

Rates	Guns	Men	Ships	Commanders.	A. D.
	45		Medway	Charles Lucas	1757.
Hof. ship	22	100	Thetis	John Moutray	
			Hunter cutter[u]		

This most respectable fleet was committed to the care of Admiral Knowles of the red division, Admiral Hawke of the blue division, and Admiral Broderick of the white division: in which commission Admiral Hawke bore the chief command at sea.

[Sidenote: Admirals.]

The land forces were also appointed and ordered to rendezvous on the Isle of Wight, and consisted of,

[Sidenote: Land army.]

Ten battalions of 700 each complete	7000 men
Two battalions of marines, viz. Effingham's and Stewart's, 700 each	1400
One troop of Light Horse ———	60
	8460

This army was supported by the following train of artillery:

[Sidenote: Artillery.]

Ordnance heavy	Proportion
Brass mounted on travelling carriages, compleated with Limbers, &c.	24 pounders ——— 6 12 ——— ——— 4
Ordnance light	
Brass mounted on travelling carriages, with Limbers, ammunition boxes and elevating screws.	6 pounders ——— 10 3 ——— ——— 6

[u] There was also the Jason, a 40 gun ship, employed as a transport for the Buffs, And the Chesterfield man of war to repeat signals.

Howitzers

A.D. 1757.

Howitzers —— — 5½ Inches — 2

Mortars on their beds — { 10 Inches —— 2
8 —— —— 2
4⅔ cohorns — 20

Gunpowder.
Horses.

N. B. The artillery carried 100 ton of gunpowder, and each regiment carried 1,100 lb. ditto. In which service there were employed 40 horses.

Transports.

For the conveyance of these troops, &c. there were hired 55 transports, making in all 15,000, contracted for five months certain, viz. from 20 August 1757 to the 20th of July 1758, at the rate of 13s per ton; with an exception to their going either to America, Africa or the East Indies. Each transport was obliged to have 500 fathom of cable [w].

Place of rendezvous.

Commander in chief.

Every thing being thus dispatched with the greatest expedition, the men of war well manned and ready to sail upon the first notice; the land forces rendezvous on the Isle of Wight, and the transports all taken up: his Majesty appointed Sir John Mordaunt, Knight of the Bath, commander in chief over the land forces, to be employed in the secret expedition; and gave him the following INSTRUCTIONS, for his better discharge of that great and important trust.

GEORGE, R.

Secret instructions to Sir John Mordaunt.

1st. YOU shall immediately upon the receipt of these instructions, repair to the Isle of Wight, where we have appointed ships to con-

---

[w] It appears by the books of the admiralty that this was the finest fleet, with the heaviest weight of metal and best found, that ever sailed from the British nation.

vey

vey you, and the forces under your command, to the coaft of France; and fo foon as the faid forces fhall be embarked, you fhall accordingly proceed, without lofs of time, under convoy of a fquadron of our fhips of war, commanded by our trufty and well-beloved Sir Edward Hawke, Knight of the Bath, admiral of the blue fquadron of our fleet; whom we have appointed commander in chief of our fhips to be employed in this expedition; the faid admiral, or the commander in chief of our faid fhips for the time being, being inftructed to *co-operate* with you, and to be *aiding and affifting* in all fuch enterprizes, as, by thefe our inftructions, you fhall be directed to undertake for our fervice.

A. D. 1757.

2d. Whereas we have determined, with the blefling of God, to profecute the juft war in which we are engaged againft the French King, with the utmoft vigour; and it being highly expedient, and of urgent neceffity, to make fome expedition, that may caufe a diverfion, and engage the enemy to employ in their own defence, a confiderable part of their forces, deftined to invade and opprefs the liberty of the empire, and to fubvert the independency of Europe; and, if poffible, to make fome effectual impreffion on the enemy, which, by difturbing and fhaking the credit of their public loans, impairing the ftrength and refources of their navy, as well as difconcerting, and, in part, fruftrating their dangerous and extenfive operations of war, may reflect luftre on our arms, and add life and ftrength to the common

A. D.
1757.

mon cause; and whereas we are persuaded, that nothing, in the present situation of affairs, can so speedily and effectually annoy and distress France, as a successful enterprize against Rochefort; our will and pleasure is, That you do attempt as *far as it shall be found practicable*, a descent, with the forces under your command, on the French coast, at or near Rochefort, in order to attack, *if practicable*, and by a vigorous impression, force that place; and to burn and destroy, to the utmost of your power, all docks, magazines, arsenals, and shipping, that shall be found there, and exert such other efforts, as you shall judge most proper for annoying the enemy.

3d. After the attempt on Rochefort shall either have succeeded or failed; and in case the circumstances of our forces and fleet shall, with prospect of success, still admit of further operations, you are next to consider Port L'Orient and Bourdeaux, as the most important objects of our arms, on the coast of France; and our will and pleasure is, That you do proceed successively to an attempt on both, or either of those places, as shall be judged practicable; or on any other place that shall be thought most adviseable, from Bourdeaux homeward to Havre, in order to carry and spread, with as much rapidity as may be, a warm alarm along the maritime provinces of France.

4th. In case, by the blessing of God upon our arms, you shall make yourself master of any place on the coast of France, our will and pleasure is, That you do not keep possession thereof; but that,

that, after demolishing and destroying, as far as may be, all works, defences, magazines, arsenals, shipping, and naval stores, you do proceed, successively, on the ulterior part of this expedition, according *as any of them shall be judged adviseable*, and may be performed within such time as shall be consistent with your return, with the troops under your command, so as to be in England at, or about, or as near as may be the latter end of September, unless the circumstances of our forces and fleet shall necessarily require their return sooner; and you are to land the troops at Portsmouth, or such other of our ports, as the exigency of the case may suggest.

5th. Whereas it is necessary, that, upon certain occasions, you should have the assistance of a council of war, we have thought fit to appoint such a council, which shall consist of four of our principal land officers, and of an equal number of our principal sea commanders, including the commanders in chief of our land and sea forces, (except in cases happening at land, relating to the carrying on any military operations, to be performed by our land forces only, in which cases you may call a council of war, consisting of such officers of our land forces as you shall think proper) and all such land and sea officers, in the several cases before-mentioned, are hereby respectively directed, from time to time, to be aiding and assisting with their advice, so often as they shall be called together by you, or by the commander in chief of our squadron for that purpose; and in all such councils of war, when assembled,

assembled, the majority of voices shall determine the resolutions thereof; and, in case the voices shall happen to be equal, the president shall have the casting vote.

6th. And whereas the success of this expedition will very much depend upon an entire good understanding between our land and sea officers, we do hereby strictly enjoin and require you, on your part, to maintain and cultivate such good understanding and agreement; and to order, that the soldiers under your command, should man the ships where there shall be occasion for them, and when they can be spared from the land service; as the commander in chief of our squadron is instructed, on his part, to entertain and cultivate the same good understanding and agreement; and to order the sailors and marines, and also the soldiers, serving as a part of the complements of our ships, to assist our land forces, if judged expedient, by taking post on shore, manning batteries, covering the boats, securing the safe re-embarkation of the troops, and such other services at land as may be consistent with the safety of our fleet: and in order to establish the strictest union that may be between you, and the commander in chief of our ships, you are hereby required to communicate these instructions to him; and he will be directed to communicate those, he shall receive, to you.

7th. You shall, from time to time, and as you shall have opportunity, send constant accounts of your proceedings, in the execution of these our instructions,

instructions, to one of our principal secretaries of state, from whom you will receive such further orders and directions as we may think proper to give you.

A. D. 1757.

G. R.

But, though both the sovereign and the minister did all in their power to carry this salutary measure into execution, with the utmost activity, and the whole nation fed their expectations with the hopes of success, it was observed that a certain set of men, not famous for their extensive knowledge, did even long before the squadron sailed, declare publicly, and offer any wager, that wheresoever was its destination, nothing would be done by it. Mankind were astonished at the boldness with which this was pronounced. **They proceeded so far as to draw from this boldness, a very ill omen of the success.** The persons who thus pronounced with so much boldness, were the same, who by their private intrigues and cabals, had, a few months before, thrown the affairs of the King and kingdom into so much confusion. For, as an ingenious writer and observer of those times, remarks, " The envy of some, who oppose the " present minister's rise to power, are likely to be " carried to such lengths as secretly to thwart and " countermine his operations[x], and blast the ex- " pedition."

Its miscarriage foretold.

---

[x] See the expedition against Rochefort fully stated and considered, &c. p. 6, 7.

The

Obstacles by the transports.

The first notorious appearance of countermining the operations, and blasting this expedition, was the delay of the transports; of which Sir John Mordaunt, in a letter[y] to Mr. Secretary PITT, complains.—On my arrival here, says Sir John, last monday, I was disappointed in finding none of the transports were come round, and more so, in that I had not yet been able to hear any positive account of them. By another letter[z] the commander in chief opens such a light into this cause of delay, in the transport service, as impeaches the understanding or bad intention of those, that made or were entrusted to make the contract for the shipping to transport the army: for he had found, "That the transports were not "sufficient for the number of troops[a]." The Lords of the Admiralty were made acquainted with this grievance by letters from Sir John Mordaunt, to Thomas Orby Hunter and Gilbert Elliot, Esqrs. Lords Commissioners of the Admiralty, then at Portsmouth, and from Sir Edward Hawke to the navy board.

This, with some other accidental delays, that happened, for a fortnight, and afterwards the winds falling contrary, the transports did not get round to Cowes on the Isle of Wight, till the 4th of

[y] Dated 11 August 1757.

[z] From Sir John Mordaunt, to Mr. Secretary PITT, dated 20 August, Newport in the Isle of Wight.

[a] "Mr. Thames, who has long been and now is agent for "the transports, came here the 7th from Portsmouth, on "purpose to inform me, The number of transports were not "sufficient for the number of troops." But this was only waiting time; for Mr. Thames was mistaken.

September;

September; which season was too far advanced to promise any great matters from almost any expedition by sea. Such an armament alarmed all Europe; but more especially the French at its first appointment, and its destination was rumoured to be against their West Indian colonies, or to the South of France, and against their Mediterranean conquest. But the knowledge of the exception mentioned in the transport contract, and the time, for which they were hired, being got abroad; the French very rationally concluded that some part of their shore, in the Channel or in the Bay, must be the object of this expedition; and the procrastination of six weeks, which were spent by the troops encamped in the Isle of Wight, confirmed that opinion more and more, and gave them time, had they embraced it, to prepare for a vigorous defence against an invasion.

On the 5th of Sept. Mr. PITT wrote to Sir John Mordaunt and to Sir Edward Hawke, putting them in mind, " That the wind had been fair for the transports ever since friday morning, and informing them, That his Majesty expected with impatience, to hear that the troops were embarked: and, if by any delay, the embarkation should not be completed, on the receipt of his letter, that it was the King's pleasure, that the most particular diligence might be employed in getting the troops on board, and proceeding without the loss of a moment, to the execution of their orders and instructions with regard to the expedition under their care."

A. D. 1757.

In embarkation.

The embarkation also took up some extraordinary time, on account, as Sir John writes [b] to Mr. PITT, "That they were obliged to march the troops and baggage five miles to the place of embarkation, and that they were then forced to put the men in small boats, in which they were rowed above a mile, before they could embark in the transports."—But why the embarkation was obliged to be put under these unfavourable circumstances does not appear: yet it is certain that it was not owing to any neglect or inactivity of the minister.

Sir John Mordaunt's doubts.

Sir John Mordaunt, during his stay at the Isle of Wight, started a doubt relative to the service he was going upon, which in some measure seems to account for the failure of this expedition—
" Having, says Sir John, since my arrival here
" conversed with Sir Edward Hawke and Vice
" Admiral Knowles, who both seem to be of
" opinion, that it is possible, from the nature of
" the navigation to Rochefort, the fleet may be
" detained even in sight of the coast of France,
" for a week or ten days, without being able to
" get into the road, or off the Isle of Aix, dur-
" ing which time an alarm will necessarily be given
" in those parts; this conjuncture and situation,
" if it should happen, appears to me so very de-
" licate, and equally to the other officers on the
" expedition, who may, by accident be the first
" in command, come to be under the same diffi-

[b] On the 6th of September 1757.

" culty

"culty (the success of our undertaking depending, A.D. 1757.
"as I apprehend, on the suddenness of its execu-
"tion) that I should be glad, if it is thought
"proper, to have a direction, how I am to act
"in that case."—

The starting of such an opinion at this juncture *Answered.* and distance of time, after every point had been well debated by, or in the presence of, this General and the other officers, at several conferences and councils held on this subject by the ministers of state, conveyed no advantageous idea of future success; or rather it indicated a fertility of invention how to exculpate a miscarriage, and to find out some incident, on which it might be thrown, in case of a failure.

Mr. PITT, in answer to this case, as stated by Sir John, says no more, but that, "I am
"commanded thereupon, by the King, to signify
"to you his Majesty's pleasure, that you or such
"other officer, on whom the command may de-
"volve, do, in conformity to the latitude given
"by his Majesty's instructions, judge of the prac-
"ticability of the service, on the spot, according
"as contingent events, and particular circum-
"stances may require: the King judging it highly
"prejudicial to the good of his service to give
"particular orders and directions with regard to
"possible contingent cases, that may arise." By which it pretty plainly appears, that his Majesty was not very well pleased with such after-doubts, that seemed to be raised by way of discouragement, and to prepare him for a failure,

U 2 that

A.D. 1757.

that did happen, and was justified chiefly upon the posture of defence, into which the enemy might put themselves from the time the English fleet appeared on their coast.

Besides; this doubt or opinion had been effectually resolved by Sir John Ligonier, in his observations or hints, read at a cabinet council and delivered to Sir John Mordaunt, at his own desire.

Sir John Ligonier's letter, explaining the instructions.

For that brave, experienced general and commander in chief of all his Majesty's forces in Great Britain, willing to remove all doubts and to clear up all difficulties in the execution of his Majesty's instructions for the land service, observed—" That there is a chance in the best concerted
" military enterprizes, which every man of long
" service must have experienced; what share then
" must be left to fortune in an expedition, where
" neither the country, nor the number of troops,
" you are to act against, is known with any pre-
" cision.

" The capacity of the generals may supply the
" want of intelligence: but to give them any
" positive plan, or rule of action under such cir-
" cumstances, I apprehend would be absurd.

" If I am rightly informed, the great point his
" Majesty has in view, by this expedition, and
" the alarming the coasts of France, is the hopes
" of making a powerful diversion in favour of
" his Royal Highness the Duke, as well as the
" King of Prussia, who desires and presses much
" this very measure.

" In

LORD VISCOUNT LIGONIER.

"In the execution of this general plan, a project of giving a mortal blow to the naval power of France is in his Majesty's thoughts, by attacking and destroying, if possible, the dock, shipping, and naval stores at Rochefort.

"A plan of that place given by one of his Majesty's engineers, who was there in 1754, seems to encourage the attempt; and it must be owned, that without such authority it could hardly be believed, that a place of that great importance could be left in so defenceless a condition.

"In all doubtful dangerous military attempts, the advantages, that may accrue from success, ought to be weighed against the damage and misfortunes, that may be the consequences of a repulse, and that well considered, may in prudence determine the choice.

"If an attempt is to be made upon Rochefort, it will be the part of the admiral to know the coasts, to bring the troops to the nearest place, to cover their landing by the disposition of his ships, and to destroy any barbet batteries, which the enemy may have upon the shore; still remembring, that if the troops are landed at too great a distance from the place, the design will become dangerous, and probably impracticable.

"Supposing the troops landed, it must be left to the consideration of the generals, whether they should not march with the proper precautions, directly to Rochefort, to prevent any succours being thrown into the place, at the
"same

"same time, that the marines should be employed in making a good entrenchment for the security of the stores to be landed from time to time, as well as of a retreat in case of necessity.

"We are told, the country in the neighbourhood is low and marshy; that circumstance might be of great advantage in this undertaking, because in that case troops cannot march by *overtures dans la campagne*, but must follow the dykes, or cawseys, which may be easily defended by coupures, or redoubts.

"A safe and well secured communication between the camp and the sea, from whence you are to receive your supplies of all kinds, is absolutely necessary; the whole depends upon it: —But this being done, I should not be much in pain for the safety of the troops, an inferior number dares not approach you, and one superior will not be easily assembled without your knowing it; and, at all events, you have secured a retreat to the ships.

"I would advise to procure guides upon the spot, and paying them greatly when faithful; there are numbers of protestants in that province, that wish you well, and would be glad to go on board with you.

"As for a *coup de main*, it may, perhaps, succeed best at your coming up, as the enemy may be in great hurry, surprize, and consternation at such an unexpected visit, and not having had time to make his dispositions; but if that is not thought proper, it may succeed as well after
"the

"the place has been thoroughly reconnoitred, and you have fixed the spots, where you design to direct your greatest efforts, and if the enemy see any preparations for a regular attack, they will lefs fufpect a *coup de main*.

"Bergen-op-Zoom was taken by a *coup de main*, after a long fiege.

"St. Philip's was taken by fcaling ladders and a *coup de main*, though the garrifon was 3000 ftrong, after a fiege of fifty-fix days.

"The necessity of dividing a fmall garrifon in a place of fuch circumference, as Rochefort, may facilitate the fuccefs of a bold attempt."

Thus provided and inftructed, the expedition fleet failed from Portfmouth [b], being firft joined by the tranfports. A letter was delivered by the agent of thofe fhips, to each of their mafters, with rendezvous at Torbay, not to be opened in cafe of feparation till they came to weftward of Scilly Iflands: and fuch care was taken by the admiral, before night came on, that floops, tenders and men of war, were ftationed on each fide, almoft in form of an octagon, with the admiral and tranfports in the centre, as crouding under his wings for protection, againft any danger or hazard of the enemy.

The advanced feafon was, before this fleet could put to fea, not the only difadvantage; its courfe to the place of its deftination was greatly delayed with contrary winds, fogs and calms: It was the

---

[b] On the 8th of September 1757.

A. D. 1757. and arrives on the French coast.

20th day of September, about one o'clock, when they arrived on the coast near the Isle of Oleron.

In their passage Captain Proby spoke with a Dutchman from Nantes to Dort, who told him "that the French expected to be attacked at Ro- "chelle, or St. Martin's, by the English, and "that an embargo was laid on all the shipping in "France."

How conducted on the French coast.

On the 21st, at seven o'clock, Admiral Knowles, who had the command of the first division, made towards the land, with full sail. At eleven a gun was fired by Admiral Hawke, and answered by Admiral Knowles, who soon after tacked and bore down, as if to speak with Admiral Hawke. The captain of the admiral's ship hoisted the bloody flag, or flag of defiance, on the fore-top-mast

---

ᶜ After the transports had been taken up, and the troops assembled near two months, we sailed, says Sir John Mordaunt, *in his Defence*, the 8th of September, and the alarm was given on the 20th, in the neighbourhood of Rochefort, by the arrival of our long expected fleet (for Captain Clevland, on the 17th of August, had spoke with a Dutch convoy from Rochelle, and was informed by the first lieutenant of a man of war, that came on board of him, that the French expected the English at Rochelle) and, continues he, from the 20th it must have been at least *eight days* before we could have come to Rochefort, nor could it be supposed, but that after so long notice of an enemy's approach, the town would be put in a good condition of defence.

N. B. At four o'clock, P. M. they espied land a-head east south-east seven leagues: And at eight at night they saw a light house and guns fire from the French coast; 225 between flash and report, or about three leagues distant.

head, at half an hour paft eleven : Then Admiral Knowles feemed to wear, as if going into the road. But Admiral **Hawke** fhortned fail about two o'clock, keeping no more than his top-fails, and fore-ftay-fails clofe in wind, and fhortly after lay too. Admiral Knowles, making full fail, all the land officers expected to land that night at eight o'clock, the foldiers provifion, arms and ammunition being put up ready ; but he, about feven P. M. making a tack, and firing again, the tranfports came to anchor near the **Ifle of Rhée.**

On the 22d, at feven in the morning, fignal to weigh anchor, and the men of war had their hammocks up, and fails crouded, ready to engage. The fleet failed into a fine bay, called *Rade de Pafque*, between the iflands of Rhée and Oleron. Every one was in expectation, that the firft divifion would prefently have cleared all obftacles, and that an attempt to land would certainly be made, that night. But the fleet was no fooner come into the centre of that fine bay, where 500 fhips might ride fafely, than a fignal was given to anchor at nine o'clock in the morning : and fo continued all the reft of the day, and the next night.

Thus it was the 23d of September before they came to action ; which delay, as it gave great anxiety to the men on board, and has been related with feveral aggravating circumftances afhore, the reader would do well to fufpend his judgment, till he has confidered the evidence given by Admiral

Arrives in Bafque Road.

A. D. 1757.

miral Knowles, on this particular charge against Sir John Mordaunt ᵈ.

In

ᵈ *Question*, What occasioned the fleet not coming into the road sooner than the 23d, seeing they made the coast on the 20th?

Answer, He will give you the best account he can, without his log-book and journal; but, for want of them, cannot be particular as to the hours.—In the morning of the 20th, Sir Edward Hawke gave him the following orders, viz.

" By Sir Edward Hawke, Knight of the Bath, Ad-
" miral of the blue squadron of his Majesty's
" fleet, &c.

" If in standing in between the isles of Rhé and Oleron, I
" shall find the winds and weather will permit of proceeding
" to Basque road, and attacking the isle of Aix, I will hoist a
" red flag on the flag-staff, at the foretop-gallantmast-head,
" and fire three guns; then you are hereby required and di-
" rected, without loss of time, to stand in as near to the said
" Isle of Aix, as the pilots will carry you, with all, or as many
" of the ships of your division, as you shall think sufficient for
" that service, and batter it, till such time, as the garrison
" shall either surrender, or abandon it. In either case you
" are to land a number of men sufficient to demolish it with
" all possible dispatch, sending me the earliest intelligence of
" your proceedings. For which this shall be your order.

" Given under my hand on board his Majesty's ship Ra-
" milies at sea this 20th of Sept. 1757.

ED. HAWKE.

" To Charles Knowles, Esq; Vice-
Admiral of the red squadron of
his Majesty's fleet.

" By command of the admiral. J. HAY."

The signal being given, the deponent, about noon, took his leave of Sir Edward Hawke, and made sail with his division,

In the morning of the 23d, it being a calm, and at anchor in sight of the isle of Aix, and so near fion. The Medway, which was a-head by Sir Edward's order to look out for the land, about two or three o'clock, as near as he can remember, made a signal for seeing the land; very soon after, the deponent saw it himself: As his own ship, and those of his division, were ordered to prepare for the attack, the lieutenant, or the captain, came to acquaint him, the ship was clear and ready for action; this was about four o'clock, the wind at that time, and to the best of his remembrance the whole day, was about north-east. As he looked upon a ship cleared, and in order for battle, to be a very entertaining sight, he desired Major-General Conway to go down to see his ship between decks: While they were viewing her, one of his lieutenants came down, sent by the captain, to acquaint him, Captain Keppel hailed the ship, and told them, there was a French man of war standing in for the fleet; for some short space of time the deponent took no notice of it, thinking it impossible, the fleet should not see her; a second message was sent him down to the same purpose, he then immediately went upon deck with General Conway, and was shewn her by his captain, when with their glasses they plainly discovered her to be a two-decked ship; she soon made a private signal, by hoisting a jack at her mizen-topmast-head; the deponent was in doubt, whether to make a signal to any of his division to chace, being ordered on a different service, which he took notice of to Major-General Conway, and to his captain; he judges, he was then at least five miles a-head of Sir Edward Hawke, and the enemy's ship much nearer to him, and his division, than they were to Sir Edward Hawke and the rest of the fleet; and he plainly saw, if some of his division did not chace her, none of the others could possibly see her, so as to chace her, when night came on. The Magnanime was then about two miles to leeward of them, on which he threw out her signal to chace, and hailed Captain Keppel in the Torbay, and directed him to chace also; observing, at the same time,

A. D. 1757.

The conquest of the Isle of Aix.

near to the French coaſt, that they could ſee the French colours hoiſted on the caſtle, and every body time, to Major General Conway and his captain, that if Sir Edward Hawke did not approve of what he had done, he would certainly call them in again; but, inſtead of that, Sir Edward threw out their ſignals to chace, by way of confirming what he had done; and in addition, made the Royal William's ſignal alſo, belonging to his diviſion; two more ſignals for ſhips in the reſt of the fleet were thrown out afterwards, and very ſoon recalled. Early the next day in the morning, Sir Edward Hawke ſent the deponent the following order, to take under his command three other ſhips in the room of thoſe three ſhips that were detached to chace, viz.

" By Sir Edward Hawke, Knight of the
" Bath, Admiral of the blue ſquadron
" of his Majeſty's fleet.

" You are hereby required and directed to
" take under your command the ſhips named
" Dublin, " in the margin; the captains of which have
" Burford, " my orders to follow your directions; and
" Achilles, " proceed, without a moment's loſs of time,
" to put in execution the orders you received
" from me yeſterday. For which this ſhall be
" your order.

" Given under my hand on board his Majeſty's ſhip Ra-
" milies, at ſea, this 21ſt of Sept. 1757.

ED. HAWKE.

" To Charles Knowles, Eſq; Vice-
" Admiral of the Red Squadron
" of his Majeſty's fleet.

" By command of the admiral. J. HAY."

In obedience to that order, the deponent proceeded with his diviſion with all the ſail they could carry, to get in, and make,

body in a hurry preparing for defence, and boats carrying men into the garrison of Aix from the coast;

make, what land it was; he judges it was about nine o'clock, when they were got within about two miles of the land, in eleven fathoms water, very hazy thick weather, so as his pilot defired, the ship might be tacked and laid with the head off till it cleared, so as he could see his marks. Whilst he was laying to, he made a signal for the captains of his division, and ordered them to send for their pilots, no two of whom agreed, what land it was; their several examinations he took down, and immediately sent them to Sir Edward Hawke, who, by that time, was advanced nearer to him by two or three miles than he was before, as he the deponent laid with his head off shore. In his letter to Sir Edward he acquainted him, that not one of the pilots would even take charge to lead in with a twenty gun ship; if they would, his division should have followed her. Soon after his boat went away, he made a signal for speaking with the admiral, seeing he continued under sail, and did not stop to take up the boat. At the same time he made sail with his division towards him, and by about twelve joined him; when the deponent got on board him, he was surprized to see Mr. Keppel on board, and also to find the Magnanime and Royal William had joined him again, which the thick weather had prevented the deponent's knowing. Sir Edward Hawke, upon the deponent's acquainting him with what had happened, (for he thinks he got on board, before his letter) immediately sent for the pilot of the Magnanime, at the same time telling the deponent, he judged, what was the matter when he saw him bring to, for his pilot had refused carrying his ship in: When the pilot of the Magnanime came on board, he immediately told them, what land it was; and after offering to carry the fleet in, returned on board his own ship, and led the deponent's division in, the admiral and the rest of the fleet following. The wind was pretty fresh all this day, till towards the evening, when about six o'clock the tide of flood being spent, the Magnanime

made

A. D. 1757.

Ships ordered on the service.

coast [c]; about ten o'clock Admiral Knowles, in the Neptune of 90 guns, and his whole division, viz. Magnanime 74, Barfleur 80, America 64, Alcide 74, Burford 74, Royal William 90, weighed and made full sail towards the front of the garrison. Captain Howe led on the starboard tack, and the America the larboard. Many guns fired from the Isle of Oleron, at two of our small vessels seeming to reconnoitre that shore.

The fort begins the fire.

Half an hour past twelve, the first gun fired from the garrison at our ships, a small battery also at the west corner of the island fired at the Jason, who had the regiment of buffs in boats ready to land, but the balls fell short of them;— vast crouds of people appear on the French coasts.

made the signal to anchor; they were then in the mouth of the Pertuis of Antioche: about eight o'clock Sir Edward Hawke made the signal for the fleet to anchor, and they continued working in, and anchored, as they came into proper births all night.—Early in the morning of the 22d the Magnanime made the signal, when the deponent weighed with his division, and Sir Edward Hawke and the rest of the fleet weighed also: About eleven o'clock it falling calm, the signal was again made to anchor; about two or three a small breeze springing up westerly, the Magnanime made the signal and weighed again, and the deponent ran in with his division, till between nine and ten o'clock at night, Sir Edward Hawke and the fleet of transports all following, when the deponent's division came to anchor.

[c] An island not above a mile long and about half a mile over, almost in an oval form, the soil barren, gravelly and sandy, and yet one continued vineyard.

The line of battle ships kept under fail, and the Jason tacked about and made up to them, not being able to land her men at the intended corner, both for the shallowness of the water, and also the fierce fire of the battery.

One o'clock the Magnanime only stood directly into the fort, and began a most heavy fire, like a continual thunder, rendering the very ship to appear as one cloud of smoke. The battery also fired very briskly, and the Barfleur at a great distance, fired some few guns. Before the attack began, Captain Howe received the fire of the garrison with great intrepidity, ordered all his men to lay down upon the decks, turned all his live cattle, fowls, and unnecessaries over board; himself only, with his speaking trumpet in hand, the pilot and the man at the helm, appearing upon deck, till he came within sixty yards of the bastions of the garrison, when he began so furious a fire, that the Monsieurs said, Something more than man must be on board that ship; the men in the garrison were so much terrified, that most of them clapped themselves down under the works of the garrison, and in the ditches, nor could be prevailed on to stand to their guns, which obliged the governor to strike the colours; and this was no sooner done, than they all jumped up, taking snuff, dancing and rejoicing, as if they had gained a victory.

The Magnanime returns the fire.

Captain Howe's bravery and conduct.

Colours of the fort struck.

The garrison ceasing fire, some sailors and mariners first landed, and the Jason, with the battalions of the buffs in boats, took possession of the island.

island. There being only two marines and one sailor killed on board the Magnanime, and one man killed in the garrison, by a ball glancing off obliquely on his breast, where it remained fixed, without force to penetrate through his body.

A. D. 1757.
Losses on both sides.

The governor, on our men taking possession, surprised them with saying to this effect, "Mes- "sieurs,"—" we expected you ere now; we had " account of your sailing from St. Helen's the " 7th, which made us remove all our valuable " effects, so that you will now find but a poor " island."

This fort, had it been compleated according to old Vauban's plan of military architecture, laid out and almost finished—might have given great trouble. The parapets were raised to their proper height, but embrazures were not yet fixed, else perhaps the French for—pusillanimity would not have been blamed; in the fort were five hundred soldiers and two hundred sailors, yet no discharge of musquetry; which, as the Magnanime was so near, might have greatly annoyed our marines on board; in the garrison were found twenty guns, eighteen pounders, eight mortars, but few bombs were thrown, all which were either taken away or rendered useless. There was a great quantity of powder, ball, and ammunition in the magazine.

Description of the fort.

Strength of the garrison.

While this conquest was in hand, Sir Edward Hawke had resolved to reconnoitre, and to sound that part of the coast, which appeared by the letter of his instructions to be the next ob-

The shore of the continent explored.

ject of the expedition. The parties employed on this service were Rear-Admiral Thomas Broderick, and the Captains James Douglas, Peter Dennis, and Matthew Buckle Esqrs; They were sent out out, on the 23d in the afternoon, and continued upon that service, all night, till three or four o'clock the afternoon following, when they returned ᶠ and made the following report to Sir Edward Hawke.

ᶠ On the 24th in the morning, the day after the attack of the Isle of Aix, signal was out on board Sir Edward Hawke, for Admiral Knowles to come on board of him; on which Major-General Conway and he went immediately; Sir Edward Hawke, on their coming on board, told the admiral, Admiral Broderick and three captains were gone reconnoitring for a landing-place, and he wished for their speedy return. As that signal, which was out on board Sir Edward, was for the rear-admiral as well as the vice-admiral, being a standard at the ensign-staff, and the vessels, which Admiral Broderick had with him, were not in sight, he begged of Sir Edward to make the signal for all land and sea general officers, which is the standard at the mizen top-mast head, that being most discernible at a distance, and to repeat firing a gun every hour, which he did: Before four, Admiral Broderick and the captains returned, very much fatigued, and drew up their report. After taking a morsel of dinner they all got into their boats and went away to the Isle of Aix (excepting Admiral Broderick) in order to collect what intelligence they could from the prisoners taken in the fort; a number of the prisoners were sent on board the vice admiral's ship, and examined, one by one, by General Conway, he speaking French, till near eleven o'clock at night, when Sir Edward Hawke and Sir John Mordaunt went away; and the admiral declared his intention of holding a council of war on board the Neptune ship the next morning, which was accordingly done.

VOL. II.   X   "We

A.D. 1757.

Order of Sir Edward Hawke for founding, &c. the coast.

"WE the under-written went and founded the French shore from Rochelle to Fort Fouras, and find as follows.

"From the south point of the entrance of Rochelle, (on which point there are twenty-seven guns mounted on barbet) to the point of the Angolin, we find it a rocky shore, and steep clifts, with shoals near two miles off; from Angolin to Chatelaillon, we find a fair, hard, sandy beach, with a flat lying off near two miles, having but three fathom at high water at that distance, but clear ground, along which beach are sand hills about fifty yards from the top of high water. On the point of Chatelaillon are two guns on barbet, which can no ways annoy the landing of the troops in the bays of either side of it; and off which point runs a riff of rocks west two miles, which are dry at low water; and round the said point, about half a mile to the eastward, there is a small sandy bay near half a mile long, and the land over the said bay rises with an easy ascent, about a quarter of a mile, to a church or convent, with a few houses near it; from the sandy bay, along to a square fort on the south part of the bay, lies a long flat mud, which is dry near two miles at low water.

"It is our general opinion, the transports cannot come nearer to either of the aforesaid bays (in order to land troops) than a mile and an half, as we found three fathoms only at that distance at high water.

"The

"The square fort on the south side of the bay we could only see two sides of; the face to the north-west had nine embrazures, and that to the north-east only two.

"Given under our hands, on board his Majesty's ship Ramilies in Basque road, this 24th of September, 1757.

> "*Thomas Broderick.*
> "*James Douglas.*
> "*Peter Dennis.*
> "*Matthew Buckle.*"

Nothing was done towards landing the army, next day, further than what was necessary to destroy the fortifications of Aix [g]. However, Colonel James Wolfe, employed as quartermaster-general on the expedition, zealous in the service, upon which he was sent, and disdaining to be idle, while others were venturing their lives, obtained leave of Sir John Mordaunt to reconnoitre the shore. He set off about one o'clock on the 23d, during the attack of the Isle of Aix, and went to the fort soon after it had surrendered.

He landed, and got upon the ramparts, and from thence viewed Fouras and the land about it; he stayed as little while as he could, and then re-

Colonel Wolfe's report of the enemy's shore.

---

[g] Miners were appointed to blow up the fortification, governor's house and the barracks, which work took them up till the 30th. In which service we lost two sailors and two soldiers blown up, and a serjeant had both his thighs broke by a stone, that fell upon him.

A. D.
1757.

turned immediately to the Ramilies, which was anchored at a confiderable diftance from the Ifle of Aix, and made a fort of a report, of what he had obferved, to Sir Edward Hawke and Sir John Mordaunt. He mentioned the fituation of Fouras, as it appeared to him, and took notice of what he thought to be the ftrength of it, to the admiral and the general: which he was induced to do, as nobody elfe within his knowledge had done it, and took the liberty of faying to Sir Edward Hawke, that he believed, if the depth of water would allow of coming near enough, a fhip would batter it down very eafily, or at leaft would fo far take the fire of the fort upon the fhip, that the troops might very fafely land round about it;—what he fpoke of the land on the other fide of the fort was from conjecture only. Sir Edward Hawke at that time feemed to embrace the propofal with a great deal of warmth, and Sir John Mordaunt approved of it. He faid to Sir Edward Hawke, that, as he fuppofed, the pilot of the Magnanime could very well inform him of the depth of water; and as the admirals and generals did not appear to difapprove of his fpeaking upon that point, he juft hinted to Sir Edward Hawke, that it might not be amifs to caufe fome diverfion on the fide of Rochelle, to divide the enemy's attention, which he apprehended might be done by means of the bombketches. Sir Edward fo far agreed to it, that he fent both for the pilot and the bomb-ketches up from the Ifle of Aix that night, he having fuggefted gested to him his opinion, that there was not a moment's time to be lost. The pilot seemed clearly to understand his notion of the attack, and of landing at the same time on both sides the fort, and said, that he could, or believed he could, take the Magnanime up to batter the fort; as also, that the landing between Fouras and la Pointe was very practicable, supposing the fort to be attacked, as proposed, at the same time.

A. D. 1757.

Yet we shall see, that notwithstanding so great an officer's opinion of the practicability of the landing, and the concurrence of Sir John Mordaunt, who acknowledged upon his trial, that he did embrace Colonel Wolfe's plan or proposition of an attack upon Fouras cheerfully, and that Sir Edward Hawke gave him room to expect, that he would next morning send up a ship to batter Fouras; it was laid aside by a council of war, on the 25th of September, on board his Majesty's ship the Neptune, at anchor off the isle of Aix [h], for the following reasons:

Remarks on the practicability of landing.

Laid aside by a council of war.

" The

[h] " Present,

" Sir *Edward Hawke*, { Knight of the Bath, Admiral and commander in chief of his Majesty's ships employed on the present expedition.

" Sir *John Mordaunt*, { Knight of the Bath, Lieutenant General of his Majesty's forces, and General and commander in chief of the troops on the present expedition.

" *Charles Knowles*, Esq; Vice Admiral of the Red.
" The Right Hon. Major General *Henry Seymore Conway*.
" *Thomas Broderick*, Esq; Rear Admiral of the White.

" Hon.

A. D. 1757. Resolutions at the council of war.

"The fortifications and island of Aix, belonging to the French King, having surrendered to his Majesty's arms, the council proceeded to take into consideration the farther steps proper to be taken, in execution of his Majesty's secret instructions to Sir Edward Hawke and Sir John Mordaunt, commanders in chief of his Majesty's forces on the present expedition; and the first object being to determine, Whether a proper place could be found for landing the troops, Sir Edward Hawke produced a report by Rear Admiral Broderick, and the Captains Douglas, Dennis, and Buckle, whom he had sent to sound and reconnoitre the coast from La Rochelle to the point of Fouras, near the embouchure of the river Charente, which report is hereunto annexed.

"The council having taken the said report into consideration, and examined the pilots, it appears, that there are but two landing places; and that the troops could not be reimbarked from either of them in bad weather, the swell of the sea making so great a surf on the shore, that no boats could be able to approach it to take the troops off; the ablest pilot having informed the council, that he had been at anchor seven weeks in this road, and not a boat been able to pass or repass: and it likewise appears to the council, that in case the troops should be

"Hon. Major General *Edward Cornwallis.*
"Captain *George Bridges Rodney.*
"Colonel *George Howard.*"

"over-

"overpowered by superior numbers of the ene-
"my, they could have no protection from the
"cannon of the fleet, the shoal water preventing
"their coming within gun-shot.

"The probability of success in the attempt
"against Rochefort, in case the landing was af-
"fected, being then taken into consideration,
"Lieutenant Colonel Clerk, chief engineer, was
"called in, and being asked his opinion, declared,
"That when he saw the place in the year 1754,
"he thought no place was more capable of being
"taken by assault; what alteration may have been
"made in the place since, he has not sufficient
"information to judge; that he does not imagine
"any regular attack was intended against that or
"any other place, the small quantity of artillery
"we have, not being sent upon that plan. Being
"asked, if the ditch were flowed with water,
"whether he should then think it practicable to
"take the place by escalade; said, he thought
"not; but that when he saw the ditch, it did not
"appear to him capable of being flowed.

"Monsieur de Bonneville, volunteer, being
"asked what he knew of Rochefort, said, that
"he was there about nine years ago; that
"the ramparts were of earth, and that there are
"sluices there, by which they can flow the ditch,
"and that it was full of water all round, when he
"was there.

"The pilot of the Neptune being called in,
"said, That he had been very frequently at
"Rochefort; that he commanded a small vessel
"there

"there many years; that they have sluices near
"the hospital, by which they can fill the ditch
"with water; that they raise them sometimes to
"cleanse the ditch, and that he has seen water in
"it quite round the town.

"The informations of some French prisoners
"were then produced confirming the same, as also
"that they had been working on the fortifications
"there for some time past.

"The intelligence received from several neutral
"vessels spoke with on the passage was also pro-
"duced, declaring, That the French had been
"for some time in expectation of a descent from
"the English in those parts[1]. All which being
"taken into consideration, together with the long
"detention of the troops in the Isle of Wight,
"and our meeting with contrary winds, fogs and
"calms upon our passage, the several informations

[1] Here also were we informed of sixteen battalions and 30,000 militia, besides the invalids and workmen at the dock of Rochefort, all which could in six hours time be assembled, to oppose our attack; that the ditch was then full of water, and by opening the sluices the country could be laid under water for five miles round. Should our infantry land at Chatelaillon,—a deep morass and rivulet would retard their march, so that the artillery could not get up without going 20 miles round into the heart of the country; that all men of war built at Rochefort, for want of water, were forced to tide it down the river at spring tides only, without guns or rigging, and be compelled with jury masts or tow, to go round to Brest to take in their guns and rigging, and that but one sixty gun ship had ever been built at Rochefort, but only 40 guns—in general, and that therefore our ships of the line, &c. could be of no use in such an attempt. See the Secret Expedition impartially disclosed, p. 44, 45.

"received

Sir PIERCY BRETT K.

"received of troops assembled in the neighbour-
"hood, and the great improbability of finding
"the place unprovided, or of surprising it, or
"consequently succeeding in an enterprize found-
"ed on the plan of an assault or escalade merely;
"and the uncertainty of a secure retreat for the
"troops, if landed; the council are unanimously
"of opinion, that such an attempt is neither ad-
"viseable, nor practicable.

A. D.
1757.

"*Edward Hawke,*
"*John Mordaunt,*
"*Charles Knowles,*
"*H. Seymour Conway,*
"*Thomas Broderick,*
"*Edward Cornwallis,*
"*G. B. Rodney,*
"*G. Howard.*"

However notwithstanding the council had been of opinion, that it was neither adviseable nor practicable to land the troops on that coast, we find that there were cutters and small vessels sent out next night and all next day to found up the river Charente, leading to Rochefort, Sir Edward Hawke did also direct Vice Admiral Knowles to carry in two bomb-ketches to try to bombard the fort; which order was immediately executed under the conduct of the Magnanime. But the Infernal bomb, which went first, run a-ground, and in that situation would have been attacked by two row galleys, had they not been beaten off by all the boats manned and armed, under the protection

Proceedings after the council for a landing.

By bomb-vessels.

of

of the Coventry, which, in attempting to get to the Infernal, ran a-ground five different times; neither could the bombs of the Infernal reach from that dangerous situation to the fort.

By orders to the soldiers.

There still remained a busling report, That something would be attempted; and on the 26th at night orders were sent to the transports for the soldiers to hold themselves in readiness, if they should be called upon to land next morning. But next day produced no further order, than to expedite the demolition of the fortifications, and for forty soldiers with ball and bayonets fixed to keep guard on deck every night, and hail every boat or vessel that passed, and to fire in upon them, if they did not give an answer in English, nor the word, after being hail'd thrice. A caution taken on a report, that the French intended to send out some galeashes, or small fire ships, in dark nights to annoy the fleet at anchor.

The spirit of the men, both of the army and fleet, was so bent upon a descent, to retalliate the French for the frequent attempts upon this island of Great Britain, that it appears, by this conduct, after the resolution of the late council of war, that they thought it hazardous to inform them with its contents, and rather waited some accident to favour the return of the fleet.

By founding the coast.

For our small cutters were employed still in sounding the coast and the Charente; and Sir John Mordaunt desired another council of war to be assembled, "To "take under consideration, whether it was advise- "able to land the troops to attack the forts lead- "ing

" ing to, and upon the mouth of the river Cha-
" rente:" which council after mature deliberation
were unanimously of opinion, " That it was ad-
" viseable to land the troops for that purpose with
" all possible dispatch [k]." And in pursuance to
this last resolution, orders were sent, at 11 o'clock
that same night, " for all the troops to debark
" from the transports on board the boats, and
" land silently."

In obedience to these orders Colonel K———y
with Lieutenant Colonel Sir William Boothby,
and Major Farquahar, who were to march at the
head of the grenadiers, took boat before twelve,
though about two leagues from shore, and a fresh
gale full against them, which would have endangered many of the boats loaded with men, so
crouded that they could only stand erect; they
were tumbled in the swell till two o'clock, none
coming to conduct them to the place of rendezvous; at last a cutter came down and said, " You

---

[k] Present,

Sir *Edward Hawke*, { Knight of the Bath, Admiral and Commander in Chief of his Majesty's
ships employed on the present expedition.

Sir *John Mordaunt*, { Knight of the Bath, Lieutenant General of his Majesty's forces, and
Commander in Chief of the troops
employed on the present expedition.

Charles Knowles, Esq: Vice Admiral of the Red.
The Right Hon. Major General *Henry Seymour Conway*.
Thomas Broderick, Esq; Rear Admiral of the White.
Hon. Major General *Edward Cornwallis*.
Captain *George Bridges Rodney*.
Colonel *George Howard*.

"are ordered to ship again, for that the other regiments cannot be ready these two hours," Colonel K———y said, "I can hardly believe it; shew me your orders," on which was shewn a written order; at which all the soldiers made a *humming noise*; and they all went to their respective transports, the boats remaining still ready.

Reasons for not landing. The reason given by Sir John[1] for putting off the landing this time, when it had been resolved to be an adviseable measure; was that a strong wind blowing from the shore, the officers of the navy, appointed to conduct the landing, represented, that it was with difficulty the long boats, which were to be towed on shore, could make way, and consequently the troops would be a long time exposed to the fire of the enemy; that the transport-boats, which were rowed by soldiers, would be still slower, and more exposed; that it would be day, before the first embarkation could get on shore, and that it would be six hours more before the troops, first landed, could be supported by a second embarkation: the generals judging the landing under these circumstances not to be expedient, agreed not to attempt it that night.

But the message sent on this occasion to Admiral Hawke, by Admiral Broderick was, "That having prepared all the boats, with proper officers to land the troops, he was now to acquaint him, That the Generals were come to a resolution not to land to night, but to wait

[1] In his defence, p. 58. of his trial.

"till

"till day light, when they can have a full view of
"the ground whereon they are to land."

A. D.
1757.

When Sir Edward Hawke saw the inftability of the orders iffued out to the land forces in purfuance of the laft council of war; and confidering that every delay was adding ftrength to the enemy, and daily increafing the hazards and dangers of the fhips in that boifterous fea, at that feafon, which he very juftly underftood to be the purport and real meaning of a letter he had lately received from Mr. Secretary PITT, to continue on that coaft fo long as there were any operations going on, agreeable to his fecret inftructions, and no longer [m];

he

---

[m] *A true copy of a letter from Mr. Secretary Pitt, to Sir John Mordaunt, dated Whitehall, 15th September 1757, (the like being at the fame time wrote to Sir Edward Hawke, mutatis mutandis.*

Mr. PITT's letter to Sir John Mordaunt.

"SIR,

"HIS Majefty, by his fecret inftructions, dated the 25th
" day of Auguft laft, having directed the return of the
" troops under your command, together with the fleet, 'fo as
" to be in England at, or about, as near as may be, the end
" of September, unlefs the circumftances of the forces and
" fhips fhall neceffarily require their return fooner,' I am now
" to fignify to you the King's pleafure, That you do not con-
" fider the above-mentioned time, limited for your return, as
" intended, in any manner, to affect or interfere with the full
" execution of the firft and principal object of the expedition,
" namely, ' attempting, as far as fhall be found practicable,
" a defcent on the French coaft, at or near Rochefort, in order
" to attack, if practicable, and, by a vigorous impreffion,
" force that place, and to burn and deftroy, to the utmoft of
" your power, all fhipping, docks, magazines, and arfenals,

"that

A. D. 1757.

he on the 29th of September, writes to Sir John Mordaunt, as follows:

"SIR,

Sir Edward Hawke's letter to Sir John Mordaunt.

"SHould the general officers of the troops have no further military operations to propose, considerable enough to authorize my detaining the squadron under my command longer here, I beg leave to acquaint you, that I intend to proceed with it for England without loss of time,

I am, Sir,

Your most obedient

Most humble servant,

EDWARD HAWKE."

Sir John in his defence, says, he wrote, in answer, that he would summon the general officers

" that shall be found there, and exert such other efforts, as
" shall be judged most proper for annoying the enemy.' And
" with regard to any other particular attempt, which, agree-
" ably to your orders, you shall have commenced, and in the
" execution whereof you shall be actually engaged, it is also
" his Majesty's pleasure, that you do not desist from, or break
" up the same, merely and solely on account of the time limit-
" ed for your return by the instructions above mentioned;—
" but that, notwithstanding the same, you do continue with
" the troops during such a farther number of days, as may
" afford a competent time for the completion of any operation
" under the above circumstances; after which you are to take
" care to return with the forces under your command, and the
" fleet, in the manner directed by your former instructions."

to confider of Sir Edward's letter, and defired A. D.
him to fignify his intention in writing: which he 1757.
did in a letter to him, the fame day. He then
applied to Sir Edward for a council of war: who
declined it, and faid, that feamen were no judges
of land operations, which were to be performed
by troops on fhore. In confequence of this Sir
John fummoned all the land officers, who had
been of the council of war, and laid Sir Edward
Hawke's letter before them. And being affembled, fays he, "We confidered the uncertainty
" of landing, if the wind fhould blow as it had
" done the night before, and the account we had
" that day received from the Captain of the Viper
" floop, who had informed Colonel Howard, that
" he had feen a confiderable body of troops near
" the landing place, whofe numbers he did not
" exactly know, but he had obferved five pair of
" colours; that he faw them in camp; that the
" next morning the view of the camp was inter-
" rupted, fo that he could not fee them again,
" which he attributed to the enemy having thrown
" up fome ground on the beach, and that he faw
" the fand hills on the beach confiderably higher
" than they were on Sunday, when he came there.
" Colonel Howard, in his return from reconnoi-
" tring, reported this to me.

" It farther appeared to us, that the attempt
" upon thofe forts at this time, could not juftify
" the ill confequences of detaining the fleet in that
" bay, at a time when, from what we had learnt
" from the converfation of the fea officers, two
" great

A. D. 1757.

"great French fleets were expected home; that at this season of the year, so near the equinox, such westerly winds were to be apprehended, as might detain the fleet there many weeks; that the foundation, upon which the resolution of the council of war upon the 28th was taken, was, that it might be done during the necessary detention of the fleet in the demolition of the fort of Aix, and thereupon was directed to be done with all possible dispatch: that the demolition of the works of the Isle of Aix was compleated that very day, and that the wind was then fair for the fleet to return; add to this, that the time limited by his Majesty's instructions was now expired, and that the time was not prolonged by Mr. PITT's letter, which allowed us only to compleat such operations, as we had already begun.

"Upon all these considerations, not thinking it a measure either adviseable or justifiable in us to take upon ourselves the consequences of detaining the fleet any longer in those parts, we came unanimously into the Admiral's proposal of returning to England."

Dispositions made by Sir Edward Hawke for returning home.

In the mean time [n] Sir Edward Hawke ordered the agent for the transports to direct them to follow

[n] When Sir Edward Hawke had received an answer from the land officers, "That they were all agreed to return directly to England," he sent a letter to Mr. PITT, which concludes with—"It was the *daily* expectation of their undertaking something, which induced me to stay here so long: As I have got their final resolution, I shall sail for England to-morrow morning."

his signal, and that no troops should disembark without further orders. And all the ships of Vice Admiral Knowles's division came down from before Aix into the open road. On the 30th the fort of Aix was blown up and in flames ° : and on the 1st of October the whole fleet got under sail and returned to England, *without making any attempt to land on the coast of France* ᵖ.

Words

° Eight mortars of 14 inch. and 30 pieces of cannon were found in the fort, i. e. 16 eighteen pounders, and 14 fourteen pounders.

ᵖ The London Gazette, of the 8th of October, has this particular article in the account of the expedition,—" On the 29th " of September the resolution was taken to return to England " the troops, *no attempt having been made to land on the coast of* " *France*." And Admiral Hawke's letter of advice concerning this service in Basque road, and his resolution to return home relates, That having maturely considered the report of the officers he had sent to reconnoitre and found the coast, he was of opinion they might land: that Sir John Mordaunt desired a council of war to consider of it, that then it was granted by every body, that the landing could be effected: that in confidence of their judgment, and knowledge of their own profession, the sea officers assented to their reasons for not proceeding to attempt taking Rochefort by escalade.—It was, says he, the daily expectation of their undertaking something, that induced me to stay here so long. Though before I came here, this place was represented, as very difficult of access, and so narrow, that ships could not lie in safety from the forts; nay the pilots made many baulks, says he, before we came in: yet I find it a safe, spacious road, in which all the navy of England, merchant ships included, may ride without the least annoyance; and that a squadron may, at any time, by laying here, prevent any armament from Rochefort, and ruin all the French trade to Rhee, Oleron, or the continent, within these islands.

A D 1757.
Difcontent at home.

Words can't exprefs the murmurings of the nation, when they heard that a fleet and army, which had coft them in this expedition, almoft a million of money, and had thrown the French miniftry, as well as their coaft, into the utmoft confufion, was returned without making one actual attempt towards executing the King's orders, except in that hour's work, in the reduction of the little ifland of Aix and its fortification.

The country exclaimed againft the commanders, and cried aloud for juftice on the delinquents. The officers in defence endeavoured to throw the blame upon the miniftry, or at leaft upon the injudicioufnefs of the plan given them to execute; and upon the variety of incidents, that concurred towars their difappointment. And each of thefe accufations and allegations being fupported by ftrong prefumptions or undoubted facts, his Majefty, to prevent any applications to him from his fubjects in their incorporate capacities, or otherwife by way of addrefs, did nominate and appoint, His Grace Charles, Duke of Marlborough, Lieutenant General, Lord George Sackville and John Waldegrave, Major Generals, to examine and enquire, and to make their report concerning the

Enquiry appointed.

iflands. And then concludes,—I beg leave to affure you, Sir, I have difcharged my duty to my King and country with fidelity, diligence, and integrity, and wifh more could have been done for the good of the fervice. The pilot of the Magnanime has behaved like a man of bravery and fkill, and as fuch I beg leave to recommend him to you.

causes of the failure in the expedition against Rochefort [q].

A. D. 1757.

The board met on the 12th of November 1757, and having ordered the papers containing all the orders and instructions, which appeared to have been signified to the commanders of the late expedition, to be read, they examined witnesses in regard to their authenticity and contents; under which examination there came out a very particular circumstance relating to the minutes of the council of war, on board the Ramillies, in Basque road, on the 28th of September. For, General Mordaunt begged leave to observe, that the minutes there produced were taken down without the knowledge of the persons, who composed the said council of war, and never seen by the gentlemen, who had subscribed them. Vice Admiral Knowles went farther, and disavowed these minutes entirely; and said he never saw them till they were shewn to him after his arrival in London, and that he did recollect, that there was a positive determination, that no minutes should be taken, but that the informations only of the persons examined should be noted down: which examinations he never heard read. This was confirmed almost literally by Major General Conway, Major General Edward Cornwallis and Colonel Geo. Howard. But Rear Admiral Broderick, said,

The board meets.

[q] This commission of enquiry was signed on 1st November 1757, and directed to Thomas Morgan, Esq; Judge Advocate, General of his Majesty's forces, or to his deputy.

A.D. 1757.

that he did observe minutes taken, that he did object to it, and that he never saw those minutes *.

The

* These are the minutes of this council, transmitted by Sir Edward Hawke to the proper office.

THE council in order to determine whether the forts leading to, and up to the mouth of the river Charante were open and capable of being attacked by land, proceeded and examined

1. Lieutenant Colonel Wolfe, who declared, that he was of opinion, that fort Fouras was not a strong place, seemingly principally fortified towards the sea: that he had seen people at work on the land side: that the taking of the barbette battery near it, would be of great use in taking the fort, provided there was proper ammunition for that purpose; and that Fouras must be taken by artillery or escalade.

2. Lieutenant Colonel Clarke, said, he could make no kind of judgment of fort Fouras, on the land side, by the help of a telescope; the only method he had ever heard of observing it.

3. A French prisoner said, Fort Fouras is a circular fort: no ditch on the back of it towards the land, when he saw it three years ago: that it mounted 24 pieces of cannon towards the sea, and had embrassures for guns towards the land: that Fort la Pointe is like Fouras circular, and mounts 22 pieces of cannon, and has a wall on the east side towards the land, like that of Fouras: that the landing in the bay of Chatelaillon is the best landing of any place here; and that when landed, and you get upon the Rochefort road, it is a fine open country: that on friday morning, the 23d Inst. he was in Fort Fouras, that there were but 22 or 24 guns in it, and not above 50 men of all kinds. That there are much about the same number of guns in Fort la Pointe, and that both forts are inclosed by a wall, in much the same manner towards the land.

The council having considered the evidence, Sir John Mordaunt declared his opinion, that something further should be attempted, and that he would give his orders accordingly that

moment,

The papers being gone through, and no body offering to give the commissioners any information touching the causes of the failure of the expedition,

moment, if any, meaning the general officers of the troops, would say it was adviseable.

Vice Admiral Knowles declared, he had received great light from the persons examined, and therefore thought something ought to be attempted.

Major General Conway, declared for the attempt merely from his own opinion, without regard to evidence.

Sir Edward Hawke, appealing to every member of the council for the truth of what he said, declared that he was now of the same opinion, which he had given both before and at the council of war of the 25th, *That the landing could be effected;* That the troops ought to be landed for some farther attempt, which was alone matter of consideration with the general officers of the troops, he, not taking upon him to be a judge of land operations, but would from a confidence in their abilities, and skill in their own profession, readily assent to any resolution they should come to, and assist them to the utmost of his power. This being settled, after some debate, Sir John Mordaunt, Vice Admiral Knowles, Rear Admiral Broderick and Captain Rodney withdrew.

The council of war being re-assembled, and the question put, whether it was adviseable to land the troops, to attack the forts leading to and upon the mouth of the river Charante?

Yes.	No.
Howard	Cornwallis, but he afterwards
Rodney	acquiesced with the majority.
Broderick	
Conway	
Knowles	
Mordaunt	
Hawke.	

N. B. This is the council of war, of which it was afterwards said, that it had been agreed to take no minutes.

A. D. 1757.

Sir J. Mordaunt's reasons for not fulfilling his instructions.

Sir John Mordaunt, as commander in chief of the land forces was called upon to shew the reasons, which prevented him from carrying his Majesty's instructions and orders into execution. To which he replied by delivering a narrative of his whole conduct from beginning to end. Which was in substance, what has been already related.

A contradiction in his defence.

In the examination of Sir John's narrative the commissioners hit upon a passage, which assigns this as a reason why the troops were not landed in the night of the 28th of September, "Because it would be day, before the first embarkation could get a-shore;" whereas in Rear-Admiral Broderick's letter to Sir Edward Hawke it is said, "That the generals were come to a resolution not to land to-night, but to wait till day-light, when they can have a full view of the ground, where they are to land." Which seeming contradiction occasioned a deal of altercation. However Admiral Broderick persisted in the truth of the letter; that he did give the letter to Sir John, and that Sir John did read it, and approve of it, before it was sent in his name to Edward Hawke.

How reconciled.

But Major-General Conway endeavoured to reconcile the passages, by saying, that he conceived Sir John's meaning was, that he would have the ground viewed in the morning, in order to embark next night; and then, after asking many questions concerning Aix, Fort Fouras, the practicability of landing, the strength of Rochefort and the informations received from prisoners concerning that town, they declined all further proceedings.

When

When the examination was finished, Sir John Mordaunt addressed himself to the board, as follows,

Sir J. Mordaunt's address to the board.

I AM conscious of having done my utmost, to the best of my judgment, for his Majesty's service, in the conduct of this expedition: and I have submitted myself voluntarily and readily to this examination. I desire no favour or partiality, and I know I shall have the most exact justice in the report this honourable board will make.

I apprehend that an enquiry into the whole conduct of an expedition, without any accusation formed, or any charge laid, is a proceeding not quite common; and however free from guilt a man may feel himself, there are few, who can stand so strict an examination.

There is nothing but the high opinion I have both of the justice and candour of this board, could make me easy in such a situation.

I therefore hope you will be indulgent to my errors; but I desire no mercy for guilt or known disobedience, and with these sentiments I submit myself to the court.

The board did then report to his Majesty, That it appeared to them, as one cause of the expedition having failed, "the not attacking Fort Fouras by sea, at the same time that it would have been attacked by land—That " another cause was conceived by them to have been; that instead of attempting to land, when the report was received

The report made to his Majesty by the board of enquiry.

A. D. 1757.

ceived on the 24th of September from Rear-Admiral Broderick, and the captains sent with him, to sound and reconnoitre, a council of war was held on the 25th; in which it was unanimously resolved *not to land*, as the attempt upon Rochefort was neither adviseable, nor practicable: because it did not appear to the board; that there were then, or at any time afterwards, either a body of troops or batteries on the shore sufficient to have prevented the attempting a descent, in pursuance of the instructions signed by his Majesty. Neither did it appear to them that there were any sufficient reasons to induce the council of war to believe, that Rochefort was so far changed in respect of its strength, or posture of defence, since the expedition was first resolved on in England, as to prevent *all attempts of an attack* upon the place, in order to burn and destroy the docks, magazines, arsenals and shipping, in obedience to his Majesty's commands. That they thought themselves obliged to remark upon the council of war of the 28th of September, that *no reason* could have existed sufficient to prevent the attempt of landing the troops previous to that day, as the council then unanimously resolved to land with all possible dispatch: and that they further observed, that after it had been unanimously resolved to land, in the council of war of the 28th, the resolution was taken of returning to England, without any regular or general meeting of the said council; and that they looked upon the expedition to have failed from the time the great object

ject of it was laid afide in the council of war on the 25th. *A. D. 1757.*

This enquiry, however well intended by his Majefty, did not anfwer the intention either of acquitting the general, or of appeafing the nation: but was productive of more public altercations. Some of which endeavoured to juftify the impracticability of the expedition-plan, and to throw the whole blame of its failure upon the Right Honourable Gentleman then at the head of the miniftry. Others as ftrenuoufly infifted upon its practicability, and without fixing the blame on any particular perfon or perfons, advanced fhrewd reafons to fufpect a fecret caufe for the failure of this fecret expedition. *Does not quiet the minds of the people.*

A right honourable author* deigned to enter the lifts amongft the firft clafs; and, with promifes not to deceive, and that he would write nothing, but the moft exact truth, begins with a fneer at the ftrength and fecrefy of this expedition, and at the expectations of thofe, who placed any hopes of advantage in its effects,—" An expedition, as
" he expreffes it, prepared with fo much often-
" tation of force, whilft its deftination was kept
" fo profound a fecret, and on which the perhaps
" over-raifed expectation of many feemed to reft
" the very iffue of the war." To back this he infinuates, that it was pretty clear, long enough before hand, that it was intended againft the weftern *Writers in defence of the land officers.*

---

* Candid reflections on the report (as publifhed by authority) of the general officers, &c.

A. D. 1757.

coast of France, and, consequently, that France could not be supposed so neglectful, as to leave Rochefort entirely out of their general plan of defence upon that coast, considering its importance.

He then collects the various opinions past by the public, on the disgraceful return of so powerful an armament, without effecting any thing answerable to the hopes or designs of its outset.

Attempt to cast the blame on Mr. Pitt.

The greater part of the nation vented their resentment on the commanders in this unsuccessful expedition, as the readiest objects. Another, by far less numerous part, did justice to the good intention, but questioned whether the projectors had sufficient ground of knowledge or information to warrant the undertaking. Some, merely guided by private attachments, or prejudices in favour of the projectors, or, at least, of the principal promoter of this attempt, extolled it to the skies, admired the activity of the new minister, that made so glorious a contrast for him to the past indolence and inaction of his predecessors; not without throwing out shrewd hints of the envy of some, who had opposed his rise to power, having been carried to such treasonable lengths, as secretly to have thwarted and countermined his operations. On the other hand, others, perhaps influenced by considerations of the like private nature by pique, prejudice, or even that envy, of which they were accused, treated, or affected to treat, the whole plan as chimerical, crude and indigested, both in the projection and appointment of the

execu-

execution, from which no better, nor other success could be expected than what befel it. Some over-refined politicians pretended to discover in the combination a tenderness for Hanover, or at least a connexion with the convention of Stade. But all ranks united in a general dissatisfaction at this enterprise, having either been so weakly projected, as not to suffer even an attempt to execute it; or at the defect of the execution itself.

{A.D. 1757.}

It is plain the fault was somewhere; and to discover where, the enquiry was appointed under such officers, as were at the head of the military profession. However this royal commission, and the characters of the officers, that filled the board, could not escape the censure of the advocates for the commander in chief; who commended him for thinking himself at liberty to call it *a proceeding not quite common*, and laying him under several disadvantages in case he should be brought to trial.

Remarks on the board of enquiry.

The impracticability of this expedition was supported by an attempt to prejudice Colonel William Clerk in the opinion of the people, as capable of giving a partial evidence in favour of the information he had given, upon which the plan was originally formed; or to create a belief that the state of Rochefort was greatly changed since he had made his observations on that town, fortifications, &c. For this purpose the French King's regular forces, which, by the memorial laid before the cabinet, did not amount to 200,000, were mounted up to 300,000 regulars in

The information of Captain Clarke questioned.

A.D. 1757.

in pay: The thirty thousand men stationed to guard the coast from Calais to Bayonne inclusive, were augmented with 100,000 militia-men, kept up in constant training, within that compass: the strength of Rochefort was magnified so much as to bid defiance to a sudden insult; as if it could be readily supplied from neighbouring garrisons with a numerous militia; and might be put in a condition of laughing at almost any number of troops, that should appear before it; especially unprovided with stores and materials for a regular assault, and situate up a river unnavigable for vessels of burden.

Impracticability affirmed.

It was further urged, that Fort Fouras must have been first taken, before the reduction of Rochefort could be attempted: But that Fouras is unexpugnable by our shipping, that the coast in Chatelaillon-Bay was covered with soldiers concealed behind sand-banks: that the information of the first suggesters of the undertaking was defective: that none but the French could have wished that our armament had proceeded further in the execution of its mission: that not a soul on board knew half the requisites to be known before any execution could be proceeded to, or even rightly planned; and at the same time, that it was no fault of *theirs* (the commanders) that they did not know them. And therefore that it might be lamented that so gallant a fleet had not been fitted out earlier against Cape Breton; as the infinite importance of America, and the actual situa-

tion

‑sion of things there loudly called for such a decisive measure.

Hence it was said, that the commanders had been acquitted with so much honour by the Board of Enquiry, That there was not a word in their report, but what they might ever glory in avowing and subscribing to: that the not attacking Fouras by sea, at the same time that it should be attacked by land, was to be laid to the charge of Thierri the pilot: at least, that in this the commanders were in no fault; nor in their resolution of the 25th, not to land; because the nature of the errand they were sent upon, and the impossibility of its execution were already plain enough, and though they might not see any troops, nor batteries on shore, it could not be supposed that there were not both, and sufficient to cut off our men, as they landed, division by division. And that from the premises it was easy to discern, whether the failure was imputable to the original sin of insufficiency in the project itself, or to the persons commissioned to carry it into execution;—whether all the requisites of knowledge were duly obtained before the dispatch in the armament, or whether a set of gentlemen, of unattainted characters, and trusted with the arms of their country, could be so grosly wanting to its honour, and to their own, as to return back with so bad a grace, if a better knowledge, and a personal view of things had not forced them to it, with a regret they rendered but too apparent by persisting in it so much beyond the bounds of their

margin: A. D. 1757. Commanders commended for not attempting to land.

their duty, that one would have thought them willing to prefer the bare opinion of others at a distance, to their own actual and palpable recognition on the spot.

Answer to this defence.

To this justification it was replied [t], That the unpromising prognostications of this expedition, and the suspicions and insinuations about a tenderness for Hanover were made and spread by a set of men, as observed before [u], not famous for their extensive knowledge, and who, by their private intrigues and cabals, had, a few months ago, thrown the affairs of the King and kingdom into so much confusion; hoping, by the same influence, by which they had put a stop to all public business, at that time, to blast the expedition

To whom the cause of the miscarriage to be imputed.

also. That a plan, (whoever projected it) approved, on the utmost deliberation, by his Majesty, and unanimously approved on by his cabinet-council; undertaken on a full examination of facts by the generals to be employed, without

Observations on the plan.

protest or remonstrance; approved and desired by the King of Prussia [w], and prepared under the immediate inspection of Sir John Ligonier, commander in chief of the King's forces, could not be a project so totally repugnant to common sense, and impracticable, as the advocates for the commanders therein chose to represent it. As to the insinua-

---

[t] In the expedition against Rochefort fully stated and considered, &c. by a country gentleman, the late ingenious Thomas Potter, Esq;

[u] On page 303.

[w] As appears in the Enquiry, p. 20.

tion

tion about the illegality or uncommonness of the proceeding against Sir John, by way of enquiry, it was observed, That this was not the first institution of a board of general officers, for the purpose of inquiry into the conduct of a commander: that it took place under the auspices of his Royal Highness William, Duke of Cumberland, at that time commander in chief of the British forces: and that an officer was judged, condemned, and ruined by such a board of enquiry, without any other trial. But that, if ever such an enquiry was right and proper, it was so in the present case, where the parties had combined in an agreement upon a total suppression of evidence. For, in the very council of war, which unanimously resolved to do nothing, far from a desire to state the evidence, on which they proceeded, and their respective opinions upon that evidence, (which one should think natural to every one, who is solicitous for his honour and justification,) the first thing resolved upon was, to take *no minutes of opinions*; and that even the informations of the persons examined should not stand part of the minutes, so as to be transmitted to any person [x].

It having been insinuated ironically, that the great officers, who were appointed for this enquiry, were not the best qualified for such an important service, it was retorted, that they could not be of Mr. PITT's recommendation, considering the known and declared friendships, con-

[x] See Enquiry, page 10. and the note on page 340.

nections and attachments of the majority of them; who most certainly had no partiality in favour of the projectors, and against those, who ought to have executed the plan of the expedition.

As to the multiplying of the military forces on the coast of France; they were so far from amounting to about 100,000 regulars, besides 100,000 militia, that there were actually but 4000 regulars, at the time our fleet came upon the coast, for the defence of all the garrisons and out-works in and near port l'Orient, la Rochelle and Rochefort; and the smaller division of these was at Rochefort. It is true there was a marshal of France to command this petty corps. But it is also as true (in the accounts given by the French themselves) that the old marshal considered all as lost, the moment the attack was pointed at Rochefort: and he was so far from making dispositions to dispute the landing of our troops, that he spent his hours in tears, and in writing expresses to his court.

Only 4000 regulars at Rochefort and on that coast.

It was observed, That the commanders could not take any refuge under the definition of a *coup de main*: which does not only mean a surprise, and that the whole prospect of success must be given up, where the opportunity of a surprise shall be lost: but that it includes every other way of attack, except by open trenches and erecting batteries; as properly explained in the advice delivered by Sir John Ligonier to Sir John Mordaunt [y]; " It may perhaps, says he, succeed *best*

Coup de main explained.

---

[y] See Enquiry, p. 22.

" at

" at your coming up, as the enemy may be in a
" great hurry, furprife and confternation, at fuch
" an unexpected vifit, and not have time to make
" his difpofitions. But if that is not thought
" proper, it (the *coup de main*) may *fucceed as well*
" *after the place has been thoroughly reconnoitred*,
" and you have fixed the fpots, where you de-
" fign to make the greateft efforts: and if the
" enemy fee any preparations for a regular attack,
" they will lefs expect a *coup de main*, &c."

A. D. 1757.

From hence it was inferred, That, if Sir John Mordaunt really thought Sir John Ligonier to be a man of that experience in the art of war, which he defcribes him to be: if he really meant to guide himfelf by the whole of his advice in the execution of the plan, and not to excufe himfelf, only by felecting certain parts of it from others, which were explanatory, and with which they were connected, how came he fo totally to have forgot this part of it, which, if any doubt had fubfifted, would have explained what was intended by a *coup de main*; and to have remembered only the recommendation to fecure a communication for a retreat: not fhewing the neceffity of Fort Fouras being taken *before the troops were landed*, in order to fecure a retreat; but fuch a retreat, as could be fecured after they were landed:—" Suppofing,
" fays Sir John Ligonier, the *troops landed*, it
" muft be left to the confideration of the generals,
" whether they fhould not march, with proper
" precautions, *directly* to Rochefort, to prevent
" any fuccours being thrown into the place, at

Remarks on Sir John Ligonier's letter.

A. D.
1757.

"the same time that the marines should be em-
"ployed for making a good *intrenchment* for the
"security of the stores to be landed from time
"to time, as well as of a retreat in case of ne-
"cessity."

Impropriety of admitting parties in evidence.

It was thought a very insufficient means, to wipe off any imputations, to attempt to invalidate the evidence and opinion of Colonel Clarke; because it was upon his representation that the expedition against Rochefort was thought of; as if he was bound in honour to support his own plan; and when the very officers, of whom the council of war was composed, were admitted to give testimony in the cause, in which they were the very parties to be tried, in case of a general misconduct.

Fort Fouras might be attacked by sea.

As to the practicability of taking Fort Fouras, the argument ran high in opposition to those, who voted against the attempt in the council of war.—It was taken for granted that the French, in matters of defence would conduct themselves on principles similar to those, which are adopted by the rest of mankind: and that, of the building a fort, it is built either to defend or offend. Thus Fouras was weak to the land, it stood at the water's edge, to guard the channel; it stood even on a bank, which ran into the water with twenty-four embrasures to the water-side[z]. Therefore its use was to guard not a sand-bank, over which scarce a Thames wherry could pass, if some accounts should be admitted; but a channel fit for

[z] See Enquiry, page 30.

large

large ships. If it had so many guns, what could be their use, if a ship could not come up within gun-shot? So that according to Admiral K———s there was no channel at all; or it lay out of gun-shot of the fort. It was further observed, That though the vice-admiral's master found no more than six feet water at high water, and a bomb-ketch, which drew but eleven feet water, went aground, at near three miles distance; the Coventry frigate did the same farther out, and the Barfleur at a still greater distance; yet *after* all this delay and hazard to the ships, that admiral thought fit to sound and try the depth of water at a distance from the fort, where no cannon could reach; and there is not one single proof given of an attempt to find the depth of water near the shore, and within gun-shot of the fort.

That there was a narrow channel, near the shore is, therefore, incontestible from the circumstance of the case: and it is demonstrable from the evidence of the French fisherman Bonneau, who knew it well, navigated it, and was examined by General Conway, &c. [a] who vouched four fathom (viz. twenty-four feet) water at half cannon shot from Fort Fouras; sufficient water for a sixty gun ship. Besides, when the public were acquainted not only with the testimony of the pilot Thierry, confirmed by Bonneau, but with Captain Colby's offer to carry the Princess Amelia [b] up to Fouras, they could not help thinking that

[a] See Enquiry, p. 53.   [b] Ibid. p. 30.

A. D. 1757.

Court martial appointed.

there was a myftery, which might be eafier gueft, than explained.

Thefe and many more difadvantageous reflexions were made on the conduct of thofe, who were entrufted with the execution of this fecret expedition againft Rochefort, and demanded a more fatisfactory proceeding to come at the caufe of this extraordinary difappointment to the nation in general. Nothing but a public trial could fatisfy the people. And it is thought that Sir John Mordaunt was no lefs folicitous for a court-martial, as the only method to eftablifh his own reputation with his countrymen. Accordingly his Majefty iffued his warrant for that purpofe on the third of December [c]; in which court he, Sir John, was charged with difobedience to his Ma-

[c] This court confifted of nine lieutenant generals, nine major generals and three colonels: viz. Lieut. Gen. James, Lord Tyrawly, prefident.—Lieut. Gen. Charles Lord Cadogan—Lieut. Gen. John Guife—Lieut. Gen. Richard Onflow—Lieut. Gen. Henry Pulteney—Lieut. Gen. Sir Charles Howard—Lieut. Gen. John Hufke—Lieut. Gen. John Lord Delaware—Lieut. Gen. James Cholmondeley—Major Gen. Maurice Bockland—Major Gen. William Earl of Panmure—Major Gen. William Earl of Ancram—Major Gen. William Earl of Harrington—Major Gen. George Earl of Albemarle—Major Gen. Henry Holmes—Major Gen. Alexander Dury—Major Gen. John Moftyn—Major Gen. Edward Carr—Colonel William Kingfley—Colonel Alexander Duroure—Colonel Bennet Noel—Charles Gould, Deputy Judge Advocate General.

Who affembled in the council chamber at Whitehall, on the 14th of December, and continued by feveral adjournments, to the 20th of December 1757.

jesty's orders and instructions. But there being no other Evidences heard on this trial, than had been admitted at the board of enquiry, except Admiral Hawke's deposition; and they all by members of the council of war, under whose resolutions Sir John pleaded authority or advice for his conduct, he was acquitted, after a defence, that differed in no essential point from the former. The court unanimously found him not guilty of the charge exhibited against him, and did therefore acquit him. But the opinion of the public remained unaltered; who, on this occasion, could not forbear throwing out some bitter speeches against the contrast, which they pretended to discover between the lenity of this sentence and the rigour of that passed upon the unfortunate admiral, who was so severely treated by the populace, and condemned and executed for not doing all that was in his power to do; or for not attempting to relieve Fort St. Philip, and for not fighting the French, who had got the heels of him, and would not stay and give him the opportunity to do all in his power to do on that occasion: and they could not even help suspecting some secret cause for the failure of this expedition, from the unprecedented measures taken by some of the courtiers, to prevent a parliamentary enquiry, which was the intention of the new ministry, to sift out the true cause. When the city of London was preparing to address his Majesty for this purpose, they were stopt by a message from the King, sent to the Lord Mayor, by Wil-

A. D. 1757.

Acquits Sir John Mordaunt.

How received by the public.

Parliamentary enquiry how stopt.

liam Blair, Efq; one of the clerks of the privy council, to acquaint him that he had given proper directions for an enquiry to be forthwith made into the behaviour of the commanding officers of the said expedition, or to that effect, which caused the motion for an address not to go on.

The nation acquit the minister.

But, though the discontent of the nation did not appear in the least to be appeased, they were far from ascribing any blame to the minister. They were satisfied, that the secret expedition had been intended, and that it was well calculated, to annoy the enemy; to make him susceptive of wounds upon his own coasts; to strike terror and dismay throughout all his subjects; to enervate and dispirit his arms, and to strike at the root of his maritime power, without which France could not possibly maintain a war, to the prejudice of England; and further they pleased themselves with the hopes, that it would conduce greatly to wipe off the disgrace of our late misconduct and miscarriages, and stimulate the British nation to exert their natural strength, and retrieve their antient glory.

What effects this expedition had on the powers of Europe.

These motives and expectations were certainly frustrated in some measure. Yet the powers of Europe interested in the sea, could discover by this specimen of the new minister's abilities, his spirit, and penetrate into the designs of his measures. They, from this moment, began to look upon the British councils with more care and circumspection; when they saw a man placed at the head

head of, and giving directions to, a warlike people, who admitted no other rule for his operations against their enemy, than conveniency. His new syſtem, reſolution and activity convinced them, that he would not be diſcouraged by the failure in his firſt attempt, however it had happened. Sweden and Denmark thought it time to arm in defence of their commerce in the Baltic, and joined their maritime force for that purpoſe, to guard againſt a ſurprize in the north. We ſaw the Italian ports taking the beſt meaſures in their power for their own ſecurity. The very Dutch could not look upon theſe proceedings without a dread, that made them propoſe an augmentation of their navy. As for France, our natural enemy, ſhe was not prepared to contend with a power, that braved every danger, had totally changed its ſyſtem, and was in a condition, and reſolved to attack her with full vigour. What ſtruck our enemies with the greateſt conſternation and dread; they perceived that no failure in the execution was able to prejudice the nation againſt this miniſter; and, for the firſt time, ſaw a Britiſh miniſter unanimouſly applauded for a meaſure, that had miſcarried. Diviſion, the grand engine of the French ſyſtem of politicks, by which they had ſo often diſgraced us abroad and diſtracted us at home, was healed. Popularity and the adminiſtration were now united: a bulwark more impregnable than our arms, and ſo eſſential in a country like England, that a miniſter, unleſs he has the power and addreſs to gain it, can never

A. D.
1757.

On France in particular.

act

A.D. 1757.

act with the strength of the whole nation, nor invigorate a true spirit in the people. This shewed the enemy that the spirit of the nation was rouzed from that stupid lethargy, in which it had continued for some years, and assured the English that their confidence was not misplaced, in a man of experience, integrity, and uninfluenced by lucrative and ambitious views; steadily pursuing their interests and happiness, and eagerly snatching at every opportunity to complete their wishes, and to preserve unanimity, as the only support against an insidious powerful enemy, and to execute the measures necessary to humble him with success.

On Great Britain.

Therefore, though the nation lamented the cause of their late discontent; they rejoiced in the administration of *one*, who had already made so great a change in the face of their affairs, and had alarmed all Europe with a sample of those great things, we are able to do with our natural strength. They had, with too much reason, run away with a despicable opinion of our degenerate strength, both in the cabinet and in the field: and now they perceived the antient spirit and military virtue of the people revive, to be once more the terror of the French.

The accounts from other parts, about this time, confirmed this opinion. Mr. PITT, in the month of February, had interest enough to forward a squadron to Jamaica, to cover our islands and trade in those seas from the injuries and danger that threatened them daily, by a superiority of the French men of war in America. Admiral Coates,

Capt. ARTHUR FORREST.

Coates [d], who commanded this squadron, detached Captain Forrest, with three frigates to cruise off cape Francois, which was the best station to intercept the French trade to Europe, and to watch their naval designs. At that time M. Kersaint, who had scoured the English settlements on the coast of Guinea, in November last, was then returned, and lay in that harbour with four men of war: and upon the first notice of Captain Forrest's appearance, the French commander strengthened his ships with an addition of sailors and soldiers, and put to sea, to attack the English frigates. Captain Forrest having descried the enemy, called his two captains on board his own ship, and said, " Gentlemen, you know your own " strength; and see that of the enemy: shall we " give them battle?" They, not regarding the vast superiority of the French, answered in the affirmative. " Then, said he, fight them we will, " there is no time to be lost: return to your ships, " and get them ready for engaging." It was done with the greatest alertness. They did not wait the attack in their station, but bore down upon the enemy with uncommon spirit, engaged them with the utmost fury for two hours and a half, in sight of the Cape, and obliged them to run back faster than they had advanced, and to seek protection in their fortified harbour, where the small squadron, under Captain Forrest, was forced to let them rest, being obliged to return

A. D. 1757.

Captain Forrest's gallant action in the West Indies.

[d] See page 152, Vol. II.

to Jamaica to repair his ships. Which done, they immediately sailed for the coast of Hispaniola; where he made up for their trouble and disappointment on the last occasion, by taking a fleet of nine Domingo men richly laden, with a single ship. This was the first effect of Mr. PITT's *first* administration, felt in the West Indies.

East Indian affairs.

About the same time that Coates was sent to Jamaica, Commodore Stevens was dispatched with another squadron to the East Indies; as related before [e]. But it is not time to expect any account of the effects of that reinforcement, ordered to join the fleet under Admiral Watson. Nevertheless this year furnisheth a variety of actions both by sea and land beyond the line.

Captain Chaillaud's relief of Trichinopoly.

The French began very early in 1757, with an attempt to surprise Trichinopoli. M. d'Autueil was charged with this service; who invested the place with nine hundred men in battalion, three or four thousand Sepoys, about one hundred Europeans and Hussars, and a much greater number of country horse. Trichinopoly, at this juncture, was not in a condition of defence against such a force, the greatest part of the garrison having marched under the command of Captain Chaillaud, who was then before Madura, a place about 100 miles from Trichinopoly, and of great consequence to the affairs of the company and their allies. However, matters were not conducted so privately by the French, but Captain Chaillaud

[e] On page 152. Vol. II.

was informed of their design, and by forced marches with all his Europeans, and one thousand of the best Sepoys, and four days provisions in their knapsacks, he was fully resolved to save the town at all events, knowing that it must be lost without his assistance. On the other hand it was the interest of the French to be as watchful and resolute to prevent his entrance into the town.

For this purpose the French formed themselves in four divisions; which formed a chain quite a-cross the plain, over which it was expected Captain Chaillaud would be obliged to attempt a passage: in the front of which their cavalry was advanced, and divided into small parties, to possess the roads and posts all round; except the plantation grounds, which extended about nine miles to the westward of the town, and was so sloughy [f], that it was impossible to march over it without being above the knee in mud at each step: and therefore deemed impassable for an army, and left unguarded.

Disposition of the French army.

Captain Chaillaud, informed by his spies, of the enemy's disposition, resolved to take his rout by this neglected and difficult way; but with such precaution as to give no suspicion of his intentions. He, to put it out of the power of spies or deserters to betray his march, kept forward in the common great road, without the least

March of the English forces.

---

[f] Occasioned by the overflowing of the waters, which is a necessary part of agriculture in these regions, and without which the rice will not grow.

A.D. 1757.

appearance of his design, till the close of the evening, when he commanded his little army to wheel off towards the rice fields. They arrived on the plantations about ten that night; and after seven hours most fatiguing march, they got, unnoticed by the enemy, within cannon-shot of the fort, and were admitted undiscovered; the enemy's attention being drawn from that quarter, not only by its difficult access, but by a detachment of two companys of Sepoys, whom the captain had ordered to march in the common road, and to alarm the enemy on the other side: which service they effectually performed, and made their own retreat good through the woods, till they found an opportunity, next night, to get into the town. When the enemy were convinced of this reinforcement's safe arrival in the town, they were too well convinced of the impossibility of their being able to take it; and of the danger they ran in continuing exposed in the field, to the enterprising genius of the brave commander, that was now in a condition to attack their camp.

Colonel Forde's unsuccessful attempt on Velloure.

M. D'Auteuil therefore resolved to return with his army to Pondicherry. Colonel Forde, who was ordered by the government of Madrafs to reduce the fort of Velloure [g], which, as apprehended, its governor Nazeabulla Cawn had, or

[g] This town is twice as large as Madrafs. It has five gates, two large and three small, surrounded by a mud wall, very broad at the bottom, and about three feet thick, on the top of the rampart; and by a dry ditch, except on the north side, which in rainy seasons has water in it.

intended to make over, with other places and ports, to the French, did not succeed so well. The colonel battered that fort three days, and on the 5th of May, he made a practicable breach, and began the assault at the break of day. Fifty Caffrees, led up by Ensign Elliot at their head, marched with great resolution to the foot of the breach. They were followed very close by three companies (300) of Sepoys, till they came within sixty yards of the breach; where they laid themselves down in a ditch, and could not be prevailed upon to advance a step further: so that the Europeans, that did not exceed 100, were obliged to march over them to the breach. This was executed with great intrepidity; and having joined the Caffrees, they advanced to the top of the breach; where they were received by the people in the fort so warmly, with pikes, fire-locks, clubs and stones, that it was impossible for such a handful to force their way over; though they maintained the assault three quarters of an hour. Then the colonel, convinced that there could be nothing done with his force against so gallant a defence, deserted also by the Sepoys, ordered a retreat; which was conducted with such good order, that not a man was hurt after they had left the attack. But in the action there were about forty Europeans killed and wounded, and about fifty Caffrees and Sepoys. They that were wounded, were rendered unfit for present service: and there was scarce any one in the breach, that escaped bruises and contusions.

Several

Various other actions.

Captain Polier.

Captain Adlercron.

Conjeveram plundered.

Several other actions happened, with various success. Our forces under Captain Polier, sent from Madrass, reduced Outremulour, a fort possessed by the French; which he entered without resistance: the French garrison consisted only of Sepoys, who abandoned the fort, upon the first notice of Captain Polier's march. But this conquest was of a very short duration. For, Captain Polier leaving no more than forty Sepoys in garrison, it was obliged soon after to submit to a detachment of one hundred Europeans and Topasses and 300 Sepoys, which marched against this fort from Allamparva. However, the situation of Outremalour gave the government of Madrass so much uneasiness, that Colonel Adlercron was immediately ordered to attempt its final reduction, and to destroy its fortifications: which he faithfully performed. From hence the colonel marched to invest Wandewash, a fortress of great importance, in the interest of France. But was deterred from making any attempt upon the place, by advice that the French army, which had been employed against Trichinopoly, was marching to its relief.

The retreat of Colonel Adlercron encouraged the enemy to follow him close, as far as Conjeveram, which they plundered; but were repulsed in their attack of the Pagoda or Fort, with the loss of an officer and six Europeans killed, and about ten wounded; though the garrison consisted of no more than a serjeant and two companies of Sepoys.

Colo-

Colonel Lawrence marched against the French at Wandewash. They were encamped and strongly entrenched about a mile from the town. The colonel took post on the 10th of June, about four miles from them, and tried every method to draw them out of their entrenchments, his men being full of spirits, and eager for engagement; but without effect—So that, as they could not be brought out into the open plain, and, they had a great superiority in numbers, and their entrenchments were defended by several batteries, it was thought proper to withdraw an army, that was obliged to remain inactive, and at an useless expence.

As for the French army it remained about Wandewash, till the 20th of September, when they marched against Chetteput with eighteen hundred Europeans. The place was defended by Nizar Mahomed Cawn, the governor, assisted by a serjeant and sixteen men from Fort St. George: who defended themselves to the last extremity, and killed a great number of the enemy. The governor being driven out of the fort, renewed the fight in the streets, and disputed every inch of ground, till a musket-ball deprived him of his life. On the report of his death, his family immediately destroyed themselves; and a vast slaughter of his troops ensued.

The desperate defence of Chetteput.

Captain Chaillaud having delivered Trichinopoly from the French, returned with the utmost diligence to his small corps, left to blockade Madura, and took such part of the garrison with him,

The siege of Madura.

as

A. D. 1757.

as could be spared, without exposing that town to a surprize from the enemy; making in all ninety military and four hundred Sepoys, supported by two twenty-four pounders. Having joined the troops under Lieutenant Rumbold, who had maintained his station before Madura, and erected a battery, he began to play his cannon from thence on the 9th of July; made a breach before noon, and without delay, to prevent new works being thrown up in the night, he formed the attack, and advanced to the breach by two o'clock of the same day. But the besieged gave them so brave a reception, that the best of his men fell in the attempt, or were so wounded, that it was not possible for him to persist in the assault. For the remainder retreated: nor was it in his power to spirit them up to a second attack, having lost between thirty and forty Europeans and Caffrees and a hundred Sepoys. However this brave and skilful officer did not despair of success, either by compelling the town to capitulate by famine, or to accept of reasonable terms to deliver up that fortress; so necessary for the security of the company's affairs, into his hands. He made the proper dispositions to reduce the place by famine. But, as this method might take up so much time, as to prolong his stay till the arrival of the French fleet, and all the strength, that could be collected, was necessary for the defence of their garrisons, against that event, he had orders to break up the blockade, and return to his command at Trichinopoly. Therefore he tried what could be done

Bravely defended.

Loss of the English.

How reduced.

by

ROBERT LORD CLIVE.

Fulta on the 15th, where Governor Drake and the gentlemen of the council waited for their arrival, on board of such ships and vessels, as had the fortune to escape the Moors. It was the 28th before the fleet could stir from hence, (the pilots absolutely refusing to take charge of such large ships till the springs were over) when he sailed with the following ships: the Kent, Tyger, Salisbury, Bridgwater, and King's Fisher sloop. The next afternoon Colonel Clive was landed, in order to march and attack Busbudgia fort by land, at the same time that the squadron appeared before the place, which anchored and began to cannonade about eight o'clock in the morning on the 30th; and, at half past eight, the King's troops were landed to support Colonel Clive. The ships soon silenced the enemy's fire; and, at seven in the evening, 100 seamen were landed under the command of Captain King. At half past eight, the body of the fort was on fire; and, immediately after, the place was deserted by the garrison; which being but few, escaped into the country. One of the company's captains was killed, and four soldiers wounded. This fort was extremely well situated for defence, having a wet ditch round it; but badly provided with cannon; only 18 guns, from 24 pounders and downwards, and about 40 barrels of powder, with ball in proportion, being found in it.

Busbudgia fort attacked.

Taken.

Situation and strength.

On the 1st of January the Kent and Tyger anchored between Tanna fort and a battery opposite to it, both which the enemy abandoned, as the ships

Tanna fort deserted.

ships approached. About 40 guns, some 24 pounders, and all mounted on good carriages, with some powder and ball, were found in this fort and battery; and the Admiral left the Salisbury as a guard-ship to prevent the enemy from regaining them.

Enemy's ships burnt.

In the night the Admiral sent the boats, manned and armed, up the river, to burn a ship and some vessels said to be filled with combustibles, which was executed without opposition.

March to Calcutta.

The next morning, early, the company's troops were landed, and immediately began their march to Calcutta. The Kent and Tyger soon after proceeded up the river, together with the 20 gun ship and sloop.

The Moors begin the fire.

At 40 minutes after nine, the enemy began to fire upon the Tyger, from their batteries below Calcutta, which they abandoned, as the ships approached.

Returned.

At 20 minutes past ten, the Tyger and Kent made a very warm fire, insomuch that the enemy were soon driven from their guns, and presently after ran out of the fort, which Captain Coote, with the King's troops, and an officer from the Kent, entered a little before eleven. Four mortars, 91 guns of different sizes, and a considerable quantity of all kinds of ammunition, were found in the fort. The ships suffered very little in their masts, yards, and rigging, and only lost nine seamen and three soldiers killed, and 26 seamen and five soldiers wounded.

Fort deserted.

An expedition was then proposed against Hughley, to be executed by the 20 gun ship and sloop, the boats of the squadron manned and armed, assisted

assisted by all the King's troops, amounting to 170, the company's grenadiers and 200 sepoys, which were to be landed under the command of Captain Kilpatrick. Every thing being prepared; they sailed under the command of Captain Smith, of the Bridgwater, on the 5th of January 1757, and attacked this city with so much spirit, as they had done the other forts, that indicated a revenge for the barbarous treatment of their countrymen, that it was also reduced without any considerable resistance. The garrison fled; and left behind them 20 guns, 24 pounders downwards, and a considerable quantity of ammunition. Nor could this satisfy the revengeful conquerors, who burnt and destroyed the city, and the granaries and storehouses of salt petre, situate on each side of the river: by which the Nabob's army was greatly distressed for subsistance in that part of the country.

A. D. 1757.

These atchievements of British valour rouzed the Moorish Prince, and convinced him of the necessity for him to provide a more respectable force to stem the progress of their arms, than the feeble garrisons of unexperienced Indians. He therefore, assisted with French officers, engineers, and gunners, resolved to take the field, with 10,000 horse and about 15,000 foot. His army took the rout of Calcutta, and on the 2d of Feb. 1757 it marched past the English camp, at the distance of about a mile, and pitched their tents on a convenient spot of ground, near the town.

The Nabob takes the field.

His force.

A. D. 1757.

Is attacked by Colonel Clive.

Colonel Clive, who had already begun to re-establish the military honour of the English, which was sinking there, as it had done in other places, did not hesitate a moment about what was to be done, notwithstanding the enemy's prodigious superiority in the field. He trusted to his faithful and brave fellows, whose valour he had so often tried and proved. He only requested such an addition of seamen, to manage his artillery, as could be conveniently spared. Accordingly Captain Warwick received orders on the 4th to take upon him the command of a detachment of 600 sailors, draughted from the several ships, to join Colonel Clive, in order to force and to drive the Nabob out of his camp.

On the 5th at one in the morning, Captain Warwick landed his men a little above Kelsal's octagon; about two he joined the Colonel, whose troops were under arms, and at three the whole army, in three columns, marched, the sailors attending the train, which consisted of six field pieces, and one haubitzer. About five, the troops in the van were charged by the enemy's horse in their camp; and by the time our rear guard were entered, the engagement became general from hedges and bushes; on which they played our artillery, defending the right and left of our army all the way through the camp, and driving the enemy before them, with great rapidity, 'till they lodged themselves in a tope, near Meter's garden, behind the hedges: from hence they detached a large body of horse, with two cannon, to the cross road of the

the Bunglo, which our men soon dislodged, and from thence marched into the fort. In this action were killed 12 seamen, two captains of the company's troops, 17 private men, and 10 sepoys. The number wounded were about 15 seamen, and 50 soldiers and sepoys. Lieutenant Ludwidge of the Salisbury, the only officer mortally wounded. Of the enemy 1300 were killed and wounded, besides horses, draught bullocks, and three or four elephants. This attack, though not attended with all the wished for success, yet it was sufficient to make the Nabob very solicitous to hasten a peace, which was concluded on, and consisted of the following articles.

A. D. 1757.
Loss on our side.

Loss of the enemy.

Articles acceded to, and signed by the Nabob of Bengal, February 9, 1757.

I. WHatever rights and privileges the King has granted the English company in their Phirmaund, and the Husbulhoorums sent from Delly, shall not be disputed or taken from them, and the immunities therein mentioned be acknowledged and stand good. Whatever villages are given the company by the Phirmaund shall likewise be granted, notwithstanding they have been denied by former Subahs. The Zemindars of those villages not to be hurt or displaced without cause.

Articles of capitulation.

Signed by the Nabob in his own hand,
 I agree to the terms of the Phirmaund.

II. All goods passing and repassing through the country by land or water, with English dustricks,

A a 4   shall

shall be exempt from any tax, fee, or imposition, whatever.

I agree to this.

III. All the company's factories, seized by the Nabob, shall be returned. All monies, goods and effects belonging to the company, their servants and tenants, and which have been seized and taken by the Nabob, shall be restored. What has been plundered and pillaged by his people, made good by the payment of such a sum of money, as his justice shall think reasonable.

I agree to restore whatever has been seized and taken by my orders, and accounted for in my sincany.

IV. That we have permission to fortify Calcutta in such manner as we may think proper, without interruption.

I consent to this.

V. That we shall have liberty to coin siccas both gold and silver, of equal weight and fineness to those of Muxadavad, which shall pass in the provinces.

I consent to the English company's coining their own imports of bullion and gold into siccas.

VI. That a treaty shall be ratified, by signing and sealing, and swearing to abide by the articles therein contained, not only by the Nabob, but his principal officers and ministers.

I have sealed and signed the articles before the presence of God.

VII. That Admiral Watson, and Colonel Clive, on the part and behalf of the English nation, and of the company, do agree to live in a good under-

understanding with the Nabob; to put an end to these troubles, and to be in friendship with him while these articles are performed and observed by the Nabob.

I have sealed and signed the foregoing articles upon these terms; that if the governor and council will sign and seal them with the company's seal, and will swear to the performance on their part, I then consent and agree to them.

The Nabob humbled, his hands tied from acting against us; and the company in possession of all their settlements and forts, it was resolved, by the commanders in chief, together with the governor and council of Calcutta, to turn their arms against the French, in those parts, and to begin with Chandenagore, a place of considerable strength, and the principal settlement of the French in that part of India; situate a little higher than Calcutta, upon the same river. Colonel Clive undertook the land service, and with 300 of the Bombay troops, 400 more Europeans and 1600 Blacks, he immediately marched to Chandenagore, before the French could expect such a visit. His first step was to make himself master of all the French outposts, which he soon accomplished; except one redoubt, situate between the river side and the walls of the fort, mounting eight pieces of cannon of 24 pounders, four of which pointed down the river. So that it was necessary to wait the arrival of the men of war. Admiral Watson undertook the attack by sea; and on the 18th came

to

A. D. 1757. Ships. River obstructed.

to an anchor with the Kent, Tyger and Salisbury, about two miles below Chandenagore; where he found the passage of the river obstructed by sinking two ships, a ketch, a bulk, a snow, and a vessel without any masts, all directly in the channel, within gun shot of the fort, and by laying two bombs moored with chains across the river,

How removed.

This obstruction caused a considerable delay. But as soon as the bombs were cut adrift, the Admiral, by sounding, found out another channel, with sufficient water for his ships to pass through. He was joined on this occasion by Admiral Pocock, who hoisted his flag on board the Tyger. So that on the 24th, at six in the morning, this petty squadron weighed and sailed up in the following order, the Tyger, Kent, and Salisbury. At ten minutes after six the enemy began firing from the redoubt, which was abandoned as soon as the leading ship got a-breast of it. At three quarters after six the ships were placed, when the signal was made for engaging, which continued very brisk on both sides till a quarter past nine. The enemy then waved over the walls a flag of truce, and desired to capitulate; and the articles being agreed upon and signed, Captain Latham, of the Tyger, was sent a-shore to receive the keys, and take possession of the fort. Colonel Clive marched in, with the King's troops, about five in the afternoon.

Attack begun.

Strength.

They had in the fort 1200 men, of which 500 Europeans and 700 Blacks; 183 pieces of cannon from 24 pounders downwards, three small mortars, and

and a considerable quantity of ammunition. Besides the ships and vessels sunk below, to stop up the channel, they sunk and run a-shore five large ships above the fort. Four sloops and a snow were taken in the harbour. The enemy had killed in the fort 40 men, and 70 wounded. The Kent had 19 men killed, and 50 wounded.

All the officers and men in general, agreeable to their usual bravery, behaved with great spirit and resolution on this occasion; as did also the land forces, who kept a good and constant fire, the whole time, from two batteries of four and two guns, which they had raised near the fort.

Articles of capitulation proposed by the Director and Council for the French East India company's affairs at Chandenagore to Vice Admiral Watson, with his answers, March 23d 1757.

Art. I. THE lives of the deserters shall be saved,

Ans. *The deserters shall be absolutely given up.*

II. All the officers of this garrison shall be prisoners on their parole of honour; that they shall have liberty to carry with them all their effects, and go where they please, on promising they will not serve against his Britannic Majesty during the present war.

The admiral agrees to this.

III. The soldiers of the garrison shall be prisoners of war, so long as the present war continues: and when peace is made between the King of France and the King of England, they shall be sent to Pondicherry, and till then be entertained at the expence of the English company.

The admiral likewise agrees, with this difference only, that instead of sending the soldiers to Pondicherry, they shall be sent to Madrass or to England, as the admiral shall hereafter think proper; and that such foreigners, who are not of the French nation, and chuse voluntarily to enter into the English service, shall have liberty.

IV. The Sepoys of the garrison shall not be prisoners of war, they shall have leave, on the contrary, to return on the coast in their country.

The admiral agrees to this.

V. The officers and men of the company's European ship St. Contest, shall be sent to Pondicherry in the first English ship, which goes to the coast.

The officers and men of the European ship shall be upon the same footing as the soldiers, and to be sent to Madrass or to England as soon as possible.

VI. The French jesuit fathers shall have liberty to exercise the functions of their religion in the house, which has been assigned them since the demolishing of their church: the silver ornaments, and every thing that belongs to the church, shall be given them, and also their effects.

The admiral cannot agree to any Europeans residing here, but that the French jesuits may go to Pondicherry, with all the ornaments of their church, or wherever they please.

VII. All the inhabitants, of what nation or quality foever, as Europeans, Muftees, Chriftians, Blacks, Gentils, Moors, and others, fhall be put in poffeffion of their houfes, and all in general as fhall be found belonging to them, either in the fort, or on their eftates.

In regard to this article, to be left to the admiral, who will do juftice.

VIII. The factories of Caffembuzar, Dacca, Patna, Jeuda, and of Bellafore, fhall remain at the command of the chiefs, who direct them.

To be fettled between the Nabob and the admiral.

IX. The director, councellors, and thofe employed under them, fhall have leave to go where they pleafe, with their cloaths and linnen.

The admiral agrees to this.

The admiral expects an anfwer by three o'clock this afternoon, and that the Britifh forces may take poffeffion of the fort by four.

The above-mentioned propofitions have been accepted of by the council; in confequence of which we have delivered up the fortrefs of **Chandenagore** to Admiral Watfon.

Chandenagore the 23d of March 1757.

P. Renault, Laportiere, M. Fournier, F. Nicolas, A. Caillott, Sugues.

Having thus made ufe of the opportunity to crufh the French power, when the Nabob was not in a condition to give them any affiftance; they now ferioufly turn their thoughts upon the conduct of the Viceroy, fince his laft folemn engagements

Ulterior proceedings in regard to the Nabob.

with

A.D. 1757.

with the English; and finding that his dilatory performance of his obligations by treaty, and his frequent prevarications and tokens of dislike, from the very moment of his signing that treaty, indicated his intention to be bad, they thought it a proper and necessary measure to renew hostilities with the Indians: the Viceroy having given them sufficient reasons to do themselves justice by way of arms.

Remarks thereon.

How a war in these circumstances would have been justified, which was to be undertaken, and must have been in a great measure depending upon the success of the army by land; an army that did not exceed 2300 men, including 1600 Blacks, against the whole strength of the kingdom of Bengal and its allies, is not conceivable. But here we may properly apply the old proverb, *Audaces fortuna juvat.* The brave are fortunate. A lucky, unforeseen, unexpected accident helps out the little army of conquerors in their desires. It was decreed that they should be the scourge of that tyrant, that inhuman barbarian, who, a few months before, took a pleasure in the tragedy of Calcutta.

Favoured by the treason of the Nabob's Greatmen.

While, therefore, the commanders, &c. were consulting about the expediency and practicability of so great and hazardous an undertaking, which, with success, would deliver the company from the difficulties, under which they were often obliged to yield to the caprice and impositions of the Nabob and his officers; and, in a manner, make them masters of the whole trade of the kingdom of Bengal:

Bengal: and on the contrary, which, if they should fail in the attempt, might be attended with the total extirpation of their nation from the Ganges, and with a prohibition of all commerce with the English for the future; Nabob Suraja Doula behaved in so tyrannical a manner to his own subjects, and especially to his great men and generals, whom he treated with indignity and contempt, for remonstrating against the measures, he was adopting and executing upon the advice of his favourites and sycophants, that there arose a general discontent; and a conspiracy was formed, to depose him, by some of his principal officers; provided they could engage the English to favour the revolution.

A. D. 1757.

How they were disgusted.

The design was communicated from the conspirators by Jaffier Ali Cawn, his prime minister, a nobleman of great authority and influence, and at the head of the conspiracy, to Mr. Watts second in council at Calcutta. An affair of this delicate nature, and proposed by a prime minister, required great consideration and penetration to guard against that deception and cunning, for which the Easterns are so remarkable in all their dealings. It was well known that the Nabob treated his subjects with a tyrannical spirit; but it was also known, that they were accustomed to slavery, and that they carried the yoke, as a matter of duty. The Nabob's haughtiness towards his great men, and his attachment to favourites of violent and perfidious principles, were no secrets: but it was running the utmost hazard to trust the deliberations

Their conspiracy communicated to the English.

A. D. 1757.

How managed by Mr. Watts.

tions of the conferences at Calcutta to the prime minister of the power, they were calculated to destroy. In this dilemma Mr. Watts managed the intercourse, he had with the prime minister, so prudently, that he drew from him sufficient conviction of his sincerity; and of the manner how the conspirators were to act their part, when matters should be brought to an open rupture between the English and the Nabob, before he would consent to lay the proposal before the council; not seeming too forward; but making a merit of, and the prime minister accountable for, every step the English should take, by this requisition, in a rupture, which, he had the address to say, was to deliver the natives from tyranny and oppression.

A treaty being settled between the council and officers of the fleet and army at Calcutta, and the conspirators; the company were to renew hostilities to oblige the Viceroy to fulfil the stipulations of the late treaty. Jaffier, on his part, promised to desert his master with the best troops in his army, on the field of battle. Accordingly Colonel Clive took the field[n] with all the force he could muster, which did not exceed 1000 Europeans, and 2000 Blacks; besides 50 seamen, under the command of a lieutenant and seven midshipmen, to manage eight pieces of cannon, the whole of their artillery, though he drew out the garrison from Chandenagore, which the Ad-

[n] On the 13th of June 1757, the army marched from Chandenagore to Muxadavat, the capital of the province.

miral

miral engaged to replace with seamen. This was the whole strength in this undertaking, except a 20 gun ship stationed above Hugly, to preserve a communication between the fleet and army. On the 18th they took Catwa by storm; and without much resistance or any loss. This was a necessary precaution, in order to secure a retreat, in case of a miscarriage; this town and fort being situated advantageously on that branch of the river, which forms the island Cassimbuzzar. Here also intelligence was expected from the conspirators, for their future conduct. But it does not appear that Jaffier dared yet to trust to his interest in the Nabob's army; which was assembling with all diligence about the capital, at the first news of the motion of the English army towards Muxadavat.

A. D. 1757.

Catwa taken by storm.

Colonel Clive continued at Catwa three days, and on the 22d crossed the river, and advanced immediately to attack the Nabob's army [b], which consisted of 20,000 men, well provided with artillery; exclusive of two divisions under the command of the conspirators. Their 24 pounders, under the direction of French gunners, began to play about seven in the morning, long before our field pieces were able to do any execution. But what carried the most disagreeable aspect in this day's service, was the behaviour of the conspirators; who, during the engagement, remained inactive spectators, leaving the whole work to be done

Strength of the Nabob's army.

[b] Encamped on the plains of Plaissey.

between

A. D. 1757.

Doubtful conduct of the conspirators.

between the Nabob's division and the English; as if they were determined to close in, and share with, the conquerors, in the triumphs of victory, on which side soever it might declare; or, if the English army had been cut off and utterly destroyed, to fall upon the Nabob's troops fatigued and wasted with the service of the day, and so work their deliverance from both the Nabob and the English.

Providential aid.

In this doubtful situation, Providence supplied the deficiency of numbers. It was desperate to march up to the mouths of so numerous an artillery. A smart shower of rain removed this difficulty and danger. The enemy drew their cannon out of the rain into the camp under cover.

Captain Clive's good conduct, &c.

Colonel Clive availed himself of this capital error, by a well placed detachment, which prevented their being brought again into action; and with a presence of mind, resolution and conduct, peculiar to himself, having hitherto covered his men from the enemy's cannon, by a favourable disposition under a mud wall, that encompassed a grove in the midst of the plain, he resolved to attack the Nabob's trenches, about four in the

Forms the attack.

afternoon. The grenadiers under the command of Major Kelpatrick were ordered to advance, with two pieces of cannon: which they performed with extraordinary resolution and bravery, doing great execution with their field pieces, in their first onset. They then made a second attack upon another quarter; and, in about half an hour, a third against a third post, the Sepoys keeping a continual fire, the whole time, into the enemy's trenches,

trenches, killed several persons of the best distinction. This dispirited the Nabob's forces: the right and center fled, abandoning their camp and artillery; which threw the whole Indian army into confusion: this was no sooner perceived than orders were given to storm the trenches; and those orders were executed with so much firmness and chearfulness, that the enemy was entirely routed, leaving behind them 42 pieces of large cannon. The Nabob had 400 men killed and 600 wounded: whereas there were not above 20 killed and 50 wounded, the greatest part of whom were Sepoys, on our part.

A. D. 1757.

The enemy routed.

Loss on both sides.

The unfortunate Nabob convinced of the treason of his principal officers, and not daring to trust himself with troops, that would not defend a fortified camp against such a handful of men, fled also with the few that continued faithful to him. Jaffier Ali Cawn and Roy Dolab, the next in command in the army, now declaring openly against their defeated sovereign, hasted away to secure the capital, and, by their own desire, were followed by the victorious army, to place Jaffier Ali Cawn, according to treaty, on the ancient throne of the Nabobs of Bengal, Bahar and Orixa.

The Nabob flies for his own safety.

The conspirators declare themselves.

Colonel Clive marched to Muxadavat, and was received into the city, with every token of joy and gratitude for the service he had done, in delivering that country from tyranny and oppression: Jaffier Ali Cawn was proclaimed Nabob; and a few days after the Nabob Suraja Doula was traced, seized

Colonel Clive's entry into Muxadavat.

Ali Cawn made Nabob.

A.D. 1757.

Old Nabob murdered.

Remarkable revolution.

and privately put to death, in the 25th year of his age.

Thus, in about thirteen days, this extraordinary revolution, in defiance of the most powerful Nabob in the east, whose dominions were not inferior to most kingdoms in Europe; in extent, in inhabitants, and in the richness of its commerce; and whose military strength was very respectable, both as to numbers, artillery and discipline, was accomplished, with less force and trouble than often is required to take a petty fortress in Germany or Flanders.

Ali Cawn ratifies his treaty.

The rejoicings at Muxadavat did not delay business. They that placed Ali Cawn on the seat of dominion, immediately exacted a ratification of the treaty he had previously signed with the company; and it was executed as far as the circumstances of the times would permit. By that treaty the former act of pacification, signed on the 9th of February 1757, by the Nabob since deposed,

The substance of the treaty.

was ratified and explained. A sum of 2,212,500 pounds was agreed to be paid in two moieties, in satisfaction of the third article of that treaty, of which one moiety was paid soon after the accession of Ali Cawn; and he assigned funds for the payment of the other moiety. The French were for ever prohibited from settling in the three provinces. The company's territories were enlarged with a very great extent. Their privileges confirmed. The Nabob divested himself and successors of all right of building new fortifications below Hugley, near the Ganges. He granted
the

the company a leafe of the Salt Petre of Patna, which had been a perpetual bone of contention between them and the Dutch; and he rewarded the army and the fleet with a prefent of 625,000 l. fterling; befides immenfe riches in jewels, &c. beftowed on the officers, amongft which was a turbant valued at 18,000 l.—It was this action that merited the public title of the *heaven born general*, which all the world can't take from the commander in chief, then Colonel, now Lord Clive, who, untutored in the art of war, performed heroic and more advantageous actions in the field than any of his cotemporaries, whofe atchievements are recorded with the blood of hundreds of thoufands left in the field of battle, at the vaft expence of many millions of money, and with the diffatisfactory accumulation of heavy taxes. Colonel Clive returned to his native country full of glory and riches, to reap the favours of a grateful nation. His Majefty created him a Lord.— The company fettled a large penfion upon him. But Admiral Watfon, after eftablifhing a great and lafting reputation for his wifdom, his courage, and his humanity, was cut off by the unwholfomenefs of the climate, very foon [p] after the days of rejoicing for this fignal victory were over. By whofe death the chief command in thofe feas devolved on Admiral Pocock.

Great as thefe advantages feem to be, they were confidered only colateral to the grand object of

A. D. 1757.

The heaven born general.

Admiral Watfon's death.

Admiral Pocock commander in chief.

Importance of this revolution to Great Britain.

[p] On the 16th of Auguft 1757.

the war, in a national light. They enriched individuals engaged in the service: they increased the riches and power of the united English East India company: they annoyed the enemy, and ruined their trade and interests, and thereby cut off the resources, they otherwise would have drawn from those distant climes, to maintain the war in Europe and America.

Affairs of North America.

But the advices from North America continued so unfavourable, that the nation received but little joy in these victorious accounts from the East. A squadron of ships had been sent ⁱ under Admiral Holborne, but to no purpose. The French, it is true, were driven off from Fort William Henry ʳ. But this was no more than a short respite, till the enemy could return with a more effectual force. — No part of our arms felt the effects of the administration after Mr. PITT was turned out, more than in North America. Every thing seemed to devolve into the old channel of discord and inactivity. Lord Loudon, on whose confidence with the American provinces depended all that part of his commission, which could not be executed without harmony and concord, lost all his popularity by laying an embargo ˢ on all the ships in North American ports, in order that the enemy might not receive any intelligence of his designs; without considering that the enemy received their intelligence chiefly, if not altogether, by land, upon that continent; and also to make provisions

How declined at Mr. PITT's dismission.

Bad effects of an embargo.

ⁱ See page 168. Vol. II.   ʳ See p. 181, &c. Vol. II.
ˢ On the 3d of March.

plenty

plenty and cheap for the army and navy; whereas he should have known, that the exports can never exhaust the great quantities of provisions which the British colonies in general produce, but more especially in this year, when the crops of corn were extraordinary. So that by this embargo the merchant, the planter and labourer all suffered, while the contractors put immense sums into their pockets: and corn became a drug in America, while England, that year, was in dread of a famine, and deprived of relief from her colonies by an ill-judged and ill-timed embargo.

The secret intended to be covered by this embargo was, a projected expedition against Louisbourg, in conjunction with a naval force expected at Hallifax. But how was this managed. As for the naval force you have already seen how it was delayed (page 168, 169). And as for the land army: Lord Loudon drew the troops from the northern frontier of the British settlements adjoining to Canada, and from other parts, till he had collected a body of 6000 men, with which his Lordship embarked at New York, on the 19th of June, under the convoy of three frigates only, it must be owned, with great intrepidity, but with manifest danger of falling into the hands of the enemy, whose superiority in those seas, at that time, proved a sufficient argument to set the expedition against Louisbourg aside, after the arrival of the squadron under Admiral Holbourn; though it was then found, that the army amounted to 12,000

A. D. 1757.

Its inutility for the end proposed.

Lord Loudon and army fail for Hallifax.

Whole force when joined with Admiral Holbourn.

12,000 effective men, and the fleet consisted of 15 sail of the line and 18 frigates, &c.

Lord Loudon arrived with his troops at Hailifax on the 29th of June, Admiral Holbourn did not make that rendezvous before the 9th of July: yet, as if delay had been an essential part of their instructions, near a month was consumed at Hallifax in exercising the troops; and by feints, accustoming them to divers sorts of attacks and defence. These steps were condemned, by some, as,—" keeping the courage of his Majesty's sol-
" diers at bay, and expending the nation's wealth
" in making sham fights and planting cabbages ᵘ,
" when they ought to have been fighting the
" enemies of their king and country in reality."

Delay at Hallifax.

Why the expedition was put off.

It was the first of August before these troops embarked, to proceed against Louisbourg. But there was still a fatal remora. A packet, supposed to be a stratagem to intimidate the British commanders, with an exaggerated account of the garrison and others bearing arms in that fortification, threw itself in the way of this fine fleet; was taken and brought in, with all her dispatches, though chased many hours, which was sufficient to suspect the contrivance; for, real packets always throw their dispatches overboard. By the letters found on board this pretended packet, the naval

---

ᵘ Alluding to a hasty expression of Lord Charles Hay, who was a Major General in this armament, and one of the bravest and best officers in this service; but was put under an arrest for some public reflexions on the conduct of affairs in America.

strength

strength at Louisbourg was fixed at seventeen ships of the line and three frigates, which might not be much exaggerated; but there was certainly a very grand augmentation in the military strength, which, upon paper, amounted to 6000 Europeans, 3000 natives and 300 Indians: with this gasconade, that the place was well supplied with military stores, and the people desiring nothing more than to be attacked.

A. D. 1757. The pretended strength of Louisbourg.

This intelligence produced a council of war; and it was therein resolved, upon the credit of this advice, to lay aside the intended expedition; a resolution that had been several times before attempted, but had been as often defeated by those, who rather chose to encounter all dangers, than to do nothing.

Resolution of the council of war.

Lord Loudon made his dispositions [w] immediately for returning to New York, where he arrived on the 30th of August. Admiral Holbourn continued, for some time, cruising off Cape Breton [x], in expectation of an opportunity to attack the French squadron in its return to Old France, and to carry some of them to England. But his hopes

Lord Loudon returns.

---

[w] He garrisoned Hallifax with three battalions, and sent two more up the Bay of Fundy.

[x] On the 20th he appeared off Louisbourg, so near as within two miles, and to see the French admiral make the signal for his ships to unmoor. At which sight the English admiral retreated, and made the best of his way to Hallifax. Where, being reinforced with four ships of the line, he returned to Louisbourg: But could not draw the French out to an equal engagement.

were rendered abortive by a violent storm [y] on the 24th of September, which dispersed [z] and shattered his fleet terribly [a]. So that being forced off his station, and some of his ships greatly distressed, he was obliged to steer away with all speed for England; but left eight men of war under Lord Colville, to protect the trade, watch Louisbourg, and to annoy the enemy.

This was not the only misfortune, that befel Great Britain this summer, in her American war. By Lord Loudon's draughting off the military from the frontiers of the northern provinces, for the expedition against Louisbourg, his Lordship left them more and more exposed to the activity and watchfulness of Montcalm, who, as soon as it was known, that the troops were embarked in

---

[y] It lasted fourteen hours: when it began the fleet was about forty leagues from Louisbourg, and towards the end of it, the ships were within two miles of the rocks and breakers: so that, had not the wind suddenly shifted from south-east to south-west, they would, in all probability, have been drove a-shore and totally lost.

[z] The Grafton of 70 guns, the Tilbury of 60, the Centurion of 50 guns, and the Ferret sloop. The Tilbury was lost, the crew were taken up by the French, and civilly treated; except Captain Barnsley; Mr. Dennis, captain of the marines; Mr. Crockson, captain of the grenadiers; Mr. Plunket, master; Mr. Jones, surgeon; Mr. Walker, purser; Mr. Smith, chaplain; Mr. Mackintosh, gunner; Mr. Truscot, midship-man, some private men to the soldiers and sailors, who all perished.

[a] Twelve ships were almost dismasted, and others very much damaged.

their way to Hallifax, prepared to take advantage of their abſence [b].

Fort William Henry, which in the ſpring of the year, had been ſtormed by the troops under M. Montcalm [c], and then eſcaped only by the vigilance of Major Ayres, the commander at that time, and through the want of many neceſſaries in the French army, who came provided only for a *coup de main*, to take it by ſurprize, or by eſcalade; became the firſt object of that general's operations. The garriſon conſiſted of 2,500 men, and General Webb was encamped with 4000 men not far off, to cover the fort from ſurprize.

M. Montcalm aſſembled an army of 10,000 men, including Cannadians and Indians [d] drawn from Crown-Point, Ticonderoga, and the adjacent poſts; but not with that ſecrecy, as to prevent an early account of his deſign and force reaching General Webb. Who, if he had given due attention to this advice, confirmed by Colonel Parker's loſs [e], and raiſed the militia in time to join his regular forces, might have obliged the French Mar-

---

[b] A peace was concluded, about this time, with the Delawares, the Ten Tribes or Nations and the Five Nations.

[c] See page 181, &c. Vol. II.

[d] Some of theſe were ſo remote that they had not learned the uſe of fire-arms, but uſed bows and arrows, and were reſerved to fall upon advanced parties.

[e] On the 21ſt of July Colonel Parker, with five companies or 350 men, made an excurſion on Lake George, to reconnoitre the enemy; next day they fell into an ambuſh of the French, who were marching againſt Fort William Henry; 150 were taken priſoners, and about 90 were killed.

quis

A. D. 1757.

quis once more to retire from before this fort. But the English general could not be persuaded of the reality of the French intentions. He could not believe that they had a force sufficient to dispute the possession of the fort with him and the garrison. However, Montcalm soon convinced Webb of his error. For on the 2d of August they appeared on the lake: which struck Webb with such a pannic, that he resolved to retire to Fort Edward that same night; but with much persuasions was prevailed upon to stay till next morning: when he marched off early, with a strong artillery, leaving the defence of the fort to Colonel Monro and Colonel Young with 2,300 men.

General Webb retires.

Strength of the garrison.

While the trenches were forming M. Montcalm, advised of the retreat of General Webb, sent the following letter, by way of summons to Colonel Monro.

SIR,   August 3, 1757.

M. Montcalm's letter to Col. Monro, by way of summons.

I Have this morning invested your place with a numerous army, a superior artillery, and all the savages from the higher parts of the country; the cruelty of whom a detachment of your garrison have lately too much experienced. I am obliged in humanity to desire you to surrender your fort. I have it yet in my power to restrain the savages, and to oblige them to observe a capitulation, as hitherto none of them are killed, which will not be in my power in other circumstances; and your insisting on your defending your fort,

can

can only retard the loss of it a few days, and must of necessity expose an unhappy garrison, who can receive no succours, considering the precautions I have taken. I demand a decisive answer immediately, for which purpose I have sent you the Sieur Funtbrune, one of my aid-de-camps. You may credit what he will inform you as from me, I am, with respect, Sir,

> Your most humble, and
>
> most obedient servant,
>
> MONTCALM.

To which the gallant commander replied, with a dignity that became one in his station.

Siege formed. The siege was regularly formed on the 3d with all the force, and a train of artillery. The Indians surrounding the breast-works of the English, whilst the French hove up trenches. The garrison behaved with courage and skill, so as to retard the enemy's works four days; during which time they had the misfortune to burst all their cannon and mortars, except two nine pounders, one four pounder and a hawitzer. Had the militia come in time to their aid, or had General Webb taken proper measures of defence upon the advice he received, it is very probable their enterprize would have been defeated: but delay, that bane of these inactive times, interposed to the ruin of the fort. For after a hot cannonading and bombarding on both sides, till the 9th, the garrison being

being informed by a letter [f] from General Webb, intercepted and sent to the commanding officer in

[f] *General Webb's letter, which contributed not a little to the surrender of Fort William Henry, was as follows:*

SIR, Fort Edward, Aug. 4. 12 at Noon.

I am directed, by General Webb, to acknowledge the receipt of three of your letters; two bearing date nine o'clock yesterday morning, and one about six in the evening, by two rangers, which are the only men that have got in here, except two yesterday morning with your first, acquainting him that the enemy were in sight. He has ordered me to acquaint you, he does not think it prudent, (as you know his strength at this place) to attempt a junction, or to assist you, till reinforced by the militia of the colonies, for the immediate march of which repeated expresses have been sent. One of our scouts brought in a Canadian prisoner last night, from the investing party, which is very large, and have possessed all the grounds five miles on this side Fort William Henry. The number of the enemy is very considerable, the prisoners say, eleven thousand, and have a large train of artillery, with mortars, and were to open their batteries this day. The general thought proper to send you this intelligence, that in case he should be so unfortunate, from the delays of the militia, not to have it in his power to give you timely assistance, you might be able to make the best terms left in your power. The bearer is a serjeant of the Connecticut forces, and if he is happy enough to get in will bring advices from you. We keep continual scouts going, to endeavour to get in, or bring intelligence from you. I am, Sir, with the heartiest and most anxious wishes for your welfare,

Your most obedient humble servant,

G. BARTMAN, Aid-de-Camp.

To Colonel Monro, or officer commanding at Fort William Henry.

the fort, by M. Montcalm, they submitted to capitulate, and obtained the following conditions.

Capitulation granted to Lieutenant Colonel Monro, for his Britannic Majesty's garrison of Fort William Henry, the retrenched camp adjoining, and all their dependencies.

Art. I. THAT the garrison of Fort William Henry, and the troops, which are in the retrenched camp, being joined, shall march out with their arms, and the usual honours of war.

II. The gate of the fort shall be delivered up to the troops of his most Christian Majesty, and the retrenched camp, immediately on the departure of the British troops.

III. All the artillery, warlike stores, provision, and in general, every thing except the effects of the officers and soldiers, shall, upon honour, be delivered to the troops of his most Christian Majesty. Provided always, that this article shall extend to the fort, retrenchments, and dependencies.

IV. The garrison of the fort, troops in the retrenchment and dependencies, shall not serve for the space of eighteen months, neither against his most Christian Majesty, or his allies.

V. All the officers and soldiers, Canadians, women, and savages, which have been made prisoners by land since the commencement of the war in North America, shall be delivered in the

space

space of three months, at Carillon; and according to the receipt which shall be given by the French commanding officers, to whom they shall be delivered, an equal number of the garrison of Fort William Henry shall be capacitated to serve, agreeable to the return given in by the English officer of the prisoners he has delivered.

VI. An officer shall be given as an hostage till the detachment returns, which shall be given for an escort to his Britannic Majesty's troops.

VII. All the sick and wounded, that are not in a condition to be transported to Fort Edward, shall remain under the protection of the Marquis de Montcalm, who will take proper care of them, and return them as soon as recovered.

VIII. Provision for the subsistence of the British troops, shall be issued for this day and tomorrow only.

IX. The Marquis de Montcalm, being willing to shew Colonel Monro, and the garrison under his command, marks of his esteem, on account of their honourable defence, gives them one piece of cannon a six pounder.

Done in the trenches before Fort William Henry, the 9th of August, 1757.

GEORGE MONRO.

Agreed to in the name of his most Christian Majesty, agreeable to the power invested in me by the Marquis de Vaudrueill, his governor-general and lieutenant-general of New France.

MONTCALM.

Notwith-

Notwithstanding this capitulation, the Indian chief insisted upon a previous agreement with M. Montcalm; who had promised him the plunder of the English, and that his men should have their agreement. Accordingly the French, generally in defiance of the faith of the capitulation and of humanity, perfidiously and inhumanly gave way to the Indian demand, and permitted the savage blood-hounds to fall upon the disarmed garrison, and all, except 300, who with their colonels Monro and Young, surrendered themselves to the French, and 600 who fled and escaped to Fort Edward, were stripped, killed and skalpt [g]. They murdered all the English Indians and Negroes found in the garrison, or made them slaves. They cut the throats of most of the women, ript open their bellies, tore out their bowels and threw them in the faces of the expiring sufferers: and taking the children by the heels, they beat their brains out against trees or stones, **so that not one was saved.**

A. D. 1757.

French suffer the Indians to break the capitulation.

Horrid barbarities.

The French general found provisions in this fort sufficient to maintain 5000 men for six months; which he carried off, as well as the artillery, ammunition and warlike stores, baggage, arms, &c. and 100 live **oxen**, besides horses, &c. But he destroyed all the boats, which **were** not wanted to

Loss on our side.

---

[g] There did not survive this massacre more than 1000 men, including the 900 above mentioned. So that they murdered, after the capitulation, 1300 men, besides women, children and other attendants.

transport

A. D. 1757.

transport the plunder; and entirely demolished the fort and the works.

Miserable state of the colonies.

This dreadful stroke, at a time there was no army to face the enemy, filled every mind with fear for the common safety. Nothing but the hopes of success against Louisbourg, appeared to keep up the spirits of the English. But when, upon the back of this loss, they were informed, that the attempt against Louisbourg was dropt, and that the troops, which had been drawn from our northern frontiers, and thereby left the country open, for the French to execute what plans they pleased against our forts and settlements, had been employed in nothing more than sham-fights, &c. at Hallifax; while the enemy were demolishing our forts, and murdering our garrisons; it extorted these melancholly reflexions,—
" God only knows where this will end—the French
" execute almost every thing they attempt: we
" neither execute nor attempt any thing but noise,
" and a prohibition to the printers to tell the
" world what they will, and do know without
" their information [h]."

Remarks on this campaign.

Such was the inglorious campaign of the year 1757, in North America. A campaign, which, by the preparations made for it, promised a total ruin of the enemy. But which, by procrastination in England, and mismanagement in America, left the security of our provinces, and the interest of our allies in a much worse situation,

[h] In a letter from New York, dated August 4, 1757.

than they were in the foregoing year. Mr. PITT, during his short administration, we have seen, formed the plan, and put it into action with a vast increase of forces, which gave us the superiority both by sea and land, to attack the French in their strongest holds, and to cut them out work to defend their own settlements. But when that administration was determined, the enemy was suffered to get the start of our armaments, and to put Louisbourg into such a posture of defence, as to defeat that well-concerted and appointed expedition. Our troops, which amounted to 20,000 regulars, and almost as many provincials, were so badly managed, that the places of greatest danger and importance, were left almost naked, or so garrisoned, as to fall a sure prey to the enemy. Our allies were deserted, and our people exposed to murder and every act of barbarity, even in sight of our troops. Our prodigious fleet failed only to become the ridicule of our enemies: And a vast tract of valuable territory followed the fate of the conquest made by M. Montcalm, at Fort William Henry. Misfortunes to be accounted for no otherwise than upon that certain maxim; where confusion and strife is there will be discord and every evil work. The political contest about power at home, the instability of the administration, and the frequent revolutions in the councils of the mother country, was the original and permanent cause of that languor, which obstructed all our military operations. When officers can keep their posts, and preserve their interest at court,

A. D. 1757.

court, without running into dangerous actions, they seldom will be forward to seek an enemy. And when a ministry is so changeable, that it is uncertain whether a service will be rewarded or condemned, a commander can have little encouragement to try the fortune of war. Besides, should the command be trusted in the hands of men subservient to the will of those, whose principles are averse to vigorous measures, there can be no expectations from the most powerful fleets and armies. Where this bane of all national virtue gets the ascendant, neither honour, nor courage, nor love of our country, will ever be able to prevail with a court-dependent to do his duty.

Affairs in Germany.

Comparative view of King of Prussia's affairs.

How unlike were these transactions to the progress made by our allies in Germany. The distress of Prussia has been already described[i]. Let us survey the Prussian dominions, and measure the remains of those possessions under that crown in April last, and which have been torn from it by the Austrians, Swedes, French and Russians, in the short space of seven months. Than which nothing can give a stronger idea of the dangerous and ruinous situation of his Prussian Majesty; deprived of the means of raising both men and money. The duchy of Guelders, the duchy of Cleves, the principality of Moers, the counties of Linger and Lipstad, the principalities of Minden, East-Friesland and Embden, part of the archbishoprick of Magdebourg, some other parts of the

[i] See page 258 and 282. Vol. II.

Marche,

Marche, ducal Pomerania, a great part of Silesia, and even of the kingdom of Prussia, including Berlin the capital; in a word, almost all his dominions were either taken from him, or laid under contributions and possessed by enemies, who collected the public revenues, fattened on the contributions, and with the money, they drew from the electorate of Hanover, and other conquests. Where was he to get recruits for his army, or the necessaries for their subsistence? Besides, he had to contend with an army of Russians, another of Austrians, another of French, another of Imperialists and another of Swedes.

Yet how much soever these prognosticated his total ruin; his Majesty met with effectual resources in the wisdom of his councils; in the fidelity and bravery of his troops, and in the protection of a good providence. He saw no alternative but to submit to inglorious terms of peace. He was not only thus beset and threatened, but he had lost the assistance of the army of observation, which had laid down their arms under a capitulation, that disabled them to assist him. He summoned all his courage, all his policy; with the former he marched to meet his enemies, and beat them: with the latter he repaired the injury, which was levelled against him by the disarming of the army at Stade.

How his Prussian Majesty conducted himself under his misfortunes.

Russia was the first object of his arms. He was resolved, if possible, to check their intrusion into the quarrels of Germany. His first essay was to try the force of sound reason, and that moderation,

A. D. 1757.

ration, which becomes a great King, renowned for his wisdom and arms. He caused the following declaration of his sentiments to preceed his army.

The King of Prussia's declaration against Russia.

"IT is sufficiently known, that the King of Prussia, after the example of his glorious ancestors, has, ever since his accession to the crown, laid it down as a maxim, to seek the friendship of the imperial court of Russia, and cultivate it by every method. His Prussian Majesty hath had the satisfaction to live, for several successive years, in the strictest harmony with the reigning Empress; and this happy union would be still subsisting, if evil-minded potentates had not broke it by their secret machinations, and carried things to such a height, that the ministers on both sides have been recalled, and the correspondence broken off.

"However melancholy these circumstances might be for the King, his Majesty was nevertheless most attentive to prevent any thing that might increase the alienation of the Russian court. He hath been particularly careful, during the disturbances of the war that now unhappily rages, to avoid whatever might involve him in a difference with that court, notwithstanding the great grievances he hath to alledge against it, and that it was publickly known, the court of Vienna had at last drawn that of Russia into its destructive views, and made it serve, as an instrument for favouring the schemes of Austria.

His

"His Majesty hath given [h] the whole world inconteſtible proofs, that he was under an indiſpenſable neceſſity of having recourſe to the meaſures he hath taken againſt the courts of Vienna and Saxony, who forced him by their conduct to take up arms for his defence. Yet, even ſince things have been brought to this extremity, the King hath offered to lay down his arms if proper ſecurities ſhould be granted to him.

"His Majeſty hath not neglected to expoſe the artifices by which the imperial court of Ruſſia hath been drawn into meaſures ſo oppoſite to the Empreſs's ſentiments, and which would excite the utmoſt indignation of that great princeſs, if the truth could be placed before her, without diſguiſe. The King did more. He ſuggeſted to her Imperial Majeſty ſufficient means either to excuſe her taking no part in the preſent war, or to avoid, upon the juſteſt grounds, the execution of thoſe engagements, which the court of Vienna claimed by a manifeſt abuſe of obligations, which they employed to palliate their unlawful views.

"It wholly depended upon the Empreſs of Ruſſia to extinguiſh the flames of the war, without unſheathing the ſword, by purſuing the meaſures ſuggeſted by the King. This conduct would have immortaliſed her reign throughout all Europe. It would have gained her more laſting glory, than can be acquired by the greateſt triumphs.

The King finds with regret, that all his precaution and care to maintain peace with the Ruſ-

[h] See page 194. Vol. II.

ſian

A. D. 1757.

sian Empire are fruitless, and that the intrigues of his enemies have prevailed. His Majesty sees all the considerations of friendship and good neighbourhood set aside by the Imperial court of Russia, as well as the observance of its engagements, with his Majesty. He sees that court marching its troops through the territories [i] of a foreign power, against the inclination of that power, and contrary to the tenor of treaties, in order to attack the King in his dominions, and thus taking part in a war, in which his enemies have involved the Russian Empire.

" In such circumstances, the King hath no other part to take, but to employ the power, which God hath entrusted to him, in defending himself, protecting his subjects, and repelling every unjust attack.

" His Majesty will never lose sight of the rules, which are observed, even in the midst of war, among civilized nations. But if, contrary to all hope and expectation, these rules should be violated by the troops of Russia, if they commit in the King's territories, disorders and excesses disallowed by the laws of arms, his Majesty must not be blamed if he makes reprisals in Saxony, and if, instead of that good order and rigorous discipline, which have hitherto been observed by his army, avoiding all sorts of violence, he finds himself forced, contrary to his inclination, to suffer the provinces and subjects of Saxony to be

[i] Poland.

treated

at five in the morning on the 30th of August, with such vehemency, that they entirely broke the whole first line of the enemy, and forced all their batteries. The Russian cavalry were routed, and a regiment of grenadiers were cut to pieces, by a regiment of Prussian dragoons, led on the service by the Prince of Holstein Gottorp, brother to the King of Sweden. But this action was of that severe kind, as made it necessary for the Prussian general to desist from any further attempt. For, he lost in this attack 3000 men (the Russian account says 10,000 killed and wounded). So that when he came up to the second entrenchment, which was stronger than the first, he prudently retired rather than expose his whole army. Which resolution he performed with excellent order, and without one attempt of the enemy to disturb his rear, only being obliged to leave behind him the artillery [1], he had taken from the first line, and eleven pieces of his own cannon, for want of proper carriages.

A. D. 1757. Attacked by Count Lehwald.

Loss of the Prussians.

This obliged the Russians to be more cautious how they traversed the distant parts of the country, in parties; and gave General Apraxin such a sample of the service he was to expect, should he proceed to favour the operations of Count Daun, as his instructions directed, that Lehwald's retreat, in a great measure, answered the purposes of a victory in favour of Prussia.

Inactivity of the Russians.

The Russians lost in this engagement 10,000, others say 14,000 men killed; but the account

Their loss.

[1] Eighty pieces of cannon.

published

A. D. 1757

published by M. Apraxin reduces them to 7000, amongst whom were three generals. Their wounded were very considerable [m], amongst these was General Lapuchin and a colonel of artillery, who with many more were made prisoners. No officer of distinction fell amongst the Prussians: nor was there any one but Count Dohna wounded.

M. Lehwald having mustered his army after this severe service in his camp, to which he returned back at Velau, changed their position for one more advantageous at Peterswald, that he might more effectually retard the further motions and progress of the enemy, in case they should make any further movements. But on the thirteenth of the next month, after the Russians had remained totally inactive from the time of this action near Norkitten, M. Apraxin broke up his strong camp, and in a sudden and surprising manner retreated out of Prussia, with such precipitation, that he left between 15 and 16000 sick and wounded, eighty pieces of cannon, and a considerable part of his military stores, behind him.

Their flight.

This flight was made in two columns, and by two [n] routs, and was managed with so much art,

by

---

[m] As appears by the number mentioned below.

[n] One proceeded towards Memel: the other took the nearest way to their own country, through the bailiwic of Absternen or through Lithuania.

It does not, to this time appear, what could be the real cause; but as the Czarina was about that time seized with an apoplectic fit, it was given out, that the army was ordered home by advancing the irregulars towards the Prussian army to cover the design, that it was not discovered till the third day. M. Lehwald upon the first notice detached Prince George of Holstein with 10,000 horse to pursue the run-aways; but they had made such forced marches, that they escaped, except a few, which the Prince made prisoners, and some stragglers, who were killed by the country people on the road to Tilsit.

A. D. 1757.

Both columns burnt every village in their way without distinction. And committed such other acts of barbarity, that they left the roads behind them strewed with dead bodies of men and horses. And thus the Russians entirely evacuated the Prussian dominions, except Memel.

Cruelty.

For this turn his Prussian Majesty was again delivered from the powerful diversion made to his arms by the Russians in favour of Austria. He had no troops to spare for the defence of his territories invaded by the French, and to give them battle. Wherefore the French marshal revelled with impunity in the open country, meeting with no opposition, and after a long blockade reduced Guelders to surrender by famine°, on the 24th of August. The whole country was now left exposed to the enemy, as far as Magdeburg, and

Guelders capitulates.

---

home to support the regulations she had made about a successor, in case of a vacancy on the throne. It is most probable that they wanted subsistence.

° By capitulation, which permitted the garrison to **march** out with honours of war, and to be escorted to Berlin. But most of them deserted before they arrived at Cologn.

the

the revenues were appointed for and received by the Empress Queen [p]. He watched the Austrians and Imperialists, and commanded M. Lehwald to chastise the Swedes, who had penetrated into Prussian Pomerania, just before the retreat of the Russians, and had laid the neighbouring country under contribution.

The Swedish general published a manifesto to justify this unexpected and extraordinary measure, in the name of the King of Sweden, setting forth, "That his Majesty in quality of guarantee of the "treaty of Westphalia could not excuse himself "from causing his troops to enter the Prussian "dominions and division of the Duchy of the "Anterior Pomerania, being by such guarantee "obliged to be vigilant in the support of the "constitutions of the Empire, at that time in- "sulted, to obtain such satisfaction as the states "of the Empire, which had suffered injury, had "a just right to expect, and to restore them the "peace, which had been infringed by the viola- "tion of the said treaty of Westphalia."

To which his Prussian Majesty replied [q], and proved in a most convincing manner, "That the crown of Sweden could not upon any legal foun- dation, lay any thing to his charge, to make it appear that he had really disturbed the peace of Westphalia: and enjoined his vassals, magistrates,

---

[p] She immediately received 200,000 crowns from Cleves and la Marcke.

[q] By his General Manteuffel, who had a command of 12,000 men in Pomerania, to cover Stetin from any surprize.

and

and subjects, in the Anterior Pomerania not to pay any regard to the Swedish declaration, but to preserve their fidelity and allegiance to him their lawful Sovereign, upon the penalty of incurring his most rigorous indignation.

Strength of their army. The Swedish army consisted of 22,000 men, under Count Hamilton; but as soon as M. Lehwald found himself at liberty, he detached 16,000 men, under Prince George of Holstein Gottorp, into Pomerania, and soon after followed with the rest of his army. He not only recovered the country they had seized on, but swept them away and added to his master's dominions all Swedish Pomerania, except the fortified town of Stralsund[r]; and with heavy contributions made the Duke of Mecklenburg repent of his alliance against his Prussian Majesty. Thus ended the Swedish campaign, who without one battle, lost half their men by sickness, desertion, &c.

How to repair the ruinous state of his territories in Westphalia was more than he could foresee, could there be found no way to prevent a neutrality for Hanover, and to prevail with the allies, that had been disarmed at Closter Seven, to re-enter the field. With those views his Prussian Majesty, as soon as he was apprized of a conven-

---

[r] The Swedes did expect to be joined by 15,000 French and 6000 Mecklenburgers: but M. Lehwald striking the blow in time prevented this junction, and reduced the Swedes to such straits, that their General was afraid of being reduced to the necessity of the garrison of Pirna; as appears from his dispatches to his court.

A.D. 1757.

tion with the French Marshal, wrote the following manly and pathetic letter, with his own hand, to his Britannic Majesty.

King of Prussia's letter to the King of Great Britain on the convention.

"I Just now hear that the business of a neutrality for the E——e of H———r, is not yet dropped. Can your Majesty have so little constancy and firmness as to sink under a few cross events? Are affairs in such a bad plight that they cannot be retrieved? Consider the step which your Majesty purposes to take, and that which you have made me take. You are the cause of all the misfortunes that are ready to fall upon me. I never would have broken my alliance with France, but for your fair promises. I repent not of my treaty with your Majesty; but do not shamefully abandon me to the mercy of my enemies, after having brought upon me all the powers of Europe. I expect that your Majesty will remember your engagements, renewed the 26th past, and that you will not listen to any engagement in which I am not comprehended."

His Britannic Majesty, in answer to this letter, ordered the following declaration to be communicated to all foreign ministers residing at the British court, on the 16th of September.

THE King having ordered an account to be given him of the representations of M. Michell, in relation to some overtures made by his Majesty's electoral ministers concerning the checks

checks received in Germany, hath commanded, that anfwer be given to the King of Pruffia's minifter, That it never was his Majefty's intention, that the faid overtures, made without the participation of the Britifh council, fhould have the leaft influence on his Majefty's conduct, as King. His Majefty fees, in the fame light as before, the pernicious effects of the union between the courts of Vienna and Verfailles, which threaten a fubverfion of the whole fyftem of public liberty, and of the independence of the European powers. He confiders, as a fatal confequence of this dangerous connection, the ceffion made by the court of Vienna of the ports of the Netherlands to France, contrary to the faith of the moft folemn treaties; and, in fuch a critical fituation, whatever may be the fuccefs of arms, his Majefty is determined to act in conftant concert with the King of Pruffia, in employing the moft efficacious means to fruftrate the unjuft and oppreffive defigns of their common enemies; and the King of Pruffia may affure himfelf that the Britifh crown will continue to fulfil, with the greateft punctuality, its engagements with his Pruffian Majefty, and to fupport him with firmnefs and vigour.

Whitehall, Sep. 16.   HOLDERNESSE.

His Britannic Majefty, in quality of Elector of Hanover, did alfo apply, by the following remarkable memorial, to the Diet of the Empire, for relief and redrefs in the diftreffed condition of his

A. D. 1757.

his Electoral dominions invaded and seized by the French.

Elector of Hanover's memorial to the Dyet of the Empire.

"THE differences, says the memorialist, arisen between the crowns of England and France had scarce been followed by some hostilities, when the latter loudly threatned to be revenged for the same on the Electoral dominions of his Britannic Majesty; and the preparations then made on the Rhine and the Moselle, together with the various motions of the French, were more than sufficient to prove the reality of that potentate's designs.

"While matters stood thus (*i. e.* towards the autumn of the year 1755) the King of Great Britain had no Electoral minister at the court of Vienna: however, his Majesty amicably expressed his sentiments to that court by the mouth of Mr. Keith, the British minister; represented to her the danger to which his German dominions and the whole Empire were exposed, and demanded the succours stipulated by the treaties of alliance and guaranty that subsisted between the two courts.

"They could not mistake at Vienna the greatness and reality of the danger, nor disown that it would be unjust, to involve, in the war, the states of the Germannic body that had no interest in the differences above-mentioned, and to molest or trouble several other considerable provinces of Germany by the march of armies; but these representations were fruitless. Far from seeing the performance of the promises of a real succour,

and

and the guaranty of his Britannic Majesty's Electoral dominions, he could not even obtain from the Empire dehortatory refcripts to the adjacent circles, in order to prevent their favouring the defigns of France, and giving her affiftance.

"In the mean while the danger greatly increafed: France fent to Berlin an envoy extraordinary, charged, no doubt, to induce, if poffible, the King of Pruffia to difturb on his part the Electorate of Hanover: at the fame time fhe went on with her preparations, and continued her menaces; and it was but too plainly perceived, the approaching winter was the only caufe that prevented her carrying them into execution. This is a true account of the fituation of affairs at that time.

"In the month of February 1756, the King of Great Britain, after a fhort negociation, concluded a treaty with the King of Pruffia, the drift of which was only to maintain the general tranquillity of Europe; to fecure, in particular, the repofe of Germany, notwithftanding the differences fubfifting between the courts of London and Verfailles; to ufe the utmoft endeavours on both fides, towards hindering their refpective allies from undertaking any thing againft the dominions of either of the contracting powers; in fhort,
" To join their forces, in order to preferve the
" tranquillity of the Empire, and to oppofe the
" paffage of foreign troops, in cafe any power,
" under any pretext whatfoever fhould march an
" army into Germany, to difturb its repofe."

"This

A. D. 1757.

"This treaty, such as it is here represented, moreover provided for the safety of all the dominions which her Imperial and Royal Majesty possesses in the Empire, and those which belong thereto;" nay, the Austrian Netherlands had even been expressly named therein, had not his Prussian Majesty grounded the exception of those provinces upon an unanswerable argument, namely, "That in all the treaties which he himself had concluded with the Empress Queen, he never guaranteed the Netherlands;" so that in treating with a third power, he could not farther extend his engagements in favour of the Empress Queen.

"The more the King flattered himself that the Emperor, as head of the Empire, would applaud this treaty, which aimed at nothing but to secure the Empire committed to his care, from a danger whose consequences might be easily foreseen, the more did he hope that the Empress Queen would acknowledge the service he rendered to the territories, which that Princess possesses in Germany: at least, his Britannic Majesty might reckon that the Germannic body would think themselves under some obligations to him, for the care he took to hinder Germany from becoming again the theatre of war, and to secure its tranquillity, as that of his own dominions.

"Nevertheless, this treaty was scarcely published, with that frankness and candour, which always accompany upright, innocent, and salutary acts, than some people began to put sinister constructions upon it, and to give out, that it teemed with secret designs respecting religion and other matters.

"His Majesty's patriotic sentimenes ought to have been better known: sentiments which never suffered him to indulge any partial views, either in political or religious affairs: they could not but know, that on all occasions he has had an eye to the maintenance of the Germannic system and constitutions, and that he has given reiterated and incontestible proofs thereof. They could not therefore, without injustice, suspect his Majesty of having designs, or being inclined to take steps, that might create troubles in the heart of the Empire, of which he is himself one of the principal members, and whose interests have ever been so dear to him, that some years ago he spared neither his treasures, nor his troops, nor even his sacred person, to deliver it from the invasion of its enemies. His Britannic Majesty nevertheless did not hesitate to inform the head and the members of the Empire of the full contents of the treaty he had recently concluded, adding to this information, such declarations, as were fit to remove every the least idea of suspicion and distrust.

"All the world knows, that soon after, *i. e.* May 1, 1756, the Empress Queen notwithstanding, concluded not only a neutrality convention, but also a treaty of union and friendship *pretendedly* defensive, with the very crown with which his Majesty, as King of Great Britain, was in open war, and which threatned to carry fire and sword into his Electoral dominions. To appearance, this treaty had been long before meditated, and had already been a considerable time on the anvil.

" 'Tis likewise well known, that as soon as this treaty was concluded, jealousies began to break out between the Empress Queen and the King of Prussia, and that they at last ended in an open war, which occasioned his Prussian Majesty to enter the Electorate of Saxony and Bohemia.

" It is moreover publicly known, that the King. was absolutely ignorant of the King of Prussia's entering Saxony; that his Britannic Majesty did not hear of it till after the event; that he detested the hostilities that broke out; that he advised the contrary; that he took no part, nor would be concerned in it; and that he would employ all his force, and bend his care to keep foreign troops at a distance from his country and the territories adjacent, and to secure his German dominions from the threatned danger.

" In this strain did his Majesty speak by his ministers at Vienna, Ratisbon, and every were else: this was the sole end of his deliberations, and of the measures he took, without concerning himself with what was doing in Saxony and Bohemia. It was in consequence of the same motive, that the King voted for the mediation of the Empire, and for restoring the tranquillity of Germany, when the affair was laid before the Dyet; because his Majesty was convinced, that this measure was the easiest and the fittest to bring about the restitution of Saxony, and the countries depending on

it,

it, and perhaps indemnifications too; whereas the other means that prevailed have produced nothing (as dire experience has shewn) but a horrible effusion of blood, with the devastation and ruin of many states and innocent subjects; nor can we yet foresee when there will be an end of these dreadful calamities.

A. D. 1757.

"It is true, that a NEUTRALITY was proposed to the King, partly immediately from the court of Vienna, and partly by the mediation of Denmark; but such conditions were tacked to THIS neutrality, as rendered the acceptance impossible. They would have had his Majesty give the French a free passage through his dominions; to furnish those troops with provisions, forage, and waggons, for almost nothing; and this at a time when his Majesty could scarce guard his subjects against a famine. They insisted upon his putting Hamelen into their hands; they wanted him to confine his troops within a narrow circle in his own dominions; they insisted, that they should be kept there almost like prisoners of war: in short, they would have deprived him of the liberty of marching a single man from one place to another, without the consent of France.

"During the negociation relative to this neutrality, France not only marched the succour of 24,000 men, stipulated by her treaty with the Empress Queen, but also sent directly into Westphalia an army of 80,000 men.

"The King's army remained till the end of April in quarters of cantonment along the We-

A.D.
1757.

fer; but the French, by exorbitant demands of provisions and waggons, which far exceeded the faculties of the country, having ruined the county of Bentheim, pitched upon the city of Munster for a place of arms, marched from all parts towards that city, and thereby evinced their design upon his Majesty's Electoral dominions; he then caused the army of observation under the Duke of Cumberland to cross the Weser, and to advance as far as Rittberg, Bielefeld, and Hervoerden: nevertheless, the King caused the most solemn declarations to be given every where, that he was very far from intending to act offensively against any of his co-estates of the Empire, or even against France; and that he had no other views than to secure from invasion, with the help of the Almighty, his own dominions, and the territories of the neighbouring Princes.

" The events that followed are too well known to need a recital here.

" The principality of East Frizeland, about which his Majesty has a suit depending in the Aulic Council against the King of Prussia, has been attacked and conquered, and its inhabitants obliged to swear allegiance to the Empress Queen.

" The countries of Hesse Cassel have been invaded by a body of 15 or 20,000 men, and wrested from their lawful master, who hath been constrained to take refuge at Hamburgh.

" At the same time another body of French troops made an irruption on the Upper Weser, took Munden, Gottingen, Nordheim, Hardeg-
sen,

fen, Hedemunden, Uſſar, and Eimbeck, cauſed allegiance to be ſworn every where to the King of France, lodged their ſick in the beſt churches, extorted immenſe quantities of proviſions and waggons, on the leaſt delay plundered whole villages, mal-treated the magiſtrates, and (to give a ſketch of French military execution) reduced other villages to aſhes, waſted or burnt the fields, and thereby deprived the wretched inhabitants of the very hope of the rich crop the land promiſed.

"In the mean time, the main body of the French army paſſed the Weſer in ſeveral places, re-aſſembled again, and then drew near the King's army of obſervation, which, on account of ſuperiority in numbers, was obliged to retire into the countries of Bremen and Verden.

"The town of Hamelen fell into the enemy's hand, and Hanover ſhared the ſame fate; ſince which time the French army arbitrarily exact contributions, proviſions, forage, waggons, &c. with a high hand; they ſeize upon all the revenues, and all the public money; in a word, they diſpoſe of the whole country, juſt as they pleaſe.

"The territories of Wolfenbuttel have in like manner been invaded and occupied, and they have left the Duke's family nothing but the caſtle of Blankenburg to reſide in.

"It is clear from this narration, which may be authentically proved, that the King did not aſſemble his troops, nor thoſe of his allies, with a view to act *offenſively* againſt any power whatever; but that his Majeſty's ſole aim was, to ſecure, as

far

far as possible, his dominions and those of his allies, from violence and unjust pretensions. And though divine Providence has not been pleased to second such just and equitable views, the King has yet the consolation of being persuaded, that the steps he has been obliged to take, will be approved by every impartial man.

"His Majesty flatters himself, that his co-estates of the Empire, and the powers that have at heart the restoration of the Germannic tranquillity, and the support of the system of the Empire, will think of applying the speediest remedies to proceedings equally harsh and undeserved, and putting an end to an opposition, which menaces Germany and all Europe with the most dismal consequences; and that they will endeavour to procure the King satisfaction adequate to the damages he has sustained."

M. D. de Richelieu pays no regard to the terms of the convention.

In the mean time M. de Richelieu was enriching himself with excessive contributions, and the plunder of the countries, which laid exposed to his arms; repairing his fortune consumed in vices at court, by the most cruel and barbarous means. He paid no regard to the conditions of the convention: but practised every art, and tried every expedient, though ever so unjust and barbarous, to fill his coffers. In which he was but too much encouraged by the dislike shewn in the French court at the articles of the convention; who expected that an army, penned up, as that at Stade was, should have surrendered at discretion, at

Encouraged therein by his court.

least

least on condition not to serve during the war against France and her allies, and insisted on disarming the auxiliary troops upon returning into their own country; and therefore seemed more willing to provoke the allied army to resume their arms, that the infringment of the convention might be thrown upon them, than to comply with the terms of the stipulated convention. On the other side, the Hanoverians were disappointed in their expectations. By laying down their arms it was their opinion, that his Majesty's Electoral dominions would have been delivered by a formal treaty, from the French invaders, and have obtained the advantages of a neutral state. But their hostile visitors took every step to secure their abode. They continued to extend their conquests. They enlarged their demands. They changed the very form of government[s]: and they, in defiance of the

A. D. 1757.

---

[s] *The authentic documents of the French administration, in his Majesty's German dominions.*

One Gautier, a farmer from Paris, having arrived at Hanover some days before Christmas, and there fixed his office, a decree of council of the King of France, appeared, dated the 18th of October 1757, the tenor of which is as follows:

" The King having charged Jean Faidy, citizen of Paris, to take upon him the receipt, and administration, of all the duties and revenues, belonging to his Majesty in the Electorate of Hanover, conquered from the King of England, Elector of Hanover, and bring to account all such persons as have had the receipt, and administration of them, since the conquest of the Electorate of Hanover; and all persons, who, before the Electorate of Hanover and the other conquered countries passed

A. D. 1757.

the late capitulation, were enforcing every means to disarm and enslave both the army and the people.

It ed under his Majesty's dominion, were employed in the direction and receipt of the revenues of the country, for all the sums they shall have received, and to receive of them the sums due for the value of their farms: and the King does hereby order, that till letters patent, sealed and registered, shall be issued forth, the said Faidy be put into possession of the direction, receipt, and administration, of all the revenues and duties in the Electorate of Hanover, conquered from the King of England, Elector of Hanover, from the time they have been subjected to his Majesty: it is his Majesty's will, that the receipt, direction, and administration, of all the revenues whatsoever, be in the hands of the said Jean Faidy, or others appointed by him; and, for that purpose, that all the papers, relating to the receipt, direction, and maintainance of the said duties and revenues, be delivered to him by those, in whose custody soever they shall be found. It is his Majesty's will and order, that all those, who have been employed in the receipt and direction of the said revenues, under what title soever, be obliged to deliver to the said Jean Faidy, or his attornies, upon their giving receipts, the accounts they have given in, their registers, land-rools, and other deeds, by virtue whereof they have received and collected the duties and revenues of the preceeding sovereign, and that the said receivers shall account for what they have received, and shall pay the sums still remaining due from them, under pain of being obliged thereto by the ordinary methods used in the King's revenues and affairs: his Majesty empowers the said Jean Faidy to remove the receivers, and all other persons, who shall have been employed in any part of the direction, receipt, and administration, of the said duties and revenues, and to place others in their room, his Majesty reserving o himself the power of ordering the vouchers of those in employment who may be removed, to be produced, and to provide

It was in this critical conjuncture, that the court of London took up the point in debate. Hanover

vide for the reimbursing them the money they shall prove to have paid, in the manner he shall judge proper: his Majesty orders, that all persons, who have been entrusted under the preceeding government with papers, relative to the revenues of the Electorate of Hanover, or those that may hereafter be so, to communicate the same to the said Jean Faidy, and to deliver authentic copies of all the papers he shall desire to have, without exemption, under pain of disobedience: his Majesty in like manner orders, under the same penalties, that the magistrates of the towns, districts and commonalities, &c. shall deliver, upon the first requisition of the said Jean Faidy, estimates, certified by them, of the produce of six years, reckoning from the 1st of January 1751, to the last of December 1756, of the duties and revenues which the said towns, districts, commonalities, and states are in possession of; that they likewise deliver to the said Jean Faidy, estimates of the sums they shall have paid to the preceding Sovereign during the said six years, and of the charges necessarily incurred during the said term, independant of the sums they have paid: it is his Majesty's intention and will, that the said Jean Faidy be put into the possession of the houses, offices, and utensils, hitherto made use of in the management of the revenues, with the direction whereof he is charged, payment being made to the proprietors for rent upon the footing he and they shall agree: his Majesty likewise orders, that all those who are actually employed in the management of the revenues of the Electorate of Hanover, after having been authorised by the said Jean Faidy, shall continue to act without being obliged to take any new oaths, and that those, who shall come in upon a fresh establishment, shall be admitted without any charges to take the oath, and discharge the duty of the employments, to which they shall be named, upon the simple presentation of the said Jean Faidy: his Majesty orders, that all those, who shall be accountable and indebted to the duties and revenues,

A. D. 1757.

over convinced, when it was too late, that there could be no safety for her, but in a vigorous exertion

revenues, of what nature soever they be, comprehended in the direction and administration, with which the said Jean Faidy is charged, shall be acquitted and discharged towards his Majesty and all others, of whatsoever they shall be found to owe, by producing receipts from the said Jean Faidy, his attornies, &c. of the accounts they shall have given in at the time they shall be balanced and acquitted: it is his Majesty's will, that any disputes, that shall arise with regard to the general administration of all the duties and revenues, of the Electorate of Hanover, wherewith the said Jean Faidy is charged, be brought before the intendant and commissary, who has the department of the *conquered country*: and adjudged by him, saving an appeal to his Majesty's council only: his Majesty enjoins the said intendant and commissary of the said department, to support the execution of the present decree, which shall be executed, notwithstanding all opposition and hindrances, of which, if any should happen, his Majesty reserves to himself and his council the cognizance, and forbids the same to all courts and judges.

Done at the King's council of state, held at Versailles, the 18th of October, 1757.

Signed   EYNARD.

Remarks.   It appears from the date and purport of this decree, that the council of Versailles was employed in framing it immediately after the convention of Bremewörde; and the said decree implies, that it was determined to change the government of the Electorate of Hanover, notwithstanding what was expressly promised by the capitulation made the 9th of August 1757, upon the surrender of the capital, and that the administration herein mentioned, with which the said Jean Faidy is charged, was to extend itself to the countries, *which might hereafter be conquered*.

If

tion of her strength against an enemy, that never quits possession of their acquisitions, whether made by force or fraud; throws herself and her cause, entirely upon Great Britain; when she had found there were no hopes left of a neutrality, nor of relief from the Dyet of the Empire.

They very justly charged Great Britain with the cause of their misfortunes: and applied to his Britannic Majesty for aid and protection. "Is it reasonable, said they, that a country, which parted with those advantages and comforts, that are enjoyed by the influence of a court, whose Sovereign resides in the heart of his native dominions, and is not embarrassed by the contending or contrary interests of an adventitious kingdom, should be ruined because it has condescended to part with those blessings? Did not Hanover, that very Electorate seized in a hostile manner by the enemies of Great Britain, give a King to Great Britain, to maintain her laws, liberty and religion, when they were endangered by a disputable succession? And is Hanover to be thus rewarded, for the refuge granted to Great Britain in her distress, as to be compelled to pour forth her

---

If so, this confession, made by the crown of France itself, cannot but be considered as an undeniable proof, that the said crown had a premeditated design of making an ill use of the cessation of arms, in order to proceed in taking possession of the provinces they had not yet seized upon, when the cessation of arms was concluded, and bring to utter destruction the Electorate of Hanover, without leaving the sovereign thereof any method of preserving it.

blood

blood and treasure in the quarrels of England? Is she to be abandoned by the only power she has a just right to apply to for help; when denied the protection of the Germannic Body, in a conspiracy with France? His Majesty by being the common father of both people, ought equally to hear the voice of distress from an Hanoverian, as from a Briton. And he has given a proof of this by leaving his Germannic counsellors to act, as they thought most conducive to their country's interest, at the late convention [t], though it has not, and cannot have their desired effect, so long as it is the interest of France to maintain war against his Britannic Majesty. The framers of the act of settlement knew that their future Sovereign was to be, and to remain Elector of Hanover: that his being so was one of their main inducements: and that the liberties of England depended upon those of the protestant interest in Europe. When was there a time to be more watchful for the protestant interest of Europe, than at a time when the natural antipathy and the opposite interests of Burbon and Austria have united, and the Aulic Council countenanceth their measures, and approves of their hostilities? Can the warmest anti-continental patriot in Great Britain affirm, that the interests of Hanover had immediately any concern in lighting up the present war? Had the Hanoverians any concern in the American disputes? Were

[t] See his Majesty's declaration in answer to the King of Prussia's letter, above on page 416, signed *Holderneſſe*.

the

the Hanoverians the primary objects of Austrian ambition, or French invasion. We tried what could be done by a neutrality, and by a convention, both have failed us. The terms of the former would have been dishonourable. The latter expedient have consigned Hanover to sufferings, that could be inflicted upon no other plea, than that the Elector is King of Great Britain. For, it cannot be thought, that France would have marched 80,000 men across such an extent of comfortless territory, to attack an Electorate, that is guaranteed to the house of Brunswick by all the solemn acts, ties and treaties, that can render possession secure. But while the enemies of Great Britain will not distinguish between the interests of the King of England and the Elector of Hanover, as separate and independant, Hanover will always be the sufferer, though she gives not the least provocation.

A. D. 1757.

Why the Hanoverians demand aid from Great Britain.

Therefore in this distressed situation, into which they had been brought solely by their connections with England, (as well as upon the faith of treaties) the regency of Hanover demanded immediate succours from the British nation. The court of London did not pretend to controvert the justice of the Hanoverian plea: they did not demur at their demand. But it was necessary, and it employed our councils for some time, so to aid, support and deliver Hanover in its present distress, as not to disable Great Britain from pursuing her own national interest, and from preserving that power, without which not only her allies, but herself must

Remarks on the conduct of the British court in regard to Hanover.

must become a prey to the ambition of France It was therefore first tried what might be effected by pacific measures. The court of London proposed to extend the convention of Stade or Closter-Seven to a general armistice, and to found thereon a negociation for a general peace. But this could not be brought about. The French had got possion, and they were determined to keep the favourite of his Britannic Majesty in hand, to more advantage; while the success of their arms in North America promised them more adequate conditions from the continuation of the war, than could be expected by a precipitate peace. The next recourse was to arms. In which the Hanoverians were justified by the breach of the convention, in so many particulars, by the French: and the British nation was obliged to succour them upon the faith of treaties, and a principle of gratitude for the sufferings they bore on the account of their connection with Great Britain: a connection not of their own seeking; but sollicited and made by British councils. (See page 432.)

Their resolutions. From these considerations it was resolved, That the Hanoverian army, who had been denied the stipulations, which they had a right to claim under the convention of Closter-Seven, should hold themselves released from all obligation, on their part; according to the example shewn them by the French; and should immediately assemble, resume their arms, and stand in the defence of their country against all invaders. And it was farther resolved, to put in motion, maintain and keep together the army

His Serene Highness **FERDINAND**
Duke of Brunswick and Lunenburgh.

army of obfervation, and to recommend a vi- A. D.
gorous execution of this meafure to the enfuing 1757.
parliament.

His Britannic Majefty immediately nominated Prince Fer-
and appointed Prince Ferdinand of Brunfwick, vefted with
(brother to the Duke of Brunfwick, and well re- the chief command.
commended for his military fkill by the King of
Pruffia) commander in chief of this army, in the
place and ftead of his Royal Highnefs the Duke
of Cumberland, who declined a command, in
which he had not met with that fatisfaction,
which is expected by an active, vigorous and vigilant commander; nor with a reception due to
his abilities, and well-meaning endeavours. A
circumftance regretted by all the fenfible part of
the nation, who have always found him a fteady
and uncorrupted friend to the intereft of England,
poffeffed of the entire affection of the troops, and
known to have been a brave officer.

This promotion was followed with a declaration of his Majefty's motives for breaking the convention of Clofter-Seven on his part, as Elector of
Hanover. In which was fet forth the naked facts
in the following words and order.

IN September 1757, a convention was agreed His Britan-
upon between the Duke of Cumberland and ty's mo-
the Marfhal Duke de Richelieu; but France was tives for breaking
no fooner informed of it, than fhe plainly mani- the con-
fefted, that fhe would not acknowledge the va- vention.
lidity of the faid convention, but, on condition
that the Hanoverian troops fhould engage not to
ferve

A. D. 1757.

serve during the present war against France and her allies. And she also insisted on disarming the auxiliary troops, upon returning into their own country.

The Duke of Cumberland, who had, on his part, fulfilled all the conditions of the convention, and caused part of the troops, destined on their return for the country of Lawenbourg, to begin their march, could not consider this new demand otherwise than as a manifest breach of the convention; the Marshal Duke de Richelieu having engaged not only to let the auxiliary troops depart freely, but the convention also setting forth in express terms, that they should not be regarded as prisoners of war, under which quality alone the condition of laying down their arms could take place. Upon this, his Royal Highness sent orders to the said troops to halt.

To reconcile this difference, expedients were proposed, which left no shadow of pretext to the opposite party. But all in vain. The troops, pent up in a narrow district, were exposed to the rigour of the season, and cut off from all necessaries and conveniences of every kind.

The French at present pretend to treat the convention as a mere military scheme; and indeed it was at first nothing more: but on account of the above declaration of the court of France, which expressly suspended its validity, and in consequence of the negociation for disarming the auxiliaries, to which the French general would give no answer categorically, without waiting for instructions

ſtructions from Verſailles, the nature of that act was totally changed; and that which was then an act between general and general, is now become a court affair.

Hard as the conditions of the convention were, for the troops of his Britannic Majeſty, Elector of Hanover, the King would have acquieſced in them, if the French had not diſcovered their deſign of totally ruining his army and his dominions; and, by the moſt evident infractions and outrageous conduct, have ſet the King free from every obligation, under which he was laid by the convention.

The great end of the conventional act (and end in itſelf of the very nature and eſſence of a proviſional armiſtice) was **to enter directly on negociations of peace,** in order **to prevent the total ruin of the Electorate of Brunſwic-Lunenbourg,** and to procure an accommodation for his Majeſty's allies. But the court of France has not only declared, time after time, that ſhe would not lend a hand towards a definitive pacification with his Majeſty, in quality of Elector, but has ſhewn plainly, by her continual violences, exceſſes, and inſupportable exactions, ſince the ſigning the convention, that her reſolution is, abſolutely to deſtroy the King's Electoral eſtates, as well as thoſe of his allies.

In the midſt of a truce, the moſt open hoſtilities have been committed. The caſtle of Schartzfels has been forcibly ſeized, and the garriſon made priſoners of war. The priſoners made by

A. D. 1757.

the French before the convention have not been restored, though this was a point expressly stipulated between the delegated generals, and was exactly satisfied on our part, by the immediate release of the French prisoners. The bailiffs of the reserved districts, into which the French troops were on no pretence to enter, have been summoned, under pain of military execution, to appear before the French commissary, with design of compelling them to deliver the domainal receipts of the public revenue, of which they are the administrators. They have appropriated to themselves part of those magazines, which by express agreement were to remain with the Electoral troops; and they still go on with seizing the houses, revenues, and corn belonging to his Majesty in the city of Bremen, in spight of the reciprocal engagement, whereby they are held to regard that city as a place absolutely free and neutral. And, lastly, they have proceeded to menaces, unheard of among a civilized people, of burning, sacking and destroying all before them without remorse.

All these violent and unjust proceedings are incontestible proofs, that the French will not admit the convention as obligatory, any farther than as it may prove ruinous to his Britannic Majesty. They deny that they are tied down to any thing, and assert a power of acting at will. To so insupportable a degree of insolence have they carried matters, that the King holds himself not only at liberty, but even necessitated, without further regard

gard to the convention, so often and so openly violated by the French, to have recourse to arms, as the means, which the Almighty has put into his hands, for delivering his faithful subjects and allies from the oppressions, with which they groan.

A. D. 1757.

As his Majesty has never thought of arming offensively against any power whatever, but solely with a view of defending himself and his allies, he reposes his confidence in God, and hopes for his benediction on the justice of his enterprizes.

As soon as it was confirmed that the Hanoverians were in motion, and repairing to the command of Prince Ferdinand, M. Duke de Richelieu wrote him this letter, as commander in chief of the Hanoverian army.

SIR,

ALTHOUGH for some days past I have perceived the Hanoverian troops in motion, in order to form themselves into a body, I could not imagine the object of these movements was to break the convention of neutrality, signed the 8th and 10th of September, between his Royal Highness the Duke of Cumberland and me. The good faith, which I naturally supposed on the part of the King of England Elector of Hanover, and of his son, who signed the said convention, blinded me so far as to make me believe that the assembling of these troops had no other design than to go into the winter-quarters that had been assigned them. The repeated advices,

Duke de Richelieu's letter to Prince Ferdinand.

which

which came to me from every quarter, of the bad intentions of the Hanoverians, at length opened my eyes; and, at prefent, one may fee very clearly that there is a plan formed to break the articles of a convention, which ought to be facred and inviolable.—The King my mafter having been informed of thefe dangerous movements, and of the infidelity of the Hanoverians, is ftill willing to give frefh proofs of his moderation, and of his defire to fpare the effufion of human blood. It is with this view that I have the honour to declare to your Serene Highnefs, in the name of his moft Chriftian Majefty, that I perfift in my refolution of fulfilling exactly all the points of the convention, provided the Hanoverian army, on its part, does the fame: but I cannot conceal from your Serene Highnefs, that, if, contrary to all expectation, it fhould take any equivocal ftep, and ftill more, if it fhould commit any act of hoftility, I fhall then pufh matters to the laft extremity, looking upon myfelf as authorifed fo to do by the laws of war; I fhall fet fire to all the palaces, royal houfes, and gardens; I fhall fack all the towns and villages, without fparing the fmalleft cabin; in fhort, this country fhall feel all the horrors of war. I advife your Serene Highnefs to reflect on all this, and not to lay me under the neceffity of taking fteps fo contrary to the natural humanity of the French nation, and alfo to my perfonal character.

RICHELIEU.

P. S.

P. S. M. Le Comte de Lynar, ambaſſador of the King of Denmark, who was mediator for the convention, has been ſo kind as to take upon him to ſay every thing in his power to your Serene Highneſs, in order to prevent the fatal conſequences with which this country is threatned.

<small>A. D. 1757.</small>

To this letter the Hanoverian general returned a very laconic and reſolute anſwer, becoming a good general and a juſt cauſe; importing that he was determined to abide by the conſequences, and would decide the diſputes, which had been unjuſtly ſtarted by the French, in perſon at the head of his army [u].

<small>Prince Ferdinand's anſwer.</small>

Matters began to ripen apace for action, notwithſtanding the advanced ſeaſon. Both armies re-enter the field. The Hanoverians, ſpirited up with reſentment for the baſe uſage they had received, were eager for an opportunity to wipe off the diſgrace of their ſummer's campaign, and to deliver their country from the unheard-of oppreſſions and cruelties exerciſed by their French invaders. They rendeſvouzed at Stade: and Prince Ferdinand marched with all expedition to ſeek the enemy, and to drive them out of the

<small>Both armies take the field.</small>

---

[u] Prince Ferdinand of Brunſwick iſſued the following orders. " All officers, magiſtrates, and other regents of his " Britannic Majeſty's German dominions, are enjoined, by " theſe preſents, not to execute any orders from the generality " or intendency of the French; but to ſend them to me im- " mediately, and to ſecure the bearers as ſpies, that they may " be treated in a manner ſuitable to their demerits."

FERDINAND.

Electorate,

A. D. 1757.

Hostilities commence.

Electorate. They presently came to blows. One division under General Count Schuylenburg, came up with 2000 of the enemy's rear at Ebstorff, as they were marching to Zell, and defeated them entirely. General Zaftrow, with another division, defeated another considerable body of the French, near the Aller. These skirmishes and advantages animated the Hanoverian army, already spirited up with revenge, and struck such a panic into the enemy, that they met with but small resistance. Harbourg, at first setting out, gave them the most trouble, by the obstinacy of the French commander, who retired into the castle, and would not surrender by capitulation, till all the fortifications were demolished. This delayed the march of the Hanoverians, and gave the French time to collect their distant parties.

Harbourg besieged.

The French army retreats.

M. Duke de Richelieu retired to Zell with as much precipitation before the Hanoverian army, as the Hanoverian army, in the summer, had retired before the French to Stade; and left in that city a most horrid example of the reality of his barbarous intentions threatned in his letter to Prince Ferdinand. Here it was thought M. Richelieu had resolved to make a stand. Here he called in his advanced parties, abandoned several magazines, burnt and destroyed the farm-houses and sheep-walks belonging to his Britannic Majesty, in defiance of the representations made on that head by Prince Ferdinand. And he gave so great a sway to his passion, that, after unmanning himself, and delivering up the city to be plundered by his troops,

Their cruelty at Zell.

against

against all the rules of war, he ordered the suburbs to be burnt to ashes, and not to spare the orphan-house of helpless children, who perished in the fire; the inhuman French marshal glutting his eyes, like another Nero, with a city in flames. Within this ruined city Richelieu entrenched his army; and by their natural situation and weight of artillery, they guarded the river so effectually, that Prince Ferdinand could not pass the Aller. The severity of the season, which set in with hard weather, forced him to retreat to Ultzen and Lunenburg for quarters, and to leave the French in possession of Hanover, in whose capital M. Duke de Richelieu fixed his head quarters; though there continued to be frequent skirmishes with various success between the out parties.

A. D. 1757.

Retire into winter quarters.

Before M. Duke de Richelieu left Zell, he published the following ordinance for collecting the public revenues of the Electorate of Hanover.

Lewis Fra. Armand du Plessis, D. de Richelieu, General of the French army in Germany.

THE breaking of the capitulation of Closter-Seven, in spite of the most solemn treaty, and the word of honour given by the generals, renders void the treaty made with the country of Hanover, when the King's army entered it; and this infraction of good faith requires the greatest rigour toward the Hanoverian army, now actually in hostilities.

Ordinance to collect the revenues.

Where-

A. D. 1757.

Wherefore we order, that all the goods, and all other effects of what nature soever, belonging to all the officers or others actually with the said Hanoverian army, be confiscated to the King's use, and that the administrator in general of the conquered countries take possession thereof, in order to collect the revenues arising therefrom, which are to be added to the contributions; and to make use of them in the most advantageous manner for his Majesty, in whatever places of the conquered countries they may be situated.

We strictly require Monf. le Duc de Randan, commander in the country of Hanover, and all other commanders, to enforce the execution of these presents, and to support the same as far as it may concern them.

Done at Zell, December 22, 1757.

(Signed)   The Marshal Duc de Richelieu.

And underneath   Le Lurez.

Remarks thereon.

After such notorious proofs of French perfidy as are here laid before the public, it is astonishing to hear these tyrants and murderers of mankind complain of the Prussians appropriating to themselves, without any declaration of war, without either reason or justice, the revenues of the duchy of Mecklenburg, whose sovereign had actually entered into a treaty to join his forces with theirs, and had marched to the assistance of the Swedes, who were at that time engaged in the conquest of Prussian Pomerania. Yet such is their way of reasoning, that it is lawful for them to invade, upon the

most

most frivolous pretences, countries in peace with all the world; but other Princes must make no attack upon their known enemies, till the mortal blow has been struck; by which they are deprived of the power to make reprisals. The city of Mecklin has undoubtedly been severely dealt with, the Duke driven from his palace, and the whole country ravaged. And the calamities of the Electorate of Saxony are not to be expressed: fathers murdered for concealing their fugitive sons; merchants plundered for not producing greater sums of money than they are worth; the real and personal estates of deserters, of whatever quality, confiscated; and the castles and palaces of the antient nobility plundered and levelled with the ground; their plantations razed, and their gardens and pleasure-houses defaced and trodden under foot by horses. These are the mildest calamities that the poor inhabitants suffer, in the countries in subjection to the conquerors in the present war. Where the French, the Austrians, or the Russians have gained the ascendancy, the most horrible barbarities are and have been committed.

Some people say, that the convention of Closter-Seven furnished a fine opportunity for breaking the chain, which bound Great Britain to a continental war, and they, with the same breath, blame the ministry for consenting to the Hanoverians resuming their arms. But those people should know, That it was not in the ministry's power to hinder the Hanoverians resuming their arms,

A. D. 1757.

arms, his Majesty, as Elector of Hanover, was not obliged to act by consent of a British privy-council, relative to the affairs of Hanover: they had no authority over his electoral subjects: he is a father to them as well as to us: and he, in that capacity, is without controul. So that, if he chose to order his Hanoverian subjects to take up arms, 'twas not in the power of a British ministry to prevent it. But the fact is this. The English approved of the measure: they humanely considered the Hanoverians, as sufferers on their account: the French had entered the Electorate merely because of the war with England, and every one pitied the unhappy calamity, which fell in a particular manner heavy on them, who were innocent sufferers in another's cause, and who had given no room for offence. The people of England, with a spirit of true benevolence, dispassionately reflected on the whole state and hardship of their unhappy condition, and on the cause, which brought upon them the worst of all miseries, that of their country being made the scene of war; and were as much rejoiced at the Hanoverians resuming their arms, as the Hanoverians could be themselves; insomuch that the parliament voted 100,000 l. for their immediate support.

Affairs of Prussia.

His Prussian Majesty being made easy, on the part of Hanover; which found sufficient employment for the French grand army, ready on the first occasion to pour down their whole force upon him, he had only the Imperialists and Austrians to guard against.

Various

Various skirmishes, and some disadvantageous actions, had followed his loss at Kolin. Gabel, an important pass, and well garrisoned with four battalions, under the command of Major-General Putkammer, situate between Bœnish Leypa and Zittau, was surprised and taken by a strong detachment under the command of the Duke d'Aremberg and M. Macguire [w]. It was with some difficulty that Prince Henry, the King's brother, ordered with a detachment to watch their motions, escaped their superior force [x], which was afterwards vented with circumstances of most horrid cruelty against Zittau, a trading town in Upper Saxony, garrisoned by six battalions. Here were several large magazines also. They, determined to carry this place, before the King of Prussia could march to its relief, attacked it with uncommon fury. They began to bombard and cannonade it on the 23d of July, without any regard to the Saxon inhabitants; and it continued with such rage, that all the garrison, except about 300 under Colonel Diricke, judged it most proper to retreat, with as much of the magazines, as they could carry off. Colonel Diricke had orders to maintain that post as long as possible. Which he would not give up till the whole place was destroyed. The cannonading began at eleven o'clock at noon, and continued no longer than till five in the evening. But such was the quantity and kind

A. D 1757.

Gabel surprised.

Zittau burnt.

Garrison escape.

[w] On the 18th of June 1757.
[x] See page 258, Vol. II.

of

A.D. 1757.

The great destruction made.

of those instruments of death and destruction, that six hundred houses and upwards, almost all the public buildings, the Cathedrals of St. John and St. James, the orphan-house, eight parsonage-houses, eight schools, the town-house, the public weigh-house, the prison, were set on fire or beaten down by 4000 balls, many of them red hot, which set fire to the houses in several places; in which conflagration were consumed, the records in the town-house, the archives and all other documents of the town council, the pictures, statues, plate and other things of value, presented to the town by Emperors, &c. And what was most deplorable, upwards of 400 citizens were killed. What escaped the flames was plundered and carried off by the Austrians, Pandours, and Sclavonians, as soon as they could force their way into the town, during the confusion of the conflagration. For, instead of assisting the inhabitants to extinguish the fire, they fell to plunder what was to be found, making no distinction between Prussians and the inhabitants of Zittau; though this town belonged to the King of Poland, their friend and ally.

M. Keith harrassed.

Marshal Keith was now ordered to quit the mountains of Bohemia, and to join the King's army: In his march his rear was much harrassed by the enemy's irregulars, who carried off some of his baggage and provisions. He met the King's army between Bautzen and Gorlitz: and the united force of these armies amounted to 60,000 men, besides twelve battalions and ten squadrons, which were stationed at Pirna, under the

Joins the King's army.

THE LATE WAR.

the Prince of Anhault Deffau, to prevent any surprise upon Dresden, to secure the passes of the mountains, and to check the incursions of the Austrian irregulars: with whom there happened daily skirmishes with various success. But these actions did not weaken the Prussian armies so much, as desertion; a misfortune that will happen to every Prince, whose army is composed of foreigners, who only serve for pay, without any regard for the interest of the king or country, in whose cause they are enlisted.

A large body of Austrians entered Silesia, and penetrated as far as Breslau; but were not in a condition to besiege it, in sight of the Prince of Bevern's army, encamped near that city. From whence they turned to Schweidnitz, an important fortress, and the key of that duchy, which was the cause of the war. They besieged this fortress in form [y]; which took them up to the 12th of November; when a garrison of 4000 surrendered themselves prisoners of war.

While the Austrians were thus employed, his Prussian Majesty endeavoured to draw their grand army into such circumstances, as might enable him to fight them with advantage. For this purpose he quitted his camp at Bautzen, and took the rout of Gorlitz; and after several other motions, he took post at Budin on the 15th of August. Here, being rightly informed of the designs of the Imperial army, in conjunction

A. D. 1757.

Daily skirmishes.

Schweidnitz besieged.

His Prussian Majesty's dispositions to attack the enemy.

[y] Opened the trenches on the 27th of October.

A. D. 1757.

with the French under the Prince de Soubife, againſt Saxony, he ſaw it was neceſſary to accelerate his own motions, and to force the Auſtrians to a battle, if poſſible, before the Imperial army, which was advancing very faſt, could arrive at the place of their deſtination. But all his art and ſtratagem could not bring it to bear. **He** drew up his army in ſight of the Auſtrians, to bid them defiance. He even detached 16000 men, under General Winterfeldt, on the other ſide the Nieſe, to take them in flank. As this would not do, no time was to be loſt. He reſolves to meet the Imperialiſts, and to bring them to an engagement; leaving 30,000 men near Gorlitz under the Prince of Bevern, Prince Ferdinand and General Winterfeldt, to obſerve the motions of the Auſtrian army; who immediately came out of their camp, when it was known, that **his** Pruſſian Majeſty had left it; and 5000 of them attacked two battalions in General Winterfeldt's diviſion, which they cut to pieces. But what was accounted the greateſt misfortune on this occaſion was the loſs of the general himſelf, who received a wound of which he afterwards died.

Dares the Auſtrians to battle.

Marches againſt the army of the Empire.

General Winterfeld attacked.

His Majeſty being informed that the army of the empire, and the forces of the Prince de Soubiſe were aſſembled at Erfurth, with a view to penetrate into Saxony, to make themſelves maſters of the Elbe, he ordered part of his army to march to Naumbourg. The light-horſe, in their march, had a ſkirmiſh with the enemy, greatly to the advantage of the Pruſſians. The army paſſed the

Sala

Sala at Naumbourg, and proceeded to Buttelftedt. Here he received advice of the convention being figned at Clofter-Seven; and of the invafion of Halberftadt by the Duke de Richelieu; againft whom he detached Prince Ferdinand of Brunfwick, who fcoured the country and beat up the quarters of the French at Egelen, and made twenty officers and four hundred foldiers prifoners: but when the grand army of France advanced againft him, he took up fuch quarters at Wanfleben, that he could hinder their receiving provifions.

A. D. 1757.

Prince Ferdinand fen againft the Duke de Richelieu.

The King having collected his forces, advanced to Erfurth. On which the Imperialifts retired, and were driven as far as the hills of Eifenach. Nothing more could be done at this time, except ftretching an advanced poft of huffars and dragoons, as far as Gotha, which maintained its ground againft a large body, under Prince Hildbourghaufen, fent to diflodge it.

King of Pruffia at Erfurth.

In this fituation the armies remained till about the laft week in October, when a body of Hungarians penetrated through Lufatia into Brandenbourg, under General Haddick, up to the gates of Berlin; which city he laid under contribution: a part of which was faved by the feafonable approach of the Prince of Anhault Deffau. In the mean time the other part of the army retired to Leipfick, under General Keith. The time was now haftening forward for action. The Imperialifts thought it moft advifeable and fafe, to feize the prefent opportunity, when the Pruffian forces were thus divided and feperated at fuch a diftance.

General Haddick penetrates to Berlin.

The Imperialifts refolve to attack General Keith.

F f 2　　　　Therefore

A. D. 1757.

Therefore they advanced by cantonments through Naumbourg, Zeets and Weiffenfels, imagining that they could make themselves masters of the course of the Sala, of Leipsic and of the Prussian magazines at Torgau.

Prussian army assemble at Leipsic.

Upon this advice, and that the Prince of Saxe-Hilburghausen and the Prince of Soubise were in full march, to attack M. Keith, the King ordered his army to assemble at Leipsic. Which was performed with such expedition, that the troops from Lusatia, and from the county of Magdebourg, arrived on the 26th of October. Every necessary disposition was made to give the enemy battle.

The Imperialists retire.

But they were still bashful; though the plains of Lutzen afforded a most spacious field of battle. On the 30th the King advanced nearer, and on the 31st he drew up his army to fall upon the enemy in their quarters; and made 500 prisoners in passing through Weiffenfels and Merseburg; but could reach no further than Lutzen. Next day, upon advice that the enemy were retiring on all sides, the King marched with the vanguard to Weiffenfels, and attacked that city with such vigour, that the Bavarian troops, and the troops of the circles, were forced to abandon the post, and to retreat, having lost 300 men, who were made prisoners. The enemy, to cover their retreat, burnt the bridge [z] on the Sala; and the position of the Imperialists on the opposite side of that river, facing Weiffenfels, behind enclosures of vineyards

Five hundred prisoners.

Three hundred prisoners.

---

[z] Which had cost above 100,000 crowns building.

and

and in huts, to prevent the repairs of the bridge, indicated their intention to difpute the paffage of the Sala with the Pruffians. M. Keith, who had advanced with the main body of the army to Merfebourg, where fourteen French battalions were pofted, found the bridge at that place burnt; and continuing his march to Hall, he found that the fame precaution had been taken by another detachment of French troops at that bridge. But M. Keith prefently repaired it, and forced the enemy to evacuate all the pofts they had on that river, and retire to Micheles. Being now in poffeffion of Hall, Merfebourg, and Weiffenfels, and their bridges repaired, the whole Pruffian army croffed the river Sala, in three columns; and they joined the fame day at the village of Rofbach, facing the enemy's camp.

A. D. 1757.

Driven from all their pofts on the Elbe.

The King went immediately to reconnoitre the enemy's fituation and ftrength; and finding that it might be attacked on the right, he propofed to do it next day. But though every difpofition was made to carry this refolution into execution; and the cavalry was put in motion in the van, it was countermanded; becaufe, upon arriving at the eminences, from whence the enemy had been reconnoitred the day before, it was found, that they had changed the pofition of their camp. It now not only faced the Pruffian army, but it was covered in front by a large hollow way. Its right was upon an eminence in a wood, fortified with three redoubts, befides barricades of trees. Which made it unadvifeable to proceed to the intended attack

King of Pruffia prepares to attack their camp.

Its fituation and ftrength.

F f 3

A.D. 1757.

The attack dropt.

attack. Therefore the infantry encamped, and the cavalry did so likewise [a]. As the reasons were not known to the enemy for this sudden alteration in the motions of the Prussian army, they, perhaps, attributed their re-encampment to a diffidence in their own strength, and upon this presumption, detached several parties to harrass them in case of a retreat.

Encouraged the Imperialists to force him to a battle.

This procrastination of the Prussian army, which till now, had given the greatest signs of an intention to force the Imperialists to an action, operated so effectually on the enemy, that it brought them to a resolution [b] not only to wait for them, to which

[a] With the loss of nine men killed by the enemy's cannon, which did no other execution, though continued the whole day.

[b] It is hardly possible to account for the conduct of the Imperialists and French, retreating so often before an enemy so much inferior to them in numbers; and whom, it was commonly thought they were sent to crush, in pursuance of the ban of the Empire. But the following letter from an officer of the combined army, dated Nov. 12, will help to set us right as to the intentions of the officers in the Imperial army, and give light in some other particulars relative to the ensuing battle.——" The Prince de Soubise having received orders from his court, not to lead the army of his most Christian Majesty beyond the Sala, but at the same time not to omit any occasion that might offer of fighting the King of Prussia on this side that river, it was judged proper, that the combined army should provide themselves with a good camp, and there resolutely wait for the enemy. In consequence of which resolution, they occupied that of Micheles, the 2d of Nov. where they were posted so as to have a wood on the right, wherein the 15 battalions of the troops of the Empire (the

rest

which his Prussian Majesty had so long in vain attempted to provoke them; but to attack them in

rest having been detached, by order of the Margrave of Baden-Durlach, along the Sala, for the security of the interior circles) had orders to continue and cover themselves by felling trees, and this place was fortified besides with some redoubts, being the only one against which the enemy could form its attack, and the intervals were guarded by several pieces of artillery. The Imperial cavalry and that of the Empire, occupied a very advantageous spot near this wood, and extremely proper for their purpose. The French troops, whose left wing was defended by an impracticable ravin, joined them; besides all which there was a corps of reserve, of eight battalions and 16 squadrons, of the same auxiliary troops, to be employed as occasion might require.

In this posture nothing could be more desirable than to be attacked. On the 3d the enemy appeared, and reconnoitred the camp from the eminences, but discovered no tokens or disposition to risque an action with the combined army so advantageously posted, but encamped near the village of Rosbach, where it was equally inaccessible both in front and flanks. This camp was on a ravin and a small eminence. A brook, no ways considerable but for its steep banks, perfectly covered either army from the other; and the troops posted in the manner of an amphitheatre, formed two lines of infantry on the hanging of the hill, and the third of cavalry, in the plain behind the two former.

It was three in the afternoon before they quitted their camp, and made a shew of retreating to Mersebourg: but taking advantage of an eminence, which intercepted them and their motions from our view, they ranged their cavalry behind it. A person of credit and distinction came in the interim, and assured the Duke of Saxe Hildbourghausen, general of the combined army, that there was scarce a handful of the enemy behind the said eminence. But bye and bye we saw them advancing

A. D. 1757.

in their camp. For, on the 5th, about nine in the morning, their infantry, which had drawn nearer, upon the rising grounds, towards the Prussian camp, filed off to the right, and the whole army was put in motion; a large body of cavalry advancing on a full gallop towards our flank. The Duke, however, gained time sufficient for forming the two Imperial regiments of cavalry on the first line, and those of the Empire on the second, by disposing the flank in front. Himself in person led on the two former regiments to the charge, and attacked the enemy with so much bravery, that we could see the two parties, for a considerable time, engaging hand in hand. At length the Imperial cavalry began to penetrate through them; but the enemy's cavalry, much superior in number to ours, found means to surround them; however, they recovered their order, and, in conjunction with the French cavalry, repulsed the enemy four times. The Marquis de Castrees signalized himself on this occasion, and received two wounds on the head from a sword.

The Prince of Saxony, in the mean while, put himself at the head of the infantry, and the officers of the French army having proposed to him to attack that of the enemy in columns, with bayonets fixt, his Serene Highness expressed his satisfaction at so vigorous a resolution, and conducted in person the regiment of Piedmont within 30 or 40 paces of the enemy; but the terrible fire which they made at once of their artillery and musquetry, obliged that brave regiment to retreat; and instantly such an universal panic possessed all the troops, that it was impossible to stop one single battalion or squadron. Our general in chief, as well as the Prince de Soubise, the French commandant, took all imaginable pains to rally the troops, but to no purpose; they were all quite overwhelmed with terror. It was therefore concluded, to contrive how to secure a retreat. The night favouring us, the combined army profited of that circumstance, and retired to Freibourg, and afterwards over the Unstrut."

the

the same time marched towards the left, directing their march all along to the rising grounds, with which the Prussian camp, that lay in the bottom between the villages of Bederow and Rosbach, was surrounded, and within the reach of large cannon. About noon the head of the columns was perceived to rise upon the extremity of the left of the Prussian army. But it was two o'clock before any certain judgment could be formed of the intention of all these movements: when it being manifest, that they by endeavouring to double the left of the Prussians, and directing their march towards Merseburg, to cut off a retreat in case of a defeat, intended to attack the King's army, and that all their dispositions were calculated with a prospect to surround them, and to open the action by an attack in the rear; his Prussian Majesty seized the critical moment, defied their art, caught them in their own imaginations, drew up his army in order of battle, and, by a half turn to the left, marched parallel with the enemy.

King of Prussia stands his ground.

In this position the King made the following speech to his army: —— " My dear friends, the
" hour is now come, in which, all that is, and all
" that ought to be dear to us, depends upon the
" swords, which are now drawn for the battle;
" time permits me to say but little, nor is there
" occasion to say much. You know that there is
" no labour, no hunger nor cold, no watching,
" and no danger that I have not shared with you
" hitherto; and you see me ready to lay down my
" life

His speech to his soldiers.

A. D. 1757.

"life with you, and for you. All I afk is the
"fame pledge of fidelity and affection that I give;
"and let me add, not as an incitement to your
"courage, but as a teftimony of my own grati-
"tude, that, from this hour, till we go into quar-
"ters, your pay fhall be double.—Acquit your-
"felves like men, and put your confidence in
"God."——The effect of this fpeech was fuch,
as can neither be defcribed nor conceived; the
general emotion burft into an univerfal fhout, and
the looks and demeanour of the men, were animated to a degree little fhort of phrenfy; and of
this difpofition, the victory may perhaps be confidered as a natural effect, notwithftanding the
fuperiority of the enemy.

Its effect.

Difpofition of his army.

His Majefty had determined to make the attack
with one wing only, and the difpofition of the
enemy made it neceffary that it fhould be the left
wing. But the very inftant the battle was going
to begin, his Majefty ordered the general, who
commanded the right wing, to decline it; to take
a proper pofition in confequence thereof, and efpe-
cially, to prevent their being furrounded. Neverthelefs, all the cavalry of the right wing, except
two or three fquadrons, had already marched to
the left, in full gallop; and formed, according to
their orders, over againft the enemy. The Pruffians by thefe motions gained the rifing grounds,
of which their cavalry made very good ufe. They
attacked the enemy's cavalry in flank. The
charge was very fierce: and feveral regiments of
the French came on with great refolution. But
they

The battle begun.

they were driven back after a few discharges; and pursued with great spirit for a considerable time, till they found an opportunity of rallying upon an eminence; where they made a stand, but were so severely handled by the victorious pursuers that they betook themselves to flight in the greatest disorder, at about four in the afternoon.

Whilst the cavalry performed wonders, the infantry opened themselves. The enemy cannonaded them briskly during this interval, and did some execution; but not with impunity, the Prussian artillery returning the loss with advantage. This prelude of cannonade having continued without intermission for a quarter of an hour, the fire of the infantry began with such activity that the enemy could not stand it, nor resist the valour of the foot, who marched up gallantly to the enemy's batteries, and carried them with an uncommon bravery, one after another, till the enemy was forced to give way in great confusion. As the left wing advanced, the right changed its position, and having soon met with a small rising ground, they availed themselves of its situation, by planting it with 16 pieces of heavy cannon. From hence they were enabled to fire upon the enemy's right, which increased their disorder, and excessively galled their left wing in front.

At five victory declared in favour of the Prussians. The cannon ceased. The enemy fled on all sides. Only six battalions of the Prussian left were engaged. The pursuit was eager: but night coming on very fast favoured the runaways, and

The Prussians victorious.

The Imperialists fl[ed]

prevented

A.D. 1757.

prevented the conquerors reaping the fruits of their victory. So that, it may be said, the night alone was the preservation of that army, which was so formidable in the morning of the same day. They took the benefit of the darkness to hurry forwards to Freybourg, and there to pass the Unstrut, which they effected next morning after a whole night's march [c].

The

[c] This narrative of the battle and victory at Rosbach, has never been contradicted; but may be explained in several particulars by the following account, given in a letter from an officer in the army of the empire, present in this battle.

At one in the morning of the 30th past, we left our quarters at Stossen, and received orders to repair to Weissenfelds: the regiment of Varell marched through the city, and over the bridge, and was cantoned at Petra; two regiments, viz. those of Nassau and Deux Ponts, and Rechman's of Bavaria, with two companies of French grenadiers remained at Weissenfelds.

On the 31st, at five in the morning, the Prussians came and attacked the city: upon this, the whole army was ordered to assemble; but Prince Hildburghausen's quarters being at half a league's distance from the city, Prince George of d'Armstadt commanded in his absence, and took every possible method to make resistance; but it was too late: they were obliged to retire, and that noble bridge, which had cost above 100,000 crowns, was burnt to secure our retreat. The Prussian artillery made a terrible fire, whilst the two regiments were passing the bridge. The regiment of Deux Ponts lost four officers and 100 private men, upon this occasion; the captains Muncherode and Dames, with two lieutenants were among the former. The loss of Rechman's regiment amounted to 200 men, of whom six were officers. The whole army continued before the town, and the Felt Marshal in his quarters at Bugerau. In the night 300 of the Wartzburg Imperial regiment were

detached

The King set out early on the 6th in the morning, with all his cavalry, supported by four battalions

A. D. 1757.
Pursued.

detached to the place where the bridge had been, in order to observe the enemy.

During the whole night, a noise was heard in the city, occasioned by the strokes of mallets; but it was not discovered till break of day, that two houses had been turned into batteries. As they were not yet finished, we easily dismounted them with our six pieces of cannon, which were sent thither; and killed them four soldiers and one workman.

The first of Nov. the fire from the artillery continued on both sides till 10 o'clock, when we began to march towards Merseburg; the baggage having gone before as far as Camburg, we were forced to lie on the ground without wood or straw. In the mean while the French were reinforced by 20 battalions and 18 squadrons, commanded by the Duc de Broglio.

The 3d of Nov. we put ourselves in a posture to wait the enemy; at one in the afternoon we retreated a league towards Freybourg, where we halted; at five we were drawn up in order of battle; and thus we advanced slowly, towards the enemy, all night. We were posted in a wood on the right, where we covered ourselves by felling trees; and batteries were placed by the French on the two eminences at each end of the wood. On the 4th we were in presence of the enemy, and cannonaded each other. The enemy's cavalry advanced, but were repulsed by ours, sustained by the fire of our artillery. The enemy's infantry then moved forwards in three columns, but were also repulsed. On the 5th the cannonading began very early in the morning on both sides. The left wing of the enemy extended as far as Legen, and their right to Schorta; and our army was posted in the wood at Waneroda. At noon, our army, as well as the French, had orders to form the line of battle, and to march out of the entrenchments which we had made. We advanced towards the enemy, keeping a little, however, to the left. The enemy made a feint of retiring, on which we redoubled our pace, but we soon found what kind

of

A. D. 1757.

talions of grenadiers, in purfuit of the fugitives; with orders for his whole infantry to follow him in two columns. But, as faid above, the enemy had paffed the Unftrut; and the Pruffians being obliged to repair the bridge at Freybourg, which the enemy had burnt, it was five in the evening before the cavalry could come up with the enemy, drawn up in an advantageous manner upon the hills of Eckerfberg, which obliged his Majefty to wait the iffue of another day. He cantoned his

of retreat they were making. In order to deceive us the more effectually, they had fent fome fquadrons towards Merfeburg; but the reft of their army was drawn up behind an eminence, which concealed them from us. It muft be confeffed, that we fell compleatly into the fnare. The firft line of the French and our cavalry continued advancing; when all on a fudden our right wing received a terrible fire from the enemy, which we returned brifkly, but as we had been obliged to advance in fome hurry, our ranks were a little difordered, which made the enemy's fire fall the more heavily upon us. Our cavalry fled the firft upon full gallop, but our artillery fupported us fome time longer: at laft the French fled likewife; and being then no longer able to refift the enemy, the rout became general. We have loft all our baggage and artillery, and at leaft 10,000 men. We marched the whole night, and paffing the river Freyberg arrived at Eckerfberg at fix o'clock in the morning. At two o'clock in the afternoon the Felt Marfhal and Prince George joined us. They had hardly fet down to dinner, but we perceived the enemy at our heels, who cannonaded us brifkly; and as our army was not got together, nothing was left for us but to retreat. Having again marched all night, we arrived at laft at Erfurth, where we now are in want of every thing, though we are rather better off than before. It is now eight days fince our men have had bread; they have lived upon turnips and radifhes, which they dug out of the earth.

army

army in the nearest villages; and the enemy having fled in the night, he contented himself with the success of his hussars, who took near 300 baggage waggons with their contents; though there were some of the irregulars, that pushed after them as far as Erfurth.

This glorious victory, glorious both in the action and in its consequences, was obtained with very inconsiderable loss of the Prussians, which did not exceed 300 men killed and wounded; amongst whom was Colonel Prignitz, killed; and Prince Henry, General Seidlitz, and General Meinecke, wounded slightly. But their enemy lost upwards of 3000 men killed upon the field of battle, and above 6000 made prisoners, amongst whom were eight French generals, besides several German generals, and 250 officers of different ranks: 63 pieces of cannon, 15 standards, two pair of kettle drums, and seven pair of colours, fell also into the hands of the Prussians, at the same time [d].

If we seriously attend to the premises, and consider the strength of both armies, either in regard to their situation or numbers, it must be ac-

[d] Some accounts raise the number of prisoners to 10,000, and the pieces of cannon to 164; 300 waggon load of wounded French and Swiss, were sent with the rest of the prisoners to Leipsick. General Revel, brother to the Duke de Broglio, died of his wounds the day after the battle at Merseburg. *N. B.* It was said, that this egregious misfortune was owing to the injudicious dispositions of the two commanders; and in part to the discontent amongst the men, who were not only badly paid, but in great want of bread, &c.

knowledged

knowledged that the battle was not to the ſtrong; but that the hand of heaven appeared viſibly in defence of Pruſſia. The enemy boaſted that they were 70,000 ſtrong. But admit that there were no more than 50,000 effective combatants on the field of battle; it was a vaſt ſuperiority. For, after the King had left five battalions for the garriſon of Leipſick, a battalion at Halle, another at Merſeburg, and another at Weiſſenfelds; and had ſtationed the regiment of Winterfield to cover the baggage during the battle, his whole force ſcarcely amounted to 18,000 effective men: upon whom the whole weight of the action fell.

END of the SECOND VOLUME,

www.ingramcontent.com/pod-product-compliance
Lightning Source LLC
Chambersburg PA
CBHW051235300426
44114CB00011B/753